The author

Gavin McFarlane, LL.M. (Sheffield), Ph.D. (London), is a barrister and Harmsworth Scholar of the Middle Temple. After wide experience in the computer and entertainment industries and in the Government Legal Service, he has joined the City firm of Titmuss, Sainer & Webb. He is the author of *Copyright: the Development and Exercise of the Performing Right* (John Offord), *The Layman's Dictionary of English Law*, *Copyright through the Cases* and *Customs and Excise Cases* (Waterlow), as well as a frequent contributor to the legal press.

Waterlow Practitioner's Library

Cases on Patents *by Brian C. Reid*
Challenging Delegated Legislation *by Keith Puttick*
Confidentiality and the Law *by Brian C. Reid*
Consumer Credit Agreements *by Jan Karpinski and Stephen Fielding*
Copyright through the Cases *by Gavin McFarlane*
Corporate Insolvency Law *by Ian Snaith*
Criminal Injuries Compensation *by Donald B. Williams*
Estate Conveyancing *by P. M. A'Court*
How to Survive your Articles *by R. N. Hill*
The Law of Co-operatives *by Ian Snaith*
Making Legal Aid Pay *by J. J. R. Dirks*
Police Powers and the Rights of the Individual *by J. B. Hill and Karen E. Fletcher-Rogers*
A Practical Introduction to Trade Marks *by Brian C. Reid*
The Probate Manual *revised by R. F. Yeldham and Angela Plumb*
Service Charges in Leases by *Gerald Sherriff*
Weapons Law *by J. B. Hill*

For further information write to Waterlow Publishers,
Paulton House, 8 Shepherdess Walk, London N1 7LB
Telephone 01-251 9442

A Practical Introduction to Copyright

Second edition

GAVIN McFARLANE
Titmuss, Sainer & Webb

WATERLOW PUBLISHERS

First edition 1982
Second edition 1989
© Gavin McFarlane 1982, 1989

Waterlow Publishers
Paulton House
8 Shepherdess Walk
London N1 7LB
A division of Pergamon Professional & Financial Services PLC

ISBN 0 08 033074 6

British Library Cataloguing in Publication Data

McFarlane, Gavin
    A practical introduction to copyright. – 2nd ed – (Waterlow
    practitioner's library)
    1. Great Britain. Copyright law
    I. Title
    344.1064'82

Printed and bound in Great Britain by
BPCC Wheatons Ltd., Exeter

Contents

Preface

The Copyright, Designs and Patents Act 1988 is of considerable significance in the field of copyright. In some areas it has swept away old and familiar principles, sometimes dating from the Copyright Act 1911 or even earlier. Certain new rights have been introduced, and there has been a laudable attempt to come to grips with the demands of new technology. But the swift changes of modern society may make a replacement Act necessary before the end of the century.

After pressing hard for new legislation over the last fifteen years, it may be churlish of me to point to defects. But the attempts to deal with moral rights do seem defective when set against Convention requirements; again, the extended criminal provisions would have bitten harder if absolute offences had been given more prominence.

Once again I must acknowledge the talents of James Lamb as my book editor. His conversion of my scripts into finished volumes of a high standard of publishing production is wholly admirable, and I am most grateful.

GMcF

Table of Cases

Table of Statutes

CHAPTER 1

The Nature of Copyright

1.01 Copyright is a field which is rapidly increasing in importance. Originally it was a quiet backwater of the law, providing protection for literary men, dramatists, composers of music and artists, together with the businessmen who published their works. Over the last century or so its scope has gradually increased to deal with a broader range of activity as the entertainment and allied industries have expanded, but the previous Copyright Act dated from 1956. Although excellently drafted, and a model for the mid-twentieth century, by the seventies it was having difficulty in coping with new developments.

1.02 In the last two decades the effect of technology on creative works has been quite drastic. At the time of the Copyright Act 1956 machinery for photocopying was still rather cumbersome and time-consuming; to make a single copy of, for example, a textbook would have been a laborious process which would hardly have justified the time and effort. Now multiple copies of a literary work can be produced swiftly and comparatively inexpensively. Efficient and rapid photocopying machines are widely used in educational establishments, libraries and offices, and in some cases the extent of this use has reduced the likely sale of the original work to the point where it simply ceases to pay the author, and perhaps more importantly the publisher also, to produce the work.

1.03 Not only literary works are threatened. The video recorder is now being enthusiastically marketed to the public at large, and the prices of the equipment have been considerably reduced. Recording equipment is called into service in many homes to tape gramophone records or broadcasts off the air. This latter development, known as time-shifting, had a profound effect on the rights position in several areas of the entertainment industry.

1.04 Such computers as existed in the early days of the 1956 Act were close to steam engines in size. The desk-top computer is now both cheap and commonplace, and computer studies appear on the courses of many secondary schools. The protection and ownership of programs has had to be provided for, as well as the effect of storing copyright works such as books in data processing equipment. It is a tribute to the flexibility of the copyright system that it has proved capable of taking these matters in its stride.

1.05 Students of copyright cannot complain that their subject has been ignored in recent years. A committee on the subject of copyright and designs law produced its report in 1977, under the chairmanship of Mr Justice Whitford, a High Court judge with considerable experience of the subject. It made recommendations for basic alteration to the 1956 Act to deal with many matters requiring urgent attention, including those outlined above. A Green Paper entitled *Reform of the Law Relating to Copyright, Designs and Performers' Protection* appeared in 1981, and in 1985 came a consultation document on *The Recording and Rental of Audio and Video Copyright Material*. Finally a White Paper on *Intellectual Property and Innovation* appeared in 1986. It is against this backcloth of government discussion papers that the Copyright, Designs and Patents Act 1988 (CDPA) was debated in Parliament and received Royal Assent. It has replaced the law in the 1956 Act in stages, as parts of the new Act have been brought into force at different dates. Most businessman using modern information technology should have some knowledge of copyright; the public at large may require a certain familiarity with its principles if they intend to use video recorders or computing equipment at home.

HISTORY OF COPYRIGHT

Early days

1.06 Whether or not a form of copyright existed in classical times is not relevant to a short practical study of the subject. Suffice to say that protection for literary works was recognised by the common law of England at an early stage. The call for effective protection in statutory form, when it came, did not emanate from the authors, a body which has historically been disinterested in acting for its own interest. It arrived eventually when commercial men moved in to develop writers' works in a saleable form, which came about with the invention of printing. Naturally the State swiftly came to appreciate the political and economic significance of the new invention, and at an early stage the king assumed the monopoly of granting licences to print.

1.07 For some time, the Stationers' Company in London purported to grant charters or licences to print by virtue of powers accorded to its governing body. In the seventeenth century a series of Licensing Acts required printed books to be registered with the Stationers' Company, but these lapsed, and the close of the century saw a confused situation in which publishers, or booksellers as they then generally called themselves, were hard put to find protection for their wares. It was the businessmen who were the moving force behind the petitions to Parliament for assistance, although they were and always have been astute enough to ask their creative colleagues to stand in the front line, a technique which has often proved effective.

1.08 Certainly it was effective at the commencement of the eighteenth century, when, following this campaign, the first copyright legislation anywhere in the world passed into law in Great Britain. It was the Copyright Act 1709, familiarly known as the Statute of Anne, which granted authors the sole right of printing their books for 21 years if already printed, and fourteen years if not then printed. This, it will be noted, was simply a protection against unauthorised reproduction, and extended no further than books, small enough by current standards, but at least it was a beginning. The extension of statutory protection was rapid, each new stage affecting a much wider number of owners and users of copyright. Now that the Copyright, Designs and Patents Act 1988 has arrived, it is likely to affect every household in the land.

The nineteenth century

1.09 The first stage of expansion came when the Copyright Act of 1814 extended the author's reproduction right to 28 years from first publication. Should the author be still living at the end of that period, the protection was to continue for the remainder of his life. The Dramatic Copyright Act of 1833 was a significant step forward, for it contained the first performing right, as opposed simply to a reproduction right, and allowed the author of a "tragedy, comedy, play, opera, farce, or any other dramatic piece of entertainment" to have as his own property the sole right of performing.

1.10 The next major measure was the Copyright Act of 1842, which extended protection to the author's life plus seven years, or a total term of 42 years, whichever should be the longer. A performing right was by this statute accorded to musical as well as to dramatic works, the term of both being the new period. By now dramatic and musical works were all covered against unauthorised reproduction, being regarded as literary works for this purpose, but at this stage protection was still largely confined to the classical productions of cultural creation. Slowly, however, industrial applications of the fine arts began to come under the umbrella of copyright law.

1.11   In the artistic field there had been Engraving Copyright Acts in 1734 and 1766, and a Prints Copyright Act in 1777. Early in the nineteenth century works of sculpture received protection under the Sculpture Copyright Act of 1814, and as the century wore on first lithographs received copyright protection in 1852; and then in 1862 photographs, drawings and paintings. Meanwhile, somewhat on its own, the field of lectures had received statutory protection quite separately by the Lectures Copyright Act 1835.

The twentieth century

1.12   When the twentieth century opened, the situation had altered dramatically. Both the gramophone and the cinema had been invented, and were beginning to be commercially exploited. Populations were becoming much more mobile, and at the same time more affluent, with increased real incomes to devote to entertainment. But the copyright laws of the United Kingdom were antique in the extreme. As early as 1876 an official survey of the subject had felt obliged to comment, "The law is wholly destitute of any sort of arrangement, incomplete, often obscure, and, even when it is intelligible upon long study, it is in many parts so ill expressed that no one who does not give such study to it can expect to understand it".[1] When the Copyright Act 1911 was passed into law, no fewer than seventeen previous British statutes relating to copyright were repealed.

1.13   The 1911 Act became the sole source of rights in the nature of copyright, and went a long way to bring matters up to the requirements of the day. Protection was extended to literary, dramatic, musical and artistic works, and this protection was for the period in operation at the present time, namely the life of the creator plus 50 years. Literary, dramatic and musical works were defined, and the full term of protection extended to both performance and reproduction of the work. Protection against unauthorised reproduction extended both to reproduction on film and on record. There was as yet no separate copyright in a motion picture, but each individual frame was regarded as an artistic work, and thus accorded protection.

1.14   Gramophone records were granted by the 1911 Act a protection which came to appear rather ambiguous, in a form which gave manufacturers no more than a reproduction right against unauthorised copying. Certainly this appeared to be the expressed intention of the record

1.   Copyright Commission (1875–76), Report, paras 7–9.

manufacturers themselves in evidence given to the Committee which had been set up to consider the form of the new copyright law.[2] Nevertheless the point of whether the manufacturers owned in addition a form of performing right in sound recordings was the subject of *Gramophone Co. Ltd v. Cawardine Ltd,*[3] and on the basis of that decision, a right of that nature was held to exist. This was to prove of enormous economic significance for the gramophone industry.

1.15 Undoubtedly the Copyright Act 1911 was an excellent piece of legislation, and the clarity of expression with which it was drafted placed Great Britain among the foremost proponents in the world of the copyright system, though in a form dissimilar to most of her European neighbours. It became a model for copyright laws in the then British Dominions, and the Act itself was applied in a large number of territories which at the time were British colonies. But as the decades of the present century passed, in its turn the 1911 Act became obviously unable to deal with new commercial developments in the entertainment world. The two world wars brought major technological advances in their wake. First sound broadcasting exploded across the continents of the world, bringing live entertainment into the most remote homes. The cinema became a mammoth industry, aimed at mass audiences, and linked to a soundtrack. Television passed from its magic lantern phase, and by the beginning of the 1950s was poised to make the greatest impact in history on the domestic circle. And at the same time the record industry was introducing the long-playing record to a younger and richer market than had ever existed before.

1.16 Against this background in the early 1950s the Gregory Committee sat to consider the reforms necessary to the British law of copyright. Its Report is still one of the cornerstones of modern copyright legislation, and makes fascinating further reading for anyone whose interest is sparked by the subject.[4] It led directly to the Copyright Act of 1956, which introduced copyright protection for such subject-matters as sound and television broadcasts, films and gramophone records, thus giving statutory confirmation to the decision in *Gramophone Co. Ltd v. Cawardine Ltd.* Once again it put the United Kingdom in the van of states supporting the notion of copyright, but with the acceleration of technological development, this position lasted scarcely longer than a decade.

2. Copyright Committee (1909), Minutes of Evidence, paras 1130–1132.
3. [1934] Ch 450.
4. Cmnd 8662.

1.17 By the mid-1960s countries such as West Germany were bringing in still more modern laws which took account of fresh changes, and after much travail the United States in 1976 at last enacted a completely new copyright law. The Report of the Whitford Committee[5] once more put this country in a position to regain its leadership of the copyright world. The 1988 Act has given effect to some of its provisions, but not all. In a number of areas quite different concepts have been introduced, and it remains to be seen whether the new Act will come to be regarded with as much respect as were its forerunners of 1911 and 1956.

CURRENT COPYRIGHT PROTECTION

1.18 The basis of copyright protection is now contained in section 16 of the Copyright, Designs and Patents Act 1988. (This basic Act will be referred to as "CDPA" throughout this book.) This provides that the owner of copyright has the exclusive right to do certain acts in relation to the work. The legislation no longer expressly states that the copyright owner has the exclusive right to authorise others to do these restricted acts, for example by licensing them, but this is to be inferred. Section 1 of CDPA tells us that copyright is a property right.

1.19 Thus there are two aspects to protection. The negative application is for the right-owner to exercise his exclusive right himself, without authorising anyone else to do the same act. While perhaps attractive to the really self-indulgent author, it is scarcely likely to allow him to derive much income from his work. This is because in its positive application it is the exploitation of the composition which gives the economic significance to copyright. Simply to prevent other people from reproducing it or from performing it prevents them from making any money out of it; this alone does not make any money for the owner of the right. His income will be derived from the licensing of his work. Thus the author will grant a publisher a licence to publish his work in book form, and the composer of a musical work will grant a music publisher a licence to publish his musical work in the form of sheet music, and, probably via the medium of the Performing Right Society, a licence enabling those who take it up to give a public performance of that musical work.

1.20 The forms of exploitation are of course not by any means confined to those listed above. There are film rights, rights to record, rights to broadcast, and depending on the nature of the original work,

5. Cmnd 6732.

a host of subsidiary rights. The significance of the copyright system to the speed of development of high technology is its ability to adapt to novel situations. New rights evolve to take account of fresh means of exploitation of copyright works, and developing almost as those inventions are taking place.

1.21 Thus, for example, a copyright-owner may place on his work some such legend as a warning that he claims not only all rights in the nature of copyright which may exist at the present time, but also those rights which may come into existence in the future. This is a wise precaution, given that for literary, dramatic, musical and artistic works the term of protection is the life of the author plus a post-mortem period of 50 years. Twenty years ago few authors would have imagined that their works could have been carried from one continent to another as part of a broadcast transmitted via a satellite, or that they would be capable of being stored in a data-processing system, or that they could be part of a copyright work recorded from a television set by a video recorder operated by the individual in the comfort of his sitting-room. But these uses now take place as a matter of course every day.

1.22 These uses now affect most people in some way or another, whether in the home, or in the office or elsewhere in the course of a businessman's life. At the present time there is a good deal of abuse of copyright, particularly in the field of unauthorised reproduction. This is very often due to the impossibility of policing the act of reproduction, and although copyright-owners have been trying for many years to grapple with what is in some cases a plague on their particular industry, direct enforcement of the existing law has not often been crowned with success.

1.23 The CDPA completely recasts the arrangement of the previous Act and copyright legislation and right owners, users and business managers who have been used to working with the 1956 Act will have to learn their way around the new statute. Section 172 provides that the relevant part of the new Act restates and amends the 1956 Act, which is completely repealed. A provision of the new law which corresponds to a provision of the previous law is not to be construed as departing from the previous law merely because of a change of expression. Decisions under existing case law may be referred to in order to establish whether a provision of the new law departs from the previous law, or in order to establish the correct construction of the new law.

FREE USE OF COPYRIGHT

1.24 Managers and executives in many areas of business need to know what remedies for copyright infringement are available, and these will be discussed later in the text. But at the same time some knowledge is useful of what unlicensed use of copyright works is allowed under the new law, the so called " free use". To a certain extent, copyright legislation holds a balance in the administration of the property rights involved between the copyright owners on the one hand, who seek as much protection as possible, and would be users of copyright on the other, who want access to copyright works on the best terms available. If that access can be free, so much the better for them. It must be said the CDPA has tilted the balance in favour of the users in a number of areas.

Fair Dealing

1.25 Some of these types of free use are rather specialised, concerning authors and publishers; they at least should be familiar with what is permitted. But CDPA, like its predecessors, is somewhat vague in these areas, and makes use of abstract expressions for which watertight definitions are not provided.

1.26 No fair dealing with a work for the purpose of criticism or review is an infringement of copyright so long as a sufficient acknowledgement is provided. There is no infringement in the case of a literary, dramatic, musical or artistic work where research or private study is involved. Other permitted acts include a wide variety of educational uses. Thus anthologies intended for use in educational establishments do not infringe copyright where a "short passage" from a published literary or dramatic work is included in a collection (section 33). The performance of a literary, dramatic or musical work before an audience consisting of teachers, pupils, and other persons "directly connected with the activities" of an educational establishment does not infringe the performing right (section 35).

1.27 These exceptions largely involve people who may be said to be professionally involved, but the guidelines for them are by no means clear. What, for example, is a "short passage" or "directly connected with the activities" of an educational establishment? The Publishers Association at one time indicated to its members that in relation to a prose work, a "short" passage should not exceed 750 words, while so far as a poetical work was concerned, a "short" passage should not exceed 75 words. But there are no hard and fast rules.

1.28 There are now quite complex rules about reprographic copying by educational establishments of passages from published works. Broadly not more than one per cent of any work may be copied by a single establishment in any quarter (section 36 CDPA). Librarians and archivists are allowed to make certain types of copy under what have the appearance of stringent conditions. A librarian or archivist who obtains a signed declaration from a person requesting a copy of a work should be in the clear, unless he is aware that the declaration is false in a material particular (sections 37–44 CDPA). Copyright is not infringed by anything done for the purposes of parliamentary or judicial proceedings, not is it infringed by anything done for the purpose of reporting such proceedings (section 45), although the author of the headnote to a law report can, it is submitted, still claim copyright. Provisions are also made about material open to public inspection or on an official register.

Criticism of concept of fair dealing
1.29 Over the years a fair amount of criticism has been voiced about the imprecision of a number of the terms employed in these sections. The very concept of "fair dealing" itself is as long as a piece of string, and it is scarcely surprising that little case law exists on the topic. Whereas if the whole of a work were to be reprinted this would hardly amount to fair dealing, at the present time there is scant guidance for an author who sees a substantial part of his work reproduced without authority as to what lesser use will be regarded by the court as fair dealing.[6] And to carry the matter into litigation in the High Court is an expensive way of finding out.

Whitford recommendations
1.30 The evidence given to the Whitford Committee amounted to demands for clarification, rather than limiting the existing fair dealing provisions[7]—"People wanted to know where they stood". After considering the various submissions made to them, the members of the Committee felt that it would be better to try to achieve clarification by having some form of exceptions, in the shape of provisions in general terms to extend to all classes of works and subject matters, and so far as is possible to have this under one heading. They used a sensible yardstick; a copyright-owner is surely allowed to complain if his market is being cut into, with the result that others are selling his work rather than their views on his work.

6. But see the case of *Sillitoe and others v. McGraw-Hill Book Co. Ltd* [1983] F.S.R. 545, where it was held that extensive quotation from school set books in a series of exam aids was *not* fair dealing.
7. Cmnd 6732, para 668.

1.31 The Committee recommended a general exception in favour of fair dealing which does not conflict with the normal exploitation of the work or subject-matter, and which does not unreasonably prejudice the legitimate interests of the copyright-owner. This is an admirable ambition, but the problem was considered 25 years previously by the Gregory Committee on copyright, which aimed at much the same target. The test lies in the draftsmanship applied to the eventual statutory provision, and so long as abstractions are used, no draftsman can clothe them with precision. The opportunity to extend the jurisdiction of the new Copyright Tribunal to settling disputes in this area was available to the legislators who considered the new measures. Unfortunately they did not avail themselves of it.

CHAPTER 2

Ownership of Copyright

2.01 This is one of the most crucial questions which arises in relation to copyright. The protection accorded by the right does not arise by virtue of registration, and in many cases the creator of a simple work of a literary or artistic nature does not bring his production into being with any conscious notion of acquiring copyright. The protection arises from the mere fact of creation itself. The moment that a work of sufficient originality comes into existence, then copyright protection automatically attaches to it.

2.02 Under the domestic law of the United Kingdom, no mark is required to be put on the work, nor any deposit or formal entry made in a central register. Moreover, the fact that a work enjoys copyright protection does not necessarily give rise to a monopoly situation, as is the case with the patent system. The general rule is that the author of a work is the first owner of any copyright in it, but as will be seen, there are a number of important exceptions to be considered.

LIBRARIES OF DEPOSIT

2.03 Although there is no central register for the deposit of copyright material in Britain, as is the case in the United States of America, nevertheless the publisher of a book is subject to certain requirements of a similar nature. The matter arises under section 15 of the Copyright Act of 1911, which has not been repealed. It has however been amended by the British Library Act of 1972. This requires that the publisher of every book published in the United Kingdom must within one month of publication deliver a copy thereof to the trustees of the British Museum. Whether adequate storage space will continue to be available is another matter. Further, if written request is made within one year after publication, the publisher must within one month deliver a further copy to the Bodleian Library at Oxford, the University Library at Cambridge, the National Library of Scotland, the Library of Trinity College in Dublin, and also in certain circumstances to the National Library of Wales.

2.04 The origin of the requirement lies in the interest of the State in earlier centuries in controlling publication and the printed word by a

11

system of licences dependent upon deposit. Its continuation is due to a desire to maintain complete archives of books published in the country, and to advance scholarship, and some such requirement is a common feature of the laws of most countries with publishing industries. Nevertheless the requirement is one which may cause hardship to publishers and their authors, and it generated quite heated argument when the matter was raised before the Whitford Committee which reported in 1977.

Cost of system

2.05 It is clearly a cause for concern to a specialised publisher of an expensive limited edition operating on narrow margins to have to provide six copies quite free. All books are caught by the requirement, so that the publisher of a multipart dictionary or encyclopedia would be liable to provide six copies of every volume. The publishing interests submitted to the Whitford Committee that editions of less than 500 copies should be exempt; this may not, however, be in the interests of either publishers or authors in the long run, if such an exemption encouraged smaller publishing companies to bring out small editions in order to avoid meeting the requirement of deposit. Printing and setting costs are proportionately much higher on short runs, and reliance thereon would probably be quite damaging to the industry.

2.06 The total cost of deposit made to the six libraries involved in 1973 was over one million pounds, since when costs have risen considerably. In times of financial stringency it is difficult to see what other source of funding the operation would be available, if it is to continue. The University Grants Committee has made it plain that neither it nor the universities would be in a position to meet the cost of the books deposited from their own resources. One of the libraries is altogether outside the United Kingdom, and in recent years the provincial universities in Britain have attained a status which would justify a claim for parity with the existing libraries of deposit.

Whitford recommendations

2.07 In the end the Whitford Committee suggested that consideration should be given to relieving publishers from the financial burden of legal deposit by some form of fiscal relief. If deemed a contribution to public funds, it could perhaps be allowed against tax liability for the appropriate period. It was further recommended that all libraries should be put on the same footing, bringing the National Library of Wales into line with the other five. The Committee members also suggested that the John Rylands University Library of Manchester should be added to the list of libraries of deposit.

2.08 At the present time there is a requirement under the Theatres Act of 1968 that anyone who presents a new play in public for the first time in this country must deliver within one month free of charge to the British Library a copy of the script upon which the performance was based. The Whitford Committee suggested that the deposit system might be extended by establishing national archives of films, and published visual and sound recordings. It is undoubtedly a logical extension of the principle at present applied to books, but it would be placing an extra expense upon the industries involved. Moreover, the establishment of these archives would call for state expenditure in the form of property with storage space and qualified staff.

2.09 However, it was decided to leave the rights of the libraries of deposit intact and CDPA has not repealed section 15 of the copyright Act of 1911.

PROOF OF A WORK'S EXISTENCE

2.10 There is one very practical aspect to the requirement of library deposit for published books, as it has the effect of establishing the existence of a work at a particular time if any question of copyright infringement or plagiarism should arise. However, the publication of a book is not usually a difficult matter to establish at the present day; it becomes harder to demonstrate that a work existed at a particular date where it is in another form, perhaps unpublished, or a musical work.

2.11 In these circumstances there are practical steps which can be taken by the copyright-owner to prove the existence of his work on a certain date. One method is to deposit it in a bank, and obtain a receipt referring by name to the work in question. As early as the seventeenth century, the Stationers' Company had passed private regulations for its members dealing with the ownership of books and printed matter. These private regulations were necessary because of the defective nature of the legislation on the subject at that time; part of the regulations called for entry of rights on the records of the Stationers' Company.

2.12 These records continued, and grew in stature. When the first Copyright Act was passed in 1709, the title to protected books had to be registered at the Stationers' Company. (It is interesting to note that by the same statute a publisher was required to deposit no fewer than nine copies of the book to various libraries). But the requirement of registration at Stationers' Hall came to an end in 1923, although the registry is still maintained at that establishment. It is very useful evidence of the existence of a work, and entry can be made on payment of a fee. The address is: Stationers' Hall Registry, Stationers' Hall Court, London EC4.

Symbol ©

2.13 Mention should also be made of the symbol ©. This does not arise from any requirement of British law, but relates to the Universal Copyright Convention (UCC), and to protection in the United States of America. Many experienced copyright-owners in the United Kingdom nevertheless recommend the addition of this symbol followed by the name of the copyright owner and the year of publication of the work. Not only does it act as a deterrent to would-be copiers, but it also goes some way towards establishing the date of creation of the work, should this ever be disputed.

COMMISSIONER OF WORK AND COPYRIGHT

2.14 By section 4(3) of the Copyright Act 1956, where a person commissioned the taking of a photograph, or the painting or drawing of a portrait, or the making of an engraving, and paid or agreed to pay for it in money or money's worth, and the work was made in pursuance of that commission, the person who commissioned the work was entitled to the copyright. It was contended by some interests before the Copyright Committee which reported in 1977 that this should be extended to cover all works ordered and paid for by a customer or client, so that all people commissioning works should become the owners of rights in them.

2.15 This did not of course affect the position that the contract or agreement relating to the commissioning of any work can always make special provision as to the ownership of copyright; quite frequently this is done.

Whitford recommendations

2.16 A majority of the Whitford Committee on the other hand recommended that, subject to any agreement to the contrary, copyright in all commissioned works should belong to the author. There were two important exceptions to this general recommendation. One was that the person commissioning the work should have an exclusive license for all purposes which could reasonably be said to have been within the contemplation of the parties at the moment of commissioning. The other was that the person commissioning should have the power to restrain any exploitation for other purposes against which he could reasonably take objection. Nevertheless these recommendations had a rather cumbersome appearance.

2.17 CDPA puts photographs and other artistic works in exactly the same position in this respect as other works. Section 11(1) states unequivocally, "The author of a work is the first owner of any copyright in it . . . " (See para 2.31 below.) This is subject to the general exception in relation to works created by employees discussed below.

EMPLOYEES AND COPYRIGHT

2.18 A further exception to the general rule as to ownership of copyright existed in section 4(2) of the Copyright Act 1956. This provided that where any literary, dramatic or artistic work was made by the author in the course of his employment by the proprietor of a newspaper, magazine or similar periodical under a contract of service or apprenticeship, and was so made for the purpose of publication in a newspaper, magazine or similar periodical, the proprietor was the person entitled to the copyright in the work in so far as it related to the publication of the work in any newspaper, magazine or similar periodical.

2.19 Section 11(2) of CDPA sweeps away the former distinction between journalists and other employees who write or draw or take pictures as part of their employment. It provides that where a literary, dramatic, musical or artistic work is made by an employee in the course of his employment, his employer is the first owner of any copyright in the work subject to any agreement to the contrary. Sections 163 to 165 make special provision in respect of civil servants and Crown and parliamentary copyright; see paras 2.33–36 below.

2.20 Whether a particular work has been made "in the course of his employment" is a question which has often led to controversy. In the first place, it is quite possible for a creative worker to make a thoroughly bad bargain, and enter a contract of employment at a relatively low rate of remuneration, during the course of which he creates for his employer top-class copyright works which greatly enrich the latter. In the second place, dispute can sometimes arise as to whether a particular contract is a contract of service. Lawyers distinguish between a contract *of service* and a contract *for services*. The distinction is of importance. A contract of service for the purposes of this discussion is one in which an employee is employed by an employer; a contract for services is one in which an independent contractor renders his services for remuneration without entering the employment of the person for whom the services are rendered.

2.21   In copyright matters the question is one of vital importance. If the author of a work is working independently, he becomes the first owner of the copyright; if employed, it is his employer who becomes the first owner of the rights. The criteria for determining whether a contract for services or a contract of service exists have altered over the years, and it is not possible to lay down hard and fast guidelines.

2.22   At one time great emphasis was laid on the degree of control exercised over the person carrying out the services. The more independence which he enjoyed, the more likely it was that he had not entered a contract of employment. If important questions were left to the individual's skill and judgement; if he were paid a lump sum as opposed to a wage or salary; if he were entitled to take other work at the same time; all these were factors pointing to a contract for services, and not employment.

2.23   But social conditions have altered, and the nature of business life as well. After the Second World War, judges began to ask whether the individual were employed as a part of the business, and his work performed as an integral part of that business. An important case is *Beloff v. Pressdram Ltd*,[1] where the judge referred to matters which he regarded as indications of a contract of service. These covered all equipment being provided by the employer, including an office on his premises and a secretary, deduction of PAYE and contributions to a pension scheme. It may be that the earlier cases tended to overcomplicate a proposition which could be quite simply posed—that is, whether the individual creating the copyright works is doing so in the course of carrying on a business on his own account. If he is, then he is the first owner of the copyright in those works.

2.24   When the question of employee works was considered by the Whitford Committee on copyright in 1977, both the British Copyright

1. [1973] 1 All ER 241.

Council and the Trades Union Congress submitted that employees should keep the copyright in works which they created. Against that the representatives of newspaper proprietors and editors argued that the employer should be given the right of reproduction in all news media; this does tend to ignore the proposition sometimes expressed that there can be no copyright in news as such.

2.25 That was the basis of the decision in *Walter v. Steinkopff*.[2] Only the literary form given to news is protected. It is of course a simple matter to rewrite an item of news so as not to infringe the wording of a report, but it cannot be reproduced verbatim, and the decision would seem to have more relevance to feature articles. The overall principle was accepted by the members of the Whitford Committee that if an employer takes a person on to produce copyright works as part of his everyday employment, for which he receives remuneration, then the employer should be entitled to the use of the work.

Whitford proposals

2.26 The Whitford Committee made a number of interesting recommendations in respect of ownership of copyright, and the creations of employees. They were:

(1) Any new legislation should make it clear that the creators of copyright works should be the owners of the rights therein, subject only to any express agreement to the contrary, and to certain other exceptions, most of which are dealt with in this chapter.

(2) In respect of works created by an employee, the rights in material created in the course of employment should be vested in the employer. If, however, such work is exploited by the employer or someone else with his permission in a way which was not within the contemplation of the employer and employee at the time of making the work, the employee should enjoy a statutory right to an award from the employer; if this cannot be settled by agreement, it should be adjudicated on by a tribunal.

(3) Rights in employee works should be defined only by reference to works created by employees in the course of their employment, and in any new legislation expressions such as 'contracts of service or apprenticeship' should be avoided.

So far as (2) above is concerned, it does appear rather unwieldy. It is doubtful if many agreements between employer and employee will specify all exploitations they had in mind at the time of creation of the

---

2. [1892] 3 Ch 489.

work. With copyright developing so fast, new applications of copyright works to the technology of the day are constantly being evolved, and it is unlikely that all will be covered in any contract. In the event of a dispute, parties in contention are hardly likely to agree on a figure by way of compensation.

THE PRESENT POSITION

2.27 As mentioned above, the whole question of ownership of copyright has now been recast. It starts with the basic proposition in section 9(1) of CDPA that "author" in relation to a work, means the person who creates it. Then section 11(1) adds that the author of a work is the first owner of any copyright, subject to certain provisos. So the basic rule is that the owner of copyright in a work is the person who creates it. But the qualifications imposed on that rule are quite substantial.

2.28 In the case of a sound recording or a film, the person who made the necessary arrangements is the "author". Unsurprisingly, it is the person making the broadcast who is the "author" of it, and in the case of a cable programme, it is the person providing the cable service in which the programme is included. There is also an important new provision in the case of a literary, dramatic, musical or artistic work which is computer-generated; in any such case the author is to be the person by whom the arrangements necessary for the creation of the work are undertaken.

2.29 By section 10, a work of joint authorship means a work produced by the collaboration of two or more authors in which the contribution of each author is not distinct from that of the other author or authors. The only alteration from the previous legislation is the rather curious substitution of "distinct" for "separate". It is now made clear by section 12(4) CDPA that where the identity of all joint authors is known, it is the life of the last of them to die which governs the term of copyright. Those connected with the music industry should note that the composer and the lyric writer do not have a joint copyright in what they produce. The composer has a copyright in a musical work, and the lyricist has a copyright in the literary work comprised by his words.

2.30 The previous rules about contracts of service and apprenticeship have been removed. The rule now is that where a literary, dramatic, musical or artistic work is made by an employee in the course of his employment, his employer is the first owner of copyright subject to any agreement to the contrary (section 11(2) CDPA). In particular the journalist is now in the same position as any other employee. If his bargaining position is strong enough, he will be able to insist on retaining his rights as a term inserted in his contract of employment.

2.31 Now a photograph is by section 4 CDPA an artistic work, so that the old exception in favour of the commissioner of a photograph has also been removed. The author of a photograph is the photographer, and as such, he is the first owner of copyright. Of course the commissioner can ask for an assignment to be made to him. By virtue of section 90(3), however, such an assignment would have to be in writing.

2.32 There is however, an interesting new right for the person who for private and domestic purposes commissions the taking of a photograph or the making of a film. Now by section 85 CDPA such a person has the right not to have copies of the work issued to the public, nor to have the work exhibited or shown in public, nor to have the work broadcast or included in a cable programme. Though well short of the right not to have one's privacy invaded which has sometimes been canvassed as a new form of tort, it goes a long way to protect the off-duty relaxation of people frequently in the public eye.

Crown Copyright

2.33 The previous position about Crown copyright has been radically altered by section 163 CDPA. Now Crown copyright in a literary, dramatic, musical or artistic work continues to subsist, if not published commercially, until the end of 125 years from the end of the year in which it was made. This finally brings to an end the concept of perpetual Crown Copyright in an unpublished work; and the general provision preserving perpetual copyright in unpublished works has also been removed, as section 12(1) CDPA provides a maximum term of the author's life plus 50 years for any work, whether published or unpublished.

2.34 It has traditionally been held that the interest of the Crown and the public were served by the widest possible dissemination of material concerned with legislation, or consultative papers and exposure drafts where the views of the public or interested parties are sought. In the past Crown copyright would not be enforced in such matters as Bills, Acts, Statutory Instruments such as Rules, Regulations and Orders, Parliamentary Reports and papers, and Hansard. Only in exceptional cases would Crown copyright be relied on, where such reproduction was in an undesirable context, or widespread piracy was resulting in loss to public funds. The Whitford Committee had reached the rather startling conclusion that "All the existing Crown copyright provisions, especially first publication provision, should be brought to an end".[3] This recommendation has not been implemented, and section 164 CDPA grants the Crown copyright in every Act of Parliament or Measure of the General Synod of the Church of England. The same Section provides that no other copyright or right in the nature of copyright subsists in an Act or measure.

2.35   A brand new provision is the creation of Parliamentary copyright by section 165 CDPA. This applies to works made under the direction or control of the House of Commons or the House of Lords. It is to endure for 50 years from the end of the calendar year in which the work was made, and will extend to any sound recording, film, live broadcast or live cable programme of the proceedings of either House. Presumably a clearing house will have to be set up in Parliament to issue licences for Parliamentary copyright, and to collect royalties.

2.36   In order to deal with copyright matters, each House is to have the capacity of a body corporate and will not be affected by prorogation or dissolution. Legal proceedings on behalf of the House of Commons are to be conducted by or in the name of the Speaker; in the case of the Lords it will be the Clerk of the Parliament.

Legal judgements and copyright

2.37   The Report of the Whitford Committee also drew attention to the confused situation existing at the present time in relation to judgments given in cases before the courts. As is pointed out, so far as is known, no judge has ever laid claim to copyright in a judgment. Some countries overseas do expressly exclude speeches and judgments in legal cases as exempt from copyright protection. Article 2*bis* of the Brussels Revision of the Berne Convention allows member states to make this exclusion in respect of speeches.

2.38   When in its written form, even if taken from a shorthand note or a tape-recording, a judgment is revised and approved by the judge who gave it before it is published. The judge would therefore appear to be the author. A publisher of law reports is entitled to the copyright in any headnote which he appends to a law report. It is submitted, however,

3.   Cmnd 6732, para 609 (ix).

that the publisher is not entitled to claim any copyright in a verbatim judgment which he reproduces. Even if he has taken an assignment from the judge of any rights in the judgment, it forms part of the record of the court, and as such is governed by the Public Record Office Acts of 1838 and 1958. A publisher would of course be entitled to claim protection for a casebook composed of abridgements or annotations of cases, but he cannot claim copyright in respect of a verbatim extract from a judgment he has published.

2.39 The Association of Shorthand Writers submitted to the Whitford Committee that a shorthand writer should enjoy copyright in his reports.[4] It based its argument on the degree of skill and/or labour involved. That Association would no doubt rely on the decision in *Walter v. Lane*.[5] The problem is that if the shorthand report is absolutely accurate, it would not appear to contain the element of originality required by section 1(1)(a) CDPA, and accordingly should not be entitled to copyright. On the other hand, an inaccurate transcription would be entitled to copyright, as it would be original by virtue of its inaccuracy. For another problem posed by this requirement of originality, see the discussion of copyright in arrangements in chapter 5.

International Organisations

2.40 Section 168 introduces copyright protection for original literary, dramatic, musical or artistic works made by officers or employees of certain international organisations which would not otherwise qualify by virtue of place of publication or the qualification of the author. It is aimed at works published by bodies such as the United Nations in circumstances which would otherwise leave them bereft of protection.

Folklore

2.41 Folklore has been tackled by sections 5, 61 and 169 CDPA. The result will not be to everyone's satisfaction, but then few solutions are in copyright. The existence of traditional airs in the folk tradition of many countries has long been the subject of plunder within the music industry. A number of melodies have risen to the top of the charts, and even passed into permanence as "evergreens", which had been previously known only in the folk repertoire of a particular locality. See the evidence in *Robertson v. Lewis*,[6] where knowledge of the tune which

4. Cmnd 6732, para 589.
5. [1900] A.C. 539.
6. The Times 1 June 1960.

became "Westering Home" appeared to have been confined for generations to a narrow circle of pipers, probably in an untranscribed form. Section 169 allows the United Kingdom to meet the requirements imposed by the Paris Revision of the Berne Convention. Section 61 allows a sound recording of a performance to be made, for the purpose of including it in an archive maintained by a body designated by the Secretary of State, without infringing copyright if certain conditions are met. The words are to be unpublished and of unknown authorship at the time of the recording, the recording is not to infringe any other copyright, and its making is not to be prohibited by any performer. We are not told whether it is considered that a tribesman performing in a remote valley in the Andes will have a copy of the Act about his person.

CHAPTER 3

Printing and Publishing

3.01 Printing was invented in the mid-fifteenth century, and brought to England by Caxton around 1451. It had an immediate impact on the social and economic structure of each state to which the new technology was in turn introduced. Multiple and comparatively swift reproduction of words and ideas meant both that writings unwelcome to established authority in Church and State could be widely distributed, and also that the means to make substantial profits became available to those who controlled the technology. Clearly the situation had to be regulated, and what better way to control it than by making it the subject of purchase from the controlling authority? Empty coffers could be replenished by the sale of licences and monopolies, and the system was quickly applied to printing. It was convenient to grant licences to print all books in a particular field, such as dictionaries and lawbooks.

3.02 Protection of the printed word now stems from section 1 CDPA, which protects both literary and dramatic works, in addition to musical and artistic works. This protection includes restrictions against reproducing the work in any material form, and also against publishing it. In practice the author, who is generally the first owner of copyright, either assigns or licenses his rights to a publisher, in order that the latter may exploit it commercially, hopefully to the benefit of both parties.

LICENCE AND ASSIGNMENT

3.03 There is an important distinction between a *licence* and an *assignment*. A licence is a limited right, allowing the person licensed (the licensee) to deal with the work in a specified way, and in some cases for a specified period of time. A licence may also be limited as to place, allowing a licensee to carry out certain acts in relation to the work in some territories only, the copyright-owner granting similar licences to others in different territories or not as he chooses. An assignment on the other hand is a complete and unreserved transfer of all interest in the work; once an assignment has been granted, the assignor has no further claim in relation to the works assigned beyond the price paid and agreed for the assignment.

3.04 There is no obvious advantage for an author in granting a publisher a full assignment of his work, and if at all possible he should try to confine matters to the grant to the publisher of a licence to print. It should also be borne in mind that section 90(3) CDPA makes it necessary for any assignment of copyright, whether total or partial, to be in writing and signed by the assignor. It is also generally an advantage for an author when entering into a publishing agreement to try to obtain a firm commitment from his publisher actually to publish the work by a certain date. If there is no such undertaking, then the publisher is not actually under any obligation to bring the work out in book form.

PUBLISHERS' CONTRACTS

3.05 Any author who intends to derive all or even part of his income from his literary activities should try to acquire some working knowledge of copyright. When offering his work for publication, particularly where this is to a magazine editor rather than a book publisher, he should make it quite plain what rights he is tendering. Generally it will be in the author's interests to ensure that he grants no more than first British serial rights for any magazine article. Formal contracts as such are not generally used by magazine editors accepting manuscripts from occasional contributing authors; when a manuscript is accepted, an author in this category should always make certain that he receives a letter setting out what rights are being acquired by the magazine, how much is being paid for the work, and when it is to be printed. The time to clarify any uncertainty is before the work is finally accepted, not after.

3.06 So far as remaindering is concerned, an author or his agent should, when entering a book contract, attempt to delay the right of the publisher to sell the work as remainders for as long as possible. Obviously this is a matter governed by the respective bargaining position of the parties, but it is certainly desirable to try to ensure a period of at least two years before this action is taken. Another contractual point which should not be missed is to write in an option for the author to purchase for himself any stock sought to be remaindered.

3.07 If submitting photographs with a manuscript for a book, an author should ensure that he does not assign the complete copyright in the photographs to the publisher; authors, certainly those writing in specialist fields, should always retain control over the selection of the illustrations to be published in the work. Any writer who is contemplating the production of a work jointly with a co-author should ensure that the contractual agreement specifies quite clearly the parts to be contributed by each author. It should also provide for what compensation should be paid by a co-author who fails to fulfil his part of the agreement. This is particularly important where a substantial advance has been paid. What may seem a good partnership when the idea for a book is first conceived may rapidly become tarnished as conflicts of approach and even style arise. Consideration should also be given to the problem of future editions, and the prospect that a co-author may have died, or even become disinclined to continue his association with the work.

WRITERS' ASSOCIATIONS

3.08 Generally speaking, authors are less well able to protect themselves than their publishers, who have access to the few specialist legal practitioners of copyright; and in the case of larger publishing houses, there will usually be several members of the permanent staff who have acquired a practical experience of copyright. But it is a wide and fast-moving world these days, and new situations are constantly being thrown up with the introduction of new technology. For the author who is confronted with a technical problem, and who cannot afford access to individual specialist advice, membership of a body such as the Society of Authors is virtually a necessity.

A highly experienced staff exists in the Society, which provides advice on technical matters affecting authorship, particularly in the areas of copyright, contract and taxation. Members are kept in touch with each other and with the work of the Society through the medium of an excellent periodical *The Author*. This carries authoritative articles on issues of current interest to authors and the world of publishing, and provides comment on proposals for new legislation relating to copyright. The staff of the Society are continually making representations for review of areas of difficulty relating to copyright. They will undoubtedly campaign vigorously for the overhaul of provisions in the new Act which they perceive to be disadvantageous for their members.

3.09 Other organisations exist which embrace similar aims. Mention may be made of the Writers' Guild, and also the Freelance Branch of the National Union of Journalists, although in the case of the latter, membership is only available to writers who derive the greater part of their income from their pen, thus excluding the large number of authors for whom writing professionally is only a part-time occupation. Publishers also have their own organisation in the shape of the Publishers

Association, which has done sterling work on its members' behalf over the years.

3.10 Reference should also be made to the Authors' Lending and Copyrights Society (ALCS). Among its activities are the collection and distribution of sums paid by countries overseas in respect of rights in the nature of public lending right which these states may operate in their own territories. ALCS has established reciprocal arrangements with foreign societies operating in this field, including those in Czechoslovakia, Italy, Portugal, Spain and West Germany. In the case of the latter, it should be noted that under West German regulations, the money due for library borrowings cannot be paid direct to an individual, but only through an authorised collecting society. In fact WORT, the West German society, was the first overseas country to make a payment to ALCS in respect of library borrowings in a foreign country by British authors.

Blanket Licensing

3.11 It may be that the traditional concept of copyright licensing, under which an individual author receives an individual payment in respect of each identifiable use of his work, will cease to be a practical proposition. As the number of potential uses multiply, and the advances of technology make individual uses harder to pinpoint, so the only resort becomes some kind of blanket licence. Then some form of measurement has to be applied to establish the relative shares of individual authors in relation to each other. Sadly, the yardstick is often going to be a rough and ready one.

PIRATED EDITIONS

3.12 Owners of rights in literary and dramatic works are at the present time under considerable pressure from the threats posed by multiple reproduction, computer use and other technological innovations, and these will be considered in more detail elsewhere in this work. But another problem which has always existed for author and publisher alike is unauthorised reproduction of complete works in the form of publication in a pirated edition, which at the present time has again become a considerable menace.

3.13 The practice was rife in the United States in the nineteenth century, when well-known literary figures such as Dickens campaigned for an international system of protection which would stamp out the loss of royalties in the parts of the English-speaking world which at that time would not pay English authors for the unauthorised publication of their works. A prohibition against the importation of pirated editions was introduced at an early date, and powers of seizure, forfeiture and prosecution in respect of infringing importations were given to the customs authorities.

3.14 Now a number of established British authors and publishers are complaining that some of their works have appeared in foreign pirated editions for which no contract has been agreed, and for which no payments have been made. Indeed, in many cases, until the matter is drawn to the writer's attention, he may have no knowledge that the edition exists, and it may well conflict with his own plans for bringing out a revised edition.

3.15 In the past the situation may have come about because a work published in the days of the old manufacturing clause in America (under which books by American authors or co-authors forfeited copyright protection unless printed in the U.S.A. or imported in only very small quantities—see chapter 17) may well never have obtained copyright protection in that country. This could have come about by failure to have the work separately manufactured there. In other cases, copyright may not have been renewed after the expiry of the first 28-year period of protection. However, now that the U.S. Copyright Act of 1976 has come fully into force the problem is unlikely to recur.

3.16 Where a situation of this kind has come about, it is not often a practical proposition for a right-owner to go to the expense, which could well be out of all proportion to the eventual compensation, of bringing an action for infringement of copyright in foreign courts. But the problem continues to grow, and it is the policy of the larger British publishing houses and the Publishers Association to mount some form of test case to remedy the position, wherever possible.

Precisely such an action formed the subject matter of *Butterworth and Others v. Ng Sui Nam.*[1] Butterworth, Longman, Lloyd-Luke, Sweet and Maxwell and Stevens joined in an action for the unauthorised reproduction of their published works. The case established that works first published in the United Kingdom do enjoy copyright protection in Singapore.

---

1. [1987] 2 F.T.L.R. 198 High Court of Singapore; see McFarlane, *Copyright through the Cases* case 7.04 (1st instance).

NEW EDITIONS

3.17   Both author and publisher should take care to provide properly for the situation where the first edition of the work has gone out of print. If the licence to print extends only to one edition, it should be made clear in the contract whether the author is entitled to require his publisher to bring out another edition. If this right is not embodied in the agreement, then a prudent author should reserve the right to go to another publisher for a second edition, in order to make the position quite clear. A publisher on the other hand may make the question of a second edition a matter entirely within his discretion, and in any case the contract should provide for the situation where the author is unwilling to carry out the necessary revisions for the preparation of a second edition.

CHAPTER 4

The Music Industry

THE STATUTORY POSITION

4.01 Together with literary, dramatic and artistic works, musical works are one of the four classic heads of copyright currently accorded protection by Part I of CDPA. The right in musical works subsists by virtue of section 1(1)(a). By section 3(1), a musical work is defined as meaning "a work consisting of music, exclusive of any words or action intended to be sung, spoken or performed with the music". The nature of the protection appears in section 16. It consists of the exclusive right to do the following acts in the United Kingdom:
  (a) copying the work;
  (b) issuing copies of the work to the public;
  (c) performing or playing the work in public;
  (d) broadcasting the work or including it in a cable programme service;
  (e) making an adaptation of the work or doing any of the acts in (a) to (d) in relation to an adaptation.

Definition of "Musical Work"

4.02 The inclusion of a definition of "musical work" in CDPA is very interesting. No definition of the term was contained in the Copyright Act 1956. However, one did appear in the Musical (Summary Proceedings) Copyright Act of 1902, since repealed. That provision was for "any combination of melody and harmony, or either of them, reduced to writing or otherwise graphically produced or reproduced". It is submitted that the 1902 version is preferable to that of 1988 (in section 3(1)), making it clear that sheet music is covered. Note that where in addition words are added to the musical work they constitute a literary or sometimes dramatic work, separate from the musical work.

Performing rights

4.03 It is the practice, however, in this country for both the composer of the musical work and the writer of the words attached to it to join the Performing Right Society (PRS), and as both assign their rights to the

PRS, that organisation is in a position to license both words and music at the same time. The music-user does not have to make separate searches for the writer and for the composer, but simply approaches the PRS for the licence he requires. This is the simplest procedure for all concerned.

4.04 Present-day lyric writers may be surprised to learn that in the early part of the nineteenth century music publishers esteemed the labours of authors of words attached to musical works so little that they made no payment for them. Even as late as 1875–76, a music publisher giving evidence to the Copyright Committee which sat then stated that the words of songs published at that time were of very little value in literary terms. Indeed, the recommendation of that Committee, which was not carried forward into law, was that the lyric-writer should not, without special agreement, enjoy a copyright in the words.[1]

4.05 Unlike the position affecting artistic works, the copyright in musical works has a highly effective positive feature, as well as the negative one of preventing unauthorised reproduction. This is the performing right, which first received statutory recognition in the Literary Copyright Act of 1842, a performing right for the written word having been introduced by the Dramatic Copyright Act of 1833. These statutes put into legislative form the decision of *Macklin v. Richardson*, which first established in the United Kingdom the principle of a performing right.[2]

4.06 The system of international accounting between collecting societies in respect of the performing right is described in Chapter 16 on copyright collecting societies; see para 16.18. From a rather hesitant beginning in both Britain and the United States in 1914, the principle has flourished to the point where composers and writers are able to expect a reasonable return from their works, and that their dependants will receive in many cases certain provision after their death. The best practical advice which it is possible to give to a newly emerged songwriter is: join the PRS, or its equivalent abroad if this is more appropriate.

Licence to Reproduce: Mechanical Right

4.07 The statutory compulsory licence available to music publishers to copy records sold by retail, known in the music industry as the mechanical right, has been very substantially affected by CDPA. Previously

1. Copyright Commission (1875–76), Report, paras 74–75.
2. (1770) 2 Amb 694.

contained in section 8 of the Copyright Act 1956, the provision is by virtue of paragraph 21 of Schedule 1 to CDPA to continue to apply only where the appropriate notice was given before the repeal of the old section 8 by CDPA. However, this is only in respect of the making of records (a) within one year of the repeal coming into force and (b) up to the number of records stated in the notice as intended to be sold. See also paras 11.21 *et seq* below.

INTERNATIONAL POSITION

4.08 In many countries outside the United Kingdom the same copyright collecting society operates in respect of both the mechanical and the performing right. There is an international organisation of mechanical right societies, which is known as the Bureau International de L'Édition Méchanique (BIEM). As with the performing right societies and CISAC (see para 16.06), BIEM links the mechanical right societies through international contracts of affiliation, so that each collects on its own territory in respect of its own members, and also on behalf of the members of each other society with which it is affiliated. By the same contract each national society is in a position to grant licences on its own territory in respect of the repertoires of each society with which it is affiliated, and thus by this system of international linkage a society is able to offer its licensees access to what is in effect a worldwide range of copyright music.

4.09 Thus a licensee in London or Paris, Sydney or New York has available effectively the entire catalogue of music which he is likely to need, in both the popular and classical fields. Admittedly, there are still some areas of the world where either states are not members of the international copyright system, or where no collecting society exists, but these lie outside the system and no societies exist in those areas which are entitled to collect on other territory. So once the licensee in any country within the copyright system organised by CISAC and BIEM has paid his royalty, he is free from the danger that remote foreign societies unaffiliated to the system will attempt to extract an additional fee from him.

Piracy

4.10 As is the case with other areas of work protected by copyright, musical works suffer considerably at the present time from the scourge of unauthorised reproduction. The piracy of sound recordings, and the question of bootlegging, involves the use of musical works which is almost invariably unauthorised by the owners of the rights in these works. The resultant loss to the copyright-owners is considerable. These right-owners also have no control over such matters as the unauthorised reproduction of television programmes and films which contain musical works, yet these represent a very considerable loss to the right-owners. Some attempt has been made to address these problems, and these will be discussed in detail in Chapter 15.

4.11 It is nevertheless particularly advisable when drawing up an assignment or licence which relates to the disposition of rights in musical works to deal expressly with the question of rights which may not exist at the present time, or which may be developed in the future. For example, the advent of satellite broadcasting has given rise to a dimension of exploitation which was in no-one's mind when contracts were being drawn up in the 1950s, and yet rights for works created then should in the normal course of events endure at least until the turn of the century. Similarly with literary works the topic of computer use was not in consideration at that time and yet it has now become of crucial importance. A contract should therefore specify whether any assignment includes both rights existing at the present time in the nature of copyright, and those rights of like nature yet to be developed.

EXTENT OF PERFORMING RIGHT

4.12 In a field of law which has seldom produced a consistent flow of important decisions, there has in the last two decades been a burst of reported decisions on copyright in the United Kingdom. Some of these are of considerable importance, and the greater part deal with musical works in one form or another.

4.13 It is frequently assumed that the extent of the performing right in musical works has for long been completely settled. Undoubtedly most of the cases establishing the limits within which it may be exercised date from between the wars, but occasionally a new area crops up which requires litigation. Often these are due to new technological developments, but sometimes they are brought about simply by more aggressive styles of marketing, with the result that the application of the musical work in this new manner requires to be considered.

PRS v. Harlequin

4.14 One such arose in *Performing Right Society Ltd v. Harlequin Record Shops Ltd.*[3] Before 1976 the PRS did not seek to license owners of record shops in respect of the playing of sound recordings on their premises. No doubt this was because for many years the vendors of gramophone records employed booths for the benefit of their potential customers, who listened to the proprietor's wares in some privacy. Generally it was impossible for the sound of the recording to be heard outside the booth, but the practice grew up of playing recordings which could be heard by all the customers in the shop, and the sound frequently spread well beyond the confines of the shop, so that it could sometimes be heard on the pavement outside.

4.15 When the PRS altered its policy and sought to claim a royalty from the defendant record shop proprietors for the performance in public of musical works controlled by the Society, they were met with the argument that the playing of the recordings promoted their sale, and therefore augmented the royalties payable to the composers. Further it was contended that the playing of the recordings did not amount to a performance in public, in that an audience whose only common factor was that they were potential purchasers of the composer's works on records was not part of the composer's public, in the sense that a composer would anticipate the receipt of a royalty from the performance of the work to them. Alternatively, it was argued for the defence that the assignment from the composer to the PRS of the rights in musical works was subject to an implied reservation of the right to license shops selling records to play recordings of the composer's works for the purpose of promoting sales. Nevertheless, the court found against the defence on all these points, and an injunction was granted in favour of the Performing Right Society preventing the playing of sound recordings in this way without the Society's licence first having been obtained.

CBS v. Charmdale

4.16 Another decision involving sound recordings upon which musical works were embodied was *CBS United Kingdom Ltd v. Charmdale Record Distributors Ltd.*[4] Charmdale had purchased in the United States and had imported into the United Kingdom for the purposes of resale sound recordings made by an American corporation, CBS Inc, who were the owners or exclusive licensees of the copyright in sound recordings. It

3. [1979] 2 All E.R. 828
4. [1980] 2 All E.R. 807

had in turn granted to its United Kingdom subsidiary, CBS Ltd, exclusive rights to manufacture and sell the same sound recordings in the United Kingdom. But the sound recordings bought and resold by Charmdale included new releases from CBS Inc which CBS Ltd meant to release in the United Kingdom at a later date.

4.17 CBS Ltd accordingly brought an action for infringement alleging that Charmdale had without the licence of the copyright-owner in breach of section 16(2) and (3) of the Copyright Act of 1956 imported an article into the United Kingdom and sold it when to the knowledge of Charmdale the making of that article would have constituted an infringement of copyright if the article had been made in the United Kingdom. Nevertheless it was held that Charmdale had not infringed copyright as CBS Ltd was not an owner of copyright within the meaning of section 16 of the Copyright Act, that company being a mere licensee with contractual rather than proprietary rights. In particular, an exclusive licensee was not the owner of the copyright within the terms of the Act.

4.18 Further, CBS Ltd was not able to claim that, for the purposes of section 16(2) and (3) of the Copyright Act 1956, the hypothetical maker of the records in the United Kingdom was the importer or any unauthorised person who might have made the records in the United Kingdom, as the hypothetical maker referred to in those subsections was taken to be the person who had actually made the sound recording overseas.

The Who v. Stage One (Records)

4.19 Another decision involving sound recordings of musical works was that of *The Who Group Ltd and Polydor Ltd v. Stage One (Records) Ltd*,[5] a decision of the Chancery Division of the High Court of England, in which the possibility of a reference to the European Court of Justice under article 177 of the Treaty of Rome was considered. An action was brought for an interim injunction to restrain the importation into the United Kingdom from Holland of sound recordings which had been lawfully made in North America, and then lawfully imported into Holland. At that stage the recordings entered into free circulation within the EEC.

4.20 One of the factors contributing to the refusal of the injunction sought was the uncertainty surrounding the movement within the Common Market of goods originating outside it, which had already been

5. [1980] 2 C.M.L.R. 429

lawfully marketed in a member state of the Community. It was contended on behalf of the defence, that by virtue of the Treaty of Rome the plaintiff company Polydor could not resist the importation and sale of such recordings in the United Kingdom once they had been freely on sale in Holland. The court felt that the point had not been sufficiently explored in any of the cases on the interpretation of the Treaty of Rome which had been cited to it. This, taken in combination with a number of other difficulties, led the court to refuse the injunction sought, but the point was left open.

4.21 The European Court has subsequently made it clear that a member state may not use copyright legislation to prevent importation into that state from another member state of any goods legitimately made in or imported into the second member state. This is recognised by section 27(5) of CDPA, which states that an article so imported is not an "infringing copy" for the purposes of the section. In other words, it is no longer possible for a copyright licencee to obtain exclusivity in the U.K. unless his exclusive licence extends to the whole of the E.E.C. See further para. 18.26.

FILM SOUNDTRACKS

4.22 At one time some conflict existed between film production and distribution companies on the one hand and the Performing Right Society on the other over the question of PRS licensing of music synchronisation rights linked to rights of public performance. That is the valuable right of incorporating music, either background or feature, in the soundtrack of cinematograph film. It is the current practice of the PRS to require those of its members owning such rights to assign to the PRS the synchronisation right. The film companies complained that the PRS declined to allow its members to license synchronisation rights to film production companies unless that company entered into an agreement with the PRS to pay licence fees for the exhibition of the film, including the soundtrack, in the United States of America.

4.23 Practically every composer of film music in the United Kingdom is a PRS member, so that there is some justice in the claim that a monopoly situation exists. The obligation to pay a royalty to the Society is passed by the film production company to the film distribution company. At one time such royalty was paid by the owners of the cinemas in the United States which exhibit the films, but because of American antitrust legislation this is not possible now. The British film production companies therefore claimed that the Society was obliging them to pay royalties which ought to be paid by cinema owners in the United States.

4.24 At that time the Performing Right Tribunal had no jurisdiction over the reproduction right in the United Kingdom, which includes the synchronisation right. Nor did it enjoy any control over the right of public performance in the United States, and clearly could never hope to do so. The Whitford Committee in considering the matter reaffirmed its view that it is an obvious advantage for music-users to be able to obtain from one source a single licence for all the music which they require. But although sympathetic to the desire of the Society to obtain royalties for the public performance of its members' music in the United States, the members did not feel that the present practice of the Society should continue to be exercised without some control.[6]

4.25 The Report therefore recommended that the jurisdiction of the Performing Right Tribunal should be extended to cover licences of the reproduction right within the United Kingdom, at least in musical works, but restricted to licensing bodies having as one of their main objects the negotiation or granting of licences in respect of the reproduction and/or performing rights of the works of several authors. Although this solution would not have any effect on the situation in the United States, it would govern the position as between the British film production companies and the composers of film music. The matter is obviously crucial to both sides, for just as the British companies complain about the monopoly of the PRS in this area, it is true also that these writers have no other outlet for their works.

4.26 By section 149(a) of CDPA, the function of the new Copyright Tribunal, which replaces the old Performing Right Tribunal, has been extended to include consideration of licensing schemes referred to it. By virtue of section 117 of CDPA, this would extend to licensing schemes operated by licensing bodies in relation to musical works, films or film sound-tracks when accompanying a film.

---

6. Cmnd 6732, para 394.

CHAPTER 5

Music Industry Problems: Reversionary Rights and Arrangements

5.01 Musical works generate large sums of money for owners of the rights therein, and there are many different applications of them. Films, sound recordings, broadcasts all make use of music in some way, and it is perhaps not surprising that the exercise of all rights in this area of copyright has given rise to some very complex questions. Undoubtedly the consideration of reversionary rights was among the most difficult of those arising in the 1970s.

LIMITATION ON POWER TO ASSIGN OR LICENSE COPYRIGHT

5.02 By a proviso to section 5(2) of the Copyright Act of 1911, the owner of copyright in a work had a limitation placed on his power to assign or license copyright for the full term. Thus where the author was the first owner of copyright, no assignment of copyright and no grant of interest by him other than by will was operative to vest any rights beyond 25 years from his death; notwithstanding any agreement to the contrary, any reversionary interest outstanding at that period was to devolve on his personal representatives as part of his estate. Indeed, any interest to the contrary was to be null and void, and the proviso finished with a form of words which was to cause much dispute, and give rise to lengthy litigation: "... nothing in this proviso shall be construed as applying to the assignment of the copyright in a collective work or a licence to publish a work or part of a work as part of a collective work."

5.03 It is thought that the main consideration behind the introduction of this measure in the statute of 1911 was a desire to protect the dependants of an author against an improvident agreement made during his lifetime, so that in such circumstances there would be an opportunity for them to negotiate a new agreement with a publisher for the remaining part of the copyright. This Act came into force prior to the existence of the Performing Right Society, indeed at a time when the performing right was not extensively exercised, and an unworldly songwriter had less access to sound professional advice than would be the case today.

Continuance of reversionary right provision

5.04 The Copyright Committee of 1952, the Gregory Committee, had recommended the omission of this proviso, and although this was accepted, a number of transitional provisions were made in the resulting Copyright Act of 1956. The upshot was that by paragraph 28(3) of Schedule 7 to that Act, the reversionary right provision re-enacted in paragraph 6 of Schedule 8 continued to apply to licences and assignments made prior to 1 July 1957. The provision was to prove considerably more enduring than must have appeared when the 1956 legislation was passing through Parliament. An assignment made immediately before 1 July 1957 by an author who had just then attained his majority would not necessarily reach the post-mortem period of 25 years until midway through the 21st century.

5.05 Little thought was given to the matter for many years after the enactment of the Copyright Act of 1956, and during that time the reversionary rights do not appear to have been much exercised, if at all. In the early 1970s, however, an astute American lady began to circulate the heirs of British songwriters pointing out the existence of the rights, and an agency was formed for the purpose of renegotiating rights for the remaining 25 years.

5.06 This caused a good deal of dismay in the publishing world, which had not expected to have to deal with the position. In fact, it seems to have been overlooked until that time, and most assignments and the contracts relating to them had been entered on the basis that copyright would endure unaffected for the full post-mortem period of 50 years. When the matter was considered by the Whitford Committee, the British Copyright Council submitted to it that the public interest had altered since 1911, and that far from protecting an author's heirs, in many cases the only practical effect of the exercise of reversionary rights had been to transfer rights between publishers without any significant benefit to the heirs.

5.07 There was pressure to alter the situation, and the British Copyright Council went so far as to suggest that it would be in the public interest to impose a form of compulsory licence in cases arising where reversionary rights were being exercised without any clear assurance that the heirs would benefit therefrom. The Performing Right Society felt that if this could not be introduced, then at the least any new legislation should limit the operation of reversionary rights in the future to the works of authors who had died before 1 July 1957.

Whitford recommendations

5.08 The members of the Whitford Committee sympathised with the views advanced by these interested bodies, but felt that they should not recommend the introduction of retrospective legislation which would affect agreements already entered into in anticipation of future benefits. They did, however, recommend to the extent that this is not already clear, that the law should provide, in the case of works caught by the reversionary rights provision, for assignments and licences in respect of the residuary period to be made at any time, either by the author, if still living, or by his heirs if he is dead.

5.09 A large number of people will already have inherited a potential reversionary right position, and as writers now alive and over the age of about 60 themselves die, their heirs will also be affected. Because it is a topic which arose rather unexpectedly, and because so many agreements were made without proper account having been taken of it, it has given rise to rather emotional discussion, and interested parties have taken up somewhat entrenched positions. Anyone confronted with a problem involving reversionary rights should seek the advice of solicitors specialising in music industry problems.

Adoption overseas of British legislation

5.10 It should also be borne in mind that after the 1956 Act was passed in the United Kingdom, a number of overseas territories adopted the British legislation as it then stood, including those provisions in the Schedules which dealt with reversionary rights. In some instances these countries will already have replaced the British Act of 1956 with legislation of their own which probably does not contain reversionary rights. Thus any contract purporting to deal with reversionary rights should consider the position arising overseas, as well as that within the United Kingdom.

Collective works

5.11 It will be recalled that the proviso to section 5(2) of the Copyright Act of 1911 referred to "collective works". In *Chappell Ltd v. Redwood Music Ltd, Redwood Music Ltd v. Francis Day and Hunter Ltd*,[1] the matter was considered in the House of Lords. The appellant music publishers had acquired over the years the copyrights in works by a large number of songwriters, and in many cases the music had been written by

1. [1980] 2 All E.R. 817.

one person and the words by another. The effect of the proviso is that an assignment prior to 1957 reverts to the author's heirs 25 years after his death, unless the work is a collective one. The respondent company had taken assignments from heirs of deceased songwriters of the words and music of many works exploited by the appellant, and the respondent claimed the copyright in these works on the ground that they were not collective, and therefore did not fall within the exception to the proviso.

5.12 The decision would be of crucial importance, for if the respondents were to succeed the effect would be that in all musical works where there was a combination of melody and words, the reversion would bite after 25 years, and the heirs and persons claiming under deceased writers' estates would be able to enter fresh arrangements about the remaining term of copyright. A very substantial proportion of popular music written before 1957 would fall into this category, with lyrics set to music and forming the same work.

5.13 Eventually the House of Lords held by a majority that the expression "copyright in a collective work" in the proviso to section 5(2) of the Copyright Act of 1911 meant that a separate copyright existed in a collective work as such, which was in addition to the copyrights existing in the constituent parts of it; in the words of Lord Russell of Killowen, it was something which by original collocation has a copyright of its own. The definition in section 35(1) of the Act referred to
   "(a) an encyclopaedia, dictionary, year book, or similar work;
    (b) a newspaper, review, magazine, or similar periodical; and
    (c) any work written in distinct parts by different authors, or in which works or parts of works of different authors are incorporated."
But the Law Lords decided that there was no third and separate copyright in the combination of the words and music of a song, and that a song was not therefore a collective work within the meaning of the proviso.

5.14 The draftsman of CDPA has incorporated the decision in the *Chappell* case in an elegant and practical manner. Paragraph 27 of Schedule 1 to the 1988 Act incorporates the provision which originally appeared in section 5(2) of the Copyright Act 1911, including the exception for assignments of copyright in a collective work. The crucial difference is that on this occasion, the vital definition of "collective work" which had appeared in section 35(1) of the 1911 Act has been applied. The result is clear: the combination of words and music of a song is not a collective work for the purposes of the reversionary right provisions.

ORIGINALITY IN RELATION TO ARRANGEMENTS
AND ADAPTATIONS

5.15 The Whitford Committee referred to another problem which has caused some confusion, both in relation to musical works, and elsewhere in the application of copyright. This concerns originality in relation to arrangements and adaptations, and there must be serious doubt as to whether the legislation as drafted correctly expresses in this connection the effect which it was desired to achieve.

Statutory position

5.16 The Act makes it quite clear that for copyright protection to attach to a literary, dramatic, musical or artistic work, that work must be original. By Section 1(1) of CDPA it is provided that "Copyright is a property right which subsists in accordance with this Part in the following descriptions of work—(a) original literary, dramatic, musical or artistic works . . ."

In the case of literary, dramatic and musical works, copyright protection granted to an original work means the right of the owner of copyright to restrict certain acts in relation to that work. These are enumerated by section 16(1) as:

(a) copying the work;

(b) issuing copies of the work to the public;

(c) performing, showing or playing the work in public;

(d) broadcasting the work or including it in a cable programme service;

(e) making an adaptation of the work or doing any of the acts in (a) to (d) in relation to an adaptation.

5.17 Section 21 spells out what is meant by an adaptation. In the case of a literary or dramatic work, it is:

(1) a translation of the work;

(2) a version of a dramatic work in which it is converted into a non-dramatic work or a version of a non-dramatic work in which it is converted into a dramatic work; or

(3) a version of the work in which the story or action is conveyed wholly or mainly by means of pictures in a form suitable for reproduction in a book, or in a newspaper, magazine or a similar periodical.

In relation to a musical work, it means an arrangement or transcription of a work. Note that in relation to a computer program a "translation" includes a version of the program in which it is converted into or out of a computer language or code or into a different computer language or code otherwise than incidentally in the course of running the program.

5.18 Thus the owner of copyright is absolutely entitled to restrict all these acts, by virtue of the originality of his works. He can either forbid anyone else completely to do any of the acts, or he can if he so desires license them. But the control of his works which the Act gives him is complete in relation to all the acts enumerated, once the originality of his work is established. It follows from the drafting of CDPA that the various acts controlled by section 16(1) are not in themselves of sufficient originality to enjoy copyright in their own right. If they were sufficiently original, any of these acts would enjoy a copyright of their own, as an original literary, dramatic or musical work, and they could not be controlled by the copyright in another original work.

The Whitford Committee

5.19 With due respect to the members of the Whitford Committee, it is submitted they were wrong when in their consideration of this question they stated "There will be the possibility, as now, of two copyrights existing in parallel, one covering the work, and the other the arrangement, but we do not think any amendment of the Act is necessary". This interpretation is a contradiction of the structure of section 2 of the Copyright Act 1956 and of section 16(1) CDPA which has replaced it, and there was nothing else in the Act to support it. It may well have been the intention of those who drafted the 1956 Act that there should be a separate copyright in all translations, dramatisations and musical arrangements of copyright works which should belong to the translator, dramatiser or arranger as the case may be. As the law now stands they have merely carried out one of the acts protected by the copyright in the original work, and to do this they must have acquired from him the right to do so, either by assignment or licence.

DIVISIBLE COPYRIGHT

5.20 By section 90(2) CDPA, copyright is divisible, and thus the owner of copyright in the original work can assign the right to translate to a translator, who thereafter is the owner of the copyright in the translation. But that assignment would be complete, and once the rights in the translation had been assigned, the assignor, in other words the owner of the rights in the original work, would have no further control over the translation.

SUFFICIENT ORIGINALITY

5.21 A further difficulty is that if any work is sufficiently original, it becomes entitled to copyright in its own right; if this is the case, the owner of copyright in another work can have no control over it. It is very difficult indeed to establish the point at which a work has achieved sufficient originality to acquire its own protection; art almost always builds on previous art to some degree, in whatever form it is expressed.

Musical arrangements

5.22 In the field of music, however, where arrangements are made of musical works which are in the public domain, in other words out of copyright, those arrangements are regarded as being entitled to copyright. It is hard to discern the justification for this in the legislation where the work is not sufficiently original. If the copyright in the original work has expired, there is no one with the power to license the making of an arrangement, or who can assign the right to make that arrangement.

Grading system by the PRS

5.23 The Performing Right Society has a well-earned reputation for its careful administration of the area of copyright committed to its care. Where arrangements of non-copyright musical works are concerned, it has set up an elaborate scheme of grading which is applied to the royalties earned by such works.[2]

Grades
5.24 A grading of 12/12 is given to those arrangements consisting of works which are not merely arrangements of non-copyright music, but which in their form are new compositions, even though based upon non-copyright themes. This clearly fits the philosophy of the Copyright Act, as the element of originality allows the arrangement to be considered as an original work in its own right. The allotment of points then diminishes, through 9/12 for what are termed "creative arrangements", and 6/12 for "straightforward concerted settings including vocal arrangements"; 4/12 is the rating granted to "simple settings for 1 or 2 instruments. For simple accompaniments in staff notation, i.e. not chord symbols", and for "simple accompanying chords or chord symbols", 2/12 is given. This also includes minor additions or alterations to melodic lines.

2. See Performing Right Yearbook (1978), p. 62.

5.25 Finally, under the heading of "simple transcriptions", the Society gives 1/20 for "unarranged transcriptions of folk-songs collected in the field". This does not accord with the decision in *Robertson v. Lewis*,[3] which established that a copyright in favour of someone who wrote down a traditional air was not proved to exist where there was no evidence of original additions or arrangements by the transcriber. Sections 61 and 169 of CDPA make limited provision for protecting musical works which are part of folklore.

Expansions and reductions of original work
5.26 The attitude of the PRS is very practical; in evaluating different kinds of "simple transcriptions", it is considered that usually expansion from a smaller medium to a larger, more complex one demands a more positive contribution from the transcriber than does a reduction, which is a matter of selection and omission. Consequently transcriptions from one medium to another of equal complexity have received lower ratings than expansions. They have, however, been rated higher than reductions, although the latter may nevertheless call for considerable ingenuity.

5.27 The approach of the PRS is a logical attempt by experienced musicians and composers to clothe with reality the situation as between the arranger or transcriber on the one hand, and the original work as it exists on the other. It is submitted however that as CDPA stands, a work is either original and in copyright, or it is insufficiently original, and therefore not entitled to copyright. The Act puts it in black and white, but the reality is one of varying shades of grey.

TRANSLATIONS

5.28 So far as translations are concerned, Professor George Steiner points to the difficulties of legislating in this area in his major work *After Babel: Aspects of Language and Translation* (1975) (1st edition, p. 403): "Too often, the translator feeds on the original for his own increase. Endowed with linguistic and prosodic talents, but unable to produce an independent, free life form, the translator (Pound, Lowell, Logue, even Pasternak) will heighten, overcrowd, or excessively dramatise the text which he is translating to make it almost his own trophy."

3. The Times 1 June 1960.

CHAPTER 6

Copyright in Artistic Works

6.01 Artistic works, with literary, dramatic and musical works, constitute one of the classical categories of matter protected by copyright. According to the European approach, it is because of their inherent qualities that an entitlement to copyright protection exists. The traditional British view had been reflected by grouping literary, dramatic, musical and artistic works in Part I of the Copyright Act 1956. The other matters which were protected appeared in Part II, did not receive the appellation of "works", and undoubtedly had a more industrial appearance. Films, sound records, broadcasts and typographical arrangements all have the characteristic of being the result of technical production, but the Part I works were the direct result of the efforts of the creative worker. As was pointed out by the Whitford Committee, this did give the impression that the matter protected by copyright fell into two classes; the Committee members rightly observed that some cinematograph films are creatively superior to certain types of literary work, such as price lists for example.[1] The distinction was certainly an unfortunate one, and the position has been rectified by grouping all works entitled to copyright together in section 1 CDPA. The old distinction between "Part I" and "Part II" works has been abolished and to the catalogue of 1956 there has now been added cable programmes.

DEFINITION

6.02 By section 4(1) of CDPA "artistic work" means
  (a) a graphic work, photograph, sculpture or collage, irrespective of artistic quality;
  (b) a work of architecture being a building or model for a building; or
  (c) a work of artistic craftsmanship.

6.03 The acts restricted by copyright in an artistic work are laid down by section 16 CDPA. They are:
  (a) copying the work;

---

1. Cmnd 6732, para 30.

(b) issuing copies of the work to the public; and

(c) showing the work in public.

In relation to an artistic work, copying includes the making of a copy in three dimensions of a two-dimensional work, and the making of a copy in two dimensions of a three-dimensional work.

GENERAL RULE

6.04   The general rule is that copyright in artistic works subsists for the life of the author, and a post-mortem period of 50 years. But there were two special cases under the 1956 Act, which need to be taken into account in respect of works existing prior to CDPA. In the case of an engraving, if before the death of the author the engraving had not been published, the copyright continued to exist until the end of the period of 50 years from the end of the calendar year in which it was first published. In the case of a photograph, copyright continued to exist until the end of 50 years from the end of the calendar year in which the photograph was first published, and then expired. By section 12(1) of CDPA, in relation to works made after its coming into force, the general rule is that copyright in all artistic works expires at the end of the period of 50 years from the end of the calendar year in which the author dies.

LIMITED NATURE OF COPYRIGHT

6.05   Clearly the extent of copyright in artistic works is rather more limited than that enjoyed by other works. The opportunities for publication, or reproduction, are scarcely applicable to the creator of a sculpture or the painter of a portrait; the potential for performance of an engraving in public does not exist. To a greater extent than elsewhere in the copyright legislation, copyright in artistic works has a negative quality. Undoubtedly the protection afforded by the law has not been responsible for generating royalties for right-owners in the way that musical and literary works have produced benefits for their right-owners.

6.06   There is also a somewhat piecemeal appearance to the section giving protection to artistic works. This is partly due to the interrelationship with design copyright (see Chapter 10 on industrial designs); and partly it is because of the history of copyright in the various categories of artistic works, which received protection by individual statutes at varying points in time. In the eighteenth century there were separate statutes for engravings (two) and prints, and in the nineteenth century there were further acts for sculpture, prints and fine art.

LEVEL OF ARTISTIC QUALITY AND COPYRIGHT

6.07 It is important to note that paintings, sculptures, drawings, engravings and photographs do not depend on the attainment of any artistic quality in order that copyright protection may extend to them. By Section 4(2) CDPA, a graphic work includes any painting, drawing, diagram, map, chart or plan and also any engraving, etching, lithograph or similar work. There is a new definition for "photograph". This means a recording of light or other radiation on any medium on which an image is produced or from which an image may by any means be produced and which is not part of a film. Finally in this connection, "sculpture" includes any cast or model made for the purposes of sculpture.

PERIOD OF COPYRIGHT PROTECTION FOR PHOTOGRAPHS

6.08 Previous to CDPA, there had been a discrepancy between the period of copyright protection for photographs and that for other artistic works. While the general rule provided for the life of the author plus a period of 50 years after his death, in the case of photographs, protection was only for a period of 50 years from first publication. Some time ago it was actually suggested that the period of protection should be reduced to 25 years, but this was not proceeded with. But under CDPA in respect of photographs made after the coming into force of the Act, protection is exactly the same as for other artistic works, namely life of the author plus 50 years. Thus a photograph is protected for longer than a film, for which copyright expires at the end of 50 years from making or release, whichever is the earlier.

POSITION IN EUROPE AND ELSEWHERE: *DROIT DE SUITE*

6.09 Partly in recognition of the fact that the opportunities for creators of artistic works to derive much benefit from their creations is limited, and partly because subsequent owners of artistic works have made large amounts from dealing in them, while the original creator has remained in comparative poverty, a doctrine has achieved some recognition in continental Europe known as the *droit de suite*. This derives from Article 14 *ter* of the Paris text of the Berne Convention, which provides that "the author, or after his death the persons or institutions authorised by national legislation, shall, with respect to original works of art and original manuscripts of writers and composers, enjoy the inalienable right to an interest in any sale of the work subsequent to the first transfer by the author of the work".

6.10 So that in countries where the *droit de suite* is acknowledged (and it depends on recognition by the domestic law) the creator of an artistic work and his heirs have a right to a percentage of the proceeds of each resale of that work. It is designed to protect an artist who may not achieve recognition until late in life to derive some benefit from the resulting enhanced value of his earlier works, which will probably have been sold at a much lower price than his later works. It is also motivated by a desire to provide for his dependants or heirs after his death.

6.11 The *droit de suite* exists in various forms in Algeria, Belgium, Brazil, Chile, Czechoslovakia, France, Italy, Luxembourg, Morocco, Norway, Poland, Portugal, Tunisia, Turkey, Uruguay and West Germany.

Consideration by Whitford Committee

6.12 The matter was considered by the Whitford Committee,[2] and, with respect to the members of that body, the analysis of the problem and the conclusions drawn from that analysis did not come up to the careful standards of the greater part of its Report. Much weight was placed on the fact that difficulty has been experienced in the collection of amounts owing, and that collection has proved to be expensive. It was pointed out that artists would have to be organised into societies in order that the right may be exercised. Furthermore, objection was raised that many artists would receive only a small amount from what would be an inconsiderable total collected.

6.13 None of these facts are very remarkable; indeed, they accord with the experience of established copyright collecting organisations in their early days. That a collecting society would be required is a truism, and in other fields such as the public lending right (PLR), it is acknowledged by the organisations representing producers of literary works such as the Society of Authors and the Writers Guild that the scheme can only be operated effectively by a collecting society, in this case the Public Lending Right Agency. Indeed, under the laws of certain foreign countries, right-owners can only participate in the fruits of the exercise of certain forms of public lending right if they are members of approved collecting societies.

2. Cmnd 6732, Ch 17.

Performing right

6.14 Of the four classes of works protected by section 1(1)(a) CDPA, artistic works alone are incapable of generating royalties for their right-owners by some means analogous to a performing right. As suggested earlier, in respect of an artistic work, copyright is largely negative. But a performing right in dramatic and literary works did not come into existence until considerable pressure for it had built up, first in France and then in the United Kingdom. Moreover, although a performing right in musical works was confirmed by the Literary Copyright Act of 1842, the right was not exercised to any extent until the formation of the Performing Right Society in 1914.[3]

6.15 Nor is it surprising that the right has not yet generated great sums of money for artists. The Whitford Committee overlooked the fact that this is the usual experience when a new right in the nature of copyright is exercised for the first time. When the Performing Right Society commenced operations in 1914, it had to enter into agreements at uneconomic rates simply to obtain recognition. In fact, no distribution was made to its members during the first three years of its existence. The total paid at that initial shareout was £11 000, a striking contrast with the £77 815 000 distributed in 1987.

For and against the introduction of the *droit de suite* in the United Kingdom

6.16 Reference was also made by the Report of the Whitford Committee to the suggestion of the Art Registration Committee that artists are unable to organise themselves. Nevertheless, submissions in favour of the introduction of the *droit de suite* were made by both the Federation of British Artists and the Royal Society of British Sculptors. Literary men and composers have also historically been poor at organising themselves, and would not achieve much in the way of exploiting their copyrights if they did not have the Society of Authors and the Performing Right Society respectively behind them.

6.17 In reaching its conclusion that the *droit de suite* should not be introduced in the United Kingdom, the Whitford Committee unfortunately relied on extremely technical objections to justify such rejection. One is left with the clear impression that undue consideration was given to the possible effect on the art market rather than the interests of the artists themselves and their dependants. At least five other member states

3. See McFarlane, *Copyright: The Development and Exercise of the Performing Right.*

of the European Economic Community recognise the right, and the United Kingdom should reconsider its position. If it does not do so, those responsible will have provided an area in which the EEC Commission could intervene. Given that the right is provided for in the Paris text of the Berne Convention, we are not at present in a strong position to resist such intervention. A percentage of the royalties collected for the artists could be ploughed back into the visual arts.

PAYING PUBLIC DOMAIN

6.18 A topic which was raised before the Gregory Committee on copyright in 1952, but not subsequently mentioned to the Whitford Committee, is that of the paying public domain, the *domaine public payant*. This is a system of not very wide application in certain states overseas whereby, after the general term of copyright has finished, persons using such works should continue to pay a royalty. This is channelled, not to the right-owners, but to a central fund which may be used either for the assistance of artists, authors and composers, or generally for the promotion of the arts. There are serious dangers for the copyright system in any scheme which gives the public the impression of an indirect tax, and it should be avoided at all costs.

6.19 Given that no paying public domain was introduced by CDPA, or even considered at any stage, it is quite inexcusable that an amendment should have been passed (now section 301) providing for royalties to be payable to the trustees of the Great Ormond Street Hospital for Sick Children arising from the use of the play *Peter Pan*, on which copyright would otherwise have expired. The author, James Barrie, had provided in his will that all royalties from the play should go to the hospital. It is an unacceptable exception to the principle of a limited life for copyright protection. It goes without saying that the Hospital for Sick Children is a deserving cause, but there are many equally deserving causes in the United Kingdom. All the experience of the taxing statutes is that once an exception to a general principle is made, it becomes very difficult to prevent a flood of similar exceptions pouring through the gap which has been made. CDPA talks in Schedule 6 of "Provision for the benefit of the Hospital for Sick Children", and that sums up the position precisely. The legislators have simply used somebody else's property to make a donation to a charity which caught their sympathy because of the imminent expiry of copyright at the time the Bill was passing through the House of Lords.

TYPE DESIGNS

Johnston Committee

6.20 The Johnston Committee on Industrial Designs which reported in 1962 gave detailed consideration to the question of type designs. Designs for individual letters could be registered under the Registered Designs Act 1949 if they possess the attribute of novelty, but generally founts of designs could not be so registered because they do not satisfy the test for registration as a set. Concluding that it was inappropriate that designs for founts should be accorded the protection of design legislation, the Johnston Committee felt that ordinary copyright law was more apt for the protection of lettering.

Vienna Agreement
6.21 After the Design Copyright Act of 1968, which has now been repealed, it appeared likely that typefaces were protected for 15 years after their first industrial manufacture. But it was doubted whether a set of lettering, as opposed to the individual letters, qualified as an artistic work within the terms of the Copyright Act 1956. Some authorities doubted whether British legislation at that time covered the position. Article 2 of the Vienna Agreement of 1973 for the Protection of Type Faces and their International Deposit defines type faces as sets of designs of:

    (a) letters and alphabets as such with their accessories such as accents and punctuation marks;

    (b) numerals and other figurative signs such as conventional signs, symbols and scientific signs;

    (c) ornaments such as borders, fleurons and vignettes; which are intended to provide means for composing texts by any graphic technique.

A state acceding to the Vienna Agreement may provide this protection either by its industrial design law, a provision for special deposit, or by means of its ordinary copyright laws, and must indicate which of these methods it intends to adopt.

6.22 Accordingly the Johnston Committee (1962) had recommended that copyright legislation should include the following provisions.[4]

    (i) copyright should subsist in every original set of lettering;

    (ii) the term 'lettering' should include letters, figures, punctuation, printing symbols, mathematic and scientific symbols;

---

4. Report of the Departmental Committee on Industrial Designs, paras 160–163.

(iii) it should be an infringement of the copyright in a set of lettering to reproduce the set, or a substantial part thereof, in any material form, including printed, written, televised, photographed and filmed representations of all kinds, regardless of the order or arrangement in which the members of the set appear;

(iv) these provisions should not prevent the subsistence of copyright in any original piece of lettering as an artistic work.

Whitford recommendations

6.23   The Whitford Committee considered the whole question in depth, and recommended that the views of the earlier Johnston Committee should be put into effect, and that the United Kingdom should ratify the Vienna Convention. Normal copyright rules should apply, and the term of protection should be 25 years.

6.24   It may be doubted whether the provision now made by sections 52, 54 and 55 CDPA, intended to implement these recommendations, successfully achieves this aim. Indeed, section 54(1) appears to prune back in the case of typefaces used in the ordinary course of printing on the extent of protection which would otherwise be accorded to an artistic work. Other aspects of industrial design are dealt with in Chapter 10.

CHAPTER 7

Copyright in Sound Recordings

7.01   Standing as we do at a point in time nine tenths of the way through the twentieth century, it is sometimes hard to credit just how long the gramophone record has been with us. Brightly packaged and presented, it carries marvellous reproductions of, according to taste, the jewels of classical music at one extreme, and the most contemporary trends in modern music at the other.

7.02   The phonograph was invented by Thomas Edison in 1877, and for almost two decades it played sound carriers in the form of cylinders. These were clumsy and jerky of tone, and were replaced by the wax disc in the 1890s. At first the discs could only carry sound on one side, but by 1905 records were double-sided, very much in the form which we knew them until the advent of the compact disc. Such original discs have become collectors' pieces, valued for their rarity and age. But in essence the gramophone record is much the same as it was in the early part of this century; precise running speeds and virtual perfection of sound have been attained, coupled with a vastly extended period of actual playing time. High quality commercially recorded audio tapes are also available, which have to some extent eroded the gramophone record's dominance; but the law makes no distinction between them as far as copyright is concerned.

7.03   As the gramophone and the sound carriers it played developed, they blossomed into a commercial proposition, and those who had invested in the prospect of commercial success naturally turned to seek protection for their wares. By the same token the owners of the rights in the musical works which were the subject of such recording also became concerned as to the extent of their own protection when the potential of the gramophone industry became apparent. For some time prior to the United Kingdom Copyright Act of 1911 a good deal of confusion reigned.

7.04   When the meetings of interested states took place which led to the establishment in 1886 of the Berne Convention on international copyright protection, Edison's patent had scarcely been developed beyond the stage of a novelty or toy. No doubt from feelings of sentiment to the

Swiss, whose Government had convened the diplomatic meetings, and whose craftsmen had established some foothold in the field of musical boxes and such novelties, the subscribing states agreed that reproduction of musical works by these means would not amount to an infringement.

The mechanical right

7.05 In 1900 the then copyright legislation, based on the Act of 1842, was held to furnish no protection for composers of musical works, in the case of *Boosey v. Whight*.[1] As the economic significance of the gramophone industry became more apparent, pressure built up from composers' representatives for more equitable treatment. Although the Copyright Committee of 1909 recommended complete control for composers over what was to become known as the mechanical right of reproduction of musical compositions on gramophone records, the Copyright Act 1911 arrived at a compromise. A compulsory licence was designed, whereby a composer of musical works who had already granted one record manufacturer a licence to record his works, was obliged to grant all other record manufacturers a similar licence to record, on payment of a statutory fee. This principle was designed to protect the small entrant to the gramophone industry against major concerns monopolising the market. Although it was carried forward with the 1956 legislation, by paragraph 21 of Schedule 1 to CDPA the mechanical right is only to continue on the limited conditions there provided for, described in para 4.07.

COPYRIGHT PROTECTION FOR RECORD MANUFACTURERS

7.06 The Copyright Act of 1911 also conferred a form of protection upon record manufacturers of their production. Contrary to the practice adopted in some other major European countries at the time, the protection was drafted in the form of a copyright, as opposed to an alternative protection as a form of industrial right. The wording of section 19(1) was to become crucial: "Copyright shall subsist in records, perforated rolls, and other contrivances by means of which sounds may be mechanically reproduced, in like manner as if such contrivances were musical works . . . "

Extension to public performance

7.07 For many years this new provision in the 1911 legislation was regarded as a reproduction right only, in other words a protection

1. [1900] 1 Ch 122.

against the unauthorised copying of the sounds recorded on the carrier. But in 1934 in a period of general recession, a gramophone manufacturer brought a claim against a company owning a tea-room in which a public performance of the sounds recorded on one of the plaintiff company's records was given.

7.08 The case was *Gramophone Company Ltd v. Cawardine Ltd.*[2] It was argued for the gramophone interests that this section accorded a performing right in sound recordings to the record manufacturers, in addition to the reproduction right which they had been exercising since 1912, and this was upheld by the trial judge in the Chancery Division of the High Court. On the face of it, this was a reasonable interpretation of the wording of the section, given that the Copyright Act 1911 granted both a reproduction right and a performing right to the owners of copyright in musical compositions. Nevertheless the report of the case does not reveal that any mention was made in court of the submissions made to the Copyright Committee of 1909 by the gramophone interests on the subject of a potential performing right.[3] These apparently amount to a disclaimer by the gramophone manufacturers of any interest in a performing right in their recordings, as they wished only to ensure at that time that the purchaser of their wares should have the right to perform them in public if he so chose.

7.09 This discrepancy was pointed out by the members of the Copyright Committee 1952 in their own Report, though after deep consideration they decided not to disturb the performing right in sound recordings as interpreted by the *Cawardine* case. It was accordingly carried forward into section 12 of the Copyright Act 1956, and the Whitford Committee did not make any recommendation for its repeal. Its preservation in the new copyright legislation is nevertheless in contrast to recent developments in other states which have modernised their copyright laws in recent years. The corresponding right which had previously existed in Canadian law was removed with effect from 1971, and a performing right in sound recordings has been expressly excluded in the United States by the Copyright Act of 1976.

Four distinct rights

7.10 In the United Kingdom a number of distinct rights exist in a sound recording by virtue of sections 1(1)(b) and 16(1) of CDPA. These

---

2. [1934] Ch 450.
3. Copyright Committee, Report, paras 1130–1132.

are copying it, issuing copies of it to the public, performing it in public, and broadcasting it or including it in a cable programme. It is vital to emphasise that the right protects the sound recording, that is the aggregate of sounds embodied on the record, as distinct from the physical record, disc or tape itself.

Phonographic Performance Ltd (PPL)

7.11   As a result of the recognition of the performing right in sound recordings in 1934 by the decision in the *Cawardine* case, the record manufacturers established a collecting society to exercise their new rights. This is known as Phonographic Performance Ltd (PPL), which issues licences to those wishing to make use of sound recordings by public performance and by broadcasting. Licences are issued, royalties collected in respect of them, and distributed among the various constituent member companies with a proportion of receipts being paid to organisations representing musicians and performing artists.

7.12   A good deal of criticism was voiced before the Copyright Committee of 1952 as to the manner in which PPL had been exercising its rights. A stark contrast was drawn by the Committee in its Report between the way in which the Performing Right Society had been conducting its operations, and those of the PPL administrators. The former never refused a licence if the appropriate fee was offered, but PPL frequently did, in spite of willingness to pay for its licences.[4] After reviewing the exercise of the rights by PPL over its whole field of operation, however, the Copyright Committee eventually decided not to recommend that the performing right in sound recordings given by the *Cawardine* case should be taken away, and PPL continues its operations at the present time.

United Kingdom and European approaches contrasted

7.13   A fundamental distinction exists between the approach of the United Kingdom and that of certain other European countries, notably France, to the concept of copyright protection. The British treatment is essentially pragmatic; if a need for protection emerges in a certain area, then Parliament should add the appropriate clause in any new copyright statute. Thus in CDPA specific provision has been made for computer programs and cable programmes. The European view is that copyright protection is inherent in respect of the products of those working in

---

4. Cmnd 8662, para 144.

certain clearly defined creative fields, such as literature, art and music. The product of a mere industrial process is, according to this view, not worthy of consideration as a subject of copyright, but must turn for its protection to the laws designed to shield manufacturing processes. It may be that if any harmonisation of domestic copyright legislation is proposed within the European Community, a good deal of conflict may take place in this area. In this connection it should be observed that the United Kingdom does not now enjoy the same domination in the record industry which was previously the case.

7.14   As early as the Berlin Conference of 1908 for the revision of the Berne Copyright Convention, the delegation of the United Kingdom had raised the question of whether it would be desirable to include in that instrument a provision giving specific protection to "gramophone discs, pianola rolls and so on". Even at that stage of development it was concluded that the matter was more appropriate to protection under industrial legislation, and this view has always subsequently been the one adopted by most members of the Berne Union.

ROME CONVENTION 1961

7.15   Attempts were made prior to the Second World War, principally by the Italian government, to draw up a separate convention giving protection to gramophone records, but these failed for lack of international support. Subsequently a convention was arranged to cover rights in sound recordings, and also two other areas which found themselves in anomalous positions internationally—performing artists, and broadcasting organisations. As a result of its deliberations the Rome Convention for the Protection of Performers, Producers of Phonograms and Broadcasting Organisations was brought into operation in 1961. It has not however achieved widespread international support. Even among the small number of adherents which it has mustered, a number have taken advantage of the opportunity to reserve on the clause most significant to record producers, so that they do not accept the principle of the performing right in records.

Broadcasting or public performance of sound recordings

7.16   Article 12 of the Rome Convention embodied the principle of remuneration for the broadcasting or public performance of sound recordings, but its effect was considerably diluted by the provisions of article 16. By this it is possible to make a complete reservation, and not apply article 12 in any way, or alternatively enter a more limited reservation, whereby a subscribing state can decline to apply the provisions of article 12 in respect of certain uses.

Reproduction of sound recordings

7.17   As a medium for the benefit of the gramophone industry, the Rome Convention proved rather two-edged. Because of widespread international reluctance to recognise the principle of remuneration in respect of the public performance or broadcasting of sound recordings, it failed to attract any significant support among the family of nations; and indeed many of the countries which simply ignored it were historically staunch adherents of the international copyright system. But in addition to its more controversial features, the Rome Convention contained a widely recognised protection for record producers in the shape of article 10. This is to the effect that record producers enjoy the right to authorise or to prohibit the direct or indirect reproduction of their sound recordings.

PIRACY

7.18   The unauthorised reproduction of sound recordings, the infamous practice of "piracy", is not merely a thorn in the side of the gramophone companies; it is now a very serious threat to their profitability. Piracy is in a number of areas of the world not a mere transient operation, with coins passing in occasional under-the-counter operations. Whole plants exist for the pressing of pirate records from matrixes which were legitimately made; packaged in their own covers, the pirate records are circulated through established channels to retail outlets only too happy to carry them—the public of course is not concerned as to the legitimacy of their origin. Indeed, in some Pacific Basin Asian states, pirate records are condoned by the authorities, who may well take the view that as their country has so few legitimate industries of substance, an industry manufacturing pirate records which provides employment and income for its inhabitants should not be too ruthlessly suppressed. In the world of literary publishing a substantial victory against the pirates has been achieved in the case of *Butterworth and Others v. Ng Sui Nam.*[5] A combination of major publishers achieved a decision that works first published in the United Kingdom do enjoy copyright protection in Singapore.

5. [1987] 2 F.T.L.R. 198; see McFarlane, *Copyright through the Cases* case 7.04 (1st instance) and para 3.16 above.

7.19 It is of crucial importance for the gramophone record interests to obtain the widest possible acceptance among all states of the need to stamp out record piracy, but because of the paucity of adherence to the Rome Convention during the 1960s, this wholly admirable principle contained therein had failed to gain much international acceptance. This resulted in huge losses by the gramophone companies as a result of the activities of the pirates.

Geneva Convention 1971

7.20 When accordingly it became apparent that the advantages to the gramophone industry from the Rome Convention were being out-weighed by the disadvantages, it was wisely decided to promote a brand new international instrument which enshrined on its own the principle that unauthorised reproductions were forbidden; divorced from the controversial provisions relating to remuneration for public perfor-mance, the Convention for the Protection of Producers of Phonograms against Unauthorised Duplication of their Phonograms was finalised at Geneva in 1971, and has since attained a fair degree of international acceptance.

BOOTLEGGING

7.21 A further problem the record industry has had to face is that of "bootlegging", which contrasts with the unauthorised reproduction known as "piracy". "Bootlegging" consists in the production in record form of extra material from official recording sessions, concerts and rehearsals, often obtained surreptitiously. If these are put on the market under the name of star artistes, they can have a very damaging effect on the profitability of the official recordings produced by the legitimate recording company, not to mention the possibly damaging effect on the performers' reputations.

℗ SYMBOL

7.22 For the purposes of international protection of a sound recording, often known internationally as a phonogram, all formalities of advising the public that it is in copyright are to be considered as fulfilled if all the copies in commerce of the published phonogram or their containers bear a notice consisting of the symbol ℗, accompanied by the name of the copyright owner and year of first publication. This of course applies only to those countries accepting the principle of international protection. This symbol is regarded as sufficient for the purposes of section 105(1) of CDPA, which sets out the information to be contained on a record label for the purposes of British law. It should be noted that neither of the major international copyright conventions (Berne and Universal Copyright Convention) afford any protection to sound recordings or phonograms.

INTERNATIONAL FEDERATION OF PRODUCERS OF PHONOGRAMS AND VIDEOGRAMS (IFPI)

7.23 The IFPI operates worldwide to promote the interests of the gramophone companies. It attempts to persuade governments to subscribe to the international conventions relating to the record industry which have been mentioned above; in particular it concerns itself with the acceptance of the principle of a performing right in sound recordings, and with the combat of piracy. It has also operated as a clearing house for the collection and distribution of royalties which have from time to time been paid by those governments overseas which have accepted the principle of the performing right in sound recordings. Since extending its sphere of operations to include videograms, there is no doubt that IFPI's operations have achieved greater success.

UNITED KINGDOM LAW

7.24 In the domestic law of the United Kingdom, protection for sound recordings stems in the first place from section 1(1)(b) of CDPA. This protection is amplified by sections 13 (duration), 16 (acts restricted by copyright) and 20 (infringement by broadcasting or inclusion in a cable programme). Copyright in a sound recording expires at the end of 50 years from the end of the calendar year in which it is made, or if released later (but before the end of that 50-year period), 50 years from the end of the calendar year in which it is released. A sound recording is released when first published, broadcast or included in a cable programme service, so long as the action in question was authorised.

7.25 "Sound recording" is defined in section 5 of CDPA as (a) a recording of sounds, from which the sounds may be reproduced or (b) a recording of the whole or any part of a literary, dramatic or musical work, from which sounds reproducing the work or part may be produced. In either case this is regardless of the medium on which the recording is made or the method by which the sounds are reproduced or produced. Note that there is no separate definition of "record" as had been the case in the Copyright Act 1956.

TAPE RECORDING OF SOUND RECORDINGS

7.26 As if the commercial copying and subsequent sale of their records by pirates was not enough, the gramophone industry has increasingly been subject to a direct loss of its profits by virtue of another illegitimate activity. This is the use of tape-recording equipment to make copies on tape and cassette of sound recordings. The threat is clearly enormous; the Whitford Committee was told of a survey which had been carried out for the gramophone industry in 1975 which established that 45 per cent of homes in the United Kingdom have access to a recording facility, and that 20 per cent of people over the age of 16 have used recording equipment at some time to make copies of commercially produced sound recordings.

7.27 With the rapid improvement of sound recording equipment, and a general reduction in price, the effect on sales of records is now very serious, and constantly increasing. So long as a free market in such recording equipment exists, it is difficult to see precisely what steps can be taken which will be of practical effect. One solution was attempted in West Germany in the Copyright Act introduced there in 1965. This was to make recording equipment subject to a levy included in the retail selling price, in return for which the purchaser of the recording equipment acquires a general blanket licence to make single copies of commercially produced records for his own use.

7.28 Whether this formula is wholly satisfactory from the viewpoint of the record manufacturers is difficult to say with any confidence. Such a levy is hardly likely to compensate entirely for the loss of sales, since it is payable only once, and the potentiality of the equipment on which it is levied to make even single copies is endless. There is also no check on multiple copies being made, and although the Whitford Committee recommend that the West German approach should be carried into the new British legislation, it is scarcely a complete solution. Not the least of the obstacles is the comparatively high cost of long-playing records relative to the cheapness of the recording equipment.

7.29 There have been experiments with sound waves built into legitimate recordings which would only become audible, to the distress of the listener, when a recording had been copied; but these efforts have not yet borne fruit. One problem is that the technology which produces such an impediment to illegal copying can also produce an antidote to it. The suggestion that persons manufacturing and selling recording equipment should refer in their advertising and sales literature to the restrictions imposed by copyright law seem to owe more to desperation than to realism.

7.30 The proposal of a levy on blank tapes was at one stage taken up by the Government. This was contained in a consultative document, *The Recording and Rental of Audio and Video Copyright Material*[6] which was published in February 1985. But when the Bill for CDPA was introduced into Parliament, the proposal for a levy had been dropped. Despite furious lobbying by interested parties it was not re-instated. Section 296 of CDPA may provide some protection against those who produce devices designed to circumvent copy protection.

7.31 So the problem grows, almost to the point where the economic viability of some forms of recording is threatened. The record manufacturers are clearly entitled to expect that the profitability of their operations should not be undermined by illicit recording to the point where they are driven out of business. Leading industrial nations have indeed a positive interest in ensuring that this does not take place. Given goodwill, a substantial improvement in the situation could be achieved by inducing the governments of such states to mount an intensified campaign of public education, coupled with the establishment and enforcement of rigorous legal provisions to stamp out the practice.

A possible solution

7.32 How can such international enforcement be achieved? It is submitted that the most likely means of the gramophone interests achieving this would be for them to drop their campaign to establish the performing right in sound recordings in return for the support from governments of the major copyright countries outlined above. Diplomatic approaches to those states in which record piracy is rife could lead to firm action; the gramophone industry has much to gain, and on its own admission little to lose from the abolition of the so-called performing right in sound recordings. As a representative of PPL said in evidence to the Copyright Committee of 1952,[7] the business of the gramophone companies is to make records

6. Cmnd 9445.
7. Cmnd 8662, para 144.

"for sale to the public for private entertainment in the home. It is in that business, and that business alone, that the industry has been built up and on which it rests today. This public performance side, despite the extra revenue it brings in, was entirely unanticipated, it is entirely ancillary, subsidiary, and relatively to the main business of the company, of little or no importance."

7.33   Note that by sections 16(1)(b) and 18(2) of CDPA, the rental of copies of a sound recording to the public is an act restricted by copyright. This also applies to the rental of films, videotapes and computer programs.

PLAYING SOUND RECORDINGS FOR CLUB OR SOCIETY

7.34   An important limitation of the performing right in sound recordings has been made by section 67 CDPA. It is not now an infringement of the copyright in a sound recording to play it as part of the activities of, or for the benefit of, a club, society or other organisation if the following conditions are met. These are (a) that the organisation is not established or conducted for profit and that its main objects are charitable or otherwise concerned with the advancement of religion, education or social welfare; and (b) that the proceeds of any charge for admission to the place where the recording is to be heard are applied solely for the purposes of the organisation.

CHAPTER 8

Cinematograph Films, Published Editions and Related Matters

FILMS

History

8.01 Films became part of the entertainment industry in the United Kingdom around 1905, when it is thought that regular public exhibition began. Although the new phenomenon spread rapidly across the country, by the time that proposals for the Copyright Act of 1911 were being considered, its impact in copyright terms had not been completely established. Those were of course the days of silent pictures, with a rather jerky quality, and at that stage its potential as a new art form was not obvious.

8.02 In the Copyright Act of 1911 section 1(2)(d) stated that copyright should include the sole right in the case of a literary, dramatic or musical work to make "any cinematograph film or other contrivance by means of which the work may be mechanically performed". In the definition section of the statute, "dramatic work" was to include "any cinematograph production", but this was qualified by the requirement that this should be only where "the arrangement or acting form or the combination of incidents represented give the work an original character". This certainly appeared to exclude from protection such material as newsreel films, which came rapidly into vogue, and were for many years a regular feature of every cinema programme.

8.03 With the advent of "talkies" in 1926 the spread of the motion picture was spectacular, but even after the Second World War, the nature of the copyright protection which they attracted in this country was obscure. A number of the constituent creative contributions of a motion picture undoubtedly enjoyed some form of rights: the narrative upon which it was based, the script itself, and the music all had copyrights independent of each other; but in the cinematograph film as a complete entity, the only copyright was in each single frame as a "still", and that only by virtue of the copyright subsisting in photographs.

Gregory Committee Recommendations

8.04 The Gregory Committee on Copyright sitting in 1952 found this quite illogical, and recommended the establishment of a separate copyright in a cinematograph film; accordingly, section 13 of the Copyright Act 1956 provided that copyright should subsist in every film of which the maker is a qualified person. The acts restricted by the copyright in a film by the Cinematograph Act 1952 were:

(a) making a copy of the film;
(b) causing the film, in so far as it consists of visual images, to be seen in public, or, in so far as it consists of sounds, to be heard in public;
(c) broadcasting the film;
(d) causing the film to be transmitted to subscribers to a diffusion service.

8.05 The Copyright Committee of 1952 did not however consider that the duration of copyright for cinematograph films or for sound recordings should be as extensive as that existing for original creative works in the fields of literature, drama, music or art. Moreover, the British Film Producers Association had gone on record as considering that most films were not alive after 10 or 15 years. This was of course before the expansion of television as a popular medium, soon to provide a vehicle for the repeated exhibition of cinematograph films of a much greater age; moreover, technical advances in production have assured a much longer useful life for the majority of feature films. When the Copyright Bill of 1956 was brought in in the House of Lords, the period of protection provided for the new right in cinematograph films was merely for 25 years, as was also the case for sound recordings. This did not meet with universal approval; it was argued that while the making of a sound recording might be a mere mechanical process, which did not in itself add anything to the work being recorded, a film came much nearer being a creative work. Moreover, it was said that a term of only 25 years would put British film producers at a serious disadvantage as against producers in those countries affording protection to films for the term of 50 years. These considerations prevailed, in days when the film industry in Britain was a good deal healthier than is now the case. The term of protection was accordingly extended for films, as it was later in the case of sound recordings by a Standing Committee of the House of Commons, during the passage of the 1956 Act.

Whitford suggestions

8.06 The efforts of the Gregory Committee did much to modernise the law relating to copyright and films, albeit somewhat belatedly. When the

Whitford Committee commenced its deliberations, there did not at that time appear to be many pressing problems in this area; the impact of video-recording on films and television programmes had not then been fully appreciated. A number of interesting and practical suggestions were, however, taken into account.

8.07 When the copyright in a cinematograph film was established in the Act of 1956, the medium was defined as:

> "any sequence of visual images recorded on material of any description (whether translucent or not) so as to be capable, by the use of that material,—
> (a) of being shown as a moving picture, or
> (b) of being recorded on other material (whether translucent or not) by the use of which it can be so shown".

"Cinematograph film" and "motion picture"
8.08 The members of the Whitford Committee believed that the intention behind that definition embodied in section 13 (quoted above) was that it should cover all video recordings, but it is unlikely that in 1952 the situation now current could have been accurately foreseen. Some concern had been expressed as to whether what is translated onto a video recording is actually a sequence of visual images. The Committee took the view that it was, but considered that the matter should be clarified in view of the doubts existing. The members of the Committee recommended that the term "cinematograph film" should be dropped, and that both films and video recordings be referred to as "motion pictures".

Illegal recording
8.09 It was a basic and laudable recommendation of the Whitford Committee that the general words of description employed in the Copyright Act should relate more closely to the way in which those words are commonly used. Certainly it is high time that the expression 'motion picture' should enter into general currency in Britain in substitution for 'film', or 'cinematograph film'. But in view of the very serious situation which has arisen since the deliberations of the Whitford Committee, in which the economic viability of the production of feature films has been threatened by the introduction of illegal video-recording equipment, it cannot be too strongly advanced that a verbal distinction between films or motion pictures on the one hand, and the video recordings made of them on the other should be maintained. To blur this distinction would make still more difficult the task of those who seek to maintain the rights of copyright-owners in an area of widespread illegal activity.

Register of films

8.10 A submission was also made to the Whitford Committee that a register of films should be established in order to control and decide questions relating to the ownership of films, and of the various elements which contributed to their production. In 1952 the Gregory Committee had added to its recommendation (that a copyright in films should be created) a further suggestion that the date of registration of all films, both British and foreign, made under the Cinematograph Films Acts of 1938 and 1948 should be adopted for the purposes of calculating the term of copyright. But a great many films are not so registrable, and in any case registration, just as first publication, can be delayed to suit commercial convenience.

Whitford's view

8.11 Attention was drawn before the Whitford Committee in its subsequent deliberations to the proposals for a Public Films Register in the Fifth Films Directive of the Council of the European Economic Community. This is designed to safeguard financial investment in films; to this end, each member state is to establish a Public Films Register in which economic rights are to be inscribed. The members of the Whitford Committee did not feel that much benefit would accrue from registration in this way. It was thought that the proposal could not be made a condition for the subsistence or exercise of copyright by virtue of the Berne Convention, and in any case they considered that the matter of registration was not really a copyright issue at all.

8.12 In view of the fact that under the Copyright Act of 1956 the term of copyright protection in a cinematograph film was in part dependent on the date of registration, this seemed an odd conclusion. At that time a substantial number of films were enjoying longer periods of copyright protection, either by virtue of delaying registration, or by not registering at all. They were securing an economic advantage, in the form of an extended period of ownership, which was not available to those which had been registered.

The Position Today

8.13 Much has been altered by CDPA. The recommendation of Whitford to use the expression "motion picture" has not been adopted. Instead "film" is defined by Section 5(1) as meaning a recording on any medium from which a moving image may by any means be produced. This undoubtedly embraces all forms of videograms, and that term is not separately defined in the Act. "Author" in relation to a film means the person by whom the arrangements necessary for the making of the film are undertaken.

8.14 Copyright in a film expires either (a) at the end of the period of 50 years from the end of the calendar year in which it is made or (b) if released before the end of that period, 50 years from the end of the calendar year in which it is released. A film is "released" for the purposes of CDPA when first published, broadcast, included in a cable programme service or first shown in public.

COPYRIGHT IN TYPOGRAPHY OF WORKS

8.15 There is a further category of material which receives its own copyright protection in sections 1(1)(c) and 8 of CDPA, and relates to the copyright in the typographical arrangement of published editions of works. Such a proposal was first raised by the Publishers Association before the Departmental Committee on International Copyright which had sat as long ago as 1934. The basis of that submission was that a considerable development had taken place in the United Kingdom between the wars in the field of typographical design, and that this had been linked to an improvement here and abroad in photolithographic processes. The result had been that certain publishers abroad were using photolithography to reproduce classical and educational works published in Britain. This process allowed them to avoid the considerable expense of typesetting.

8.16 Where the works copied were literary, dramatic or musical works which were in copyright, this activity would require the consent of the copyright-owner. This would also apply to editions reproducing as illustrations artistic works which were still in copyright. But where the work which was made the subject of this process was out of copyright, there was no remedy, save in the limited number of foreign countries where a law of unfair competition then operated.

8.17 An interesting analogy was drawn between the work which the publisher puts in to the production of his edition, including the typesetting, and the work of the manufacturer of gramophone records in making the sound recording of a musical work. Although no effect had been given to the British proposal in the revision of the Berne Convention which took place in 1948, the recommendation of the Departmental Committee of 1934 was taken up by the Gregory Committee of 1952, and it passed into law in 1956.

EEC interest

8.18 In admitting the claims of publishers to this protection, the members of the Gregory Committee accepted that they were using copyright to fill gaps in the then laws of unfair competition relating to the copying of certain types of industrial articles.[1] They had also proposed a term of 25 years' protection for copyright in films and sound recordings, although these were extended to 50 years in both cases in Parliament. The Commission of the European Economic Communities is keenly interested in questions of copyright by virtue of its economic importance. When it comes to consider the question of harmonisation of the various copyright laws of the member states of the Common Market, there is certain to be some conflict between the British view that such matters as typographical arrangements and sound recordings are properly included in copyright legislation, and the standpoint of certain Western European states, that they are merely industrial questions, which should be dealt with in the law of unfair competition.

8.19 Section 1(1)(c) of CDPA gives copyright protection to the typographical arrangement of published editions. "Published edition" in this context means (section 8) a published edition of the whole or any part of one or more literary, dramatic or musical works. The period of protection has been retained at 25 years from the date of first publication (setion 15) which certainly makes it appear rather exposed.

DIFFICULTIES OF LEGISLATING FOR COPYRIGHT

8.20 CDPA gives protection to a curious jumble of works. The classic products of the creative individual—literary, dramatic, musical and artistic works – rub shoulders with a number of far more prosaic items—sound recordings, films, broadcasts, cable programmes and typographical arrangements. These have a close affinity to industrial production or manufacture. Within these broad headings the categories of material eligible for protection by copyright legislation are being constantly extended, to take account of fresh developments and applications to technology. But the overall effect has been to create a very patchwork appearance. The view that computer programs benefited from the protection given to literary works under the previous law was widely held. But this conclusion was open to debate, as such cases as *Sega Enterprises Ltd v. Richards*[2] and *Thrustcode Ltd v. W. W.*

1. Cmnd 8662, paras 307, 308.
2. [1983] F.S.R. 73.

Computing Ltd[3] demonstrate. Although the point was confirmed by the Copyright (Computer Software) Amendment Act 1985, and has been carried into section 3(1)(b) of CDPA, earlier clarification by statute would have been desirable.

Whitford deliberations

8.21   The Whitford Committee was keenly aware of the criticisms to which the current legislation is open. The authoritative voice of the British Copyright Council had suggested to it that any new copyright legislation should express the rights of the creators in general terms of principles. The alternative was to set out in meticulous detail the exact limits of control and free use, and given the current rate of advance, these would be out of date before such legislation could come into operation.

8.22   The Whitford Committee had found the system of definitions used in the Copyright Act 1956 inexplicable "even to the extent to which it is comprehensible." The members of the Committee felt that some set principle of definition should be employed. They considered that instead of trying to set out a comprehensive definition of what works were protected by copyright, the new legislation should furnish examples of subject-matter included in the general definition of works, such as written works and musical works, without going into too much detail.

8.23   In this area at least a substantial improvement has been made. Of necessity definitions, often highly technical, are scattered throughout CDPA. Frequently they are expressed as being for the purposes of a particular part of the Act although in practice they will have a wider application. But section 179 of CDPA is an index of defined expressions for the lengthy Part I of the statute showing where the definition of each expression is located.

POSSIBLE EXTENSIONS TO COPYRIGHT PROTECTION

8.24   It will be of practical use to collect here under one section for the benefit of easy reference a number of matters which have been refused copyright protection. The promoters of sporting events made representations to the Gregory Committee in 1952 that their promotions should be under some form of control; their contention was that the heavy

3.   [1983] F.S.R. 502.

production costs which they incurred should not be prejudiced either directly, by reduced attendances at the event itself, or indirectly, by reduced attendances at other events of a similar nature taking place at the same time. But it was decided that there never has been a copyright in a sporting event, and that there should be none in the future. The promoters had a remedy in contract when they made their agreements with the broadcasting authorities. The answer is for them to make an agreement which will compensate them sufficiently, or to refuse to license the broadcasting of the spectacle.

Copyright in performances

8.25 For many years the same principle was applied to performers, such as actors, singers and artistes of the variety stage. They did not enjoy any rights in their performances in the nature of property rights enforceable by civil law. If they had not protected themselves by contract (and given the weakness of their bargaining position, it was unlikely that in many cases they had done so), their remedies were to bring criminal proceedings under the Performers' Protection Acts of 1958 and 1963. When the Whitford Committee had considered the question, it had concluded that to give a performer copyright in his performance could lead to practical difficulties.

8.26 But now the whole of Part II of CDPA is devoted to what are called "rights of performances", a phrase which may lead to confusion with the performing right. Section 180 confers rights on performers, by requiring their consent to the exploitation of their performances. It also confers rights on a person having recording rights in relation to a performance in relation to recordings made without his consent or that of the performer.

8.27 A performance means a dramatic performance, including dance or mime, a musical performance, a reading or recitation of a literary work or a performance of a variety act or any similar presentation. Note that although the new provisions cover performances given before the Act comes into force, no act done before that time can be regarded as an infringement. A performer's rights are infringed by recording the performance, broadcasting it live, showing or playing it in public and also by importation. These rights last for 50 years from the end of the calendar year in which performance takes place, and they are not assignable, although they may be transmitted by will. An infringement of any of the rights of a performer is actionable as a breach of statutory duty. Section

198 of CDPA provides for criminal offences in respect of illicit recordings. The Performers' Protection Acts are repealed.

"Elaborated ideas"

8.28   Certain other proposals for the extension of copyright protection were considered by the Whitford Committee. One was that it should be extended to "elaborated ideas". Ideas as such have never been the subject of copyright protection, and it would be very hard to form an effective definition of this concept. No change in the law was recommended, and it was observed that there may be protection under other heads of the law.

Character rights

8.29   Another suggestion was the adoption of so-called character rights to supplement the copyright work in which the character features. It is not easy to perceive the advantages which would flow from such an innovation in most cases. In literary and dramatic works the plagiarism of a character would generally amount to an infringement, and this would probably be true of most artistic works as well. If the character claimed to be infringed is not immediately recognisable, there is little hope of getting an action off the ground. See now *Re American Greetings Corporation's Application.*[4] Popularly known as "the Holly Hobbie Case", it was an attempt to use trade mark registration to protect character and copyright in manufactured articles bearing the likeness of the little girl Holly Hobbie who had acquired considerable vogue in the USA as a character. The application failed on the basis that it was trafficking in a trade mark, though it was suggested that many marks involved in character merchandising might be protected by copyright. This is another area where a law of unfair competition might be more appropriate.

Copyright in a title

8.30   It is a basic principle of the law of copyright in this country that there is no copyright in a title. However, some relief may be available outside copyright in the law of passing-off. The Whitford Committee did not recommend any alteration to the position; as it was rightly observed, it would be dangerous to accord copyright protection to a title of one or two words. They were also concerned that any material which was to

4. [1984] 1 W.L.R. 189

receive copyright protection must have involved a sufficient degree of skill and labour, which would not necessarily have been involved in the forming of a title, or even of a slogan. Although the nature of a literary work has been subject to wide interpretation in the courts of the United Kingdom, the Court of Appeal has confirmed in *Exxon Corporation v. Exxon Insurance Consultants International Ltd*[5] that a single invented word such as "Exxon" is not an original literary work. It may, however, be possible to register it as a trade mark.

News and copyright

8.31   Finally, it should be emphasised that there is no copyright in news as such. It is a matter of history, and does not constitute a literary work. There is on the other hand a copyright in the manner of its expression. An editor cannot therefore lift a news feature directly from the publication of a competitor and reprint it word for word, as his own.

---

5.   [1982] R.P.C. 69.

CHAPTER 9

Sound and Television Broadcasts and Cable Programmes

DEVELOPMENT OF SOUND BROADCASTING

9.01 In November 1922 sound broadcasting began in London. The station, the first in the world, was known as 2LO. It was situated on top of Marconi House in the Strand, and the first programmes, of varying audibility, were transmitted to the 8000 listeners who had contributed 15 shillings a head for what was known as a "constructor's licence." These early listeners, so it was said, were sometimes kept waiting while the studio piano was moved; bystanders in the studio were on occasion heard to pass remarks that certainly were not intended to be broadcast; but no one complained, for it was surprising that anything was transmitted at all.

9.02 The use of copyright works on the radio, principally musical works, but also material in the realm of drama and literature, was an activity clearly requiring authorisation by the owner of the rights. A factor which contributed greatly to the secure establishment of the Performing Right Society was the agreement by the infant British Broadcasting Company, as it was then known, to take a PRS licence as early as 1923. The BBC had made use of gramophone records in its programmes from the first, and also as a matter of policy became a leading patron of classical music.

9.03 Sound broadcasting grew from a small new industry to revolutionise home entertainment; television made a flickering beginning before the outbreak of the Second World War, but this was of very limited significance, and was received only in a few hundred homes in the environs of London. It was reintroduced in 1947, and two years later a nationwide service commenced operations. The figure of 10 million sound licences and 7500 television licences in 1947 had by 1951 grown to $11\frac{1}{2}$ million and half a million respectively. Thereafter the increase in viewing exploded, and by 1957 there were as many television viewers as there were listeners to sound broadcasts. The Independent Television Act 1955 introduced commercial television and this stimulated an expansion of watching in the home which has never abated. New advances follow on the heels of each technical development to the point at which innovation has become almost commonplace. Satellite broadcasting, cable programmes and sky satellite television have followed in rapid succession, the latter as a fixed satellite service (FSS).

STATUTORY PROTECTION

9.04 The Broadcasting Committee sat in 1949 under Lord Beveridge, and the British Broadcasting Corporation put before it a submission that a copyright should attach to broadcasts. The medium had of course not been invented at the time of the previous Copyright Act of 1911, otherwise such protection might have been granted to the broadcasts then. Even in 1949, the BBC submitted that "It is clearly anomalous and inequitable that . . . sound and television programmes on which the BBC has expended much creative effort and incurred considerable expense should be freely available for third parties to use for their own pecuniary advantage." As will be seen, this complaint has been raised again in recent years because of new threats from audio-visual recording equipment.

9.05 The BBC told the Beveridge Committee that the establishment of a right in broadcasts would be the only effective means of safeguarding its programmes against unauthorised use by third parties. Its inability to control the use made of its programmes sometimes caused difficulties in clearing the necessary rights needed for their production. Sometimes performers would refuse to make a programme for a broadcasting organisation if they feared that the production would be pirated.

9.06 Submissions along the same lines were made by the broadcasters to the Gregory Committee on Copyright in 1952, and the Copyright Act of 1956, contained the protection sought in section 14. The position is now governed by section 1(1)(b) of CDPA, and by section 14(1), copyright in a broadcast expires at the end of the period of 50 years from the end of the calendar year in which the broadcast was made.

9.07 By section 6(1), a "broadcast" is defined as a transmission by wireless telegraphy of visual images, sounds or other information which (a) is capable of being lawfully received by members of the public and (b) is transmitted for presentation to members of the public. It thus includes television as well as radio broadcasts. An encrypted transmission can only be lawfully received if decoding equipment has been made available to the public with the authority of the person making the transmission, or the person providing the contents of the transmission.

9.08 Where CDPA refers to "the person making a broadcast" or "broadcasting a work" or "including a work in a broadcast", these are references to (a) the person transmitting the programme, if he has responsibility to any extent for its contents, and (b) any person providing the programme who makes with the person transmitting it the arrangements necessary for its transmission.

9.09 By section 9 CDPA, an author in the case of a broadcast is "the person making the broadcast" according to the definition set out in the previous paragraph. The only exception is in the case of a broadcast which relays another broadcast by reception and immediate retransmission, in which case the author is the person making that other broadcast.

Rome Convention 1961

9.10 The new protection for broadcasts which had been introduced by the Copyright Act of 1956 was to prove quite satisfactory for some years. The Rome Convention of 1961, which in its more controversial aspects dealt with the rights of producers of sound recordings (see paras 7.15–20), also dealt with performing artistes and broadcasting organisations. This Convention gives broadcasting organisations the right to authorise, or to prohibit, in subscribing states accepting the Convention:

(a) the rebroadcasting of their broadcasts;

(b) the fixation of their broadcasts;

(c) the reproduction:

    (i) of fixations, made without their consent, of their broadcasts;

    (ii) of fixations, made in accordance with the provisions of the Convention, of their broadcasts if the reproduction is made for purposes different from those referred to in those provisions;

(d) the communication to the public of their television broadcasts if such communication is made in places accessible to the public against payment of an entrance fee; it is a matter for the domestic law of the member state where this right is claimed to determine the conditions under which it may be exercised.

9.11 Protection under the Rome Convention lasts for 25 years from the end of the year in which the broadcast took place. The United Kingdom adheres to the Convention, but largely because of the international unpopularity of its provisions on a performing right in sound recordings, the Convention has not secured wide acceptance among the family of nations; the worthwhile provisions on such matters as the protection of broadcasters and performers have suffered accordingly.

SATELLITE BROADCASTS

9.12 As time passed, the broadcasters had to meet new difficulties. The pirate radio stations broadcasting outside the territorial waters of Britain and other Western European countries in the 1960s were not so much a problem for the legitimate broadcasting organisations as for the owners of the rights in the musical works and sound recordings which they made use of. But when in 1957 Yuri Gagarin made the first manned journey into space, a completely new situation arose for the broadcasters.

9.13 Earth-to-earth satellite broadcasts, put in their most simplified form, pass through an earth transmitting station into space, and return via the satellite out in space to earth, where they then pass either through an earth receiving station to be transmitted by the television organisations of the receiving country, or through a "dish" aerial to be received directly by the TV set of the subscribing customer. The difficulty for the broadcasting organisations which produce the programmes is that there is at present no means of preventing unauthorised receipt of the programme back on earth—they can be taken in at any earth receiving station. Thus, although a broadcasting organisation in the United Kingdom may have an entirely satisfactory licensing agreement with a broadcasting organisation in the United States whereby the latter (in consideration of a substantial sum) agrees to receive, say, a programme on the Derby, yet once it is put into space, there is no means of preventing it being intercepted by receiving stations in other countries.

9.14 This practice if unchecked would represent a huge loss of revenue for broadcasting organisations which had invested large sums in the production of such programmes, particularly if they hoped to recoup some of the cost by licensing it overseas via the satellite. Because of the weakness of the Rome Convention 1961, this could not be brought to bear on the problem, so a new international solution had to be found.

Brussels Convention 1974

9.15 The solution to this dilemma lay in the drawing-up of a new international agreement on the subject, and this was done at Brussels in 1974, when the Convention Relating to the Distribution of Programme-carrying Signals Transmitted by Satellite was drawn up. This has gone some way towards achieving the effect intended, and has been ratified by a fair number of states. The moving force behind international protection for broadcasting organisations such as the Brussels Convention is the European Broadcasting Union (EBU); virtually as much as is possible in this area has been brought about by the efforts of the EBU. But broadcasting organisations are in many countries part of the apparatus of the state, and if a state-backed organisation in a country not adhering to the Brussels Convention transmits satellite broadcasts without authorisation, there is unfortunately no other legal remedy.

Statutory difficulties

9.16   So far as the United Kingdom is concerned, however, difficulties arose under the Copyright Act 1956 which set up a barrier to ratification. In that statute section 14 defined "television broadcast" as

> "visual images broadcast by way of television, together with any sounds broadcast for reception along with those images . . . and for the purposes of this Act a television broadcast . . . shall be taken to be made by the body by whom, at the time when, and from the place from which, the visual images or sounds in question, or both, as the case may be, are broadcast."

As the Whitford Committee pointed out in 1977, it was not clear whether transmissions to satellites fell within this definition, and it recommended that in new legislation it should be established that the distribution by satellite of programmes meant for public reception, with or without the intervention of a ground receiving station, is to be deemed to be broadcasting within the meaning of the Copyright Acts.

9.17   Section 6(4) of CDPA now provides that the place from which a broadcast is made is, in the case of a satellite transmission, the place from which the signals carrying the broadcast are transmitted to the satellite. So the state in which the satellite broadcast is made is the one in which the earth transmitting station is located. "Satellite broadcast", however, is not separately defined in CDPA.

ASSOCIATION FOR PROTECTION OF COPYRIGHT IN SPORT

9.18   There is in connection with television and sound broadcasting no right in the nature of copyright which attaches to sporting and similar events. At one time after the Second World War the lobby for a right of this kind was so strong that an Association for the Protection of Copyright in Sport was formed by organisations with interests in this field. Submissions were made on the point to the Broadcasting Committee of Lord Beveridge. The members of that Committee did not see why the promoters of sporting events should require any powers other than those already available in civil and criminal law to prohibit the appearance of television cameras in the venue where a particular sporting event was held, but the contention was carried to the Copyright Committee of 1952 (the Gregory Committee).

9.19 The reasons for the claim of the Association were economic; on the one hand, to make sure that promoters of sporting events participated in whatever profits were made from the public performance by means of television of such events; on the other, to effect some form of control over these performances. With excellent perception, they were looking forward to such situations as exist in the present day where transmission of events like world-title boxing matches are shown to audiences in cinemas by means of closed-circuit television or under the latest developments on encrypted transmissions which require the application of some kind of decoding equipment.

9.20 But the Copyright Committee of 1952 were not anxious to extend the principles of copyright to this arena. They realised that, once established, there was a grave danger of the new right spilling over into areas far wider than those purely of sport, and even if by chance they managed to confine it to sporting events, there was a strong possibility that a multiplicity of collecting societies would spring up vying with each other to administer the new right. So the Copyright Committee of 1952 made a strong recommendation that the concept of a copyright in the sense of a right to prevent or control the copying or recording of a spectacle or a sporting event should not be extended in the way suggested by the sports promoters. This recommendation was followed in the Copyright Act of 1956, and it is now highly unlikely that any right of this nature will come into being. Promoters of sporting fixtures who are worried about these matters should seek the advice of lawyers and accountants specialising in this area; there is now a good deal of expertise available in the matter of broadcasting contracts, and suitable compensation against subsequent uses should be provided for in any agreement.

CABLE TV AND COPYRIGHT

9.21 Under the Copyright Act 1956 the distribution of copyright works to subscribers to a cable programme, or diffusion service as it was known at that time, was only a restricted act in relation to literary, dramatic, musical and artistic works. There was no protection for record manufacturers or broadcasting organisations. Moreover the diffusion of broadcast or other programmes as an incidental service to keeping hotel rooms or letting flats or other places where people reside or sleep was not under the 1956 Act an infringement of copyright, and could be carried on without restriction.

Whitford Recommendations

9.22 By the time that the Report of the Whitford Committee was published in 1977, the urgency of the situation had become apparent. Cable broadcasting was about to grow, and grow rapidly. Some kind of protection against piracy was overdue, particularly in such areas as sporting events. The Committee recommended that there should be a new copyright for cable programme companies analogous to the copyright in sound and television broadcasts which the broadcasting companies enjoyed.

Cable Programmes and CDPA

9.23 In the event the recommendation of the Whitford Committee that the new right should be in respect of "communication of works or subject-matter to the public by wire" was not taken up. The basic protection to "cable programmes" is granted by section 1(1)(b) CDPA, and by section 14(1), it expires at the end of the period of 50 years from the end of the calendar year in which the programme was included in a cable programme service.

9.24 "Cable programme service" is defined by section 7(1) and means a service which consists wholly or mainly in sending visual images, sounds or other information by means of a telecommunications system, otherwise than by wireless telegraphy. This is subject to two qualifications in respect of reception. The service must be either (a) receivable at two or more places (whether for simultaneous reception or at different times in response to requests by different users) or (b) for presentation to members of the public. In addition, it must not fall under one of the exceptions to the definition of a cable programme service described below.

Exceptions to Definition of "Cable Programmes Service"
9.25 These exceptions appear in section 7(2) of CDPA and are as follows:
   (a) A service or part of a service of which it is an essential feature that while visual images, sounds or other information are being conveyed by the person providing the service, there will or may be sent from each place of reception, by means of the same system or the same part of it, information for reception by the person

providing the service or other persons receiving it—in other words a two-way radio installation or interactive computer system. Signals sent for the operation or control of the service are not included in "information" for these purposes.

(b) A service run for the purposes of a business where the following 3 conditions are all satisfied: (i) No person except the person carrying on the business is concerned in the control of the apparatus comprised in the system; (ii) the visual images, sounds or other information are conveyed by the system solely for purposes internal to the running of the business and not by way of providing a service or amenities for others; and (iii) the system is not to be connected to any other telecommunications system. This covers typically business closed-circuit TV systems or linked computer terminals.

(c) A service run by a single individual where the following 3 conditions are all satisfied: (i) all the apparatus in the system is under that person's control; (ii) the visual images, sounds or other information conveyed by the system are conveyed solely for that person's domestic purposes; and (iii) the system is not connected to any other telecommunications system.

(d) A service where: (i) all the apparatus comprised in the system is situated in, or connects, premises which are in single occupation; and (ii) the system is not connected to any other telecommunications system. This does not extend to services operated as part of the amenities provided for residents or inmates of premises run as a business (such as a hotel), so the old exception under section 48(3) of the Copyright Act 1956 (which allowed hotels to escape from the copyright net) has been abolished.

(e) Services which are run for persons providing broadcasting or cable programme services or providing programmes for such services.

Other Provisions about Cable Programmes

9.26 Note that copyright does not subsist in a cable programme (a) if it is included in a cable programme service by reception and immediate retransmission of a broadcast, or (b) if it infringes the copyright in another cable programme or in a broadcast. In the case of a cable programme, the person providing the cable programme service in which the programme is included is the author for the purposes of CDPA.

VIDEO RECORDERS

9.27 Broadcasting, in particular television broadcasting, is one of the sectors of copyright most affected by the explosion of technology. The problems posed by video recording apparatus were considered by the Whitford Committee, but matters have been overtaken by the rapid spread of such equipment in the few years since the Whitford Committee reported. Improvement in their function coupled with simplification of operation and reduction in price has made them generally available in the home. As their popularity spread, it was noticeable that the promotional publicity did not lay much emphasis on the obligations of the purchaser to the owner of the copyright works under the law as it stood prior to CDPA. A widespread and aggressive advertising campaign has brought the video recorder to the point where it is as commonly found in the homes of Britain as the record player, radio and television.

Whitford recommendations

9.28 The Whitford Committee directed its deliberations to audio and visual recording together, but placed the emphasis on audio recording. Although a curse to the gramophone industry, the tape recorder did little real damage to broadcasters. The Committee noted the problem of video-recording, but clearly did not appreciate the impact it was to have within months of the publication of its Report. It based its recommendations largely on the provisions of the Copyright Act 1956 of West Germany, and concluded that a levy system similar to that provided in the German legislation should be introduced, applying to the sale of all equipment capable of private recording. This would take the form of a single levy on the retail selling price of the equipment, raised at the point of sale and paid for by the consumer as part of the retail selling price. The Committee further recommended that a rate-fixing body such as the Performing Right Tribunal should be given jurisdiction over the rate of the levy, its application, and the distribution of the sums raised between the collecting societies representing the different classes of copyright owner.

9.29 With respect to the members of the Committee, this did not come to grips with the problem as it now exists. The direction of their comment was substantially towards private recording; they tended to look at non-private recording as a legitimate commercial venture which would be subject to normal licensing procedures. But unfortunately for the copyright system, the reverse has proved to be the case.

BBC complaints

9.30 A senior official of the BBC has complained that great concern was felt by the broadcasting organisations about the immense sums invested in the production of television programmes and series, which are illegally copied directly off the air, and sold in commercial numbers. This is using property of many different groups of right-owners, who as matters stand have no chance of recovering any royalties. The broadcasting organisations, the film producers, writers, composers and record producers may all be deprived of their legitimate income, which can well lead to the destruction of the material copied as an economic substance for the right-owner.

9.31   As an example, the classic full-length feature films of the Disney Organisation, beloved of several generations of children, are subject to a policy of re-releasing them on cinema circuits in turn every seven years or so. But once copied off-air from a television showing, and sold illegally in multiple copies, their continuing value is likely to be considerably reduced, perhaps even to the point where re-release would be futile.

Proposals for a Point-of-Sale Levy

9.32   There has been a remarkable amount of vacillation in Government circles over the correct policy to apply to the problem. Apart from the consideration devoted to it in the context of general copyright problems, a consultative document entitled *The Recording and Rental of Audio and Video Copyright Material*[1] was published in 1985. This document arrived at the firm conclusion that copyright owners were entitled to payment for the home taping of their material, and that a levy on blank audio and videotapes was the only practicable way of providing such payment. Statutory maximum rules were to be established, with exemptions in respect of certain uses. Collective administration by the right owners would be necessary, with provision for the arbitration of disputes. The Government appeared to take the view that if commercial renting of particular products could not be prevented contractually, the argument for an exclusive rental right was strong.

Developments in Case Law

9.33   In *CBS Inc v. Ames Records and Tapes Ltd,*[2] a record lending library was introduced as an alternative to direct sales, and the plaintiff company brought an action claiming infringement of its copyright by this commercial hiring out of certain of its recordings. Although only dealing with audio recording, the decision was of considerable significance. It was held that once the plaintiff company had parted with its

1.   Cmnd 9445.
2.   [1981] R.P.C. 407.

records by sale, the purchaser was perfectly entitled to sell them, give them away, hire them or destroy them, and lending tapes for a subscription was not an infringement of copyright, although it was admitted that the proprietors of the lending library were aware that the tapes were being copied by its customers.

9.34 This should be compared with the American decision in *Sony Corporation of America v. Universal City Studios.*[3] There it was decided that the sale of video recording equipment did not create a vicarious liability of the manufacturer for infringements of copyright by those who purchased recording machines from him.

CDPA: The Final Result

9.35 It came as a considerable surprise in many quarters when the proposal for a tape levy was not incorporated in the new legislation. This result had the appearance of a last-minute change of heart. In an area of intense lobbying by the various industrial interests, somebody had produced an ace when serving on match point! But this is a problem which is not going to evaporate, and it is likely to be re-opened in the future.

9.36 There is, however, a rental right, which has been achieved by section 18 of CDPA. This provides that in relation to sound recordings, films and computer programs, the restricted act of issuing copies to the public includes any rental of copies to the public. On the basis of this section, the plaintiff in *CBS Inc. v. Ames Records and Tapes Ltd* would now succeed in an action for infringement of copyright.

---

3.   (1984) No. 81–1687, 52 U.S.L.W. 4090.

CHAPTER 10

Industrial Designs

10.01 The law on industrial designs lies somewhat apart from the other subjects protected in CDPA. Its development has sometimes followed a different course, and the materials which it aims to cater for are generally the products of manufacturing industry and design. There has in addition existed at times an overlap in the legislation relating to design copyright and general copyright in artistic works which has made for unnecessary complexity. In order to appreciate the position, it is helpful to trace the development of the law in some detail, as the Whitford Committee devoted close scrutiny to the situation in 1977.

DEVELOPMENT OF STATUTORY PROTECTION

10.02 There was no protection for designs until the eighteenth century in this country. Extending at first only to designs for fabrics, it was opened up by a series of statutes during the nineteenth century to most subjects of manufacture, and a scheme of registration was established under the supervision of the Patent Office. Thus there was built into the system relating to designs a monopoly element, similar to the protection afforded by the patent system, and contrasting with the general scheme of things in copyright; in the latter the tradition in the United Kingdom has always been based on originality, and there is no requirement of registration for such matters as books, plays, sheet music and works of art in order that they may acquire the protection of copyright.

10.03 However, the concepts of artistic works in the general copyright legislation of 1911 and 1956 included protection against the reproduction of that artistic work in a material form. By section 48(1) of the Copyright Act 1956, "reproduction" in the case of an artistic work included a version produced by converting the work into a three-dimensional form, or if it was in three dimensions, by converting it into a two-dimensional form. However section 10 of the 1956 Act excluded from the protection of general artistic copyright all designs applied to industrial usage and not registered under the Registered Designs Act of 1949.

10.04 By the Registered Designs Act 1949 (in its original form) monopoly protection was granted for up to fifteen years for registered designs. They must possess the quality of novelty, and by section 1 (as originally drafted) they had to possess:

> "features of shape, configuration, pattern or ornament applied to an article by an industrial process or means, being features which in the finished article appeal to and are judged solely by the eye, but does not include a method or principle of construction or features of shape or configuration which are dictated solely by the function which the article to be made in that shape or configuration has to perform."

10.05 A good deal of adjustment took place between designs law and general copyright law to try to accommodate their overlap, and to avoid the problems of double protection. It is beyond the scope of this book to give a detailed historical account of the various amendments which were made, but uncertainty reigned over the interpretation of the Registered Designs Act of 1949, and an attempt to clarify the position which was made by section 10 of the Copyright Act 1956.

Consideration by the courts

10.06 The extent of section 10 was considered in *Dorling v. Honnor Marine Ltd*,[1] where it was held that unregistered designs were not debarred from copyright protection by that section, but maintained it for the full term of life plus 50 years. This meant that drawings of articles and machine parts which were purely functional were admitted to the protection of the Copyright Act 1956.

10.07 The matter was taken further by the decision in *Amp v. Utilux*,[2] which had the result that no registered design existed within the meaning of the Registered Designs Act of 1949 where an article was made in a particular shape by a designer solely to fulfil a particular functional requirement, and was not in any way designed to attract the eye of a potential customer. The result was that a large number of designs which were purely functional enjoyed the full term of copyright protection by virtue of being unregistrable. This situation was clearly anomalous, for aesthetic creation should surely be rewarded with a longer term of protection rather than a shorter one, and designs which are merely mechanical ought to be excluded from such protection.

10.08 In *Re Coca-Cola Co*,[3] the Coca-Cola organisation attempted to register as a trade mark the well known and distinctive shape of the

1. [1965] 1 Ch. 1
2. [1972] R.P.C. 103
3. [1986] W.L.R. 695

bottle in which the beverage is contained, protection under the registered design legislation having run out. But the attempt was rejected by the House of Lords. The bottle was a container for the liquid and not a mark applied to the liquid. See also *Interlego AG v. Tyco Industries Inc.*[4] The Lego building bricks are well known to several generations of children throughout the world. They had been protected by copyright in the drawings, but that had run out. New drawings were produced in an attempt to get another term of protection but it was held that they were not original. As the Lego organisation had not wished to make physical alterations to their bricks, so the new drawings contained no modifications, and were not entitled to protection as artistic works.

The Johnston Committee

10.09   In 1962 the Johnston Committee had been set up to consider the confused situation surrounding legislation on industrial designs, and in its Report it produced the following recommendations. A system of design copyright should be established in parallel with the monopoly scheme for registered designs already existing under the Act of 1949. The new system would be dependent upon deposit, and should provide protection for a term of 15 years only. Moreover, the definition of "design" was to be "features of shape, configuration, pattern or ornament applicable to articles, in so far as such features appeal to and are judged solely by the eye": This was clear acceptance of the principle of double protection under two systems simultaneously but there was no immediate response in the form of legislation.

Design Copyright Act 1968

10.10   A bill brought in by a private member passed through all its stages in Parliament to become the Design Copyright Act 1968. Its sponsors introduced it with the principal intention of protecting decorative and ornamental articles (jewellery in particular), but like much else in the field of design legislation, in practice it extended far beyond its original *raison d'être*. In essence, it amended section 10 of the Copyright Act 1956 to allow works registered or capable of being registered as designs to be protected under the 1956 Act, in addition to the registered designs legislation, for a term of 15 years from first exploitation. It did not do anything to remove the conflict between two terms of protection, or the possibility of the longer term of copyright protection for artistic works being accorded to articles whose shape or configuration was

4.   [1988] 3 W.L.R. 678

dependent only on the job which that article was designed to carry out.

10.11 So despite the attempts to patch the matter up by legislation, the recommendations made by the Johnston Committee were not fully implemented, and the matter continued to be a muddle, at the cost of considerable uncertainty in the relevant Industries. The 1968 Act was eventually repealed by CDPA.

Dress designing

10.12 An area of industry where the application of the law was particularly confused was dress designing. Dress patterns, as two-dimensional drawings, were protected by the Copyright Act 1956 as artistic works; the position was more difficult in respect of made-up dresses. The matter is of practical importance because of the ease with which *haute couture* designs can be quickly made up in cheaper material, and rapidly marketed over a wide area. In *Burke v. Spicer Dress Designs*,[5] it was decided that a dress copied by the defendants from the plaintiff's dress was not an infringement of the copyright in a sketch of a girl wearing the plaintiff's dress, because the dress was not considered to be a reproduction of the sketch. It was also decided in that case that a dress made up by employees of the plaintiff from a third party's sketch was not a work of artistic craftsmanship. This was because the dress drew any artistic merit from the sketch, and it was doubtful if a dress could ever be regarded as a matter of artistic craftsmanship. One of the complications in this field is that dresses can be made up in forms which are very similar, if not identical, but based on sketches which are not identical.

Fabric designs

10.13 Fabric designs, if of sufficient originality, are entitled to protection under copyright law as artistic works, although in their industrial application they become the subject of wide multiplication. Thus in *Infabrics Ltd v. Jaytex Ltd*,[6] a design on printed fabric showing three racehorses with their jockeys passing a winning post in a dead-heat finish was the subject of copyright as an artistic work. This took account of the fact that the design in its industrial application was repeated on the fabric at particular intervals and in a particular relationship. The decision demonstrated how strained the concept of artistic copyright had become when applied to subjects of manufacturing industry; by selling

5. [1936] Ch. 400
6. [1980] 2 W.L.R. 822

shirts bearing this design in the United Kingdom, the plaintiffs' copyright in the design would have been infringed, such sale being regarded as publication within the meaning of the Copyright Act 1956.

10.14 This decision of the Court of Appeal was overturned by the House of Lords.[7] The Law Lords did not consider that what had been done by Infabrics Ltd amounted to publishing. In relation to copyright, whether under common law or statute, "publishing" and "publication" were fundamental expressions meaning making available to the public and there was a strong *prima facie* case for interpreting publication as making available to the public something unpublished. Accordingly the sale in the United Kingdom of shirts with this design did not constitute an infringement of copyright, and Infabrics Ltd were not entitled to an injunction restraining Jaytex Ltd from infringing copyright. A distinction between published and unpublished works lay at the roots of the law. The Copyright Act of 1911, the forerunner of the 1956 Act, had been drafted wholly in accordance with the traditional concepts which stemmed from the earlier common law.

10.15 The Copyright Act 1956 did not contain a positive definition of "publication" as such, although there was a certain amount of guidance of a negative nature in section 49. But now by section 175 of CDPA there are positive definitions of both "publication" and "commercial publication". The former is basically the issue of copies to the public, while the latter is basically the issue of copies of the work to the public at a time when copies made in advance of the receipt of orders are generally available to the public. The definitions only apply to Part I of CDPA.

10.16 In *Roberts v. Candiware Ltd*,[8] an interlocutory injunction was granted to a designer of garments who produced and sold pattern books with instructions for knitting the garments which she designed. It was to restrain the defendant company from reproducing the garments using the pattern books and selling them when made up.

Automatic copyright protection

10.17 One argument put to the Whitford committee in support of automatic copyright protection for the design of industrially produced articles was based on the small distinction in principle between the industrial exploitation of artistic works, and such matters as the printing

7. [1982] A.C. 1
8. [1980] F.S.R. 352

of books. Indeed, the subjects of copyright protection in Part II of the 1956 Act such as gramophone recordings and typographical arrangements were more akin to products of manufacturing industry than many artistic works which have been exposed to industrial exploitation. Why should copyright protection be accorded to a mere catalogue or calendar, but not to the products of skilled design in furniture? As the Report of the Whitford Committee put it, "What is the difference in principle between a large greenhouse, which is regarded as a work of architecture, and a small garden frame, which is an industrial design?"

Spare parts

10.18 An area of industry which is particularly affected by the problem of design protection is that of spare parts. Some interested parties have suggested that purely functional designs at least should be subject to registration in order to obtain protection, while others have contended that no protection at all should attach to spare parts. The Consumers Association suggested to the Whitford Committee that there should certainly be no protection for replacement machine parts, particularly for motor vehicles and domestic machinery. They argued that to allow protection would enhance the monopoly position of manufacturers and encourage a two-tier pricing system of low initial prices and high replacement costs; alternatively it would tend to restrict consumer choice because spares might not be freely available.

10.19 One omission from the Design Copyright Act 1968 was that there was no provision for compulsory licences in cases where the demands of the market were not fulfilled. It was suggested to the Whitford Committee that in the area of spare parts either the demand of the market was not fulfilled, with the possible intention of forcing the public to buy new equipment in situations of built-in obsolescence; alternatively, it was suggested that spare parts were supplied at relatively high prices. These allegations were strenuously disputed by the manufacturing sector of the motor industry, which contended that their prices were little if at all higher than the prices of those who copy their parts. They were anxious to put the matter into perspective, bringing forward evidence that 15 per cent of items on the spares list of one manufacturer represented 80 per cent of the total sales value. Against that it was suggested that copiers of parts frequently only carry some 1 per cent of the possible range.

10.20 Matters came to a head in *British Leyland Motor Corporation Ltd v. Armstrong Patents Ltd.*[9] The effect of this judgement of the House

9. [1988] A.C. 577

of Lords was to remove the protection of the copyright system from spare parts. Basically a manufacturer of products such as spare parts gives up the right to interfere with the purchaser's subsequent use of the article. This decision if extended generally would shoot down claims such as that of the record industry to a performing right in sound recordings, if statutory protection had not been granted.

The Log-Jam and How to Break It

10.21 For a major industrial country the position surrounding the protection of industrial designs in the United Kingdom prior to CDPA was quite simply inadequate. What was at one time a system based on a limited monopoly period linked with registration had been opened up in a haphazard manner to a variety of forms and periods of protection, not necessarily dependent on registration or giving a monopoly. A great deal of the confusion was due to the failure to implement the recommendations of the Johnston Committee made in 1962. The situation demanded firm and prompt action along the lines subsequently recommended by the Whitford Committee in 1977,[10] the main points of which are summarised below.

Whitford recommendations
10.22 In relation to designs consisting only of surface pattern and the shapes of three-dimensional articles of which the aesthetic appearance would influence a potential buyer in making a purchase, it was recommended that:
1. At least the aesthetic elements of these designs should be accorded protection in respect of their appearance (but not in respect of any underlying idea or principle) under the general law of copyright, without the formality of registration or deposit. All the members of the Whitford Committee, save two, recommended protection for the design viewed as a whole, subject to the understanding that copyright protection does not, in the case of any design, protect the underlying idea or principle.
2. The term of protection should be 25 years from marketing, once the design has been industrially applied.
3. To ensure adequate notice of the claim to protection, damages should not be recoverable in respect of infringement committed before specific notice of the claim to copyright or unless notice has been given by way of marking on the article or, where this is not possible, on the packaging for the article or any literature issued with the article.

10.   Cmnd 6732, paras 200–203

10.23 In relation to designs being shapes of three-dimensional articles where the appearance of the article does not influence the purchaser, who buys it only in the expectation that it will do the job for which it is intended, the members of the Committee were divided in their opinions:

1. Two wished to exclude such designs altogether from copyright protection.
2. Four wished to accord to such designs the same protection and on the same basis as the majority recommended for designs consisting only of surface patterns and shapes of three-dimensional articles where the aesthetic appearance will influence the potential purchaser.
3. Three wished to protect such designs only under a system of design deposit copyright with a period of protection between fifteen and 25 years, according to the basis recommended earlier by the Johnston Committee.

10.24 In addition, the members of the Whitford Committee recommended unanimously that:

1. Registered design monopoly protection, as currently provided by the Registered Designs Act of 1949, should be repealed; this was subject, in the view of two members, to the introduction of a design deposit system which provides a satisfactory alternative basis for claims for priority overseas under the Paris Industrial Property Convention.
2. Copyright should subsist in original works which start their life in three-dimensional form, as well as those starting in two-dimensional form; this should be so whether or not such works could now be described as works of sculpture or "works of artistic craftsmanship".
3. In the case of designs which are shapes of three-dimensional articles the appearance of which does not influence the purchaser, it should be possible to obtain compulsory licences on the ground that the market in the United Kingdom is not being adequately supplied by the rate of manufacture within the European Economic Community.
4. The Crown should have powers equivalent to those it then enjoyed as regards registered designs under the then current version of Sch 1 to the Registered Designs Act 1949.
5. The current position with regard to the term of protection for artistic works such as drawings should continue, so that they would enjoy protection for the life of the author and a post-mortem period of 50 years.
6. Certain works of an artistic character should continue to retain full copyright protection even after they have been subjected to mass-production, as was then provided for in the rules made under section 1(4) of the Registered Designs Act 1949 (now section 1(5)).

7. The "non-expert test", as established under section 9(8) of the Copyright Act 1956, should be repealed.
8. Nationals of the Paris Industrial Property Convention countries should not enjoy automatic copyright protection (which is not dependent upon deposit) for their designs in the United Kingdom unless they enjoy such protection for the same designs in their own countries.
9. There should be statutory prohibition in respect of unjustified threats of proceedings for infringement of copyright over the whole field of copyright, but not in respect of threats made to the primary infringer.

10.25 The content of (9) above is of considerable importance to all owners and users of copyright, and is not confined merely to the field of industrial designs. Although there was not very much discussion of the point in the Whitford Committee Report, the recommendation extended to unjustified threats of proceedings in respect of all types of works, including the basic categories of literary, dramatic, musical and artistic. The Report merely spoke of "statutory prohibition", and was not specific as to the form which such prohibition should take. There is a good deal of merit in the proposal, but a number of considerations should be taken into account. A criminal sanction in respect of such unjustified threats would scarcely be practical; the prohibition should not extend beyond the possibility of civil action. In the case of both patents and registered designs legislation there is already provision for application to the court for an injunction to restrain such threats; there is also provision for damages unless the right-owner can demonstrate either that no such threat was made, or alternatively that it was justified.

10.26 But both patents and registered designs involve registration; copyright does not. Is a claim to copyright which is unjustified to be actionable? At present, claims are frequently made on the face of a work that it is subject to copyright, and that a particular individual or corporation is the owner of copyright. If such a statement is false, it may be that the situation would be caught by the prohibition, and an action might lie.

10.27 The matter was raised in *Gramby Marketing Services Ltd v. Interlogo A.G.*[11] where the defendant company sought to warn potential purchasers of the plaintiff company's products against making such purchases because by doing so they might infringe copyright. It was decided that without specific proof of malice, the defendant company

---

11. [1984] R.P.C. 209

could not be held liable. But there is a remedy for groundless threats of infringement proceedings in respect of design rights, and this is contained in section 253 of CDPA.

THE NEW LAW: THE DESIGN RIGHT

10.28 Unfortunately the legal position after enactment of CDPA remains highly complex, although some of the worst anomalies have been removed.

10.29 Part III of CDPA introduces the design right as a new property right subsisting in original designs recorded or put into production after this part of CDPA came into effect (section 213(7)). It does not subsist until the design has been recorded in a design document or until an article has been made to the design (section 213(6)). The designer is the person who creates a design, and is the first owner of any design right (section 215(1)) in a design not created in pursuance of a commission or in the course of employment (in which case the design right belongs to the employer or customer). The right expires 15 years from the end of the calendar year in which the design was first recorded in a design document or an article first made to the design, if that event took place earlier. But if articles made to the design are made available for sale or hire within five years from the end of the (15th) calendar year, then design right expires ten years from the end of the calendar year in which that first occured (section 216(1)).

10.30 The owner of a design right has the exclusive right to reproduce the design for commercial purposes by making articles to the design or by making a design document recording the design for the purpose of enabling such articles to be made (section 226(1)). It follows that anything within these exclusive rights done without licence constitutes an infringement. Where copyright subsists in a work consisting of or including a design in which design right subsists, it is not an infringement of design right in the design to do anything which is an infringement of the copyright in that work (section 236).

10.31 The essential difference between this new design right and the right to register a design under the 1949 Act is that the new right applies to the design of any aspect of the shape or configuration (internal or external) of the whole or part of an article (section 213(2)), whereas the registered design right refers to "external" features of shape, configuration, pattern or ornament of a decorative or aesthetic character. Surface decoration is expressly excluded from the new right (section 213(3)(c)).

Registered Designs

10.32   Part IV of CDPA contains amendments to the Registered Designs Act 1949, although these can hardly be described as substantial. Note that the provisions are by way of amendment to the 1949 Act, rather than free-standing sections. Section 1(2) now requires only that a design be new in order to be registered. Section 8 relating to duration of a right in a registered design has been subject to substantial alteration. The initial period of five years may be extended for a second, third, fourth and fifth period of five years, thus making a maximum of 25 years potential registration, if the relevant conditions are fulfilled.

Transitional Rights

10.33   Important transitional rights are contained in Schedule 1 to CDPA. By section 51 it is no longer an infringement of copyright to make up an object from design documents (such as technical drawings) or models, even though the drawings or models themselves may still enjoy copyright protection as artistic works. But this does not apply for ten years after commencement of the new copyright provisions in relation to a design recorded or embodied in a design document or model before commencement. During those ten years the design right provisions about availability of licences of right and application to the Comptroller to settle the terms of a licence of right apply to any relevant copyright as in relation to design right.

10.34   By paragraph 20 of Schedule 1, where section 10 of the Copyright Act 1956 (which related to the effect of the industrial application of a design corresponding to an artistic work) applied in relation to an artistic work to any time before the commencement of CDPA, the period of 15 years is to be substituted for the 25 year period which would otherwise be applied by section 52(2) of CDPA. In other words, in these cases the work may be copied without infringement after a period of only 15 years.

CHAPTER 11

Rate Fixing Bodies

MONOPOLY SITUATIONS

11.01 One of the difficulties raised by the operation of the copyright system is that it gives rise to monopoly situations. Over the last few decades there has been rapid progress in the development of anti-monopolistic legislation, first in the United States, and more recently in Europe. British adherence to the Treaty of Rome has meant our acceptance of the provisions of that instrument aimed at controlling restrictive practices in the commercial field; these in themselves are very much more extensive than those which previously existed in the law of the United Kingdom.

PERFORMING RIGHT SOCIETY AND BRITISH MUSIC UNION LTD

11.02 The only effective way for particular groups of right-owners, especially in the area of musical composition, to hope to exploit their right economically is via the medium of a collecting society such as the Performing Right Society. Clearly such an organisation, operating a monopoly right backed by the force of law, is going to attract a certain amount of criticism from disgruntled would-be-users of the music it controls. There is every reason to suppose that in the early years of its existence, just as now, the PRS was eminently reasonable in its negotiations with potential licensees, but some would no doubt always be dissatisfied with the terms they secured, and willing to complain about the manner in which the monopoly was exercised.

11.03 The early history of the exercise of the performing right has been examined in more detail elsewhere.[1] But the PRS having been set up in 1914, by 1919 a group of its strongest opponents among music-users had set up the British Music Union Ltd. It conducted a campaign of lobbying against the Society through its supporters in Parliament, operated a catalogue of free music in an attempt to undermine the

---

1. See for example: McFarlane, *Copyright: The Development and Exercise of the Performing Right.*

Society, and in 1927 developed into the International Council of Music Users Ltd. In this form it tried to force the PRS into granting bulk discounts, and when it failed in that enterprise, it persuaded a Member of Parliament to bring in privately the Musical Copyright Bill in 1929.

11.04 One of the requirements proposed by this measure was that any musical work which wished to obtain the protection of the performing right should have a notice of that reservation printed on it. This would have been in contravention of British obligations under the Berne Copyright Convention. More damaging still was the second proposal. This was that a maximum fee of 2 old pence was to be payable as consideration for the perpetual right to perform any musical work, which would be payable on the purchase of a copy of that work. A professional artiste buying just one copy of a new song would have thus been able to give a limitless number of performances of it to audiences on a national scale for the payment of a single fee of 2 old pence, less than 1p in today's currency.

11.05 Had this measure been passed, it would undoubtedly have destroyed both the Performing Right Society and the occupation of songwriter as a means of gainful employment. But half a century later much the same single payment was being proposed as the only solution to the problems confronting copyright-owners by copying and reproductive equipment (see chapter 9).

11.06 The Bill was given a second reading, and at that stage passed to a Select Committee of the House of Commons, which agreed that a fixed fee could not be applied to all the circumstances of public performance if the composer was to obtain a reasonable remuneration. It concluded that the formation of an association such as the PRS was virtually a necessity to composer and music publisher, and also felt it was vital to the interests of the music-user, who would otherwise have considerable trouble in negotiating separately for every piece of music that he wished to perform: "If such an association is to function effectively, it must obtain as near a super-monopoly as is possible of the monopolies conferred upon composers by the Copyright Acts".[2] But at the same time, the Committee registered its view that such an association or super-monopoly could abuse its rights by declining to grant licences on reasonable terms so as to be contrary to the public interest. Accordingly it recommended that persons so prejudiced should be able to appeal to arbitration or some other tribunal against such alleged abuse, but only

2. Report of the Select Committee on the Musical Copyright Bill (1930).

in cases where the ownership or control of copyright had passed to an association.

Canadian position

11.07 This recommendation in Britain was followed by the setting up in Canada in 1931 of a scheme for the licensing of any organisation in the nature of a copyright collecting society. This followed the commencement of operations in Canada in 1925 of such an organisation for composers, authors and publishers of music, now known as CAPAC. As part of the same scheme there was also established the Copyright Appeal Board which hears objections to fees proposed, among its other functions.

Postwar developments

11.08 Because of the outbreak of the Second World War, no further steps were taken in the United Kingdom at that stage, although as a result of the Report of the 1930 Select Committee it had been decided at the next meeting for the revision of the Berne Copyright Convention to press for freedom for the British government to deal as it saw fit with any abuse of the monopoly of rights in the nature of copyright. When hostilities ceased, and the member states of the Berne Union met for the purposes of revision in 1948, the British delegation therefore added to its acceptance of exclusive right for authors of musical and dramatico-musical works the understanding that the British government was free to enact such legislation as it considered necessary to prevent or deal with any abuse of monopoly rights.

11.09 In 1951 a Copyright Committee began to consider evidence in relation to a new copyright law, and in its Report it made it clear that it had been confronted with a large amount of criticism from various areas of the way in which performing rights had been exercised. The members of the Committee indeed were in little doubt that there was justification in the criticism. It was felt that the Appeal Board set up in Canada had provided an excellent precedent, and the Committee recommended that the same principle should be introduced into this country.

PERFORMING RIGHT TRIBUNAL

11.10 Section 23 of the Copyright Act 1956 accordingly provided for setting up the Performing Right Tribunal, which had jurisdiction in three types of case only; the performing right in literary, dramatic or musical works; the right to cause a sound recording to be broadcast or heard in public; and the right to cause a television broadcast to be seen or heard in public. This jurisdiction bore only on the operation of licensing organisations, in other words copyright collecting societies. On the one hand, it confirmed or varied licensing schemes being operated by such an organisation; on the other hand, it ruled upon complaints made by applicants for licences who had been aggrieved by the refusal of such a body to grant them a licence.

Adjudications

11.11 During the existence of the Performing Right Tribunal in the period up to the CDPA there were not a large number of adjudications. The chairman sat on a part-time basis, assisted by other members appointed by the Department of Trade and Industry. Applications to the Tribunal were made by users of copyright, and PPL and the Performing Right Society were by their nature the licensing bodies involved. Adjudications were very much rate-fixing exercises, and a very specialised practice grew up in matters referred to the Tribunal.

Representation

11.12 In theory, an applicant to the Performing Right Tribunal was not obliged to be represented by counsel or solicitors, although in practice this was almost always done. In general however the parties to the adjudications of the Tribunal have been substantial commercial organisations which have retained lawyers specialising in copyright. If an individual had decided to appear in person, he would nevertheless have found that only a modest fee would have been levied for the application; and had he been ultimately unsuccessful, the likelihood was that costs would not have been awarded against him.

Whitford recommendations

11.13 When the Whitford Committee came to consider the Tribunal in the light of experience gained since the passing of the Copyright Act 1956, there were very few complaints, and it was clear that its existence had done much to clear up the bitter complaints which had earlier been made to the Gregory Committee about the activities of the collecting societies, notably Phonographic Performance Limited (PPL). But a number of suggestions had been made to the Whitford Committee that the jurisdiction of the Tribunal should be extended.

11.14 In addition, a number of the more important conclusions reached by the Committee in its Report had specified that certain matters should be ultimately controlled by the Performing Right Tribunal, and some of these related to control of the impact of technology on copyright-owners. So far as reprography is concerned, the Committee had formed the view that blanket licensing provided the only hope, and in this connection recommended provision for a form of arbitration. The Tribunal should have the power to decide rates of payment for such blanket licence, and also should be able to decide on the terms and conditions of its exercise, according to the Whitford Committee.

11.15 In the area of audio and video-recording, a single levy had been recommended by the Whitford Committee members, along the lines of that introduced earlier in West Germany. This would relate to domestic and private use only, and it was recommended that the Performing Right Tribunal should control not only the rate of the levy, but also its application, and the distribution of the receipts between collecting societies representing different categories of right-owners. In this recommendation lies the germ of considerable potential trouble, for the German experience has led to a certain amount of conflict between various collecting societies; there is the further problem in blanket licensing that it is impossible to identify individual uses, and so the scheme of establishing how the sums eventually finding their way into the coffers of individual societies is to be allocated among its members provides a further potential source of dispute. In the event, no levy was included in CDPA in respect of audio or video recording. This was not because of the difficulties alluded to here, but as a result of conflict between the commercial interests involved, as described in Chapter 9.

11.16 It is tempting for the authority legislating for such a new concept to include as part of the package provisions of a 'social' nature, as for example has been the case with the majority of states which have brought in a form of payment for the public lending right. This could take the form of the subtraction of a specific percentage of the receipts for the maintenance of indigent or aged right-owners or their dependants, and another device is to weight larger percentage payments in favour of right-owners not earning as great an income as those more successful in their occupation.

11.17 In relation to the "synchronisation right", which film-makers have to clear before they can link music to the soundtrack of a motion picture, it was recommended that the Tribunal should enjoy a jurisdiction to cover the reproduction right in the United Kingdom for licences, certainly in musical works at least. This would be limited to licensing bodies meaning to negotiate or grant licences in respect of the reproduction and/or performing rights in works of a number of authors. The Tribunal would then have jurisdiction for licences relating to one single work, or to the works of one single author.

11.18 Important extensions of the Tribunal's jurisdiction were recommended in a number of other areas. In relation to the licensing scheme proposed by the Whitford Committee in respect of recording, it suggested that the Tribunal should be vested with the power to arbitrate between collecting societies and educational users; this would no doubt provide a fertile field for dispute. And in any reference on the subject of the royalty to be paid by broadcasters in respect of the broadcasting of any works within the United Kingdom, the Tribunal would be specifically required to take account of the full audience potential, both for reception off the air and by means of cable broadcasts.

11.19 On the subject of copyright clearance, complaints had been made to the Whitford Committee that there were difficulties in ensuring that all rights were cleared in advance of the broadcasting of programmes. The Independent Television Companies Association had suggested to it that there should exist some form of machinery for ensuring the fixture of a fair remuneration in cases where advance clearance is not obtained, in other than deliberate cases. The Whitford Committee did not favour any provision for clearing copyright after the event, but did recommend the creation of a statutory power vested in the Tribunal, on such terms as to the reservation of payment or otherwise as it in its discretion considered appropriate. This in fact recommended the delegation of a very wide power in this area to the Tribunal.

11.20 As a tidying-up exercise, the members of the Whitford Committee also suggested that in relation to the reproduction right generally, the jurisdiction of the Performing Right Tribunal should be enlarged to cover all situations where a body or organisation of any description in practice controls the "going rate" for a number of works, and in these cases it should be endowed with a general jurisdiction in respect of licences granted by organisations issuing blanket licences as part of their business. The Tribunal should not, however, have its power extended to deal with cases other than those referred to it, but it was recommended that the name of the forum be changed to that of the "Copyright Tribunal".

MECHANICAL RIGHT

11.21 The mechanical right involved a compulsory licence to make a sound recording, which had to be granted by the owner of copyright in a musical work which had already been recorded with the consent of the copyright owner. Under section 8 of the Copyright Act 1956, if it appeared to the Department of Trade and Industry that the statutory rate of royalty had ceased to be equitable, either generally or in relation to any class of records, it could hold a public enquiry. Over the years a number of reviews were held, which were sometimes lengthy and expensive, but did not often produce great change. The Whitford Committee took the view that the procedure for reviewing the statutory rate of royalty was cumbersome and recommended that supervision by the new Copyright Tribunal would be more appropriate.

11.22 However, when CDPA was passed, the statutory licence to copy records sold by retail was abolished. The casual reader of the new legislation would find it hard to discover what has happened. Schedule 8 to CDPA repeals the Copyright Act 1956 in its entirety. But paragraph 21 of Schedule 1 to CDPA gives a saving for the statutory recording licence where notice was given under the 1956 Act before its repeal, but only in respect of the making of records within one year of the repeal coming into force, and only up to the number of records stated in the notice as intended to be sold. In the United Kingdom everyone, both lawyer and layman, is presumed to know the law. No lawyer knows all the law, although a good lawyer knows where to look for it. But the layman, confronted with a highly technical statute such as CDPA, having no fewer than 306 sections in the main body of the text, has little chance of picking up a provision of such importance when it is tucked away in one of eight schedules which themselves account for a further 88 pages of legislation.

THE COPYRIGHT TRIBUNAL

11.23 Chapter VIII of Part I of CDPA deals with the Copyright Tribunal. Effectively the old Performing Right Tribunal has been renamed. The important innovation is the widening of its jurisdiction. By section 149 its function is to hear and determine proceedings under the following heads: (a) references of a licensing scheme; (b) applications with respect to entitlement to a licence under a licensing scheme; (c) references or applications with respect to licensing by a licensing body; (d) appeals against orders as to the coverage of a licensing scheme or licence; (e) applications to settle the royalty or other sum payable for the rental of a sound recording, film or computer program; (f) applications to settle the terms of a copyright licence available as of right; (g) applications to give consent to the exploitation of his performances by a performer; and (h) determinations of royalty or other remuneration to be paid to the trustees for the Hospital for Sick Children.

11.24 Note that the Copyright Tribunal enjoys the power to order the costs of one party to proceedings to be paid by the other party (section 151(1)). It does not automatically follow that the loser will pay the winner's costs, but the new Tribunal may adopt this practice. Obviously it will not want to deter potential customers from coming to it. No doubt the members of the Copyright Tribunal will be anxious to avoid a series of determinations building up which are perceived as merely "splitting the difference" between the parties in dispute.

Summary

11.25 The recommendations made by the Whitford Committee provided the stimulus for the new provisions relating to the Copyright Tribunal which appear in CDPA. The various matters to be adjudicated on, particularly as between right-owner and right-user on the subject of rates, are likely to provoke a greater volume of applications than has previously been the case, and a great deal more employment is liable to be created for the copyright Bar, still a rather slender specialisation for lawyers.

THE AMERICAN POSITION

11.26 The monopolistic aspects of the exercise of copyright have attracted a certain amount of attention since British adhesion to the European Economic Community, and this will be considered elsewhere in the text (Chapter 18). In the United States, antitrust legislation was developed at a much earlier date; the first anticartel legislation in that country was the Sherman Act of 1890, and by the time that the first restrictive trade legislation was brought in in Britain, the American situation was very much more sophisticated.

11.27 The American Society of Composers, Authors and Publishers was the original copyright collecting society in the United States, having been set up in 1914, as was the PRS. Known generally as ASCAP, it was in 1941 subjected to enquiry under the antitrust legislation, as a result of which a consent decree was reached. Moreover, as a result of the opposition to ASCAP from the American broadcasting stations, another copyright collecting society was set up, known as Broadcast Music Inc., otherwise BMI. So the situation in the United States with regard to copyright monopoly is not parallel to that generally existing in most other major copyright countries.

11.28 Reference was made in para 7.09 to the American Copyright Act of 1976. This was the fruit of the extensive review and debate on new legislation in the field of copyright which had been taking place in the United States during the two previous decades. One of the principal measures it introduced was the Copyright Royalty Tribunal by section 801. Completely new to American law, it is cast in the mould first set by the Canadian Appeal Board, and followed in the United Kingdom by the Performing Right Tribunal established by the 1956 Act.

11.29 However, the new American model goes further than did the old PRT, and extends to a wider range of material. No doubt what was contained in the new American Act influenced to some extent the thinking of the Whitford Committee. The American Tribunal extends to the consideration of copyright rates in more general terms, and sets out the criteria which are to govern its deliberations. These are to include the maximising of the availability of creative works to the public; and to afford the copyright-owner a fair return for his creative work, balanced against a fair income to the copyright-user under existing economic conditions.

11.30 Such considerations were not conspicuous in the decisions of the Performing Right Tribunal in the United Kingdom, and they did not loom large in the deliberations of the Whitford Committee. Sometimes the decisions of the British Tribunal discussed "striking a bargain between a willing buyer and a willing seller", but this is a concept very difficult to translate into copyright terms. If the principles now embodied in American law can be made to work in the new British Tribunal, a fair measure of success will have been achieved.

CHAPTER 12

Public Lending Right

THE NEED FOR A PUBLIC LENDING RIGHT

12.01 Authors will not need to be told that theirs is an occupation for which the financial returns have decreased consistently and steadily. Not that a literary career ever meant large financial rewards for any but a very fortunate minority, but in recent decades the returns for traditional outlets even in once remunerative areas such as textbooks have declined even for the moderately successful.

12.02 There are a number of reasons for this phenomenon. The nature of the publishing industry has changed considerably, and cuts in public spending have led to sharply reduced purchasing by educational authorities and libraries. The hardback has been assailed by the cheaper paperback edition selling at a fraction of the cover price of the established form of binding. Social changes this century have led the market of potential consumers to such recreations as television, the cinema and popular motor transport, so that less leisure time is devoted to reading. And on top of all this, the plague of unauthorised copying of such literary works as are actually published erodes still further any prospect of worthwhile royalties which might have existed.

12.03 To those representing the interests of authors, it has been apparent for some time that not only is action required to protect the literary world from direct assault in the nature of unauthorised and wide-scale infringements of copyright involved in multiple reproduction, but at the same time new sources of income are required to replace the potential sales which have been lost. The acts which in relation to a literary work such as a book are protected by CDPA section 16(1) are those of copying the work, issuing unauthorised copies of the work to the public, performing or reading the work in public, broadcasting the work or including it in a cable programme service, and making an adaptation of the work and doing any of these things in relation to the adaptation. Sale, hiring or loan of legitimately printed copies to the public is, however, specifically excluded by section 18(2). To authors it has long seemed that this list was incomplete, and that they should receive some form of remuneration in respect of loans of their works to the public for which they receive no royalty, by means of a public lending right (PLR).

THE CAMPAIGN FOR PLR

12.04 The campaign for the introduction of this new right began in about 1951, when the author John Brophy suggested that authors should receive some form of recompense for loans to the public. His idea at that stage was that one old penny should be levied from the borrower on each occasion that he borrowed a literary work from a public library. This was known as the "Brophy penny", but it failed to achieve widespread support, and the original proposal faded away. The factor which told most heavily against it was the opposition of the library authorities to the notion of a charge to the borrower. The free public library system in the United Kingdom has deep roots, and they were to prove impossible to disturb.

12.05 This initial setback in the campaign to establish what by now had become known as the public lending right was followed by a number of other attempts in the following years. There was a proposal to bring in a direct amendment to the Copyright Act 1956, which failed, as did two Bills to bring about the new right by amendment of the legislation relating to public libraries. But a steady and calculated momentum was continued which kept the matter in the public eye, and ensured that it was a topic of discussion in political circles. This was to prove invaluable when the matter later became the subject of fierce debate in Parliament.

12.06 The proponents of the public lending right were fortunate in having among their number the late Sir Alan Herbert, a skilled publicist and negotiator who was himself a leader of the authors' interests. He was well aware that no hope existed of basing a scheme upon a charge to the borrower of the literary work; he therefore came up with the alternative concept of a fixed annual charge per reader, and drew attention to it in a booklet published in 1962, which was circulated under the title of *Libraries: Free for All?*

12.07 This stimulated the debate considerably, and in 1964 a Public Libraries and Museums Bill was introduced in Parliament, containing a public lending right as a fixed annual charge. But this too was defeated, so a completely fresh approach was initiated, bringing a movement away from the notion of direct compensation along traditional copyright lines, which until then had proved the main stumbling block.

Administrative committee proposal

12.08 The new proposal was to elect an administrative committee on which would sit the representatives of the three main interested groups: authors, librarians and publishers. Both authors and publishers would have been obliged to provide lists of their work currently in copyright, and the whole scheme would have been under the wing of the Department of Education and Science. From the information provided the committee would have drawn up a consolidated register to be forwarded to three representative library authorities. It was intended that they in turn would have made a schedule of the number of copyright books appearing on this register which they had on their shelves.

12.09 The library authorities would have been made up of one county, one large town and one Greater London Council borough, and each year one of these authorities would have been changed for another in the same category. This would have meant that no one authority would have been called upon to serve for a longer period than three consecutive years. The basis of payment would have been on the stocks held on the library shelves rather than on any estimate of lendings over a certain period, and this data would have been used to gross up the sample returns in ratio to the total stocks held by all library authorities; the payment due on each book would then have been worked out in relation to the total sum available for the operation of the scheme.

12.10 Of the amount available for the right-owners, 25 per cent would have been distributed to the publisher, and 75 per cent to the author. A variable rate was proposed according to the numbers of the work published. Thus the full rate would have been paid to the first 2000 copies of any work, the slice between 2000 and 5000 would have received half-rate, and any further copies over 5000 would have been paid at a quarter-rate. This was a considerable shift from the conventional system of copyright compensation, which is not subject to any limitation on the size of the fee, or the number of works on which it is paid, or the number of uses made during any particular period.

12.11 The authors' representatives came up against yet another barrier at this point. The amount of work involved for any of the three selected library authorities would have been very considerable, too large to have been covered by a system of manual accounting, and requiring a level of data processing above the power of computerisation most library authorities enjoyed in those days. Quite apart from the work involved, the expense of the scheme would have been prohibitive, and this, coupled with the reluctance of the librarians to become involved in extra work of this kind, spelled disappointment yet again for the authors.

Authors' need for PLR

12.12 The measure of the authors' need lay perhaps in the persistence with which their claim was repeatedly pressed. By 1970 the proposals had been modified yet again in an effort to meet the objections of the library authorities, and to divert any extra work away from the library staffs. Certain information was available from the statistics held by publishers which could show both the titles and numbers of copies sold to the twenty main wholesalers supplying the public libraries. Again, it was contemplated that the fruits of this scheme would be distributed in the ratio of 25 per cent to publishers and 75 per cent to authors.

12.13 By the early 1970s there seemed to be increasing governmental support for the idea of a public lending right, and in its early stages Mr Heath's administration appeared on a number of occasions to lend its weight to the idea. But as time passed it became less probable that the necessary legislation would be brought in in governmental time; the supporters of PLR realised eventually that they would have to gain the support of an individual Member of Parliament who had been lucky in the private members' ballot.

PLR Bill 1973–74

12.14 By the autumn of 1973 such an individual had been found. Mr Ernle Money, who at that time was the Conservative Member for Ipswich, had drawn fourth place in the ballot, and elected to introduce his Public Lending Right Bill. This proceeded on the apparently simple basis of adding to the rights restricted by copyright in the Copyright Act 1956 the right of lending the work to the public. Indeed, by February of 1974 the Bill had fared so well that it was on its way to a third reading; just at that time, however, Parliament was dissolved and as Mr Heath's government was defeated at the polls, Mr Money's Bill lapsed.

12.15 Had this Bill succeeded in the form in which it was drafted, it would have had the following effects. There would have been no obligation on an author to operate his rights through the medium of a collecting society, and accordingly he would have been entitled to levy a royalty in theory on each occasion that his book was lent, with no limit on the number of royalties he could have drawn in, and no limit on the amount he could have charged. This is the very essence of the concept of copyright as enshrined in successive Copyright Acts. Moreover, had he so chosen, he could have declined altogether to allow his work to be lent to the public, for copyright is a negative as well as a positive right. As the Performing Right Tribunal only had jurisdiction in cases where schemes were being operated by licensing bodies, it would have been unable to interfere in such circumstances. While the jurisdiction of the Copyright Tribunal under CDPA is wider, it still does not extend to any schemes apart from those provided for, and certainly not to a public lending right.

PLR Bill 1976

12.16 However, after the victory of the Labour Party in the second General Election of 1974, fresh attempts were made to bring in the public lending right, but it was not until 1976 that another Bill was introduced into Parliament. At this point, it started to become a very controversial measure indeed. One side embraced the fervent supporters of the proposal, among these the Society of Authors, armed with statistics pointing to the low earnings of authors; on the other were to be found a small band of Members of Parliament who maintained a fierce opposition to the measure, vigorously contesting its progress at every stage in both the House of Commons and the House of Lords. On this occasion the Bill made a fine start in the Upper Chamber, and was read a second time in the Commons. But at the committee stage it ran into serious difficulty, and its opponents put down a very large number of amendments. Eventually, faced with a large number of undiscussed amendments, and with this backlog threatening to drain away precious parliamentary time, the Government abandoned the Bill prior to the completion of the report stage and the third reading.

PLR ACT 1979

12.17 After this protracted struggle, and the bitter defeat of the session of 1976, it was rather surprising that yet another Bill for a public lending right passed into law as an Act of Parliament late in 1979, just before the dissolution of Mr Callaghan's administration. Some of the more controversial points of drafting which had handicapped earlier Bills had this time been dropped, and the measure did not on this occasion meet with the fierce opposition which it had previously provoked. Thus only authors, and not publishers, were to be the beneficiaries, and the drafting did not afford opportunity for discussion of the merits of paying foreign authors, or music publishers and manufacturers of sound recordings.

12.18 The right, known as "public lending right", is conferred on authors and illustrators by section 1(1) of the Public Lending Right Act 1979 and unlike copyright is not assignable. It consists of the entitlement to receive from time to time from a central fund payments in respect of the author's books which are lent by local library authorities in the United Kingdom to the public. A local library authority means either a library authority under the Public Libraries and Museums Act 1964, a statutory library authority under the Public Libraries (Scotland) Act 1955, or an Education and Library Board within the Education and Libraries (Northern Ireland) Order 1972. Thus the right does not extend to the private book-lending carried on for subscription by certain types of smaller shops as a sideline.

12.19 The technique of the Public Lending Right Act 1979 is to set up the framework of the measure in the statute itself, but to leave a very large part of the flesh to be filled in by a scheme brought into operation by the Secretary of State for Education and Science. So the classes, descriptions and categories of books in respect of which the right subsists are specified by this scheme, as are the means of payment to be made in respect of it from the Central Fund. This Central Fund, constituted by the Secretary of State and under the control and management of the PLR Registrar, is provided by Parliament. Funding is decided by the Secretary of State with the approval of the Treasury. The Act originally provided in section 2(2) that in respect of the liabilities of one financial year the total was not to exceed £2 million; however the Secretary of State may and has from time to time with the approval of the Treasury increased by statutory instrument the limit on the sums payable.

Operation of the Scheme

12.20 For the sixth year of operation of the public lending right scheme, that is from 1 July 1987 to 30 June 1988, the fund was set at £3,500,000, an increase of 27% over the previous limit of £2,750,000. The rate per loan was set at 1.45 pence, with an upper limit of £6,000 and a lower limit of £5 per individual author. The application of this limit to the 67 authors who came up against it meant that a further £344,000 was available for redistribution to other authors. Critics might argue that the figures represented by the fund are pitifully low. However the introduction of the scheme established the principle. The amount available for distribution has recently been increased by a figure above the current rate of inflation. It may be that this trend will continue, if economic expansion is maintained. The PLR Registrar has done much to ensure the smooth operation of the public lending right scheme in its formative years.

12.21 Loans are recorded by computer at a representative sample of libraries (changed annually) and grossed up by a factor to give an equivalent figure covering all public libraries in the U.K. The cost of loan recording is borne by the PLR Fund. The results are published (as well as distributed to authors with their payments) and have produced much useful information about the relative popularity of different authors and the reading habits of the British public.

12.22 Entitlement to PLR is contingent on registration, and thus eligibility to register is one of the key aspects of the scheme. Some apparently arbitrary rules and exclusions are designed to reduce administrative cost and ensure that the largest possible slice of the "cake" is available for distribution to authors. At present authors must be resident in the U.K. and their books must be published there; it is hoped to extend eligibility to nationals of foreign countries where British authors are entitled to PLR when funds allow. The book must bear an international standard book number (used for identification by libraries) and the author's name must appear on the title page (special rules apply to pseudonyms). A maximum of four authors may register per volume. Provided they satisfy these rules, illustrators may register as well as authors. The fact that a book is out of print or was published before the scheme came into operation is no bar to registration. At first the scheme was confined to living authors, but books published after a previously registered author's death may now be registered. The Scheme is set out in a statutory instrument (SI 1982/719), subsequently amended in 1983 and 1984. A helpful booklet *PLR in Practice* is available from the PLR Registry, Bayheath House, Prince Regent Street, Stockton-on-Tees, Cleveland TS18 1DF.

PLR AND COPYRIGHT

12.23 PLR is not a branch of copyright, and it is clear from the structure of the legislation that the word "right" is something of a misnomer. The public lending right is not an unrestricted right to do or to prevent others from carrying out certain acts, which is of course the basic principle of copyright legislation; the latter places no limitation on the amount which a copyright owner can earn from the exercise of his copyright, being controlled wholly by the number of uses of the work made by the licensees, and the amount which any outright purchaser is prepared to pay.

12.24   PLR, on the other hand, is subject to governmental control on the total amount distributed to be shared among the entitled authors. This has to be divided up among them according to the terms of the statutory scheme, and to that extent payment is made according to entitlement founded on use of their works. However there can be no dispute but that the money provided is undoubtedly a grant from the Government, certainly not a payment by the user. If the same principle were to be applied to copyright generally, it would certainly not be to the advantage of right-owners.

12.25   Where no sum has become due in respect of a work for a period of at least ten years, it may be removed by the Registrar, a provision which is directly contrary to the principle of copyright law. Both this, and the requirement of registration, make the public lending right a concept with sharp contrasts to copyright as envisaged by the Berne Convention and CDPA. In the Public Lending Right Act 1979 section 4(7) creates a criminal offence in respect of any false statement made knowingly in relation to any entry of any nature in the register. These procceedings are to be brought in the magistrates court, and the maximum fine is £1000. It is unclear from the Act whether these proceedings are to be brought by the Registrar or the aggrieved right-owner; if the latter, it is unlikely that many prosecutions will be initiated, if the number of private prosecutions brought under the criminal provisions in the Copyright Act 1956 is any guide.

PLR IN OTHER COUNTRIES

12.26   The United Kingdom was not the first country in the field. Various forms of compensation exist in West Germany, Holland, Finland, Sweden, Denmark, and Australia. In only one of these states, West Germany, is the right incorporated into the domestic copyright law of the country. Even there the right has not been able to free itself entirely from the socioeconomic emphasis which distinguishes it from true copyright. The public lending right in West Germany can only be exercised by a collecting society, and not therefore by an individual. A number of collecting societies participate in the amount made available, and a proportion of the money is diverted into a social fund for needy authors. Payments under the German system will be made to qualifying foreign authors, who will need to be represented by their national collecting society. This function could eventually be fulfilled in Britain by the Authors' Licensing and Collecting Society (ALCS).

12.27 Even in West Germany, however, the money for the right is provided from central funds; in some of the other states it is frankly a subsidy for authors, and outside West Germany the benefits are confined to nationals, which is contrary to the basic concept of copyright. Understandably, no government finds it desirable to provide significant sums to fund a form of public lending right, only for a substantial section of those funds to be carried overseas to benefit foreign nationals whose own countries do not acknowledge a public lending right. The United States does not possess a public lending right, but American authors are heavily represented on the shelves of the whole English-speaking world. They would inevitably benefit substantially from unrestricted public lending rights in Britain and the Commonwealth countries.

Hope for an international convention

12.28 At the present time, there is no central authority controlling the various national public lending rights, in the way that the Berne and Universal Conventions govern international copyright. If a new convention could amass enough signatories as a result of a diplomatic conference on public lending right, reciprocity could be made a feature of this agreement. This would lead to the abandonment of nationality between ratifying states, and could pave the way for international accounting for the public lending right in the same way that the scheme for copyright payments currently exists. Once it is seen to operate smoothly, governments might be more prepared to make larger sums available.

Position of publishers under the PLR Act

12.29 Most of the states operating some form of public lending right specifically exclude publishers from the benefits. The prime exception to this rule is Australia, where publishers can claim a fee for each qualifying book, which is approximately one quarter of the fee which the author may claim. There is also an element of participation by publishers in West Germany.

12.30 In the Public Lending Right Act 1979 of the United Kingdom however, section 1 confers the public lending right on authors, and this appears to be exclusive; a publisher will not be able to participate in the benefits. This factor probably contributed to the eventual passage of the Act, for in earlier Bills provision for payments to publishers had caused great controversy.

Rental right

12.31 The comment must be made that the complete exclusion of public lending right from the general scheme of copyright contained in CDPA seems a little anomalous, in view of the introduction of rental rights for sound recordings, films and computer programs.

CHAPTER 13

Copyright and Data Processing

13.01 One of the factors which has contributed greatly to the projection of the topic of copyright into a central position on the legal stage in recent years is the realisation of its application to the problems posed by the use of computers. There are two distinct aspects to the matter—both the extent to which computer programs can be protected against copying and other unauthorised acts, and also the extent to which copyright works, generally in the literary field, can be protected from unauthorised computer use.

13.02 Computers have been with us in a commercially viable form for less than 50 years, but the rate of expansion in their use has been phenomenal. In this area of technology as in a number of others there has been a reduction over the years in the physical size and relative cost of the equipment, and a consequent increase in their accessibility. "Software" is the general term for what is fed into the computer, whereas the machines themselves are known as the "hardware". Thus the question of the extent to which proprietary rights may exist in computer programs has become known as "software protection". When the 1956 Copyright Act was being drawn up computers were still few in number, cumbersome and very expensive and it is hardly surprising that the Act failed to tackle the problem.

PATENT PROTECTION FOR COMPUTER PROGRAMS

13.03 There had been hopes in the early days that the patent system might be adapted to afford protection to computer programs, but this was first doubted in cases tried under United States law, and then so far as the United Kingdom is concerned, was put into a firm recommendation in the Report of the Banks Committee on the British patent system[1]: "A computer program, that is a set of instructions for controlling the sequence of operations of a data processing system . . . should not be patentable". The international investment in computer software is massive, and in the absence of protection under the

---

1. Report of the Banks Committee (1970), para 487.

patent system the situation existing in copyright law is therefore of crucial importance to the data processing industry.

THE CONCEPT OF COMPUTER SOFTWARE

13.04 In its broad sense, the term "software" includes not only the programs themselves, but also the documents and operating manuals connected therewith, together with the papers relating to the programming of the computer. There is a very wide range both in the instructions which go to make up a program, and the form in which they are manifested. There is also a considerable difference in the sophistication of the various "languages" which have been developed. Of great importance to the topic of software protection is the fact that programs themselves may be stored on a variety of carriers and in a number of forms. They can, for instance, be punches on paper tapes or cards in the form of holes, or recorded on magnetic tapes, discs and cards. It is theoretically possible for a very experienced programmer to read the symbols or indentations made on these media but it is hardly an easy task.

13.05 The difficulties posed for the judiciary by the concepts of software were highlighted in the case of *Thrustcode Ltd v. W W Computing Ltd.*[2] Megarry VC in the Chancery Division pointed out that in normal cases where infringement is claimed, the two articles could be put side by side for purposes of comparison. In considering software "many different processes may produce the same answer and yet remain different processes that have not been copied from one another". Legislating to make software subject to the laws of copyright protection does not necessarily get over the evidential difficulties canvassed in that case.

WHITFORD DELIBERATIONS

13.06 It was suggested to the Whitford Committee that programs should be covered in any new copyright legislation by treating them as a separate category of work, with its own definitions. The members were urged that the definition of "literary work" should be extended to include "any written computer program", and the definition of "writing" to include "notation expressed in the form of punched holes or of magnetic signs or symbols". This would require consequential definitions for the expressions "computer" and "computer program".

---

2. [1983] F.S.R. 502.

13.07 In its Report the Committee rejected these proposals, although without giving any very extensive explanation of why it had done so.[3] It took the view that copyright should exist in any original work which is fixed in such a way that the recorded information can be reproduced, and that therefore there is no requirement for a special provision.

> "We feel the existing categories of literary and (where appropriate) artistic works are sufficiently wide to cover computer programs already, and that the only amendment necessary is to make it clear that copyright subsists in any work recorded in such a way that it can be reproduced; in saying this we would emphasise that, in our view, it is quite immaterial that a program may not be visible to or readable by the human eye or be directly understandable by the human brain. There can be no doubt that a literary work is protectable notwithstanding that it is in code."

13.08 The view of the Whitford Committee was endorsed by subsequent case law in many jurisdictions. In the U.K. it was incorporated into statute by the Copyright (Computer Software) Amendment Act 1985. This principle was carried forward into CDPA, in which computer programs are specifically included in the definition of literary works by section 3(1)(b).

UNITED STATES POSITION

13.09 The draftsmen of the new Copyright Act of the United States in 1976 also felt that the matter required clarification. That law states at section 102 that: "Copyright protection subsists ... in original works of authorship fixed in any tangible medium of expression, now known or later developed, from which they can be perceived or otherwise communicated, either directly or with the aid of a machine". And in section 101, "literary works" are defined as "works, other than audio-visual works, expressed in words, numbers, or other verbal or numerical symbols or indicia, regardless of the nature of the material objects, such as books, periodicals, manuscripts, phonorecords, film, tapes, disks, or cards, in which they are embodied".

"USE RIGHT"

13.10 The Whitford Committee also considered the matter of a "use right", by which there would be an express restriction on the use of a program to control or condition the operation of a computer. A majority of the members came down in favour of such an express right,

---

3. Cmnd 6732, para 492.

taking the view that the whole point of the creation of works in this form is to exploit them by use, and from this use the author will derive any revenue for the work he has created. In making this majority recommendation the Committee returned to the traditional view of copyright as a source of income for the author which is generated by individual and identifiable uses. But the objection to the proposal throws into relief the problem confronting the whole copyright system today.

13.11 Use of computer programs in such ways as running them through the computer almost invariably takes place in private. How then is such use to be detected, let alone policed? The Committee members did not attempt to provide an answer to the problem, which they merely noted. But the majority of areas of modern technology which affect the copyright system have one factor in common, namely the difficulty of showing that any infringing use has taken place. A practical solution has to be found very rapidly, and the creation of rights which are little more than lip-service to the system without any possibility of significant return is not in the short term likely to be of much practical assistance to the owners whose rights are being infringed. This comes back to the problem raised by Vice-Chancellor Megarry in *Thrustcode v. W W Computing Ltd* (see para 13.05).

13.12 Section 17 of CDPA is important. Subsection (2), which provides that copying in relation to a literary, dramatic, musical or artistic work means reproducing the work in a material form, adds that this includes storing the work in any medium by electronic means. Subsection (6) adds that copying in relation to any description of work includes the making of copies which are transient or incidental to some other use of the work. So in the case of programs, substantial measures for the control of their use have been fed into the law, but the problems of detection of abuse still remain.

Databases

13.13 The problem of databases was also considered by the Whitford Committee, and it came to a similar view to that reached in the case of software. The two cases it found were very similar, and it was considered that databases should be regarded for copyright purposes in the same way as was recommended for computer programs. They will be treated as literary works if a sufficient amount of skill or labour, or both, has been devoted to their preparation. This would seem to have the same objections as have been noted above in the case of software protection; in view of the great investment of time and money involved, any doubts should be resolved through the medium of clear legislative drafting. Unfortunately CDPA is not so specific here, particularly where the material has not previously existed in a form (such as print or paper) giving rise to copyright protection in its own right.

13.14　As the capacity and power of data-processing equipment has developed, so the kind of material to which its powers can be applied has also expanded. The world's store of learning is contained on printed pages, together with its great works of literature and drama. Music too is contained in notation on printed pages, and all can be easily converted into a form readily assimilated by a computer. This gives rise to the problem of the computer use of copyright works. Textbooks, reference works, encyclopaedias and all kinds of manuals can be fed into data-processing equipment, and authors and owners of the rights in such works may fear that such operations will lead to a decline if not an extinction of their incomes. There is little doubt that databases will in many cases by formed either from entire copyright works or from compilations. Section 17 of CDPA will certainly apply here.

Threat of computer technology to copyright-owners

13.15　So long as computer use is confined to storage or running for the use of that particular computer installation, probably not much harm is done. A use is made which is probably an infringement of copyright, but little real income is lost to the author, and as previously noted, such use is very hard to detect. But the peril lies in the ongoing developments of computer technology. It is the power of these new machines to multiply the transmission of data not just a few hundred times, but many-fold, and at the immediate behest of the user, so that the potential economic value to the right-owner is completely destroyed.

13.16　Change in this field is so rapid that one can only note that technological development may before long replace newspapers and postal communications, and eventually printed works altogether. The Whitford Committee foresaw a situation in which all homes and offices throughout the country are linked to a national computing centre through the medium of viewer/printer consoles. As is noted in the Report[4]: "Works of reference would in that case be particularly vulnerable. The sale of just one copy of a work to the national centre would result in its contents, or a selection thereof, being made available throughout the country". Such a system is now technically feasible.

4.　Cmnd 6732, para 506.

Destruction of authorship as an occupation
13.17 Clearly such a situation without effective copyright protection would destroy authorship as an occupation from which any income would be derived, and it is obvious that no one would write or compose with a view to earnings through the copyright system based on per-use compensation if the sale of only one copy of the work was likely.

13.18 The problems posed to copyright by other technological developments are considered at various points in this book, but there is no doubt that the current threat is immense. The Whitford Committee stated its view that in almost all cases of any practical significance the input of copyright material into a computer will involve reproduction in a material form, and that storage of copyright material in a computer store should be clearly restricted. This has undoubtedly been done in CDPA, but substantial questions of administration and evidence remain.

Measure of compensation
13.19 These remedies are largely academic if such uses are unauthorised by the owner of copyright, and at the same time incapable of detection. And even in the case of the reproduction of vital parts of a work on a viewer/printer console via a national computer centre, what is to be the measure of compensation? A single lump sum payment is hardly going to be adequate compensation, and even if such payments are provided for in the law, there is some doubt as to how they will be equitably divided up.

13.20 If for example a major reference work is produced in several volumes which in its successive editions represents a lifetime's work for its sole author, he is not going to be content with a small fraction of the fruits of an annual payment made by the computing centre to a representative collecting society. The computing centre on the other hand will not have time to arrange individual contracts with all authors of major reference works which it wishes to use. But the use of the work by the computing centre may destroy all other potential sales of the work.

13.21 Reference works and textbooks seem to be most at risk. Only the most pessimistic would conclude that the future holds the prospect of no further publication of fresh novels and dramas, belles-lettres or major descriptive works of non-fiction. There will always be a market for certain types of book, simply because the work which they contain lends itself to being read principally through the medium of the printed page. No one, it is surmised, is going to sit down and read a Scott Fitzgerald work from a computer console, and then follow this with, for example, one of Trollope's novels.

Licensing

13.22 If the development of desktop computers is carried through to the point where all homes and offices are linked to a national centre, some solution may be found in licensing the home installation on an annual basis in respect of copyright use. I have always argued that any dividing line between a copyright royalty with the force of statutory backing, and a tax or duty also having the force of statutory authority in the Finance Acts is very slender indeed. True, in the case of the latter, the revenue raised goes to the national exchequer, while in the former it largely finds its way into the accounts of individual copyright owners, but there are many analogies.

13.23 If copyright-owners are to derive any protection against the real threats now posed to them by technology, they may have to abandon the nice distinctions raised by the purists among them, and press for annual licensing backed by the force of the state in the form of sanctions for non-compliance. It is far better to move now, while there is time to negotiate successful terms, than argue for some years until it is too late to affect the issue, and a solution is imposed by Parliament, which may not be of the greatest benefit to copyright owners.

13.24 It would, for example, be highly desirable for them to ensure that control of any such licensing operation remained under the control of copyright-owners, through some such central collecting society as the PRS or ALCS. If it were left in State control, it would run the danger of being regarded as just another indirect tax, subject to economic regulation according to Treasury direction, and liable to have a proportion directed to coffers other than those of copyright interests. It will be recalled that the road fund tax was originally earmarked for the improvement of Britain's road system.

13.25 It is also of vital importance for copyright interests to ensure that no disputes arise between various parties as to the division of any fruits of such licensing. This has taken place abroad in relation to various forms of the public lending right, where rival author's societies have entered litigation over the revenues derived from such new rights. The blanket licensing schemes operated by ALCS in Chapter 16, to which indirect statutory backing is available through sections 116–143 of CDPA, are a limited but significant development in this direction.

CHAPTER 14

International Protection

14.01 Of the many international organisations which have mush-roomed in the last century or so to attempt to control the economic and social behaviour of mankind, arguably the two principal bodies which govern the international copyright system have been the most consistently successful. Indeed one of them, the Berne Copyright Union, is among the oldest of such organisations. By and large it has secured the compliance of its members with the rules which have been agreed upon, and in particular the Berne Union has a striking record throughout its existence of regular and practical adaptation to the changing requirements of society.

HISTORICAL DEVELOPMENT

14.02 A detailed account of the development of the Berne Union is given by Dr Stephen Ladas in his standard work, *International Protection of Literary and Artistic Property*. More briefly, it will suffice to note that among the great publishing nations there existed by the middle of the nineteenth century considerable dissatisfaction with the quality and extent of the copyright protection afforded to their productions outside their national territory. Some of these states had concluded treaties between each other to attempt to govern the position, but this did nothing to alleviate the situation in third countries with which no treaty existed.

Berne Convention

14.03 In 1885 a conference of the interested powers met to attempt to reach common ground, and from their deliberations was forged the Berne Convention of 1886. The nine original signatories comprised the major publishing countries of Great Britain, France, Germany and Italy, together with Belgium, Spain, Haiti, Switzerland and Tunis. The original instrument was regularly and frequently overhauled: at Paris in 1896, Berlin in 1908, again in Berne in 1914, Rome in 1928, and Brussels in 1948. More recently there were important conferences at Stockholm in 1967 and Paris in 1971, but first some mention must be made of the second important international body, the Universal Copyright Convention (UCC).

Universal Copyright Convention (UCC)

14.04 Although by 1948 a substantial number of states had adhered to the Berne Convention, notable exceptions were the United States and the USSR. The standards imposed on its members were of a high order, and neither country had been prepared to accept them—even in Tsarist days Russia had demonstrated no interest. A major problem in the United States was the existence of the protectionist "manufacturing clause" in domestic law (see para 3.15) which the Americans were not prepared to forsake.

14.05 In the hope of inducing at least the United States to come into the international copyright club, a new international organisation was established in 1952 under the auspices of UNESCO. This was the Universal Copyright Convention, demanding a lower standard of reciprocal protection than the Berne Union. It asked of its members only that published works, if first published outside the territory of the member state and not the work of one of its nationals, are to enjoy protection without any formality, save that all copies should carry the symbol ©, together with the name of the copyright-owner and the year of first publication. This would allow published works of nationals of other member states wherever first published the same rights as it allowed the nationals of its own who had published a work for the first time in its territory.

Conflict between Berne Convention and UCC

14.06 This proved sufficiently attractive to the United States to tempt it into membership of the UCC, and since that time the symbol © has become familiar in publishing quarters as a tribute to the wide membership and rapid growth of the UCC. But when in 1967 the Stockholm Conference met to revise the Berne Copyright Convention, ripples of dissent for the first time disturbed the calm of the international copyright system. On the one side were ranked the developing countries, conscious of their recent colonial past and avid for access to textbooks and the storehouse of world literature at prices which they could afford; on the other stood the major publishing countries, highly developed and disinclined to permit unrestricted access to the works of their authors which would sap the economic return from this export market.

14.07 The conflict stemmed directly from the relinquishment of their former imperial glories by states such as the United Kingdom and France. In colonial days many developing countries had acquired their copyright law as a result of the governing power imposing its own copyright law upon the colony, together with at the same time membership of the high standard Berne Copyright Union. Understandably newly independent states were not keen on being bound by laws which had been enacted for them; and, unhappily, when the colonial power left, little was done to give the newly independent power an insight into the benefits which could accrue from the international system of copyright.

14.08 In 1961 Ghana brought in a new copyright statute to replace the copyright legislation which had been inherited from the United Kingdom. This reduced considerably copyright protection in Ghana's domestic law, and set a precedent which was followed over the next few years by a number of other countries including Kenya, Malawi, Uganda and Zambia. To the distress of the developed nations, in 1963 a Draft African Model Copyright Law was produced, and a similar instrument for East Asian states appeared in 1967. Both had the aim of pruning back sharply the high standards of copyright protection advocated by the developed states, with highly organised publishing and entertainment industries.

14.09 The Stockholm Conference met in 1967 against this disturbing background of the newly independent member states asserting themselves in opposition to copyright statutes which had been created *for* them, rather than *by* them. The economic factor played a significant part, reflected in the balance of payment of trade between the various countries. Those states exporting copyright material, drawn substantially from the ranks of the developed world, would enjoy very favourable balances of trade; against this the copyright importing countries were frequently undeveloped, and their balance of payments so far as copyright material was concerned would generally be in deficit. The grievance was not therefore entirely a matter of pride.

Protocol regarding developing countries

14.10 While these developing states were anxious to maintain their membership of the high level Berne Convention, or in some cases even to join it, they were very keen to secure considerable relaxations of the requirements of the Convention for so long as they stayed in conditions of development. To the new text of the Berne Convention as revised at

Stockholm there was appended a Protocol regarding developing countries. The proposal was that this became an integral part of the revised text, and that any country adopting the revised text was obliged at the same time to adopt the Protocol.

14.11 But these new provisions were less than attractive to the developed exporting states. Developing countries were accorded the right to reduce the period of copyright protection by up to 25 years, to cut back severely the rights of translation, and to augment considerably the various forms of free use for educators, broadcasters and other users of copyright. The copyright-exporting states indicated that they could neither accede to the Protocol nor the substantive provisions of the revised text which accompanied it. Deadlock seemed inevitable, and for the first and only time the harmony, and indeed the very continuation of the international copyright system, was threatened.

14.12 While the developed countries staunchly declined to accept the Stockholm Protocol, the developing states, however, indicated that this stance might result in their withdrawal from the Berne Union to establish with other countries in their category a new, low-standard convention to meet their particular requirements. But a major obstacle to any withdrawal from the Berne Convention was the safeguard clause in the Appendix Declaration to Article XVII of the Universal Copyright Convention. This was to the effect that a country which left the Berne Convention would not be entitled to claim protection on the basis of the Universal Copyright Convention from other Berne Convention states.

Temporary stalemate

14.13 This was by far the most dangerous crisis which the international system had ever been obliged to face, and for some time the stalemate appeared to be hardening into a permanent impasse. But a good deal of frank negotiation took place away from the public glare of the conference halls, and eventually this was rewarded with a measure of success. At a joint meeting of the Intergovernmental Committee of the UCC and the Permanent Committee of the Berne Convention at Paris in February 1969, the former body elected to convene a conference to revise Article XVII and the Appendix Declaration. At the same time a joint study group was set up to examine the entire field of international copyright, and to consider means of settling the dispute.

Washington Recommendation

14.14 The first meeting of the joint study group took place in Washington in September 1969, and it produced the Washington Recommendation. This called for the revision of both the UCC and the Berne Convention at conferences to be held at the same time and at the same place. It also suggested that Article XVII of the UCC, the safeguard clause, should be removed in respect of countries in a state of development, that certain rights not previously appearing in the UCC should be written into its text, and that both Conventions should included less extensive concessions to developing countries.

Paris Revision

14.15 After a series of preparatory meetings, the conference for the joint revision of the Berne and the UCC texts started in Paris on 5 July 1971. The revised versions of both texts were signed there just three weeks later, and this finally put paid to the Stockholm Protocol. The valuable innovations which had been worked out in Stockholm in 1967 were largely incorporated into the Paris revisions. The crux of the concessions made to the developing countries is the preferential treatment accorded to them in the area of translation and reproduction; effectively the same system has been introduced into both Conventions.

THE POSITION TODAY

14.16 In addition, a scheme of compulsory licences has been worked out in respect of both translation and reproduction rights, and these represent considerable concessions by both sides. In practice, these rules have established the borderlines inside which negotiations between copyright-owner and copyright-user can take place. While the United Kingdom has acceded to each revised text of the Berne Convention up to that of Brussels in 1948, it has not ratified in full the Paris revision of 1971; in accordance with the Washington Recommendation, the revised text of the Berne Convention could not come into effect until France, Spain, the United Kingdom and the United States had all ratified the new UCC.

14.17 The Paris revision of the UCC text, which gave wider compulsory rights for translation and reproduction, did not call for any alteration in the domestic law of the United Kingdom, and thus there was an early ratification by this country. But a number of minor changes to domestic British copyright law were called for in order for the UK to ratify the Paris revision of Berne. For example, an alteration to the statutory protection for choreographic works was required to accord with the Convention description of "fixed in some material form" (Article 2). It is thought that the extension of the definition of literary work in section 3(1) CDPA to any work, spoken or sung, will cover the situation.

Architecture, Films and Folklore

14.18 Further alterations to the previous law have been made in these areas by CDPA. These are designed to support United Kingdom ratification of the Paris Revision of the Berne Convention.

Droit Moral

14.19 It had long been felt in some quarters that British copyright law did not fully take account of Convention obligations in respect of the *droit moral* or "moral right" of authors to be acknowledged as such and not have their work altered without consent. False attribution of authorship, which appeared in section 43 of the Copyright Act 1956, was by no means analogous and the situation was not fully covered by the law of defamation. The Whitford Committee recommended that the general philosophy of the *droit moral* should be introduced into British law, though rendering it subject to waiver in certain circumstances. This view was in keeping with British membership of the European Community, and differed from the line taken by the Gregory Committee a quarter of a century earlier.

14.20 Extensive provision for moral rights is now made in Part I of CDPA, specifically in Chapter IV. Now the author of a copyright literary, dramatic, musical or artistic work, and also the director of a film, has the right to be identified as such, but that right must be specifically asserted. This may be done by a statement in an assignment, or a written instrument signed by the claimant. Special provisions exist for making such an assertion in relation to the public exhibition of an artistic work. But there is no right to be identified as an author or director in the case of a computer program, the design of a typeface, or a computer-generated work. A wide number of permitted uses such as fair dealing reduce the value of the right quite considerably.

14.21 Similarly, the author of a copyright literary, dramatic, musical or artistic work, and also the director of a film, enjoy the right not to have their work subjected to derogatory treatment. This means any addition to, deletion from, alteration to or adaptation of the work. Translations are not "treatment" for these purposes, nor are arrangements or transcriptions of musical works involving no more than a change of key or register. "Derogatory" treatment involves distortion or mutilation of the work, or treatment otherwise prejudicial to the honour or reputation of the author or director. There are also wide exceptions to this right.

14.22 Protection against false attribution of authorship is preserved in section 84 of CDPA, and by section 85, a person who for private and domestic purposes commissions the taking of a photograph or the making of a film has, where copyright subsists in it, certain rights to privacy. In the case of photographs, this includes the right not to have copies issued to the public. None of these moral rights are assignable. However, the value of these moral rights have been very considerably nullified by qualifications and exceptions.

MEMBERSHIP OF THE CONVENTIONS

14.23 Most of the civilised nations of the world are members of either the Berne Convention or the UCC, and many are members of both, although they may have ratified different revisions of the Berne Convention. The chief differences between the two instruments are that the term of protection is longer under the Berne Convention, being normally a minimum of life plus 50 years, and no formality may be imposed as a condition of the grant of copyright protection. The UCC in contrast calls for a minimum period of protection of 25 years in addition to the life of the author, with lesser periods of ten years for such matters as photographs. The formality which any member country may demand as a condition of copyright protection is the application to copies of the symbol ©, with the year of first publication, and the copyright-owner's name.

14.24 The most striking aspect of recent developments in international copyright has been the effect on the major countries which were lukewarm to the system, or which had remained outside it altogether. China is not a member of either Convention, though it is hoped that this situation will be rectified when she has enacted an adequate domestic copyright Act. The United States came late into the fold. For long only a member of the lower-standard UCC, the new copyright statute of the United States passed in 1976 gave extended protection designed to bring that country more into line with the standards offered by the other great publishing nations. America eventually joined the Berne Convention with effect from 1 March 1989, as a result of further amendments made to domestic law.[1]

Soviet Union

14.25   By far the most significant event in the Soviet Union's copyright relationship with the outside world was her ratification of the UCC. This completely altered her historic approach to the subject. Before the 1917 Revolution, Russia was the only major European power to remain outside the international system, and even after the Second World War of the Communist countries in Europe only the USSR and Albania belonged to no copyright convention at all. Bulgaria, Czechoslovakia, Hungary, Poland, Romania and Yugoslavia all maintained the membership of the Berne Convention which each had entered between the two world wars; indeed, in the majority of these states there are internationally affiliated author's societies which are in a position to account externally for royalties which have arisen from the public performance of musical works.

14.26   However, until the recent adhesion of the Soviet Union to the Universal Copyright Convention there did not exist in that country any authors' society with international affiliations which could receive on behalf of its members any royalties transferred from foreign authors' societies in respect of performances in their territories of Russian works. This was of course a grave disadvantage to Russian authors and composers, but it had a conversely adverse affect on Western copyright-owners. At that time no foreign works were protected within Russian territory by the copyright law of the Soviet Union, and thus no Russian society could make reciprocal payments to authors' societies outside Russia in respect of performances of foreign works within the USSR.

14.27   Before the ratification of the UCC in 1973, there had been a civil code containing provisions on copyright in each of the 15 Soviet Federated Republics. Each of these codes also contained model publishing agreements which had the force of law, and which governed relations between author and publisher. However, protection could be accorded to a foreigner's works only if they had first been published in the Soviet Union, and even then it was unlikely that royalties could have been legally remitted outside the country.

---

1. Public Law 100–568 of 31 October 1988.

14.28   The only exception to this state of affairs was a bilateral treaty which Russia had entered in 1968 with Hungary, another member of COMECON, by which each of the two countries acknowledged the copyright of resident nationals of the other state in respect of works which had first been published in that other state. But the effect of joining the UCC is that the Soviet Union has now accepted the principle that each member state must accord to the unpublished works of the nationals of all other UCC member states the same protection as it grants to the unpublished works of its own nationals. Moreover, it grants to the published works of nationals of other member states wherever first published, and to published works of the nationals of any country if first published in one of the UCC member states, the same rights as it grants to works first published in its own territory.

14.29   Already this ratification has had a practical result for Western authors and publishers. A copyright collecting society with the title of *Vsesojuznoje Agentstvo po Avtorskim Pravam* (VAAP) has been established in Russia, and it has entered into a contract of affiliation with the Performing Right Society in London. This means that British copyright-owners will be able to have remitted to them royalties in sterling in respect of protected performances of their works in Russia. British and other publishers now enter into normal publishing agreements with their Soviet counterparts, directly or through VAAP.

14.30   This is not as wide a provision as it might be, for as the domestic law of the Soviet Union now stands, a royalty can only be exacted in respect of live performances, for example concerts or variety shows, or by bands in restaurants and hotels. It does not include any provision for payment in respect of performances by mechanical means, such as records, broadcasts or film soundtracks. But it is a great advance for Western right-owners, who may now expect to enjoy some income in respect of performances of their works in Russia. Certain types of western music enjoy a considerable vogue there, and the composers and authors of these works should benefit accordingly.

SUMMARY

14.31   Thus the Berne Convention and the Universal Copyright Convention are the two instruments which dominate the international copyright system. There are a number of more specialised conventions relating to such matters as the use of gramophone records and the sounds recorded on them, and broadcasts. These are dealt with in the chapters on those subjects, but mention must be made of some minor conventions which have an international flavour.

14.32 These all came into existence as a result of conventions held in various parts of the American continent. To none of them is the United Kingdom a party, and their importance would in any case seem to be diminishing with the spread of ratifications of the two main instruments discussed above. The Pan-American Conventions resulted from a series of conferences held in the first two decades of this century at Mexico City, Rio de Janeiro, Buenos Aires, Havana and Washington, and have not been ratified by any state outside the Americas. There is, in addition, a Montevideo Convention dating from the close of the nineteenth century which a number of European states did ratify, but it is not of practical significance to the British entertainment or publishing industries.

14.33 As the member states of the European Community move towards closer integration, greater interest is being taken by the Commission in copyright matters. It has issued a Green Paper entitled *Copyright and the Challenge of Technology – Copyright Issues requiring Immediate Action*.[2] Some interests will submit that if harmonisation takes place within the EC, it should be upwards to the highest standards prevailing in the domestic systems of member states.

14.34 Interestingly, in *EMI Electrola GmbH v. Patricia Import and Export*,[3] the European Court held that a restriction on Community trade could not be justified on the ground of a disparity in the period of protection granted by national copyright laws, where this constituted a means of arbitrary discrimination or a disguised restriction on trade between member states.

14.35 The Commission also contends that intellectual property should be governed by the basic GATT principle of equal national treatment. These proposals are on a worldwide footing, and are relevant to problems of counterfeiting which arise outside the Community.

2. Comm (88) 172, June 1988.
3. The Times 13 February 1989.

CHAPTER 15

The Menace to the System: Authorised and Unauthorised Reproduction

15.01 At the beginning of the 1980s the copyright system stood at the crossroads. A wrong turning could have resulted in a system loosely based on equitable remuneration for identified uses foundering. At worst, this could even have dragged down to destruction several industries based on the system.

15.02 At the heart of the problem was the arrival of certain types of equipment with the capacity to make multiple copies or uses of works protected by copyright. All too often these copies or uses would be incapable of identification, so that no claim could be made by the copyright owner; in other cases the sheer extent of the potential reproduction is such that in most instances the only practical form of copyright payment – a lump sum imposed at the point of retail sale – could not provide a realistic compensation to the right owner for the loss of potential sales.

15.03 These matters have been considered as they have occured in connection with the subject-matter of each chapter heading. It is hoped in this chapter to put the matter into some form of perspective, and consider the solutions put forward by the Whitford Committee, together with those adopted in CDPA.

WHITFORD DELIBERATIONS

15.04 In its deliberations on the subject of reprography, the Whitford Committee drew attention to the fact that over the previous two decades the cost of photocopies had decreased considerably in relation to that of conventional printing.[1] In addition to the well-known processes of photocopying, there existed a number of non-light systems producing facsimiles of one kind and another, and the Committee decided to apply the generic term "reprography" to them. Its members made two significant comments on the situation. One was that "The widespread copying of textual matter is clearly here to stay". With that proposition there can be no argument. The second was that " . . . publishers of books and periodicals have been watching these developments closely".

1. Cmnd 6732, para 205.

15.05 Both publishers and authors are now watching the situation with a great deal of anxiety, linked to a growing feeling of helplessness. Books in the educational field were increasingly exposed to being reproduced in multiple form on the photocopying equipment of educational establishments, frequently by educationalists well aware of the requirements of copyright legislation. Sad to record, it seems that in a number of cases, the infringing reproductions were being made by copying the book sent to the educational establishment for inspection. It took some time for the seriousness of the matter to be fully understood, but publishers' sales in this field were plummeting, and the moment for concerted action had arrived while a mass publishing industry still existed. At the least, it is unlikely that educational publishers will continue to carry in their lists books for teachers which carry detailed instructions on how to make infringing copies.[2] The falling sales of books were not entirely due to a surplus of titles on the market, or to a lack of public funds. The serious situation in which many publishers found themselves was substantially due to loss of sales from unauthorised copying, and unless dramatic steps were taken to eradicate the practice, more publishers' lists were going to be slashed, and more publishing staff made redundant.

15.06 The educationalists submitted to the Whitford Committee that they required more freedom of action, and that teachers and their support staff should be able to make copies without having to go to the trouble of seeking permission. To the extent that educationalists are prepared to acknowledge the copyright system, and go through the formalities provided by the law, nothing should be done to discourage them, and if any simplification of the position would be of assistance to them, then it should be put in hand. But as the Whitford Committee acknowledged, the potential for infringement is enormous, and a great deal of infringing copying was taking place.

15.07 One of the factors which had altered the position for the educationalists was the introduction of "resource-based learning", which reduces considerably the need for textbooks in classes. Not only does this lessen radically the potential for sales, but if the substituted material is taken from a large variety of sources which are copyright-protected literary works, the loss to author and publisher is going to be painful; if it continues at the present rate of development, the publication of certain categories of reference work will simply cease to be an economic proposition.

2. See case cited in *The Author*, Autumn 1980, page 14.

THE STATUTORY POSITION

15.08 The statutory provision about anthologies now appears in section 33 of CDPA. Subsection (1) makes provision about the inclusion of a short passage from a published literary or dramatic work in a collection which both (a) is intended for use in educational establishments and is so described in its title, and in any advertisements issued by or on behalf of the publisher, and (b) consists mainly of material in which no copyright exists. Where these conditions exist, then the short passage does not infringe the copyright in the work if the work itself is not intended for use in such establishments, and the inclusion is governed by a sufficient acknowledgement. This does not authorise the inclusion of more than two excerpts from copyright works by the same author in any collections published by the same publisher over any period of five years.

15.09 Section 6(6) of the Copyright Act 1956 was the forerunner of this provision. Although it appeared to be dealing with published anthologies, and intended for collections largely of non-copyright works, the Whitford Committee regarded it as the only provision in the Copyright Act 1956 of direct application to reprography in the educational field. With respect to the members of the Whitford Committee, to allow multiple photocopying of literary and dramatic works for use in schools by virtue of this provision was to strain its meaning.

15.10 What was promising to develop into jungle warfare between copyright owners and would-be educational users has now been made the subject of further control. Section 32 of CDPA takes things done for the purpose of instruction and examination outside the ambit of copyright. Section 34 does the same for performances of works in the course of the activities of an educational establishment. Similarly, recordings by educational establishments of broadcasts and cable programmes do not infringe copyright if within section 35. Finally, section 36 allows photocopying by an educational establishment for the purposes of instruction, where not more than one per cent of a work is copied by an establishment in any quarter. But this does not cover copies if licences are available authorising it, and the person making the copies ought to have known that.

15.11 Recently there have been indications that the voluntary licensing arrangements between the two sides described in Chapter 16 may take the heat out of the matter. Both sides are aware that the jurisdiction of the new Copyright Tribunal has been considerably extended, and will be anxious to avoid it.

RECORD PIRACY AND BOOTLEGGING

15.12 The record industry has described as a "prevalent and virulent disease" the two activities of record piracy and bootlegging. The former is the act of making unauthorised reproductions of sound recordings, the latter is the illicit recording of performances. They have been dealt with in some detail in Chapter 4 relating to the record industry but it suffices to record again that they are prominent factors in the fall of the profits of the gramophone companies in recent years. There is enormous investment in certain types of recording, particularly in some areas of classical music, where the assembly over a substantial period of time of symphony orchestras and operatic companies is a very expensive exercise. Clearly the sales potential in this area is not so high as on the side of popular music, where individual singles can achieve a million copies. To their lasting credit, the record companies subsidise to a certain extent the classical catalogue from their popular successes.

15.13 It follows that if a major classical work is subject to piracy, any profit which might have accrued from its legitimate sales will evaporate; if the popular side of the record company's business has sustained severe inroads from the pirates, the amount available to subsidise the classical recordings will be diminished. Record piracy is an infringement of copyright in the sound recording. Bootlegging had previously been subject to the penalty provisions of the Performers' Protection Acts of 1958 and 1963, but now falls to be dealt with under Part II of CDPA — rights in performances. Now it is an infringement of the rights of someone having recording rights in relation to a performance to make a recording of it without consent, other than for private and domestic use. It may be infringement of this right to show, play or broadcast such a recording, thus striking at media collaboration. However, some kind of knowledge of the illegality seems to be required. Importation is an infringement as well. There is a right to seize illicit recordings, and coupled with the criminal provisions, this package of measures should hit the bootleggers fairly hard.

BROADCASTING

15.14 The problems of broadcasters have been referred to in Chapter 9 on copyright in sound and television broadcasts. The damage from satellite broadcasts being illegally taken during transmission has to a certain extent been controlled by international convention; but the great threat to the makers of television programmes is the new and mush-rooming capacity to take programmes and televised films off the air by means of video recording equipment. The threat does not end with the TV companies, but extends to film-makers, gramophone companies and owners of rights in literary, dramatic and musical works.

15.15   The major broadcasting organisations and film distribution com-panies have diversified into the field of video cassettes as a further outlet for their productions of television programmes and feature films. They are of course still subject to protection under the Copyright Act, but just as the original transmissions are illicitly recorded off the air, so too these programmes in cassette form are copied by video recorders. There are now several million of these machines on the market, some of which have been bought outright, others merely hired. The definition of "film" has been widened in section 5 CDPA so that it clearly takes in video cassettes. It covers a recording on any medium from which a moving image may by any means be produced. After considerable vacillation, the government decided not to introduce any kind of levy, either on cassettes or tapes, or on the equipment on which they are played, in the Act.

15.16   A spin-off is the vexed question of time-shifting, whereby some-one records a programme or film from his television set, in order to watch it at a later time. In *Sony Corporation of America v. Universal City Studios*[3] the U.S. Supreme Court decided that the sale of audio-visual equipment to the public did not in itself amount to contributory infringement of copyright in television programmes, and that there was no evidence that the practice would diminish the market for copyright works. In the United Kingdom, *CBS Songs Ltd v. Amstrad Consumer Electronics plc*[4] saw confirmation by the House of Lords of the same principle. Manufacturers and retailers of recording equipment which allowed the purchasers to copy tapes and sound recordings in breach of copyright under the legislation in force at the time did not authorise such breaches, and were not joint infringers with the purchasers. But the Law Lords added that this position was lamentable, and that a copyright law which was treated with such contempt by home copiers should either by amended or repealed. Under section 70 of CDPA, time-shifting no longer infringes copyright in any way, provided the recording is solely for private and domestic use. Mr Eric Forth, in defending the new copyright legislation (*The Independent* 3 February 1989), said it would be

3. (1984) No 81–1687, 52 U.S.L.W. 4090.
4. The Times 13 May 1988

inconceivable that the government would set out to encourage piracy. Against that it must be observed that it has done very little to discourage it in CDPA.

15.17 At a certain level of copying, both for private use and illegal profit, the plunder would be so vast as to threaten the funding of future production at the level now known. At one time, the major feature film *Star Wars* was available in illegally copied form on cassette in London shops some days prior to the London première of the film, and the resulting losses were estimated at hundreds of thousands of pounds. The most popular programmes made by the BBC and ITV were similarly widely available in pirated form, but from these sales neither the broadcasting companies, composers, writers or performers derived any benefit. It is obvious that if the profit is diminished, the quality of future productions, both as feature film and television programme, will tumble; this may already have started. In any field of the entertainment industry where the profit vanishes altogether, in the present economic climate the production will soon disappear also, be it film, book or record. The solution to this problem was seen to lie in stiffer criminal sanctions, and these have been incorporated into CDPA (see paras 15.24 *et seq.* below).

LEVY SYSTEMS

15.18 The proposal for a levy on sales of blank audio and video tape contained in the White Paper was ultimately abandoned and no such provision appears in CDPA. Nevertheless the idea is an interesting one and worth examining in some detail. The notion of a levy was considered in detail by the Whitford Committee.[5] It was looked upon in certain quarters as the best hope of salvation, for all types of equipment capable of multiple use and reproduction of copyright material. For example, the Interim Action Committee on the film industry under the chairmanship of Sir Harold Wilson regarded a levy on blank tapes as a solution to the problem. The statutory precedent for the idea lies in article 53 of the Copyright Act 1965 of West Germany. This provides (in translation) as follows:

> "If from the nature of the work it is to be anticipated that it will be reproduced for personal use by the fixing of broadcasts on visual and sound recordings, or by transfer from one visual or sound recording to another, the author of the work shall have the right to demand from the manufacturer of equipment suitable for making such reproductions a

5. Cmnd 6732, para 301.

remuneration for the opportunity to do so ... The right may only be enforced through collecting societies. By the way of remuneration, each copyright owner shall be entitled to an equitable participation in the proceeds realised by the manufacturer from the sale of such equipment, the total claims of all copyright owners, including performers, manufacturers of sound recordings and film producers, shall not exceed 5% of such proceeds."

Whitford recommendations

15.19 The Whitford Committee recommended the adoption of a levy system for private audio and video recording on the sale of all suitable equipment, and a levy on the sale of equipment for educational recording. But for reprographic equipment the Committee ruled out the idea of a levy on the ground that many may never, or only infrequently, be used to infringe copyright. This seems a remarkably complacent view of the position, but having reached the conclusion the Committee felt that the only possible solution to the problem of photocopying lay in blanket licensing. In relation to the computer use of copyright works, beyond saying that both input and storage should be restricted (in other words, protected by the copyright system), no clear solution was offered as to how the copyright-owners were to be remunerated, or even how such use is to be controlled and identified.

15.20 There are serious objections to these solutions. In the case of sophisticated and expensive video recording equipment, the price has fallen considerably in recent years; the same may prove true of the "desktop" consoles which are thought likely to appear in many homes in the country in the next few years. With falling prices availability increases, and the damage to the copyright-owners is multiplied. Even when the retail selling price of equipment is high, a 5% levy will fail to produce a sum sufficiently high to compensate copyright-owners for their loss. And as the cost of the equipment falls, so the return from such a levy would fall in line with it, unless the percentage of that levy were increased very greatly, at which point consumer resistance might be encountered, and the producers of the electronic equipment would be threatened.

Collecting societies

15.21 Difficulties arise when sums of this nature are levied by collecting societies. Where a single society is collecting in respect of a single monopoly right, such as the Performing Right Society, there is no real difficulty, but where a number of categories of right-owner have to depend on getting their share through collecting societies, then serious problems are met. Disputes between collecting societies and between categories of right-owner took place in West Germany following the introduction of a public lending right, and if the collecting society attempted to hold a proportion of the sum collected back, the more powerful right-owners such as broadcasting organisations and film production companies could legitimately complain. It is difficult to reconcile the arbitrary division of such a levy with the concept of copyright based on compensation for each use; nevertheless it must be accepted if it is the only practical way. But there are serious doubts as to whether it would generate enough revenue to compensate for the losses to right-owners sustained by the use of such equipment, and there are always certain entitled right-owners who cannot be identified, but in respect of whom funds have accrued.

15.22 Blanket licensing as a solution for photocopying and reprographic equipment is subject to the objection that it is impossible to establish the extent of copying of protected material which takes place on individual equipment; no doubt the new Copyright Tribunal will be kept fully occupied with these matters in the early years of its existence. There is no doubt that now educationalists have started to pay, as they should, for their use of copyright material, a good deal of extra money is going to be needed to meet the cost, but this should not be used as an excuse for depriving copyright-owners of their legitimate entitlement; otherwise, certain types of copyright work might simply not be available for copying, whether legitimately or otherwise. If this solution proves practical for reprographic equipment, there is no reason why something similar should not be introduced for computer installations. The scope for a collecting society in these areas in considerable.

Levies as indirect taxation

15.23 These solutions may eventually work, but whether they will be in time to save those areas currently under heaviest attack is not certain. Despite heavier criminal sanctions in CDPA, these are not necessarily going to deter the hardened copier. An objection to a levy is that it looks more like an indirect tax than a royalty earned by a use of copyright, and the further the movement from that position, the greater the reduction of the independence of the copyright-owners. Already the payment in respect of the public lending right has some resemblance to a subsidy from central government; there is a danger that if the levies imposed on recording, copying and other equipment look like indirect taxes, it will be felt that copyright-owners are simply receiving direct support from the state. In the case of creators such as writers and composers, this will merely compromise their independence; but in the case of manufacturing right-owners such as publishers, film producers, broadcasting organisations and record companies, there is a danger that they will appear to be gaining an unfair advantage over other sectors of industry.

CRIMINAL SANCTIONS

15.24 Even under the Copyright Act 1956, the criminal sanctions were very feeble indeed. There was considerable reluctance among copyright owners and their representative organisations to be seen in the criminal courts. This was not because of the weakness of the offence provisions, but apparently because it was somehow considered not to be very dignified to be seen prosecuting copyright matters in the criminal courts. Despite these reservations, matters became so bad that eventually prosecutions were brought in cases such as *R v. Lloyd, Bhuee and Ali*.[6] Here prosecutions were brought under the Theft Act, as a conspiracy to steal contrary to section 1(1) of the Criminal Law Act 1977. This attempt failed, and coupled with *Rank Film Distributors Ltd v. Video Information* Centre[7] highlighted the paucity of remedies available for combating infringement, and the need for new legislation. (See paras 15.28–33 below.)

15.25 The extent of criminal sanctions has been greatly widened by CDPA. By section 107, the following are made offences when done without the authorisation of the copyright owner:

(a) making for sale or hire;

(b) importing other than for private use;

(c) possessing in the course of business with a view to infringing copyright;

(d) in the course of business, selling or letting, or offering or exposing for sale or hire; or exhibiting in public or distributing;

(e) distributing other than in the course of business to the prejudice of the copyright owner;

(f) making or possessing an article specifically designed or adapted for copying a particular copyright work; there must be knowledge or reason to believe that it is to be used to make infringing copies for sale or hire or use in the course of a business; and

---

6. [1985] Q.B. 829.
7. [1981] 2 All E.R. 76 H.L.

(g) causing an infringing performance, playing or showing of a literary, dramatic, musical or artistic work, sound recording or film; here also there must be knowledge or reason to believe that copyright would be infringed.

The offences are triable either way, with a fine or imprisonment for up to 6 months or both in the magistrates court, and if tried in the Crown Court, a fine or imprisonment for up to 2 years, or both.

15.26 An order may be made by the trial court for delivery up of infringing copies (section 108), and there is a power to issue search warrants (section 109). On giving notice to the Commissioners of Customs and Excise infringing copies may be treated as prohibited goods, and liable to seizure on importation (section 111).

15.27 By section 198 of CDPA, criminal offences have been created which relate to the new rights for performers, and here also the offence is triable either way, with fines being available to the sentencer, together with a maximum of 6 months' imprisonment in the magistrates court, and 2 years' in the Crown Court.

An Example of Lack of Sufficient Civil and Criminal Protection

15.28 The higher judiciary has drawn attention to the fact that the civil law provisions of copyright legislation were in a number of situations failing to protect the right-owner, and that the criminal provisions were incapable of furnishing any assistance. The serious nature of the lacuna was highlighted by comments made in *Rank Film Distributors v. Video Information Centre*.[8]

15.29 The plaintiffs were the owners of copyright in a number of cinematograph films, unauthorised copies of which were being made by the defendant firm in breach of that copyright. The plaintiffs made an *ex parte* application before a judge (an application made without notice of it being served on the defendants) and they obtained an order allowing them to enter the defendants' premises to seize infringing copies, and requiring them to divulge information about the supply and sale of the infringing copies. The defendant first made an unsuccessful application to have these orders set aside on the basis that by complying with them, the defendants might expose themselves to criminal proceedings.

8. [1980] 3 W.L.R. 487 A.C.; [1981] 2 All E.R. 76 H.L.

15.30 The matter came before the Court of Appeal, where it was held by a majority of the three judges that, although there was undoubtedly jurisdiction to make the orders, any person defending an action for the infringement of copyright could claim to be privileged from giving the information sought on the ground that to do so would incriminate him. The House of Lords agreed. Sections 99 and 100 of CDPA confirm that interpretation of the law—infringing copies may be seized with a court order, but there is no requirement to divulge information on sales. In the Court of Appeal, a number of observations were made by the judges on the unsatisfactory state of the law as a weapon to deal with the abuse which they were considering.

15.31 The judge whose refusal to set aside the orders was eventually overturned by the Court of Appeal appeared to take the view that copyright-owners were not limited to the feeble provisions of the Copyright Act 1956. He spoke not only of possible offences under that Act, but also of charges of conspiracy either under the Criminal Law Act of 1977 or conspiracy to defraud at common law, on the basis of the arguments which had been put to him by counsel. He then expressed the view that:

> "The manufacture and sale of infringing copies may well lead to criminal proceedings under the Copyright Act 1956 or, in my judgement, under the Theft Act 1968, having regard to the provisions of section 1 of that Act. This relates that 'A person is guilty of theft if he dishonestly appropriates property belonging to another with the intention of permanently depriving the other of it; and "thief" and "steal" shall be construed accordingly.' "

15.32 This is one of the first judicial suggestions of the kind of remedy which is required to combat the menace, made, it should be noted, by Mr Justice Whitford, who chaired the Copyright Committee of 1977. And on appeal, although his view was not upheld on the main issue, Lord Denning spoke eloquently about the operations of the pirates.

> " 'It is, it is a glorious thing, to be a Pirate King,' said W. S. Gilbert: but he was speaking of ship pirates. Today we speak of film pirates. It is not a glorious thing to be, but it is a good thing to be in for making money. Film pirates plunder the best and most recent films. They transpose them onto magnetic tape: and then sell video tapes on the black market ... this black market makes huge inroads into the legitimate business of the film companies. They have been put to great expense in producing the best films: they have the copyright which gives them the sole and exclusive right to reproduce them. Yet here are the pirates plundering it—stealing all the best films."

15.33 Having summarised the pirates' activities, Lord Denning then demonstrated how little can be done against them at the present. He continued:

> "But the criminal law does not provide an adequate remedy for the film companies. The Committee to consider the Law on Copyright and Designs . . . reported that '. . . the criminal provisions are of little use and little used'. The criminal law is too low and the penalties too small. Section 21 creates only a summary offence. [The offence is regarded so lightly that it was not included when other penalties were increased by section 30 of the Criminal Law Act 1977.] The fine for an offence under the Copyright Act 1956 is still only £50. That is a small price for a film pirate to pay. He can look upon it as one of the incidental expenses of his trade. In any case it is very difficult to catch the real people behind this illicit traffic. As a rule the only people who can be caught are small traders in back streets. They may sell video cassettes to an inquiry agent who gives a 'trap' order. But as soon as legal proceedings are in the offing, the stock of the street trader disappears. He protests his innocence, says that he had no knowledge that there was any infringement of copyright."

15.34 Lord Denning's assessment of the situation was, as ever, powerfully accurate. It was to prevent this escape that there was an urgent need for the introduction of an absolute criminal offence for possession of unauthorised copies for which knowledge does not have to be proved. The judicious use of this weapon against the pirates would go a long way towards stamping out this problem, particularly when coupled with a more serious offence involving terms of imprisonment where knowledge can be proved.

15.35 The suggestion about using the Theft Act 1968 linked with conspiracy under the Criminal Law Act of 1977 received a considerable setback in *R v. Lloyd, Bhuee and Ali*.[9] The prosecution in that case failed (on appeal) because films which had been borrowed without permission from a cinema in order to make pirated copies were returned unharmed a few hours later. There was thus no intention permanently to deprive which is an essential ingredient of the offence of theft. Nor were the owners deprived of their copyright by the copying, even though its value may have been diminished. Since then, the new criminal provisions of CDPA have been introduced. In every case under section 107, some kind of criminal intention is required. Proof of guilty knowledge about infringement in intellectual property cases is likely to be very hard to establish.

15.36 It would have been far more effective to have provided a series of absolute offences, with realistic penalties attached. These would not have

9. [1985] Q.B. 829

required proof of guilty knowledge, and would have been far more effective in tackling the problem of copyright theft. When further legislative reform is being contemplated, consideration should be given to the introduction of civil penalties, which could be subject to appeal to the Copyright Tribunal. The removal of conversion as a civil remedy in copyright cases has worsened the overall position of copyright owners.

Audio and video recording at home

15.37 Although time-shifting (home taping of radio or TV broadcasts for viewing or listening at a later time) is no longer an infringement of copyright, the home taper should realise clearly that copying of records, films, videos or audio tapes, whether bought, borrowed or hired, most definitely is, under section 17 of CDPA. If this is done commercially, or on such a wide scale as to prejudice the rights of the copyright owner, it also constitutes a criminal offence under section 107(1). However, it is necessary for the prosecution to prove that the alleged offender knew or had reason to believe that the work in question was in copyright. Most commercial publishers make this clear on the label. Nevertheless, the need to prove the point is a potential weakness in the new legislation.

15.38 Clearly in the case of a sound recording, film, or video which has been purchased or hired, the private taping is in order for it to be played elsewhere, or in other circumstances. This deprives the right-owners of a potential further sale. Until a satisfactory means of compensating the right-owners for such losses is devised, a more effective criminal sanction should be created to enable the right-owners to protect their property. If it said that such a power would be used oppressively, it should be borne in mind that there is no obligation upon a prosecuting authority to bring a prosecution simply because there is evidence of an offence. An element of discretion is always present, and no doubt would be exercised with care by those having the power to mount such prosecutions. But the failure of the authorities to include a levy on blank audio and video tapes in CDPA is a considerable blow to copyright owners.

CHAPTER 16

Copyright Collecting Societies

EXPLOITATION OF COPYRIGHT BY OWNER

16.01 As the true significance of copyright to the owner of the right lies in its positive economic exploitation, rather than the power to prevent potential users from dealing with the protected work, his thoughts will turn to how best to carry out this exploitation. The obvious procedure would be for him to present a bill to everyone who has performed or published or recorded his work, or put it to any of the other protected uses. But the practical question for the busy author or songwriter must be how to discover who those users are. Having discovered them, how much should they pay, and how can that payment be enforced if the user proves to be recalcitrant?

16.02 Obviously in most cases this procedure is simply not possible. The creative worker would simply find that his entire day had slipped away in this administrative work, and even if he did work in some rare field where he could conduct his own collection, the financial expense of doing so might prove to be out of all proportion to the sums eventually received. This is particularly true in the field of music, where a popular song may be performed literally thousands of times in the course of one day. How could the songwriter hope to recover personally more than a tiny fraction of the moneys due to him?

Representation in France

16.03 The solution is not much younger than the concept of copyright itself, for at quite an early stage right-owners appreciated that they would only obtain their dues by banding themselves together, and by negotiating rates collectively. In 1847 the French composer Bourget set in motion litigation in France in respect of the unauthorised performance of his works, a French law of 1791 having accorded copyright protection to musical as well as literary works. Subsequent to his success in this suit, Bourget with some of his colleagues established a copyright collecting society for musical works in 1851. Known as the *Société des Auteurs, Compositeurs et Éditeurs de Musique*, it was to lead the way for a movement which spread all over the world.

Representation in the United Kingdom

16.04 In 1914 the Performing Right Society was set up in London to collect within the United Kingdom in respect of protected musical works. From a rather slow beginning, its influence has spread to the point where in 1987 the total royalty income of the Society was over £90,000,000, of which over £60,000,000 represented public performance and broadcasting royalties in Great Britain and Ireland, while almost £30,000,000 was received from foreign affiliated societies.[1]

NATIONAL COLLECTING SOCIETIES

16.05 Organisations such as the Performing Right Society (PRS) have been established in all countries which recognise in their law the concept of copyright. They constitute a separate body which the potential user can approach to obtain a licence. This is an advantage to the user of the protected work, as otherwise he would incur heavy administrative costs to discover who the right-owner was, negotiate with him, and pay for the work on a per-use basis. But the blanket licence granted by the copyright collecting society gives the licensee access to the whole repertoire of protected works, not only in this country, but in the repertoires of all affiliated societies abroad. For a single annual royalty, the user can make use of the entire stock of protected works, as often as he cares during the currency of the licence.

INTERNATIONAL ORGANISATIONS

16.06 These national collecting societies, or authors' societies as they are sometimes known, are linked together by international contracts of affiliation. By this means, each society collects on its own territory in respect of the works of its own members, and also in respect of the members of each other national society abroad with which it is affiliated. By the same contract of affiliation each national collecting society is empowered to grant, to users, licences on its own territory in respect of the repertoires of each other society with which it is affiliated.

16.07 To control the scheme of international affiliation, international organisations exist in certain fields. Thus in respect of the performing right organisations, such as the PRS in London, CISAC is the

---

1. *The Performing Right Society Yearbook* 1988–89, p. 11.

appropriate body—the *Confédération Internationale des Sociétés d'Auteurs et Compositeurs*. The mechanical right societies have a similar network of affiliated national collecting societies, and the international organisation in respect of these is BIEM—the *Bureau International de l'Édition Méchanique*.

16.08 Most authors and composers elect to belong to their own national collecting society, but some find it an advantage to belong to a foreign society, such as one of those in the United States. This may be the case for example where the works of a national right-owner are substantially performed in a single foreign country. So far as collections in respect of the performing right in musical works are concerned, there is one single national authors' society in virtually every country which subscribes to the system, with the notable exception of the United States of America.

United States—ASCAP

16.09 The first collecting society in the United States in respect of musical works was formed in 1914, in fact at the same time as the PRS in London. It was known as ASCAP, the American Society of Composers, Authors and Publishers. Its formation was very close in time to the rapid development of popular music in the United States, this spread being carried along by the gramophone record, then broadcasting and the talking motion picture with synchronised soundtrack. A very large number of broadcasting stations were set up in the United States shortly after radio was introduced, more than 500 starting up in the first year.

16.10 The broadcasting stations were not uniformly willing to accept that a royalty was payable to ASCAP for the broadcasting use of its repertoire, and the first American society was obliged to wage a long and expensive series of actions through the courts in order to consolidate the position it had gained prior to the invention of sound radio. The battle smouldered on for a number of years, with ASCAP unable to establish a process of licensing broadcasting stations on a non-variable lump sum basis until the year 1932.

16.11 At that time the society sought to introduce instead a royalty for broadcasting licences based on a percentage of the broadcasting station's revenue. This was anathema to the National Association of Broadcasters. They had at this stage no alternative but to accept grudgingly the terms offered by ASCAP, which they did until 1940, when ASCAP tried to introduce fresh terms for its broadcasting licences. This time the members of the National Association of Broadcasters agreed to boycott all music in the repertoire of ASCAP. This was to be achieved by broadcasting music in the public domain which had fallen out of copyright protection, and by commissioning new music especially composed for the broadcasting stations which would not fall into the ASCAP repertoire.

16.12 ASCAP enjoyed at that time a very wide repertoire, backed by the monopoly position which is today generally to be found in most other states. Although the radio stations were not given much hope of succeeding, they set up a rival copyright collecting society to administer the rights in the new repertoire which they gradually acquired as a result of their own boycott. This was known as Broadcast Music Inc (BMI), and it had a remarkable success.

16.13 Unfortunately for ASCAP, the United States Department of Justice at the same period initiated action against it under the anti-trust laws of the United States. This is the American anti-monopoly legislation, long established in that country, and allowing government intervention to promote competition where it was felt to be necessary. Faced with this action, ASCAP settled the matter by submitting to a consent decree, which meant that no public judgment was given, and no evidence taken. At the same period, ASCAP decided to settle its differences with the broadcasting orgainsations, so the BMI was not only able to continue in existence, but managed to establish itself on a permanent basis. Since that time it has remained in competition with ASCAP, although it operates a smaller repertoire.

Position of BMI
16.14 Subsequently BMI also was obliged to submit to a consent decree under the anti-trust laws, perhaps in itself some acknowledgement of the public acceptance which the younger society had achieved. A writer or publisher may not belong to both BMI and ASCAP at the same time, but he is allowed to resign from one organisation in order to join the other. Both are affiliated to authors' societies abroad, and in many cases both have contracts of affiliation with the same foreign society.

16.15 A feature of the BMI organisation is that it operates as a private company. This means that it is sometimes more able to alter its rules to meet market conditions than the normal society of which the writers and publishers are members, and which may of necessity have a less flexible approach. A British composer who intends to join an American society should seek expert advice on the spot, for the advantages and disadvantages which meet his particular case may well fluctuate from time to time.

SESAC

16.16   To complete the rather complex situation in the United States, mention should be made of a third and much smaller authors' society operating in the area of collecting for public performance of musical works. This is the body now known as SESAC, formed in 1930, and previously known as the Society of European Stage Authors and Composers. In the private ownership of one family, it is operated as a private licensing company which controls the catalogues of a number of music publishers who have entrusted their works to its care. While both BMI and ASCAP levy their royalties on the basis of a percentage of the licensee's revenue, the charges of SESAC are on the basis of a fixed lump-sum payment in each case.

16.17   This takes into account such factors as the location of a broadcasting station, its output in terms of hours of broadcasting, and its range. Some feeling of the relative size of each operation can be derived from a comparison of the receipts of each society in respect of performing right royalties collected. In 1963, for example, ASCAP took in 38 million dollars, BMI some 15 million dollars, and SESAC had around one million dollars. Nevertheless most broadcasting organisations in the United States feel it worthwhile to take out the SESAC licence.

Collection in Respect of Mechanical Right

16.18   The societies which collect in respect of public performances of musical works are more widely established across the world than any other kind of authors society, and they deal in the largest sums. But the societies collecting in respect of the mechanical right in relation to musical works and sound recordings made of them have set up an effective network of organisations along similar lines (see Chapter 7). In a number of countries outside the United Kingdom the same organisation collects in that state in respect of both the performing right and the mechanical right; for example, this is the case in West Germany, where GEMA performs both functions. The international organisation controlling the mechanical rights societies is BIEM, as noted above. It must be borne in mind that in the U.K. on the coming into force of CDPA, the statutory right to copy records sold by retail, previously existing in section 8 of the Copyright Act 1956, has been abolished, though there is a limited saving in respect of certain cases where notice had been given prior to the repeal.

PERFORMING RIGHT IN SOUND RECORDINGS

16.19 In Chapter 7 on sound recordings, mention has been made of Phonographic Performance Ltd. This is the organisation which collects from users of the performing right in sound recordings granted by sections 19 and 20 of CDPA. The right-owners are the record manufacturers, and the royalties they collect are distributed among themselves, with some percentages of the receipts being given to recording artistes and musicians. The system of international affiliation between societies is not so firmly established as is the case with the performing right in musical works, largely due to the right in sound recordings being less widely accepted internationally. Although the right has been pruned back somewhat abroad in recent years, similar organisations to Phonographic Performance Ltd do exist in Australia, Germany, India, and New Zealand, and there is one body dealing with the whole of Scandinavia.

THE WRITTEN OR SPOKEN WORD

16.20 When we move away from the area of music to the written or spoken word, we see that the need for collecting societies is less pressing. Musical performances are transient and individually generally unadvertised, so that the individual composer cannot practically keep track of what is happening to his works. But with a literary work the situation is quite different. The performances of plays are widely advertised by name, and public performances of other literary works are generally sufficiently known to make it feasible for a writer or his agent to handle the matter satisfactorily at the present time.

16.21 This may be partly due to the contraction of the live theatre in the provinces and the concentration of opportunities for significantly earning performances in the West End and the major broadcasting stations. In fact during the nineteenth century there did exist a collecting society specifically to gather fees for the use of the works of British dramatists from the management of theatres which had staged their plays. It was remarkably sophisticated for its time, and a number of the techniques which it pioneered have passed into the general use of modern copyright collecting societies. This organisation was known as the Dramatic Authors Society.[2]

2. For a full examination of the history of the Dramatic Authors Society, see McFarlane, *Copyright, The Development and Exercise of the Performing Right*, Chapter 4 (John Offord/City Arts).

Use of representatives

16.22   One of these techniques is the use of representatives, such as the PRS currently employs. The collecting society assigns to each representative or licensing inspector a particular territory, within which it is his responsibility to seek out and sign up potential and actual users of the performing right in musical works. While the great majority of users of the "commodity" of the collecting societies are comparatively happy to enter into a licensing agreement in respect of their access to the protected works, there is a small but recalcitrant minority which will not voluntarily seek an agreement with the copyright-owners; such users need to be firstly sought out and secondly persuaded to sign an agreement. Clearly the representatives require qualities of both diplomacy and detecting abiltiy, and it is not surprising to find that a number of them are drawn from the ranks of retired policemen.

Public lending right

16.23   The Public Lending Right Act 1979 made provision for the establishment of a central fund to be administered by a Registrar. Although he controls the moneys provided by Parliament for the operation of the public lending right, and he also makes the necessary payments out of the central fund in respect of the right, this cannot be described as a collecting society. The scheme has been described earlier at paras 12.17–25.

Authors' Lending and Copyrights Society Ltd (ALCS)

16.24   This collecting society was established in 1977 to try to solve the problem of collection and distribution of payments which copyright owners cannot collect individually. It has already signed agreements with the relevant collecting societies in Belgium, Denmark, West Germany and Holland; ALCS distributes to its members revenue from the public lending right in West Germany, and for the simultaneous cabling of BBC television programmes in Belgium, Denmark and Holland.

16.25   The Society is operated on a non-profit basis, and both the Society of Authors and the Writers Guild of Great Britain are represented on its Council of Management. It is affiliated to CISAC (see para 16.07 above). Its activities are aimed at foreign public lending right schemes, the reprography right in published works, the private and off-air recording right, and the cable TV right. The Society does not intervene where the right can be exercised by an individual.

16.26 At the present time it is not too difficult for a writer or his literary agent to keep track of the copyright uses made of his work, by contrast with the sheer impossibility for a composer of music of achieving the same end. But the situation will become much harder for the literary world with the introduction of new uses, many connected with data processing and the world of computers. Already there is widespread abuse of photocopying and other reproduction equipment, and if proper compensation is introduced to control this, the authors will need to have an efficient clearing house. Compensation will be required for such uses as storing literary works in data banks, and for reproducing them on video screens, and the individual author will simply not be able to handle this aspect of matters.

16.27 The philosophy behind the establishment of the Authors Lending and Copyrights Society is that the organisation will eventually be in a position to collect in respect of all these uses which may become protected in the future, and will distribute the proceeds to each author member who is entitled to a share. As matters stand at present, it would appear to be very much in the interests of every author to join this new collecting society if he or she lives and works in the United Kingdom. Not only will it represent his or her best hope of receiving any income from these new and technological uses, but the more members to which the organisation can point, the more muscle it can pack in negotiations with government and other bodies. Writers who are interested in joining should contact the Secretary General of ALCS, 7 Ridgemount Street, London WCIE 7AE.

The Copyright Licensing Agency Ltd (CLA)

16.28 The Agency is primarily aimed at licensing copyright users in the fields of education, government, industry and libraries. A three-year voluntary licensing agreement with local education authorities came into force in April 1986 covering all state colleges and schools and has since been extended. Licences also exist for the private education sector, and a scheme is available for universities in the United Kingdom.

16.29 It licenses users for copying extracts from copyright books, journals and periodicals, and has a variety of basic blanket schemes on offer. Its first distribution of £518,000 was made in October 1987, and a second of £897,000 in March 1988. Payments to right owners are now made every 6 months.

16.30 So far the schemes have operated on a voluntary basis. Users or their representative organisations enter into a contract with CLA and in return for an annual fee are granted permission to copy the works covered by the scheme in the manner specified, and thus gain immunity from being sued by copyright owners. However, CDPA provides them with indirect statutory backing. Disputes are bound to arise, and sections 117 – 135 make detailed provision for settling them by reference to the Copyright Tribunal, which is also given power to alter the terms of existing or proposed schemes if it thinks them unfair to a given class of user or against the public interest.

16.31 It is possible for a licensee to become confused over which works, and which dealings with them, are covered by a scheme, perhaps because the terms of the scheme have not been clearly drafted; section 136 of CDPA creates an implied immunity for the user in these circumstances. It is also possible for a good scheme to be put at risk by a major copyright owner (such as a large educational publisher) refusing to join. So far as photocopying in schools is concerned, section 137 gives the Secretary of State power to make an order extending the scheme to the excluded works; sections 138 and 139 deal with variation and discharge of the order and appeals against it to the Copyright Tribunal. He can also set up a new scheme (under section 140) and issue statutory licences (section 141). It is too soon to tell what the practical effect of these provisions will be.

POSITION IN THE FUTURE

16.32 For the future, the probability is that collecting societies of one form or another will come more and more to operate on behalf of copyright-owners. A glance at the standard copyright notice now carried in most books will show why. Usually these days it is something to the effect that, "No part of this publication may be reproduced or transmitted in any form or by any means, including photocopying or recording, without the written permission of the owner of the copyright. Such permission must also be obtained before any part of this publication is stored in retrieval system of any kind". The introduction of such warnings shows the threats to publication by these uses, and others which may soon be developed. Not only does the right-owner need to band together with his fellows in order to gather in such royalties as may be available in respect of these uses, but he also needs the strength of his colleagues in order to present a solid and recognisable front in the hard negotiations which undoubtedly lie ahead to preserve some tangible protection for creative workers.

CHAPTER 17

American Copyright

17.01 A knowledge of American copyright law has always been vital for British authors and publishers; not only does the U.S.A. provide a major outlet for works in the English language with a market of some 220 million potential consumers, but unfortunately in the past copyright-owners in the U.K. and elsewhere have felt that infringement of their works has taken place in the United States with very little opportunity for redress. Complaints of this nature were voiced by writers from Dickens onwards, and with some justification. Much of the difficulty was due to the historical reluctance of the United States to join the system of international copyright relations, and also to a domestic American copyright law of extreme antiquity.

NEW AMERICAN COPYRIGHT LAW

17.02 These grounds for complaint have now substantially disappeared. For many years the United States has been a member of the Universal Copyright Convention (UCC), although for long she held back from adherence to the higher standard Berne Convention. With the passing of a new domestic Copyright Act in 1976 to replace the previous legislation which had endured with modifications from 1909, the scene was set for further change. The new law not only brought the American situation into line with contemporary standards, but introduced concepts which were later to be followed in the United Kingdom in CDPA. For these reasons, and because it covers a wide range of subject-matters, many of which are in the field of high technology, some familiarity with the situation in the United States is desirable for those working in a number of important business areas, for example the data processing industry.

"Manufacturing clause"

17.03 One of the great difficulties for English language authors and publishers outside the United States had always been the "manufacturing clause". This was in essence a piece of protectionist legislation; in its original form it meant that any book published in the United States

154

which was in the English language had to be printed from type set in the United States and in addition the printing and binding had to be carried out in America. This meant that at its worst, virtually every English-language book written by a non-American author was entirely without copyright protection. This changed for the better after America joined the Universal Copyright Convention in 1955, for thenceforward any work covered by the Convention was specifically exempted from the effect of the manufacturing provisions.

17.04 The effect of the new American law on the manufacturing requirements is that they have been phased out. Before 1 July 1982, the importation into or public distribution in the United States of a work mainly comprising non-dramatic literary material in the English language was forbidden unless the parts consisting of such material had been manufactured either in the United States or in Canada or unless on the date on which importation was sought or public distribution in the United States was made, the author of any substantial part of such material was not a United States national, or if he was, where he had been domiciled outside the United States for a continuous period of at least one year immediately prior to that date.

17.05 From 1 July 1982 the manufacturing requirements of American law were discontinued altogether. Even prior to that date the manufacturing clause had been effectively discontinued in respect of British authors. Now with American adherence to the Berne Convention, the formalities of copyright notice, registration and deposit have been significantly diluted.

Adherence to the Berne Convention

17.06 On 16 November 1988 the government of the United States deposited its instrument of accession to the Berne Convention, in the form of the Paris revision of 24 July 1971. The Paris Revision accordingly entered into force as regards USA on 1 March 1989. Public Law 100–568 of 31 October 1988 makes the necessary amendment to Title 17 of the U.S. Code, the American domestic copyright law.

17.07 The general effect is that the provisions of the Berne Convention are not to be enforceable in any action brought on the provisions of the Berne Convention itself. Adherence of the United States does not expand or reduce any right of an author to claim authorship or to object to any distortion, mutilation or derogatory action in relation to the work which would prejudice his honour or reputation. No right or interest in a work eligible for protection under Title 17 may be claimed by reliance on the Berne Convention.

17.08 Minor alterations have been made to the subject matter and scope of copyright. Paragraph 116A has been inserted to deal with negotiated licences for public performances by means of coin-operated phono-record players (generally known as juke boxes). Limitations are placed on the exclusive right if the fees are not negotiated.

Notice of Copyright

17.09 Even under the new American copyright law, all publicly distributed copies of works protected under it were required to carry a notice of copyright, until recent adjustments were made under an amendment of 31 October 1988.[1] This had to consist of (a) either the symbol © or the word "copyright" or the abbreviation "copr", together with (b) the year of first publication of the work, and also (c) the name of the owner of the copyright. Now the copyright notice has been made discretionary, so that the United States could adhere to the Berne Convention.

Registration

17.10 Although the question of registration had already been made optional in the United States, prior to the amendments of 1988 to facilitate entry to the Berne Convention the fact that no action for infringement could be brought until the formalities of registration had been complied with rendered this option largely illusory. But now the requirements of registration have been substantially modified, and it is no longer a problem for copyright owners outside the United States.

MAIN TYPE OF WORKS RECEIVING COPYRIGHT PROTECTION

17.11 The main types of works which receive copyright protection under American law include the following categories: (a) literary works, (b) musical works, including any accompanying words, (c) dramatic works, including any accompanying music, (d) pantomimes and choreographic works, (e) pictorial, graphic and sculptural works, (f) motion pictures and other audio-visual works, and (g) sound recordings.

---

1. Public Law 100–568, amending Title 17 of the U.S. Code.

17.12 Two important factors are: that in relation to sound recordings the American law only amounts to a right against unauthorised reproduction, and does not extend to the performing right known in British law; also that literary works are works, other than audio-visual works, expressed in words, numbers, or other verbal or numerical symbols or indicia, regardless of the nature of the material objects, such as books, periodicals, manuscripts, phonorecords, film, tapes, discs, or cards in which they are embodied. This is of much concern to computer men, because it clearly extends copyright protection to software. In *Whelan Associates Inc v. Jaslow Dental Laboratory Inc* [2] it was held that copyright in a computer program could be infringed even in the absence of copying of the literal code if the structure was part of the expression of the idea behind the program, rather than the idea itself. The Semiconductor Chip Protection Act 1984 adds to the Copyright Statute a new chapter on the protection of semiconductor chip products.

PERIOD OF PROTECTION

17.13 A major defect in the former American law prior to 1977 was that there were potentially two terms of copyright protection. There was an original term of 28 years from the date of first publication, with a right to renew for a second period of 28 years. Quite apart from anything else, this prevented American adhesion to the Berne Copyright Convention. One of the most important alterations brought about by the new law was that in principle copyright in a work created after 1 January 1978 lasts for the author's life, plus a post-mortem period of 50 years. Thus the United States law comes into line with that of most other countries in the civilised world, certainly with all those which have a substantial publishing industry.

17.14 There are important provisions in the law for owners of existing US copyrights. Thus any copyright, the first term of which under the previous law was still subsisting on 1 January 1978, is to endure for 28 years from the date when it was originally secured, and the copyright-owner or his representative may make application for a further period of 47 years within one year prior to the expiry of the original term. In the absence of any such application, the copyright is to end at the expiry of 28 years from the date when copyright was originally secured. Any copyright, the renewal term of which was subsisting at any time between 31 December 1976 and 31 December 1977 is extended for a term of 75 years from the date that copyright was originally secured.

2. [1987] F.S.R. 1

SECTIONAL INTERESTS

17.15　One of the reasons for the delay in the enactment of a modern copyright statute in the United States was that there had taken place throughout the late 1960s, and increasingly through the 1970s, a series of bitter clashes between various sectional interests. Generally these were between a group of copyright-owners on one side, ranged against an equally partisan group of copyright-users which did not wish to allow any further encroachment upon what they regarded as their right of access to a particular form of creative work.

17.16　While these battles were going forward, the basic American law remained the same, and was growing increasingly incapable of meeting the requirements of an advanced modern society. Amendments had been built into the Act from time to time, but the situation was highly unsatisfactory, particularly as the deadlock required the passage of a series of extensions to keep in force copyrights which would otherwise have expired.

17.17　Happily, many of these disagreements were reconciled by the new law, especially in those areas touched by the music industry. The concept of public performance in the United States is no longer tied to the notion of profit; now it is to include performances at places open to the public or any place where a substantial number of persons outside a normal family circle and its social acquaintances are gathered. So far as owners of rights in musical works are concerned, this should open up a wider source of potential income than existed previously in the United States, and wider source of potential income than existed previously in the United States, and should certainly increase the receipts of those who are members of the appropriate collecting societies.

EXEMPTIONS

17.18　It should be noted that copyright is not to be infringed by performances of works of a religious nature in the course of church services and similar assemblies. There is also an exemption for certain kinds of charitable and other performances, where the performers give their performances without fee. These provisions do not have an equivalent in British law at the present time, although the copyright collecting societies generally do not enforce their rights in such cases.

LIMITED NATURE OF COPYRIGHT IN SOUND RECORDINGS

17.19 An important distinction between British and American law is that the copyright in sound recordings is specifically limited to a reproduction right. It is stated in terms in the law that the rights in sound recordings do not include any right of performance.[3] In this connection it has followed the position in Canada, where the previously existing performing right in sound recordings was removed, following consideration of the issue by the Economic Council of Canada.[4]

JUKEBOXES

17.20 An important new source of revenue for right-owners in musical works, which will of course include many British popular composers, is that the operators of coin-operated record players are now obliged to pay a royalty of $8 per machine each year. These jukeboxes or "nickelodeons" are a bulwark of twentieth-century American culture, and their introduction into the system of royalty payment is a significant advance for songwriters. Until the new law was passed in 1976, the jukebox lobby had always packed sufficient political influence in the United States to be able to maintain its exemption from the obligation to pay for its use of musical works.

MECHANICAL RIGHT

17.21 The royalty in respect of the mechanical right, which is the right accorded to record manufacturers by compulsory licence to make records of works which have been previously recorded and distributed to the public, was fixed by the new law at a rate of either $2\frac{3}{4}$ cents per work, or $\frac{1}{2}$ cent per minute of playing time, whichever is the larger. In the United Kingdom the equivalent rate for this right before its abolition was $6\frac{1}{4}$ per cent of the retail selling price of the record. The British approach would appear to have offered a better bargain to the owner of the rights in the musical work in times of inflation.

"FAIR USE"

17.22 In American law the equivalent of the British "fair dealing" is "fair use", and it is restricted in much the same way by the abstract

---

3. US Code, Title 17, s 114.
4. Economic Council for Canada, *Report on Intellectual and Industrial Property* (1972).

nature of the concept. The balance to be struck between the anxiety of copyright owners to gain financially from their work by extending the frontiers of copyright protection as far as possible and the wish of copyright-users to obtain access to copyright material for as little as possible gave rise to much debate, if not dispute, and contributed greatly to the controversy which held up the new law.

17.23 The basis of the law now is that the fair use of a copyright work, including such use by reproduction in copies or on records, for such purposes as criticism or comment, news reporting, teaching (including multiple copies for classroom use), scholarship or research is not an infringment of copyright. Clearly the question of multiple copying in the classroom could have a devastating effect on the survival of a standard educational work. There are therefore a number of limitations attached to fair use. Thus in determining whether in any particular case the use made of a work is a fair use, the factors to be considered include:
  (a) the purpose and character of the use, including whether such use is of a commerical nature or is for non-profit educational purposes;
  (b) the nature of the copyrighted work;
  (c) the amount and substantiality of the portion used in relation to the copyrighted work as a whole; and
  (d) the effect of the use upon the potential market for or value of the copyrighted work.[5]

Copyright Royalty Tribunal

17.24 It remains to be seen in the future how the qualification about effect on potential market or value will be determined by the courts. At this point it becomes relevant to consider a novel feature of the new American law. This is the establishment of the Copyright Royalty Tribunal. Although there had previously been no equivalent body in the United States, the authority of the Tribunal extended further than the jurisdiction of the Performing Right Tribunal under the old United Kingdom law. Now the CDPA has introduced a modern Copyright Tribunal into Britain, the differences between the two countries in this area are less marked.

17.25 The intention behind the creation of this body is to make reasonable copyright royalty rates in respect of the exercise of particular rights, which are mainly in the music industry. The new United States

5. US Code, Title 17, s 107.

law spells out the economic objectives which the Copyright Royalty Tribunal is to apply in calculating the applicable rates. These are

(a) to maximise the availability of creative works to the public;

(b) to afford the copyright-owner a fair return for his creative work and the copyright-user a fair income under existing economic conditions;

(c) to reflect the relative roles of the copyright-owner and the copyright-user in the product made available to the public with respect to relative creative contribution, technological contribution, capital investment, cost, risk and contribution to the opening of new markets for creative expression and media for their communication; and

(d) to minimise any disruptive impact on the structure of the industries involved and on generally prevailing industry practices.

Terms of reference

17.26 There is scope within its terms of reference for the American body to provide a useful and comparatively cheap service to the large copyright community in America. In particular its interpretation of the economic parameters laid down in the statute will be awaited with keen interest.[6] The law specifically provides that the Tribunal may take account of national monetary inflation and, somewhat optimistically, deflation, in arriving at its decisions on how rates should be adjusted.

ANTITRUST LAWS

17.27 A major distinction between the copyright situations in the United States and the rest of the world community relates to the copyright collecting societies which exist to gather in for composers, authors and publishers of music the fees due to them in respect of the performances of their works. As has been seen, in the greater part of the world, and particularly in Europe and the English-speaking former Dominions, within each territory there exists what is in reality a monopoly (see Chapter 16). In America alone of the major countries of the world the situation is entirely different.

17.28 The American Society of Composers, Authors and Publishers (ASCAP) was established in 1914, the same year as the Performing Right Society in the United Kingdom, and its spread was very rapid. Soon after its creation there took place two events in the United States

---

6. US Code, Title 17, s 801.

which were to be of enormous significance in the spread of popular music. The first was the forcible closure by the Government of the United States of the Storyville quarter of New Orleans in 1917—the red light district patronised by the U.S. Navy. This forced the black musicians who had made their living there out across the highways and byways of the continent, to St Louis, Chicago, New York, and the West Coast, where they had a radical effect on the development of Tin Pan Alley, and the cultural revolution it brought about.

17.29 The second was the introduction of radio broadcasting, which in America was followed by the rapid establishment of literally hundreds of local radio stations, using the ASCAP repertoire as the mainstay of their programmes. As described in Chapter 16 above, this resulted in antitrust action taken by the Department of Justice against ASCAP, and the submission of the latter to a consent decree.

CHAPTER 18

The Impact of the European Economic Community (EEC)

EUROPEAN COMMUNITIES ACT 1972

18.01 By virtue of the European Communities Act of 1972, the United Kingdom became a member state of the EEC and acknowledged the supremacy of the Community as a legislative body in areas of law to which it extended. Since the date of British adherence to the EEC, in one field after another, directly applicable legislation has been drafted and passed into law in Brussels. It has in certain cases thereafter had direct effect in the various member states. For the United Kingdom, this has been a wholly fresh experience, with which many of its inhabitants have not yet fully come to terms. But now that the Single European Act has been signed, attitudes are changing fast. As we move towards 1992, with harmonisation in many areas, and physical restrictions being renewed, there are signs that former reservations are dying out.

ROMAN LAW AND COMMON LAW

18.02 Although all EEC member states belong to the Berne Union, distinct differences in approach have grown up between the countries basing their legal systems on what may be broadly called the Roman law approach, and those stemming from the common law of England and Wales. Nowhere is this more true than in the realm of copyright, where the major Western European countries, particularly those of Latin temperament, favour a philosophical approach. This considers that the true copyright is an author's right, *le droit d'auteur*, which is in some way the inherent right of the creator. This contrasts with the more pragmatic British approach, based as it is on the fact that all rights in the nature of copyright must by virtue of section 171(2) of CDPA be contained in that Act. The abolition of the Performers' Protection Acts of 1958 and 1963, which did not create rights in the nature of copyright, should be contrasted with the new performers' rights in Part II of CDPA, which are certainly very similar to copyright. Note that section 194 makes an infringement of any of the civil rights in a performance actionable as a breach of statutory duty. By virtue of its inclusion in section 1(1)(b) of CDPA, the performing right in sound recordings is in the United Kingdom accorded the status of a copyright, which is the opposite of the view taken by some Latin states in Western Europe. There is no performing right as such for sound recordings in French copyright law.

DROIT MORAL

18.03 Prior to CDPA, there had been a good deal of criticism of the fact that British domestic copyright law did not provide cover for the *droit moral*. The need became still more pressing after the Stockholm Revision of the Berne Convention provided that:

> "independently of the author's economic rights, and even after the transfer of the said rights, the author shall have the right to claim authorship of the work, and to object to any distortion, mutilation or other modification of, or other derogatory action in relation to the said work, which would be prejudicial to his honour or reputation."

The new provisions about moral rights now appear in Chapter IV of Part I of CDPA, between sections 77 and 89. They are dealt with in greater detail at paras 14.19–22 above. Although the United Kingdom should now be able to adhere to the Stockholm Revision, there is a substantial body of opinion in the country which considers the rights to be of little value, due to the substantial number of qualifications and exceptions which have been included. Surprisingly, in the United Kingdom, an author is entitled to waive his moral rights, which rarely occurs elsewhere.

APPROXIMATION OF COPYRIGHT LAWS

18.04 The Commission of the European Communities has been interested in the question of copyright for a number of years. For much of that time, this interest has been manifested by enquiries into the monopoly aspects of the exercise of copyright. However on 10 July 1980 Monsieur Davignon of the Commission was asked by written question whether the Commission intends to propose the approximation of the laws of the members states on copyright, when it envisaged making such a proposal, and when it would enter into force.[1] The reply was as follows: "Yes. The approximation of copyright laws will be the subject of a series of proposals, the first of which will deal with artists' resale rights and the duration of protection respectively ... The Commission considers a gradual approach in this area preferable to a comprehensive

1. *Official Journal* C 269/28, written question 792/80.

proposal." Monsieur Davignon went on to state that the Commission was currently engaged in preliminary consultations with the circles concerned. Draft directives would be drawn up in the light of these meetings and would then be examined by a working party of government experts appointed by member states. He concluded that it was difficult to foresee the date of entry into force of the eventual approximated law.

18.05   Matters have moved forward since then. In November 1987, Mr Willy de Clercq, then European Commissioner for external trade, tabled the EEC proposals for world-wide protection for intellectual property rights. They were tabled in negotiations on the General Agreement on Tariffs and Trade (GATT). The EEC contended that intellectual property should be governed by GATT's general principle of equal national treatment. This is designed to ensure that foreign intellectual property receives that same legal protection as that given to domestic nationals.

18.06   Later on, in June 1988, the Commission prosecuted proposals for discussion in its Green Paper *Copyright and the Challenge of Technology – Copyright Issues Requiring Immediate Action*. Consultations are taking place, and representations are being received from interested parties. When these have been analysed, draft directives on copyright issues may be produced. These would eventually have a profound effect on the domestic legislation of member states.

Stricter interpretation of law by the United Kingdom and Ireland

18.07   Nevertheless, it must be recorded that in many areas of economic life for which it has attempted to legislate, the Commission of the EEC has caused a great deal of dissatisfaction. This reaction has been particularly marked in the United Kingdom, where, together with Ireland, we alone of the member states of the Community operate legal systems based on common law rather than Roman law principles. The common law approach puts much more weight on strict interpretation of the letter of the law, and the judges have evolved a set of highly technical rules for statutory interpretation. By contrast the Roman law countries attack questions of interpretation from a different direction. The matter has been summed up succinctly by Lord Denning in *H. P. Bulmer Ltd v. J. Bollinger S.A.*[2]

> "The European judges did not go by the literal meaning of the words or the grammatical structure of the sentence. They went by the design or

---

2.   [1974] Ch 401.

purpose which went behind it. They asked 'What is the sensible way of dealing with this situation so as to give effect to the presumed purpose of the legislation?'

They laid down the law accordingly. The decisions of the European Court did that every day. To our eyes, shortsighted by tradition, it was legislation pure and simple. To their eyes, it was fulfilling the true role of the courts. They were giving effect to what the legislature intended, or might be presumed to have intended. In interpreting the Treaty of Rome, which was part of our law, we should adopt the new approach. In Rome one should do as Rome did."

18.08 This is undoubtedly the correct approach of the other ten member states, and it is the technique which will be applied in the European Court in the cases which go to it from the United Kingdom and from Ireland. But although Lord Denning has firmly recommended that this technique should be used in British courts when trying issues under Community legislation, this approach does not seem to be approved of by the House of Lords. Thus in *James Buchanan Ltd v. Babco Forwarding and Shipping (UK) Ltd*,[3] the late Viscount Dilhorne said emphatically:

"I am not competent to speak on European methods of interpreting legislation but I know of no authority for the proposition that one consequence of this country joining the European Economic Community is that the courts of this country should now abandon principles as to construction long established in our law. The courts have rightly refused to encroach on the province of Parliament and have refused to engage in legislation."

18.09 There is some ground for thinking that section 3 of the European Communities Act 1972 supports Lord Denning's view, and that interpretation should be along European lines, but the very fact that there should be such wide differences of opinion among the most eminent judges illustrates the complexities of trying to impose the Community view on an existing British situation. As to the quality of the legislation produced by the Commission of the EEC, a great deal of criticism has been generated.

GEMA CASE: RESTRICTIVE TRADE PRACTICES

18.10 One of the key objectives of the Treaty of Rome is the elimination of restrictive practices. The often monopolistic powers wielded by copyright collecting societies have thus come under close scrutiny in the EEC. The long drawn out battle between the EEC Commission and the

3. [1977] 3 WLR 907.

German national collecting society GEMA ended finally in a recognition that the need for a simple and effective (and indeed compulsory) system for central enforcement of authors' rights and collecting payments outweighed any disadvantages stemming from lack of freedom for users. It is worth examining in detail, together with other similar cases, as a vivid illustration of the difficulties of applying in practice the anti-monopoly provisions of the Treaty, without doing more harm than good.

18.11 The sophisticated system of international accounting for copyright royalties between national collecting societies has been explained in Chapter 16. Prior to the date of the entry of the United Kingdom to the European Economic Community, on 3 June 1970 the Commission commenced proceedings against the powerful West Germany collecting society, GEMA (*Gesellschaft für musikalische Aufführungs- und mechanische Vervielfältigungsrechte*). The decision given on 3 June 1970 is one of the most important of its decisions on restrictive trade practices.[4]

18.12 GEMA was the only copyright collecting society in West Germany functioning in respect of performing rights in musical works, in common with all the other member states of the Community at that time, and the same situation existed in the United Kingdom in respect of the Performing Right Society. Its operations nevertheless were held to infringe a number of the provisions of the Treaty of Rome dealing with monopolies, in particular under article 86. The Commission found it objectionable that any publisher, author or composer in West Germany would in practice be obliged to join GEMA to exploit their rights, as no competing collecting society existed.

18.13 The Commission further found it objectionable that a composer or publisher in another member state who had joined GEMA could only become an associate member and not a full member of GEMA. It was found as a fact that GEMA constituted an undertaking for the purposes of article 86, and was exploiting in an improper manner a dominating position within a substantial part of the Common Market, namely West Germany. The practice of the German collecting society of taking from its members an assignment of copyright for the entire world, in respect of all categories of works, was regarded by the Commission as particularly objectionable.

18.14 The Commission considered that members of GEMA should be at liberty to decide whether they wanted to assign to GEMA or to a

---

4.   *Re GEMA (No.1)* [1971] C.M.L.R. D35.

foreign collecting society all or any part of their rights in those countries in which GEMA did not operate directly. Such members should be free to decide if they wished to assign the whole of their rights in the countries where GEMA operated directly, or if they wanted to split them up by category among a number of collecting societies. A member should also be at liberty whether he wished to withdraw any category of works from GEMA after due notice, and without penalty.

18.15 The social fund operated by GEMA was criticised, in relation to the way in which the society classified certain types of light music and sought at the same time to exclude any recourse by members to the courts. The payment of loyalty bonuses restricted only to certain classes of members was likewise found objectionable. GEMA had also sought to deny certain classes of writers and publishers the status of ordinary membership, and that even if granted, such a status could be withdrawn if the member became automatically dependent on a music-user, such as a recording company. The Commission, while recognising the need to control certain types of activity, decided that GEMA should in future end the various practices which it had found objectionable, and should alter its constitution to take these matters into account. The administration of GEMA after long consideration decided not to appeal and made the necessary alterations to its rules.

18.16 This decision threw the continued operation of such schemes, and the whole fabric of mutual international co-operation woven round them (described in Chapter 16), into jeopardy. Throughout the seventies all copyright collecting societies watched anxiously for further signs of the Commission's attitude; eventually they came in 1982 in the shape of *Re the GEMA Statutes* – see para 18.23 below.

18.17 Meanwhile in *Belgische Radio en Televisie v. SABAM and NV Fonior*,[5] the Court of Justice of the European Communities had decided in relation to Community law on restrictive practices that when deciding whether a national copyright collecting society is imposing unfair trading conditions on either its own members or on third parties, account must be taken of all the relevant interests to ensure a balance between the need for maximum freedom for composers and authors to dispose of their works on the one hand, and for effective management of their rights by the collecting society to which they have assigned their rights when there is no practical alternative to doing so. In such circumstances it is desirable to decide whether the practices in dispute go beyond the limit absolutely necessary for the attainment of that objective.

5. [1974] 2 C.M.L.R. 238.

18.18   This might appear to have been some slight relaxation of the rigidity of the GEMA case, but the other parts of the SABAM decision did not support this interpretation. Thus it confirmed that a compulsory assignment by a composer to a collecting society enjoying a dominant position of all that composer's rights both present and future, with no distinction between the various forms of exploitation, may amount to an unfair condition under article 86; this is particularly so if such an assignment is taken for an extended period of time after any withdrawal by the member from the society. The inequitable nature of such provisions must be decided by the relevant court, taking into account both the intrinsic individual effect of such clauses and their joint effect when combined.

18.19   If abuses are held to exist under article 86, the national court must decide whether and to what extent they affect the interests of authors or third parties, in order to decide the consequences on the validity and effect of the contracts in dispute. It can constitute an abuse if an undertaking entrusted with the exploitation of copyrights which occupies a dominant position within the meaning of article 86, imposes on its members obligations not absolutely necessary for the attainment of its objective, and which therefore encroach unfairly on the freedom of a member to exercise his copyright. Copyright collecting societies moreover were held not to be exempt from EEC anti-monopoly law by article 90(2) of the Treaty of Rome.

18.20   If anything, the later decision went further than the earlier one in limiting the traditional practices of European collecting societies. In the intervening years, the collecting societies have been careful to ensure that their activities did nothing further to bring down on them the wrath of the Commission. An uneasy peace settled over the question, and in general a single national collecting society continued to operate within each territory; however, the rules governing their administrations were trimmed considerably to the will of the Commission.

18.21   Another example of the attitude of the European Court to the activities of performing right and copyright collecting societies was provided by the cases of *Greenwich Films SA v. SACEM*.[6] This concerned the French national copyright collecting society which brought two actions in France in respect of royalties for the public performance of two films produced by Greenwich and exhibited in two member states of the Community. The music had been written for the films by two

6.   [1979] 2 C.M.L.R. 535 and [1980] 1 C.M.L.R. 629.

French composers who had assigned to SACEM the exclusive right to authorise or to prohibit the performance in public of their works throughout the whole world. Greenwich, having commissioned this music, claimed the rights in it, and resisted SACEM's claim on the ground that this assignment amounted to an abuse of article 86 of the Treaty of Rome.

18.22 On a reference from the national court to the European Court, it was held that in deciding whether the abuse by an undertaking of a dominant position in the EEC was such as to effect trade between members of the Community, regard was to be had to the consequences of that undertaking's conduct for the effective competitive structure within the Community. There was accordingly no need to distinguish either between production intended for sale within the Community and production destined to be exported. Applying these principles to the present case, there was no need to distinguish between the provision of such services as the management of copyright inside and outside the EEC. The operations could result in the partitioning of the market, which would restrict the freedom to provide services and affect trade between the member states.

18.23 GEMA's revised constitution was considered by the EEC Commission in *Re GEMA Statutes*.[7] The Commission now recognised that the basis for any effective activity on the part of a copyright collecting society was the collective administration of rights for the purpose of joint exploitation of the use of those rights. It also recognised that practices which in other circumstances would amount to an abuse of a dominant position would not be so regarded it they were necessary to carry out the essential purposes of an authors' society, and were not excessive.

18.24 In *Hérault v. SACEM*[8] this position was endorsed in the French Cour de Cassation. It was held that where a copyright collecting society is in a monopoly situation in respect of licensing the works of its members for public performance in France, this is not incompatible with article 86 of the Treaty of Rome. For an interesting decision on the rights of performing artistes, see *Interpar v. GVL*.[9]

18.25 It is clear that these later cases represent a considerable retreat from the EEC Commission's earlier position. Indeed, without them it is

7. [1982] 2 C.M.L.R. 482.
8. [1983] 1 C.M.L.R. 36.
9. [1982] 1 C.M.L.R. 221.

unlikely that the statutory provision for collecting societies in other fields contained in CDPA (see paras 16.30–31 above) could have been brought into effect.

EXCLUSIVE MARKET RIGHTS

18.26 Traditionally authors have granted exclusive rights to different publishers in different markets. One example was Dutch language books being published or distributed by one publisher in the Netherlands and another in Belgium. In *VBVB and VBBB v. E.C. Commission*[10] (the Dutch Books case) the Belgian and Dutch trade organisations failed to convince the European Court that the Commission was wrong in holding that the restrictions on cross-border trade which the system had imposed were unjustifiable in the light of article 85. This decision will have considerable impact on the British book trade, because traditionally authors have signed agreements whereby the continent of Europe has been treated as an open market in which British and American editions of the same book may be sold side by side, whereas the British publisher has had an exclusive right to sell the book in Great Britain and Ireland. The Commission has refused a block exemption for such agreements. The EEC's position is indirectly endorsed by section 27(5) of CDPA, which provides that copyright law may not be used to prevent the import into one member state of goods which are legitimately on sale in another. In other words British publishers cannot now prevent import of American editions from continental Europe unless they have negotiated an exclusive licence covering the whole of the EEC.

ABUSE OF DOMINANT POSITION

18.27 The Commission has also intervened to override national copyright law where it considered that otherwise there would have been abuse of dominant position. The position under British law has always been that compiled works such as directories, mathematical tables and lists of football fixtures enjoy the same protection as more "literary" compositions. In *BBC and ITV v. Time Out*,[11] for example, the plaintiffs sucessfully prevented publication by *Time Out* of their TV and radio programme schedules. However, the EEC Commission's decision in *Magill TV Guide v. ITV, BBC and RTE*[12] was that, in the circumstances,

10.   [1984] E.C.R. 19.
11.   [1984] F.S.R. 64.
12.   21 December 1988 (21.3.89 OJ L 78/43).

to prevent the Irish plaintiff company from publishing programme schedules amounted to an abuse of dominant position and thus was against article 86 of the Treaty of Rome. The defendants have appealed and obtained a temporary suspension of the order, but if the original decision is upheld, it will represent a significant challenge to copyright law. In September 1989 the British Home Secretary indicated that the forthcoming Broadcasting Bill would contain a provision forcing all broadcasters to license publication of their programme schedules. It seems likely that the Copyright Tribunal would adjudicate failing agreement on a fair price.

LENGTH OF COPYRIGHT PROTECTION

18.28   In *EMI Electrola GmbH v. Patricia Import and Export VmbH*[13] the question of a disparity in the period of copyright protection between member states was considered, in relation to the reproduction and distribution of musical works performed by Cliff Richard. It was held by the European Court of Justice that a restriction on Community trade could not be justified on the grounds of a disparity in the period of protection granted by national copyright laws, where it constituted a means of arbitrary discrimination or a disguised restriction on trade between member states.

COMPETITION ACT 1980, SECTION 30

18.29   In the United Kingdom, the anxiety which has been felt by copyright-owners on the application of restrictive practices legislation and the possibility of investigation under anti-monopoly powers has to some extent been allayed by section 30 of the Competition Act 1980. This has inserted a provision into the Restrictive Trade Practices Act 1976 to the effect that the latter statute is not to apply to certain licences granted by the owner or a licensee of any copyright, assignments of copyright, or agreements for such a licence or assignment. The Restrictive Trade Practices Act 1976 and Part I of the Restrictive Trade Practices Act 1956 shall be deemed never to have applied in relation to any of the cases set out above by virtue only of restrictions being accepted or information provisions being made under it in respect of the work or other subject-matter in which the copyright subsists.

13.   The Times 13 February 1989.

CHAPTER 19

Immorality, Obscenity and Public Policy

19.01 The Copyright, Designs and Patents Act 1988 was supposed to tidy up the uncertainties which new technology had introduced to the field of intellectual property, particularly copyright. While solutions have in many cases been put forward, in others the gratuitous introduction of new concepts has simply created new problems. The draftsman is not to blame, for he acts on the instructions he receives, but where new material has been put in which is clearly out of step with the general philosophy of copyright, the overall impression is of lack of research. All too often ideas seem to have been thrown in simply because they appeared attractive at the time, and because no one was present in Parliament or the responsible Department to demonstrate why the idea should not have been included.

MORAL RIGHTS

19.02 A glaring example lies in the field of moral rights. The United Kingdom had long been criticised for its stand on this issue. The provision made under previous Copyright Acts was not sufficient to discharge our obligation under the Berne Convention. Accordingly substantial alterations have been made in Chapter IV of Part I of the 1988 Act. The right to be identified as author or director has been included, together with the right to object to false attribution of work, the right to privacy of certain photographs and films, and the right to object to derogatory treatment of one's work.

19.03 This new right to object to derogatory treatment accrues to the author of a copyright literary, dramatic, musical or artistic work, and the director of a copyright film. "Treatment" broadly means any addition to, deletion from or alteration or adaptation of the work. It is derogatory if it amounts to distortion or mutilation of the work, or is otherwise prejudicial to the honour or reputation of the author or director. But a number of exceptions have been drafted into the Act, and this is where the problem arises. It is provided in section 81(6) that the right is not infringed by anything done for the purpose of, in the case of the British Broadcasting Corporation "avoiding the inclusion in a programme broadcast by them of anything which offends against good taste or decency or which is likely to encourage or incite to crime or to lead to disorder or to be offensive to public feeling."

19.04   Why this exception should be limited to the BBC is unclear. If it has to be introduced at all, it should in logic have been extended to commercial broadcasting interests. That apart, it is repugnant as imposing an unwarranted form of censorship. The point was not one made in the sensible Report of the Whitford Committee on Copyright in 1977; if the legislation had been based on the recommendations of that excellent Committee, how much better matters would be today! It is not in response to any need to control a situation which had been perceived by the general body of Parliamentarians. It is drafted as an absolute power in the hands of the BBC, which the officials of that body can exercise without let or hindrance. Worst of all, there is no right of appeal against it. As matters stand, the BBC may make deletions or omissions from a programme which in the author's view ruin the production, but he has no redress against it.

19.05   There really is no excuse for introducing the matter in this way, particularly when it is linked to the abstract expression "offends against good taste or decency", which is undefined. Whose standards are to apply? Clearly not those of the author, and probably not objective standards of the public at large. Will there be a special department in the BBC to administer the new provision, or will it be the province of some more sinister force controlling the Corporation?

OBSCENE, BLASPHEMOUS AND LIBELLOUS WORKS

19.06   Copyright lawyers are well aware that there was a line of cases which suggested that no copyright could exist in works which were libellous, immoral, obscene or irreligious. There were two serious objections to this doctrine as a proposition appropriate to modern situations. The doctrine was only to be found in case law, and section 46(5) of the Copyright Act 1956 provided that no copyright, or right in the nature of copyright, was to subsist "otherwise than by virtue of this Act or of some other enactment in the behalf." The doctrine was not to be found in any enactment.

19.07   The case law, such as it is, is revealing, for those cases where the judges confidently disallowed copyright on some moral ground are antique by modern standards, and could scarcely be mounted seriously today. The first judgement of real substance which puts forward the doctrine is *Stockdale v. Onwhyn*.[1] It was an action for damages for the loss alleged to have been sustained by the plaintiff, who was the first publisher of *The Memoirs of Harriet Wilson*. It was found that the work was the history of the amours of a well-known courtesan of the times, that some parts of the book were libellous in respect of named individuals, and that other parts were very licentious. Because of the nature of the work, it was held that the first publisher, who would normally be entitled to copyright, could not maintain an action against someone who published an unauthorised edition. It was in respect of this book that the Duke of Wellington commented "Publish and be damned!"

19.08   In *Glyn v. Western Feature Film Company*[2] an action had been brought over alleged infringement of copyright in the novel *Three Weeks*. The subject-matter was the life of a young man whose standards, even by those prevailing in 1916, were unremarkable. The episode to which objection was particularly made was a liaison at a country hotel with a lady who was not his wife. She later returned to the country of which she was queen, gave birth to a child, and was murdered by her husband. Younger J. felt able to observe:

> "It is in my opinion grossly immoral in its essence, in its treatment, and in its tendency. Stripped of its trappings, which are mere accident, it is nothing more or less than a sensuous adulterous intrigue . . . Now it is clear law that copyright cannot exist in a work of a tendency so grossly immoral as this . . . This renders it necessary for me to say a word about the film . . . There are in it isolated incidents and movements which in my judgement are more than vulgar; they are indecently offensive. The presence of these incidents in the film I think disentitles it in its present form to protection in this court."

Earlier, on the subject of defamation, Lord Elleborough had stated in *Hime v. Dale*[3] that if a composition in respect of which copyright protection was sought appeared on the face of it to be a libel so gross as to affect public morals, he would have advised the jury to give no damages.

19.09   The best consideration given to the topic in modern times was in *Chaplin v. Leslie Frewin (Publishers) Ltd.*[4] Charles Chaplin's son Michael produced his biography through ghost writers. After signing proofs but prior to publication, he sought to repudiate the agreement on the ground *inter alia* that the work was defamatory. Danckwerts L.J. commented

1. (1826) 29 R.R. 207.
2. [1916] 1 Ch. 261.
3. (1809) 2 Camp 27n.
4. [1966] 1 Ch. 71.

that the book itself was "worthless from a literary point of view, and in addition to its many other shortcomings, contains . . . passages of cheap and silly blasphemy . . . " Winn L.J. added that it was the plaintiff's choice that the blasphemous passages referred to should be retained in the script. The Court held that the contract should stand. This is the clearest recent finding at this judicial level that passages in a literary work in which copyright was claimed were blasphemous. But nowhere in the report is any suggestion made that the work should for that reason be deprived of copyright. Given the strong views expressed by the members of the Court of Appeal about the lack of any merit in the text on that ground, it seems safe to conclude that the doctrine, last advanced in *Glyn v. Western Feature Film Company* in 1916, that copyright will not be enforced in a work of libellous, immoral, obscene or irreligious tendency, can no longer be regarded as sound law. The doctrine as such is not included anywhere in the 1988 Act as a provision by which a copyright owner may be deprived of his copyright. It will be interesting to see if the BBC ever attempts to use section 81(6) of the new Act to justify tampering with an author's work.

19.10   The literary and publishing world will regard it as an outrage if the Corporation ever does seek to rely on the new provision. The question did arise under the previous legislation in *Frisby v. British Broadcasting Corporation,*[5] where the plaintiff wrote a play for television containing the line to be spoken by a female character in relation to sexual intercourse "My friend Sylv told me it was safe standing up." At a late stage in production the BBC sought to remove the words "standing up". One of the findings was that the plaintiff had made out a case for relief, on the basis that the deletion of the words "standing up" from the line in question would constitute a structural alteration. At the time it appeared that the United Kingdom was ignoring its obligations to allow an author to object to distortion, multilation or other modification of his work. Now that a provision has been introduced in the 1988 Act, albeit in a truncated form, there is no justification for the exceptions which have been added to qualify the right. Once again, we appear to be in breach of our international obligations under the Berne Copyright Convention.

THE PUBLIC POLICY ASPECT

19.11   The editors of *Copinger and Skone James on Copyright*[6] suggest that where the courts have refused to intervene in such cases, it was

5. [1967] 2 All E.R. 106.
6. 11th edn, para 224.

probably on the ground that it was against public policy to protect rights of publication and sale of works, where this would be against the public interest; "not that there is no copyright in the work, but that the courts will not enforce such copyright." That is a very fair rationalisation. Nevertheless, there was no provision as such in the Copyright Act of 1956 which deprived a copyright work of protection on the ground that public policy demanded it.

19.12   In fact this point arose under the 1956 Act in relation to breach of confidential information in *Lion Laboratories Ltd v. Evans*.[7] Two employees of Lion left the company, and contacted certain newspapers with copies of some of Lion's internal documentation, which cast doubts on the effectiveness of its breathalysing equipment. Lion obtained an ex parte injunction. Eventually in the Court of Appeal, the injunction was discharged. Griffiths L.J. observed "I am quite satisfied that the defence of public interest is now well established in actions for breach of confidence and, although there is less authority on the point, that it also extends to breach of copyright". But copyright is and always has been in this country a right of property. Under the Copyright Act of 1956, no qualification was made anywhere about public interest. At the time of the *Lion* case, there was no principle which Griffiths L.J. could invoke in support of an extraordinary finding.

19.13   That this was the case appears to have been acknowledged by the insertion of section 171(1)(e) into the Copyright, Designs and Patents Act 1988. This is to the effect that nothing in Part I of the Act affects the operation of any rule of equity relating to breaches of confidence. It would seem that the weakness of the justification advanced by Griffiths L.J. for his decision in the *Lion* case has been recognised. At least Parliament has not gone so far as to attempt an exemption from copyright protection on the general ground of public policy.

7.   [1984] 2 All E.R. 417.

APPENDIX

Copyright, Designs and Patents Act 1988

(CHAPTER 48)

ARRANGEMENT OF SECTIONS

PART I

COPYRIGHT

CHAPTER I

SUBSISTENCE, OWNERSHIP AND DURATION OF COPYRIGHT

Introductory

CHAPTER II

RIGHTS OF COPYRIGHT OWNER

178

CHAPTER III

ACTS PERMITTED IN RELATION TO COPYRIGHT WORKS

Introductory

General

Education

Libraries and archives

PART I: COPYRIGHT

CHAPTER I

SUBSISTENCE, OWNERSHIP AND DURATION OF COPYRIGHT

Introductory

Copyright and copyright works

1.—(1) Copyright is a property right which subsists in accordance with this Part in the following descriptions of work—

    (a) original literary, dramatic, musical or artistic works,

    (b) sound recordings, films, broadcasts or cable programmes, and

    (c) the typographical arrangement of published editions.

(2) In this Part "copyright work" means a work of any of those descriptions in which copyright subsists.

(3) Copyright does not subsist in a work unless the requirements of this Part with respect to qualification for copyright protection are met (see section 153 and the provisions referred to there).

Rights subsisting in copyright works

2.—(1) The owner of the copyright in a work of any description has the exclusive right to do the acts specified in Chapter II as the acts restricted by the copyright in a work of that description.

(2) In relation to certain descriptions of copyright work the following rights conferred by Chapter IV (moral rights) subsist in favour of the author, director or commissioner of the work, whether or not he is the owner of the copyright—

    (a) section 77 (right to be identified as author or director),

    (b) section 80 (right to object to derogatory treatment of work), and

    (c) section 85 (right to privacy of certain photographs and films).

Descriptions of work and related provisions

Literary, dramatic and musical works

3.—(1) In this Part—

"literary work" means any work, other than a dramatic or musical work, which is written, spoken or sung, and accordingly includes—

    (a) a table or compilation, and

    (b) a computer program;

"dramatic work" includes a work of dance or mime; and

"musical work" means a work consisting of music, exclusive of any words or action intended to be sung, spoken or performed with the music.

(2) Copyright does not subsist in a literary, dramatic or musical work unless and until it is recorded, in writing or otherwise; and references in this Part to the time at which such a work is made are to the time at which it is so recorded.

(3) It is immaterial for the purposes of subsection (2) whether the work is recorded by or with the permission of the author; and where it is not recorded by the author, nothing in that subsection affects the question whether copyright subsists in the record as distinct from the work recorded.

Artistic works

4.—(1) In this Part "artistic work" means—

(a) a graphic work, photograph, sculpture or collage, irrespective of artistic quality,

(b) a work of architecture being a building or a model for a building, or

(c) a work of artistic craftsmanship.

(2) In this Part—

"building" includes any fixed structure, and a part of a building or fixed structure;

"graphic work" includes—

(a) any painting, drawing, diagram, map, chart or plan, and

(b) any engraving, etching, lithograph, woodcut or similar work;

"photograph" means a recording of light or other radiation on any medium on which an image is produced or from which an image may by any means be produced, and which is not part of a film;

"sculpture" includes a cast or model made for purposes of sculpture.

Sound recordings and films

5.—(1) In this Part—

"sound recording" means—

(a) a recording of sounds, from which the sound may be reproduced, or

(b) a recording of the whole or any part of a literary, dramatic or musical work, from which sounds reproducing the work or part may be produced,

regardless of the medium on which the recording is made or the method by which the sounds are reproduced or produced; and

"film" means a recording on any medium from which a moving image may be any means be produced.

(2) Copyright does not subsist in a sound recording or film which is, or to the extent that it is, a copy taken from a previous sound recording or film.

Broadcasts

6.—(1) In this Part a "broadcast" means a transmission by wireless telegraphy of visual images, sounds or other information which—

(a) is capable of being lawfully received by members of the public, or

(b) is transmitted for presentation to members of the public;

and references to broadcasting shall be construed accordingly.

(2) An encrypted transmission shall be regarded as capable of being lawfully received by members of the public only if decoding equipment has been made available to members of the public by or with the authority of the person making the transmission or the person providing the contents of the transmission.

(3) References in this Part to the person making a broadcast, broadcasting a work, or including a work in a broadcast are—

    (a) to the person transmitting the programme, if he has responsibility to any extent for its contents, and

    (b) to any person providing the programme who makes with the person transmitting it the arrangements necessary for its transmission;

and references in this Part to a programme, in the context of broadcasting, are to any item included in a broadcast.

(4) For the purposes of this Part the place from which a broadcast is made is, in the case of a satellite transmission, the place from which the signals carrying the broadcast are transmitted to the satellite.

(5) References in this Part to the reception of a broadcast include reception of a broadcast relayed by means of a telecommunications system.

(6) Copyright does not subsist in a broadcast which infringes, or to the extent that it infringes, the copyright in another broadcast or in a cable programme.

Cable programmes

7.—(1) In this Part—

    "cable programme" means any item included in a cable programme service; and

    "cable programme service" means a service which consists wholly or mainly in sending visual images, sounds or other information by means of a telecommunications system, otherwise than by wireless telegraphy, for reception—

        (a) at two or more places (whether for simultaneous reception or at different times in response to requests by different users), or

        (b) for presentation to members of the public,

    and which is not, or so far as it is not, excepted by or under the following provisions of this section.

(2) The following are excepted from the definition of "cable programme service"—

    (a) a service or part of a service of which it is an essential feature that while visual images, sounds or other information are being conveyed by the person providing the service there will or may be sent from each place of reception, by means of the same system or (as the case may be) the same part of it, information (other than signals sent for the operation or control of the service) for reception by the person providing the service or other persons receiving it;

(b) a service run for the purposes of a business where—

(i) no person except the person carrying on the business is concerned in the control of the apparatus comprised in the system,

(ii) the visual images, sounds or other information are conveyed by the system solely for purposes internal to the running of the business and not by way of rendering a service or providing amenities for others, and

(iii) the system is not connected to any other telecommunications system;

(c) a service run by a single individual where—

(i) all the apparatus comprised in the system is under his control,

(ii) the visual images, sounds or other information conveyed by the system are conveyed solely for domestic purposes of his, and

(iii) the system is not connected to any other telecommunications system;

(d) services where—

(i) all the apparatus comprised in the system is situated in, or connects, premises which are in single occupation, and

(ii) the system is not connected to any other telecommunications system,

other than services operated as part of the amenities provided for residents or inmates of premises run as a business;

(e) services which are, or to the extent that they are, run for persons providing broadcasting or cable programme services or providing programmes for such services.

(3) The Secretary of State may by order amend subsection (2) so as to add or remove exceptions, subject to such transitional provision as appears to him to be appropriate.

(4) An order shall be made by statutory instrument; and no order shall be made unless a draft of it has been laid before and approved by resolution of each House of Parliament.

(5) References in this Part to the inclusion of a cable programme or work in a cable programme service are to its transmission as part of the service; and references to the person including it are to the person providing the service.

(6) Copyright does not subsist in a cable programme—

(a) if it is included in a cable programme service by reception and immediate re-transmission of a broadcast, or

(b) if it infringes, or to the extent that it infringes, the copyright in another cable programme or in a broadcast.

Published editions

8.—(1) In this Part "published edition", in the context of copyright in the typographical arrangement of a published edition, means a published edition of the whole or any part of one of more literary, dramatic or musical works.

(2) Copyright does not subsist in the typographical arrangement of a published edition if, or to the extent that, it reproduces the typographical arrangement of a previous edition.

Authorship and ownership of copyright

Authorship of work

9.—(1) In this Part "author", in relation to a work, means the person who creates it.

(2) That person shall be taken to be—

(a) in the case of a sound recording or film, the person by whom the arrangements necessary for the making of the recording or film are undertaken;

(b) in the case of a broadcast, the person making the broadcast (see section 6(3)) or, in the case of a broadcast which relays another broadcast by reception and immediate re-transmission, the person making that other broadcast;

(c) in the case of a cable programme, the person providing the cable programme service in which the programme is included;

(d) in the case of the typographical arrangement of a published edition, the publisher.

(3) In the case of a literary, dramatic, musical or artistic work which is computer-generated, the author shall be taken to be the person by whom the arrangements necessary for the creation of the work are undertaken.

(4) For the purposes of this Part a work is of "unknown authorship" if the identity of the author is unknown or, in the case of a work of joint authorship, if the identity of none of the authors is known.

(5) For the purposes of this Part the identity of an author shall be regarded as unknown if it is not possible for a person to ascertain his identity by reasonable inquiry; but if his identity is once known it shall not subsequently be regarded as unknown.

Works of joint authorship

10.—(1) In this Part a "work of joint authorship" means a work produced by the collaboration of two or more authors in which the contribution of each author is not distinct from that of the other author or authors.

(2) A broadcast shall be treated as a work of joint authorship in any case where more than one person is to be taken as making the broadcast (see section 6(3)).

(3) References in this Part to the author of a work shall, except as otherwise provided, be construed in relation to a work of joint authorship as references to all the authors of the work.

First ownership of copyright

11.—(1) The author of a work is the first owner of any copyright in it, subject to the following provisions.

(2) Where a literary, dramatic, musical or artistic work is made by an employee in the course of his employment, his employer is the first owner of any copyright in the work subject to any agreement to the contrary.

(3) This section does not apply to Crown copyright or Parliamentary copyright (see sections 163 and 165) or to copyright which subsists by virtue of section 168 (copyright of certain international organisations).

Duration of copyright

Duration of copyright in literary, dramatic, musical or artistic works

12.—(1) Copyright in a literary, dramatic, musical or artistic work expires at the end of the period of 50 years from the end of the calendar year in which the author dies, subject to the following provisions of this section.

(2) If the work is of unknown authorship, copyright expires at the end of the period of 50 years from the end of the calendar year in which it is first made available to the public; and subsection (1) does not apply if the identity of the author becomes known after the end of that period.

For this purpose making available to the public includes—

    (a) in the case of a literary, dramatic or musical work—

        (i) performance in public, or

        (ii) being broadcast or included in a cable programme service;

    (b) in the case of an artistic work—

        (i) exhibition in public,

        (ii) a film including the work being shown in public, or

        (iii) being included in a broadcast or cable programme service;

but in determining generally for the purposes of this subsection whether a work has been made available to the public no account shall be taken of any unauthorised act.

(3) If the work is computer-generated neither of the above provisions applies and copyright expires at the end of the period of 50 years from the end of the calendar year in which the work was made.

(4) In relation to a work of joint authorship—

    (a) the reference in subsection (1) to the death of the author shall be construed—

        (i) if the identity of all the authors is known, as a reference to the death of the last of them to die, and

        (ii) if the identity of one or more of the authors is known and the identity of one or more others is not, as a reference to the death of the last of the authors whose identity is known; and

(b) the reference in subsection (2) to the identity of the author becoming known shall be construed as a reference to the identity of any of the authors becoming known.

(5) This section does not apply to Crown copyright or Parliamentary copyright (see sections 163 to 166) or to copyright which subsists by virtue of section 168 (copyright of certain international organisations).

Duration of copyright in sound recordings and films

13.—(1) Copyright in a sound recording or film expires—

(a) at the end of the period of 50 years from the end of the calendar year in which it is made, or

(b) if it is released before the end of that period, 50 years from the end of the calendar year in which it is released.

(2) A sound recording or film is "released" when—

(a) it is first published, broadcast or included in a cable programme service, or

(b) in the case of a film or film sound-track, the film is first shown in public;

but in determining whether a work has been released no account shall be taken of any unauthorised act.

Duration of copyright in broadcasts and cable programmes

14.—(1) Copyright in a broadcast or cable programme expires at the end of the period of 50 years from the end of the calendar year in which the broadcast was made or the programme was included in a cable programme service.

(2) Copyright in a repeat broadcast or cable programme expires at the same time as the copyright in the original broadcast or cable programme; and accordingly no copyright arises in respect of a repeat broadcast or cable programme which is broadcast or included in a cable programme service after the expiry of the copyright in the original broadcast or cable programme.

(3) A repeat broadcast or cable programme means one which is a repeat either of a broadcast previously made or of a cable programme previously included in a cable programme service.

Duration of copyright in typographical arrangements of published editions

15. Copyright in the typographical arrangement of a published edition expires at the end of the period of 25 years from the end of the calendar year in which the edition was first published.

CHAPTER II

RIGHTS OF COPYRIGHT OWNER

The acts restricted by copyright

The acts restricted by copyright in a work

16.—(1) The owner of the copyright in a work has, in accordance with the following provisions of this Chapter, the exclusive right to do the following acts in the United Kingdom—

    (a) to copy the work (see section 17);

    (b) to issue copies of the work to the public (see section 18);

    (c) to perform, show or play the work in public (see section 19);

    (d) to broadcast the work or include it in a cable programme service (see section 20);

    (e) to make an adaptation of the work or do any of the above in relation to an adaptation (see section 21);

and those acts are referred to in this Part as the "acts restricted by the copyright".

(2) Copyright in a work is infringed by a person who without the licence of the copyright owner does, or authorises another to do, any of the acts restricted by the copyright.

(3) References in this Part to the doing of an act restricted by the copyright in a work are to the doing of it—

    (a) in relation to the work as a whole or any substantial part of it, and

    (b) either directly or indirectly;

and it is immaterial whether any intervening acts themselves infringe copyright.

(4) This Chapter has effect subject to—

    (a) the provisions of Chapter III (acts permitted in relation to copyright works), and

    (b) the provisions of Chapter VII (provisions with respect to copyright licensing).

Infringement of copyright by copying

17.—(1) The copying of the work is an act restricted by the copyright in every description of copyright work; and references in this Part to copying and copies shall be construed as follows.

(2) Copying in relation to a literary, dramatic, musical or artistic work means reproducing the work in any material form.

This includes storing the work in any medium by electronic means.

(3) In relation to an artistic work copying includes the making of a copy in three dimensions of a two-dimensional work and the making of a copy in two dimensions of a three-dimensional work.

(4) Copying in relation to a film, television broadcast or cable programme includes making a photograph of the whole or any substantial part of any image forming part of the film, broadcast or cable programme.

(5) Copying in relation to the typographical arrangement of a published edition means making a facsimile copy of the arrangement.

(6) Copying in relation to any description of work includes the making of copies which are transient or are incidental to some other use of the work.

Infringement by issue of copies to the public

18.—(1) The issue to the public of copies of the work is an act restricted by the copyright in every description of copyright work.

(2) References in this Part to the issue to the public of copies of a work are to the act of putting into circulation copies not previously put into circulation, in the United Kingdom or elsewhere, and not to—

(a) any subsequent distribution, sale, hiring or loan of those copies, or

(b) any subsequent importation of those copies into the United Kingdom;

except that in relation to sound recordings, films and computer programs the restricted act of issuing copies to the public includes any rental of copies to the public.

Infringement by performance, showing or playing of work in public

19.—(1) The performance of the work in public is an act restricted by the copyright in a literary, dramatic or musical work.

(2) In this Part "performance", in relation to a work—

(a) includes delivery in the case of lectures, addresses, speeches and sermons, and

(b) in general, includes any mode of visual or acoustic presentation, including presentation by means of a sound recording, film, broadcast or cable programme of the work.

(3) The playing or showing of the work in public is an act restricted by the copyright in a sound recording, film, broadcast or cable programme.

(4) Where copyright in a work is infringed by its being performed, played or shown in public by means of apparatus for receiving visual images or sounds conveyed by electronic means, the person by whom the visual images or sounds are sent, and in the case of a performance the performers, shall not be regarded as responsible for the infringement.

Infringement by broadcasting or inclusion in a cable programme service

20. The broadcasting of the work or its inclusion in a cable programme service is an act restricted by the copyright in—

(a) a literary, dramatic, musical or artistic work,

(b) a sound recording or film, or

(c) a broadcast or cable programme.

Infringement by making adaptation or act done in relation to adaptation

21.—(1) The making of an adaptation of the work is an act restricted by the copyright in a literary, dramatic or musical work.

For this purpose an adaptation is made when it is recorded, in writing or otherwise.

(2) The doing of any of the acts specified in sections 17 to 20, or subsection (1) above, in relation to an adaptation of the work is also an act restricted by the copyright in a literary, dramatic or musical work.

For this purpose it is immaterial whether the adaptation has been recorded, in writing or otherwise, at the time the act is done.

(3) In this Part "adaptation"—

(a) in relation to a literary or dramatic work, means—

(i) a translation of the work;

(ii) a version of a dramatic work in which it is converted into a non-dramatic work or, as the case may be, of a non-dramatic work in which it is converted into a dramatic work;

(iii) a version of the work in which the story or action is conveyed wholly or mainly by means of pictures in a form suitable for reproduction in a book, or in a newspaper, magazine or similar periodical;

(b) in relation to a musical work, means an arrangement or transcription of their work.

(4) In relation to a computer program a "translation" includes a version of the program in which it is converted into or out of a computer language or code or into a different computer language or code, otherwise than incidentally in the course of running the program.

(5) No inference shall be drawn from this section as to what does or does not amount to copying a work.

Secondary infringement of copyright

Secondary infringement: importing infringing copy

22. The copyright in a work is infringed by a person who, without the licence of the copyright owner, imports into the United Kingdom, otherwise than for his private and domestic use, an article which is, and which he knows or has reason to believe is, an infringing copy of the work.

Secondary infringement: possessing or dealing with infringing copy

23. The copyright in a work is infringed by a person who, without the licence of the copyright owner—

(a) possesses in the course of a business,

(b) sells or lets for hire, or offers or exposes for sale or hire.

(c) in the course of a business exhibits in public or distributes, or

(d) distributes otherwise than in the course of a business to such an extent as to effect prejudicially the owner of the copyright,

an article which is, and which he knows or has reason to believe is, an infringing copy of the work.

Secondary infringement: providing means for making infringing copies

24.—(1) Copyright in a work is infringed by a person who, without the licence of the copyright owner—

(a) makes,

(b) imports into the United Kingdom,

(c) possesses in the course of a business, or

(d) sells or lets for hire, or offers or exposes for sale or hire,

an article specifically designed or adapted for making copies of that work, knowing or having reason to believe that it is to be used to make infringing copies.

(2) Copyright in a work is infringed by a person who without the licence of the copyright owner transmits the work by means of a telecommunications system (otherwise than by broadcasting or inclusion in a cable programme service), knowing or having reason to believe that infringing copies of the work will be made by means of the reception of the transmission in the United Kingdom or elsewhere.

Secondary infringement: permitting use of premises for infringing performance

25.—(1) Where the copyright in a literary, dramatic or musical work is infringed by a performance at a place of public entertainment, any person who gave permission for that place to be used for the performance is also liable for the infringement unless when he gave permission he believed on reasonable grounds that the performance would not infringe copyright.

(2) In this section "place of public entertainment" includes premises which are occupied mainly for other purposes but are from time to time made available for hire for the purposes of public entertainment.

Secondary infringement: provision of apparatus for infringing performance, &c.

26.—(1) Where copyright in a work is infringed by a public performance of the work, or by the playing or showing of the work in public, by means of apparatus for—

(a) playing sound recordings,

(b) showing films, or

(c) receiving visual images or sounds conveyed by electronic means,

the following persons are also liable for the infringement.

(2) A person who supplied the apparatus, or any substantial part of it, is liable for the infringement if when he supplied the apparatus or part—

(a) he knew or had reason to believe that the apparatus was likely to be so used as to infringe copyright, or

(b) in the case of apparatus whose normal use involves a public performance, playing or showing, he did not believe on reasonable grounds that it would not be so used as to infringe copyright.

(3) An occupier of premises who gave permission for the apparatus to be brought onto the premises is liable for the infringement if when he gave permission he knew or had reason to believe that the apparatus was likely to be so used as to infringe copyright.

(4) A person who supplied a copy of a sound recording or film used to infringe copyright is liable for the infringement if when he supplied it he knew or had reason to believe that what he supplied, or a copy made directly or indirectly from it, was likely to be so used as to infringe copyright.

Infringing copies

Meaning of "infringing copy"

27.—(1) In this Part "infringing copy", in relation to a copyright work, shall be construed in accordance with this section.

(2) An article is an infringing copy if its making constituted an infringement of the copyright in the work in question.

(3) An article is also an infringing copy if—

(a) it has been or is proposed to be imported into the United Kingdom, and

(b) its making in the United Kingdom would have constituted an infringement of the copyright in the work in question, or a breach of an exclusive licence agreement relating to that work.

(4) Where in any proceedings the question arises whether an article is an infringing copy and it is shown—

(a) that the article is a copy of the work, and

(b) that copyright subsists in the work or has subsisted at any time,

it shall be presumed until the contrary is proved that the article was made at a time when copyright subsisted in the work.

(5) Nothing in subsection (3) shall be construed as applying to an article which may lawfully be imported into the United Kingdom by virtue of any enforceable Community right within the meaning of section 2(1) of the European Communities Act 1972.

(6) In this Part "infringing copy" includes a copy falling to be treated as an infringing copy by virtue of any of the following provisions—

section 32(5) (copies made for purposes of instruction or examination),

section 35(3) (recordings made by educational establishments for educational purposes),

section 36(5) (reprographic copying by educational establishments for purposes of instruction),

section 37(3)(b) (copies made by librarian or archivist in reliance on false declaration),

section 56(2) (further copies, adaptation, &c. of work in electronic form retained on transfer of principal copy),

section 63(2) (copies made for purpose of advertising artistic work for sale).

section 68(4) (copies made for purpose of broadcast or cable programme),

or

any provision of an order under section 141 (statutory licence for certain reprographic copying by educational establishments).

CHAPTER III

ACTS PERMITTED IN RELATION TO COPYRIGHT WORKS

Introductory

Introductory provisions

28.—(1) The provisions of this Chapter specify acts which may be done in relation to copyright works notwithstanding the subsistence of copyright; they relate only to the question of infringement of copyright and do not affect any other right or obligation restricting the doing of any of the specified acts.

(2) Where it is provided by this Chapter that an act does not infringe copyright, or may be done without infringing copyright, and no particular description of copyright work is mentioned, the act in question does not infringe the copyright in a work of any description.

(3) No inference shall be drawn from the description of any act which may by virtue of this Chapter be done without infringing copyright as to the scope of the acts restricted by the copyright in any description of work.

(4) The provisions of this Chapter are to be construed independently of each other, so that the fact an act does not fall within one provision does not mean that it is not covered by another provision.

General

Research and private study

29.—(1) Fair dealing with a literary, dramatic, musical or artistic work for the purposes of research or private study does not infringe any copyright in the work or, in the case of a published edition, in the typographical arrangement.

(2) Fair dealing with the typographical arrangement of a published edition for the purposes mentioned in subsection (1) does not infringe any copyright in the arrangement.

(3) Copying by a person other than the researcher or student himself is not fair dealing if—

    (a) in the case of a librarian, or a person acting on behalf of a librarian, he does anything which regulations under section 40 would not permit to be done under section 38 or 39 (articles or parts of published works: restriction on multiple copies of same material), or

    (b) in any other case, the person doing the copying knows or has reason to believe that it will result in copies of substantially the same material being provided to more than one person at substantially the same time and for substantially the same purpose.

Criticism, review and news reporting

30.—(1) Fair dealing with a work for the purpose of criticism or review, of that or another work or of a performance of a work, does not infringe any copyright in the work provided that it is accompanied by a sufficient acknowledgement.

(2) Fair dealing with a work (other than a photograph) for the purpose of reporting current events does not infringe any copyright in the work provided that (subject to subsection (3)) it is accompanied by a sufficient acknowledgement.

(3) No acknowledgement is required in connection with the reporting of current events by means of a sound recording, film, broadcast or cable programme.

Incidental inclusion of copyright material

31.—(1) Copyright in a work is not infringed by its incidental inclusion in an artistic work, sound recording, film, broadcast or cable programme.

(2) Nor is the copyright infringed by the issue to the public of copies, or the playing, showing, broadcasting or inclusion in a cable programme service, of anything whose making was, by virtue of subsection (1), not an infringement of the copyright.

(3) A musical work, words spoken or sung with music, or so much of a sound recording, broadcast or cable programme as includes a musical work or such words, shall not be regarded as incidentally included in another work if it is deliberately included.

Education

Things done for purposes of instruction or examination

32.—(1) Copyright in a literary, dramatic, musical or artistic work is not infringed by its being copied in the course of instruction or of preparation for instruction, provided the copying—

    (a) is done by a person giving or receiving instruction, and

    (b) is not by means of a reprographic process.

(2) Copyright in a sound recording, film, broadcast or cable programme is not infringed by its being copied by making a film or film sound-track in the course of instruction or of preparation for instruction, in the making of films or film sound-tracks, provided the copying is done by a person giving or receiving instruction.

(3) Copyright is not infringed by anything done for the purposes of an examination by way of setting the questions, communicating the questions to the candidates or answering the questions.

(4) Subsection (3) does not extend to the making of a reprographic copy of a musical work for use by an examination candidate in performing the work.

(5) Where a copy which would otherwise be an infringing copy is made in accordance with this section but is subsequently dealt with, it shall be treated as an infringing copy for the purpose of that dealing, and if that dealing infringes copyright for all subsequent purposes.

For this purpose "dealt with" means sold or let for hire or offered or exposed for sale or hire.

Anthologies for eductional use

33.—(1) The inclusion of a short passage from a published literary or dramatic work in a collection which—

(a) is intended for use in educational establishments and is so described in its title, and in any advertisements issued by or on behalf of the publisher, and

(b) consists mainly of material in which no copyright subsists,

does not infringe the copyright in the work if the work itself is not intended for use in such establishments and the inclusion is accompanied by a sufficient acknowledgement.

(2) Subsection (1) does not authorise the inclusion of more than two excerpts from copyright works by the same author in collections published by the same publisher over any period of five years.

(3) In relation to any given passage the reference in subsection (2) to excerpts from works by the same author—

(a) shall be taken to include excerpts from works by him in collaboration with another, and

(b) if the passage in question is from such a work, shall be taken to include excerpts from works by any of the authors, whether alone or in collaboration with another.

(4) References in this section to the use of a work in an educational establishment are to any use for the educational purposes of such an establishment.

Performing, playing or showing work in course of
activities of educational establishment

34.—(1) The performance of a literary, dramatic or musical work before an audience consisting of teachers and pupils at an educational establishment and other persons directly connected with the activities of the establishment—

(a) by a teacher or pupil in the course of the activities of the establishment, or

(b) at the establishment by any person for the purposes of instruction,

is not a public performance for the purposes of infringement of copyright.

(2) The playing or showing of a sound recording, film, broadcast or cable programme before such an audience at an educational establishment for the purposes of instruction is not a playing or showing of the work in public for the purposes of infringement of copyright.

(3) A person is not for this purpose directly connected with the activities of the educational establishment simply because he is the parent of a pupil at the establishment.

Recording by educational establishments of broadcasts and cable programmes

35.—(1) A recording of a broadcast or cable programme, or a copy of such a recording, may be made by or on behalf of an educational establishment for the educational purposes of that establishment without thereby infringing the copyright in the broadcast or cable programme, or in any work included in it.

(2) This section does not apply if or to the extent that there is a licensing scheme certified for the purposes of this section under section 143 providing for the grant of licences.

(3) Where a copy which would otherwise be an infringing copy is made in accordance with this section but is subsequently dealt with, it shall be treated as an infringing copy for the purposes of that dealing, and if that dealing infringes copyright for all subsequent purposes.

For this purpose "dealt with" means sold or let for hire or offered or exposed for sale of hire.

Reprographic copying by educational establishments of passages from published works

36.—(1) Reprographic copies of passages from published literary, dramatic or musical works may, to the extent permitted by this section, be made by or on behalf of an educational establishment for the purposes of instruction without infringing any copyright in the work, or in the typographical arrangement.

(2) Not more than one per cent, of any work may be copied by or on behalf of an establishment by virtue of this section in any quarter, that is, in any period 1st January to 31st March, 1st April to 30th June, 1st July to 30th September or 1st October to 31st December.

(3) Copying is not authorised by this section if, or to the extent that, licences are available authorising the copying in question and the person making the copies knew or ought to have been aware of that fact.

(4) The terms of a licence granted to an educational establishment authorising the reprographic copying for the purposes of instruction of passages from published literary, dramatic or musical works are of no effect so far as they purport to restrict the proportion of a work which may be copied (whether on payment or free of charge) to less than that which would be permitted under this section.

(5) Where a copy which would otherwise be an infringing copy is made in accordance with this section but is subsequently dealt with, it shall be treated as an infringing copy for the purposes of that dealing, and if that dealing infringes copyright for all subsequent purposes.

For this purpose "dealt with" means sold or let for hire or offered or exposed for sale or hire.

Libraries and archives

Libraries and archives: introductory

37.—(1) In sections 38 to 43 (copying by librarians and archivists)—

    (a) references in any provision to a prescribed library or archive are to a library or archive of a description prescribed for the purposes of that provision by regulations made by the Secretary of State; and

    (b) references in any provision to the prescribed conditions are to the conditions so prescribed.

(2) The regulations may provide that, where a librarian or archivist is required to be satisfied as to any matter before making or supplying a copy of a work—

    (a) he may rely on a signed declaration as to that matter by the person requesting the copy, unless he is aware that it is false in a material particular, and

    (b) in such cases as may be prescribed, he shall not make or supply a copy in the absence of a signed declaration in such form as may be prescribed.

(3) Where a person requesting a copy makes a declaration which is false in a material particular and is supplied with a copy which would have been an infringing copy if made by him—

    (a) he is liable for infringement of copyright as if he had made the copy himself, and

    (b) the copy shall be treated as an infringing copy.

(4) The regulations may make different provision for different descriptions of libraries or archives and for different purposes.

(5) Regulations shall be made by statutory instrument which shall be subject to annulment in pursuance of a resolution of either House of Parliament.

(6) References in this section, and in sections 38 to 43, to the librarian or archivist include a person acting on his behalf.

Copying by librarians: articles in periodicals

38.—(1) The librarian of a prescribed library may, if the prescribed conditions are compiled with, make and supply a copy of an article in a periodical without infringing any copyright in the text, in any illustrations accompanying the text or in the typographical arrangement.

(2) The prescribed conditions shall include the following—

    (a) that copies are supplied only to persons satisfying the librarian that they require them for purposes of research or private study, and will not use them for any other purpose;

    (b) that no person is furnished with more than one copy of the same article or with copies of more than one article contained in the same issue of a periodical; and

    (c) that persons to whom copies are supplied are required to pay for them a sum not less than the cost (including a contribution to the general expenses of the library) attributable to their production.

Copying by librarians: parts of published works

39.—(1) The librarian of a prescribed library may, if the prescribed conditions are complied with, make and supply from a published edition a copy of part of a literary, dramatic or musical work (other than an article in a periodical) without infringing any copyright in the work, in any illustrations accompanying the work or in the typographical arrangement.

(2) The prescribed conditions shall include the following—

(a) that copies are supplied only to persons satisfying the librarian that they require them for purposes of research or private study, and will not use for any other purpose;

(b) that no person is furnished with more than one copy of the same material or with a copy of more than a reasonable proportion of any work; and

(c) that persons to whom copies are supplied are required to pay for them a sum not less than the cost (including a contribution to the general expenses of the library) attributable to their production.

Restriction on production of multiple copies of the same material

40.—(1) Regulations for the purposes of sections 38 to 39 (copying by librarian of article or part of published work) shall contain provision to the effect that a copy shall be supplied only to a person satisfying the librarian that his requirement is not related to any similar requirement of another person.

(2) The regulations may provide—

(a) that requirements shall be regarded as similar if the requirements are for copies of substantially the same material at substantially the same time and for substantially the same purpose; and

(b) that requirements of persons shall be regarded as related if those persons receive instruction to which the material is relevant at the same time and place.

Copying by librarians: supply of copies to other libraries

41.—(1) The librarian of a prescribed library may, if the prescribed conditions are complied with, make and supply to another prescribed library a copy of—

(a) an article in a periodical, or

(b) the whole or part of a published edition of a literary, dramatic or musical work,

without infringing any copyright in the text of the article or, as the case may be, in the work, in any illustrations accompanying it or in the typographical arrangement.

(2) Subsection (1)(b) does not apply if at the time the copy is made the librarian making it knows, or could by reasonable inquiry ascertain, the name and address of a person entitled to authorise the making of the copy.

Copying by librarians or archivists: replacement copies of works

42.—(1) The librarian or archivist of a prescribed library or archive may, if the prescribed conditions are complied with, make a copy from any item in the permanent collection of the library or archive—

(a) in order to preserve or replace that item by placing the copy in its permanent collection in addition to or in place of it, or

(b) in order to replace in the permanent collection of another prescribed library or archive an item which has been lost, destroyed or damaged,

without infringing the copyright in any literary, dramatic or musical work, in any illustrations accompanying such a work or, in the case of a published edition, in the typographical arrangement.

(2) The prescribed conditions shall include provision for restricting the making of copies to cases where it is not reasonably practicable to purchase a copy of the item in question to fulfil that purpose.

Copying by librarians or archivists: certain unpublished works

43.—(1) The librarian or archivist of a prescribed library or archive may, if the prescribed conditions are complied with, make and supply a copy of the whole or part of a literary, dramatic or musical work from a document in the library or archive without infringing any copyright in the work or any illustrations accompanying it.

(2) This section does not apply if—

(a) the work had been published before the document was deposited in the library or archive, or

(b) the copyright owner has prohibited copying of the work,

and at the time the copy is made the librarian or archivist making it is, or ought to be, aware of that fact.

(3) The prescribed conditions shall include the following—

(a) that copies are supplied only to persons satisfying the librarian or archivist that they require them for purposes of research or private study and will not use them for any other purpose;

(b) that no person is furnished with more than one copy of the same material; and

(c) that persons to whom copies are supplied are required to pay for them a sum not less than the cost (including a contribution to the general expenses of the library or archive) attributable to their production.

Copy of work required to be made as condition of export

44. If an article of cultural or historical importance or interest cannot lawfully be exported from the United Kingdom unless a copy of it is made and deposited in an appropriate library or archive, it is not an infringement of copyright to make that copy.

Public administration

Parliamentary and judicial proceedings

45.—(1) Copyright is not infringed by anything done for the purposes of parliamentary or judicial proceedings.

(2) Copyright is not infringed by anything done for the purposes of reporting such proceedings; but this shall not be construed as authorising the copyright of a work which is itself a published report of the proceedings.

Royal Commissions and statutory inquiries

46.—(1) Copyright is not infringed by anything done for the purposes of the proceedings of a Royal Commission or statutory inquiry.

(2) Copyright is not infringed by anything done for the purpose of reporting any such proceedings held in public; but this shall not be construed as authorising the copyright of a work which is itself a published report of the proceedings.

(3) Copyright in a work is not infringed by the issue to the public of copies of the report of a Royal Commission or statutory inquiry containing the work or material from it.

(4) In this section—

"Royal Commission" includes a Commission appointed for Northern Ireland by the Secretary of State in pursuance of the prerogative powers of Her Majesty delegated to him under section 7(2) of the Northern Ireland Constitution Act 1973; and

"statutory inquiry" means an inquiry held or investigation conducted in pursuance of a duty imposed or power conferred by or under an enactment.

Material open to public inspection or on official register

47.—(1) Where material is open to public inspection pursuant to a statutory requirement, or is on a statutory register, any copyright in the material as a literary work is not infringed by the copying of so much of the material as contains factual information of any description, by or with the authority of the appropriate person, for a purpose which does not involve the issuing of copies to the public.

(2) Where material is open to public inspection pursuant to a statutory requirement, copyright is not infringed by the copying or issuing to the public of copies of the material, by or with the authority of the appropriate person, for the purpose of enabling the material to be inspected at a more convenient time or place or otherwise facilitating the exercise of any right for the purpose of which the requirement is imposed.

(3) Where material which is open to public inspection pursuant to a statutory requirement, or which is on a statutory register, contains information about matters of general scientific, technical, commercial or economic interest, copyright is not infringed by the copying or issuing to the public of copies of the material, by or with the authority of the appropriate person, for the purpose of disseminating that information.

(4) The Secretary of State may by order provide that subsection (1), (2) or (3) shall, in such cases as may be specified in the order, apply only to copies marked in such manner as may be so specified.

(5) The Secretary of State may by order provide that subsections (1) to (3) apply, to such extent and with such modifications as may be specified in the order—

    (a) to material made open to public inspection by—

        (i) an international organisation specified in the order, or

        (ii) a person so specified who has functions in the United Kingdom under an international agreement to which the United Kingdom is party, or

    (b) to a register maintained by an international organisation specified in the order,

as they apply in relation to material open to public inspection pursuant to a statutory requirement or to a statutory register.

    (6) In this section—

    "appropriate person" means the person required to make the material open to public inspection or, as the case may be, the person maintaining the register;

    "statutory register" means a register maintained in pursuance of a statutory requirement; and

    "statutory requirement" means a requirement imposed by provision made by or under an enactment.

    (7) An order under this section shall be made by statutory instrument which shall be subject to annulment in pursuance of a resolution of either House of Parliament.

Material communicated to the Crown in the course of public business

    48.—(1) This section applies where a literary, dramatic, musical or artistic work has in the course of public business been communicated to the Crown for any purpose, by or with the licence of the copyright owner and a document or other material thing recording or embodying the work is owned by or in the custody or control of the Crown.

    (2) The Crown may, for the purpose for which the work was communicated to it, or any related purpose which could reasonably have been anticipated by the copyright owner, copy the work and issue copies of the work to the public without infringing any copyright in the work.

    (3) The Crown may not copy a work, or issue copies of a work to the public, by virtue of this section if the work has previously been published otherwise than by virtue of this section.

    (4) In subsection (1) "public business" includes any activity carried on by the Crown.

    (5) This section has effect subject to any agreement to the contrary between the Crown and the copyright owner.

Public records

    49. Material which is comprised in public records within the meaning of the Public Records Act 1958, the Public Records (Scotland) Act 1937 or the Public

Records Act (Northern Ireland) 1923 which are open to public inspection in pursuance of that Act, may be copied, and a copy may be supplied to any person, by or with the authority of any officer appointed under that Act, without infringement of copyright.

Acts done under statutory authority

50.—(1) Where the doing of a particular act is specifically authorised by an Act of Parliament, whenever passed, then, unless the Act provides otherwise, the doing of that act does not infringe copyright.

(2) Subsection (1) applies in relation to an enactment contained in Northern Ireland legislation as it applies in relation to an Act of Parliament.

(3) Nothing in this section shall be construed as excluding any defence of statutory authority otherwise available under or by virtue of any enactment.

Designs

Design documents and models

51.—(1) It is not an infringement of any copyright in a design document or model recording or embodying a design for anything other than an artistic work or a typeface to make an article to the design or to copy an article made to the design.

(2) Nor is it an infringement of the copyright to issue to the public, or include in a film, broadcast or cable programme service, anything the making of which was, by virtue of subsection (1), not an infringement of that copyright.

(3) In this section—

"design" means the design of any aspect of the shape or configuration (whether internal or external) of the whole or part of an article, other than surface decoration; and

"design document" means any record of a design, whether in the form of a drawing, a written description, a photograph, data stored in a computer or otherwise.

Effect of exploitation of design derived from artistic work

52.—(1) This section applies where an artistic work has been exploited, by or with the licence of the copyright owner, by—

(a) making by an industrial process articles falling to be treated for the purposes of this Part as copies of the work, and

(b) marketing such articles, in the United Kingdom or elsewhere.

(2) After the end of the period of 25 years from the end of the calendar year in which such articles are first marketed, the work may be copied by making articles of any description, or doing anything for the purpose of making articles of any description, and anything may be done in relation to articles so made, without infringing copyright in the work.

(3) Where only part of an artistic work is exploited as mentioned in subsection (1), subsection (2) applies only in relation to that part.

(4) The Secretary of State may by order make provision—

(a) as to the circumstances in which an article, or any description of article, is to be regarded for the purposes of this section as made by an industrial process;

(b) excluding from the operation of this section such articles of a primarily literary or artistic character as he thinks fit.

(5) An order shall be made by statutory instrument which shall be subject to annulment in pursuance of a resolution of either House of Parliament.

(6) In this section—

(a) references to articles do not include films; and

(b) references to the marketing of an article are to its being sold or let for hire or offered or exposed for sale or hire.

Things done in reliance on registration of design

53.—(1) The copyright in an artistic work is not infringed by anything done—

(a) in pursuance of an assignment of licence made or granted by a person registered under the Registered Designs Act 1949 as the proprietor of a corresponding design, and

(b) in good faith in reliance on the registration and without notice of any proceedings for the cancellation of the registration or for rectifying the relevant entry in the register of designs;

and this is so notwithstanding that the person registered as the proprietor was not the proprietor of the design for the purposes of the 1949 Act.

(2) In subsection (1) a "corresponding design", in relation to an artistic work, means a design within the meaning of the 1949 Act which if applied to an article would produce something which would be treated for the purposes of this Part as a copy of the artistic work.

Typefaces

Use of typeface in ordinary course of printing

54.—(1) It is not an infringement of copyright in an artistic work consisting of the design of a typeface—

(a) to use the typeface in the ordinary course of typing, composing text, typesetting or printing,

(b) to possess an article for the purpose of such use, or

(c) to do anything in relation to material produced by such use;

and this is so notwithstanding that an article is used which is an infringing copy of the work.

(2) However, the following provisions of this Part apply in relation to persons making, importing or dealing with articles specifically designed or adapted for producing material in a particular typeface, or possessing such articles for the purpose of dealing with them, as if the production of material as mentioned in

subsection (1) did infringe copyright in the artistic work consisting of the design of the typeface—

> section 24 (secondary infringement: making, importing, possessing or dealing with article for making infringing copy),
>
> sections 99 and 100 (order for delivery up and right of seizure),
>
> section 107(2) (offence of making or possessing such an article), and
>
> section 108 (order for delivery up in criminal proceedings).

(3) The references in subsection (2) to "dealing with" an article are to selling, letting for hire, or offering or exposing for sale or hire, exhibiting in public, or distributing.

Articles for producing material in particular typeface

55.—(1) This section applies to the copyright in an artistic work consisting of the design of a typeface where articles specifically designed or adapted for producing material in that typeface have been marketed by or with the licence of the copyright owner.

(2) After the period of 25 years from the end of the calendar year in which the first such articles are marketed, the work may be copied by making further such articles, or doing anything for the purpose of making such articles, and anything may be done in relation to articles so made, without infringing copyright in the work.

(3) In subsection (1) "marketed" means sold, let for hire or offered or exposed for sale or hire, in the United Kingdom or elsewhere.

Works in electronic form

Transfers of copies of works in electronic form

56.—(1) This section applies where a copy of a work in electronic form has been purchased on terms which, expressly or impliedly or by virtue of any rule of law, allow the purchaser to copy the work, or to adapt it or make copies of an adaptation, in connection with his use of it.

(2) If there are no express terms—

> (a) prohibiting the transfer of the copy by the purchaser, imposing obligations which continue after a transfer, prohibiting the assignment of any licence or terminating any licence on a transfer, or
>
> (b) providing for the terms on which a transferee may do the things which the purchaser was permitted to do,

anything which the purchaser was allowed to do may also be done without infringement of copyright by a transferee; but any copy, adaptation or copy of an adaptation made by the purchaser which is not also transferred shall be treated as an infringing copy for all purposes after the transfer.

(3) The same applies where the original purchased copy is no longer usable and what is transferred is a further copy used in its place.

(4) The above provisions also supply on a subsequent transfer, with the substitution for references in subsection (2) to the purchaser of references to the subsequent transferor.

Miscellaneous: literary, dramatic, musical and artistic works

Anonymous or pseudonymous works: acts permitted on assumptions
as to expiry of copyright or death of author

57.—(1) Copyright in a literary, dramatic, musical or artistic work is not infringed by an act done at a time when, or in pursuance of arrangements made at a time when—

    (a) it is not possible by reasonable inquiry to ascertain the identity of the author, and

    (b) it is reasonable to assume—

        (i) that copyright has expired, or

        (ii) that the author died 50 years or more before the beginning of the calendar year in which the act is done or the arrangements are made.

(2) Subsection (1)(b)(ii) does not apply in relation to—

    (a) a work in which Crown copyright subsists, or

    (b) a work in which copyright originally vested in an international organisation by virtue of section 168 and in respect of which an Order under that section specifies a copyright period longer than 50 years.

(3) In relation to a work of joint authorship—

    (a) the reference in subsection (1) to its being possible to ascertain the identity of the author shall be construed as a reference to its being possible to ascertain the identity of any of the authors, and

    (b) the reference in subsection (1)(b)(ii) to the author having died shall be construed as a reference to all the authors having died.

Use of notes or recordings of spoken words in certain cases

58.—(1) Where a record of spoken words is made, in writing or otherwise, for the purpose—

    (a) of reporting current events, or

    (b) of broadcasting or including in a cable programme service the whole or part of the work,

it is not an infringement of any copyright in the words as a literary work to use the record or material taken from it (or to copy the record, or any such material, and use the copy) for that purpose, provided the following conditions are met.

(2) The conditons are that—

    (a) the record is a direct record of the spoken words and is not taken from a previous record or from a broadcast or cable programme;

    (b) the making of the record was not prohibited by the speaker and, where copyright already subsisted in the work, did not infringe copyright;

    (c) the use made of the record or material taken from it is not of a kind prohibited by or on behalf of the speaker or copyright owner before the record was made; and

    (d) the use is by or with the authority of a person who is lawfully in possession of the record.

Public reading or recitation

59.—(1) The reading or recitation in public by one person of a reasonable extract from a published literary or dramatic work does not infringe any copyright in the work if it is accompanied by a sufficient acknowledgement.

(2) Copyright in a work is not infringed by the making of a sound recording, or the broadcasting or inclusion in a cable programme service, of a reading or recitation which by virtue of subsection (1) does not infringe copyright in the work, provided that the recording, broadcast or cable programme consists mainly of material in relation to which it is not necessary to rely on that subsection.

Abstracts of scientific or technical articles

60.—(1) Where an article on a scientific or technical subject is published in a periodical accompanied by an abstract indicating the contents of the article, it is not an infringement of copyright in the abstract, or in the article, to copy the abstract or issue copies of it to the public.

(2) This section does not apply if or to the extent that there is a licensing scheme certified for the purposes of this section under section 143 providing for the grant of licences.

Recordings of folksongs

61.—(1) A sound recording of a performance of a song may be made for the purpose of including it in an archive maintained by a designated body without infringing any copyright in the words as a literary work or in the accompanying musical work, provided the conditions in subsection (2) below are met.

(2) The conditions are that—

    (a) the words are unpublished and of unknown authorship at the time the recording is made,

    (b) the making of the recording does not infringe any other copyright, and

    (c) its making is not prohibited by any performer.

(3) Copies of a sound recording made in reliance on subsection (1) and included in an archive maintained by a designated body may, if the prescribed conditions are met, be made and supplied by the archivist without infringing copyright in the recording or the works included in it.

(4) The precribed conditions shall include the following—

    (a) that copies are only supplied to persons satisfying the archivist that they require them for purposes of research or private study and will not use them for any other purpose, and

    (b) that no person is furnished with more than one copy of the same recording.

(5) In this section—

    (a) "designated" means designated for the purposes of this section by order of the Secretary of State, who shall not designate a body unless satisfied that it is not established or conducted for profit,

(b) "prescribed" means prescribed for the purposes of this section by order of the Secretary of State, and

(c) references to the archivist include a person acting on his behalf.

(6) An order under this section shall be made by statutory instrument which shall be subject to annulment in pursuance of a resolution of either House of Parliament.

Representation of certain artistic works on public display

62.—(1) This section applies to—

(a) buildings, and

(b) sculptures, models for buildings and works of artistic craftsmanship, if permanently situated in a public place or in premises open to the public.

(2) The copyright in such a work is not infringed by—

(a) making a graphic work representing it,

(b) making a photograph or film of it, or

(c) broadcasting or including in a cable programme service a visual image of it.

(3) Nor is the copyright infringed by the issue to the public of copies, or the broadcasting or inclusion in a cable programme service, of anything whose making was, by virtue of this section, not an infringement of the copyright.

Advertisement of sale of artistic work

63.—(1) It is not an infringement of copyright in an artistic work to copy it, or to issue copies to the public, for the purpose of advertising the sale of the work.

(2) Where a copy which would otherwise be an infringing copy is made in accordance with this section but is subsequently dealt with for any other purpose, it shall be treated as an infringing copy for the purposes of that dealing, and if that dealing infringes copyright for all subsequent purposes.

For this purpose "dealt with" means sold or let for hire, offered or exposed for sale or hire exhibited in public or distributed.

Making of subsequent works by same artist

64. Where the author of an artistic work is not the copyright owner, he does not infringe the copyright by copying the work in making another artistic work, provided he does not repeat or imitate the main design of the earlier work.

Reconstruction of buildings

65. Anything done for the purpose of reconstructing a building does not infringe any copyright—

(a) in the building, or

(b) in any drawings or plans in accordance with which the building was, by or with the licence of the copyright owner, constructed.

Miscellaneous: sound recordings, films and computer programs

Rental of sound recordings, films and computer programs

66.—(1) The Secretary of State may by order provide that in such cases as may be specified in the order the rental to the public of copies of sound recordings, films or computer programs shall be treated as licensed by the copyright owner subject only to the payment of such reasonable royalty or other payment as may be agreed or determined in default of agreement by the Copyright Tribunal.

(2) No such order shall apply if, or to the extent that, there is a licensing scheme certified for the purposes of this section under section 143 providing for the grant of licences.

(3) An order may make different provision for different cases and may specify cases by reference to any factor relating to the work, the copies rented, the renter or the circumstances of the rental.

(4) An order shall be made by statutory instrument; and no order shall be made unless a draft of it has been laid before and approved by a resolution of each House of Parliament.

(5) Copyright in a computer program is not infringed by the rental of copies to the public after the end of the period of 50 years from the end of the calendar year in which copies of it were first issued to the public in electronic form.

(6) Nothing in this section affects any liability under section 23 (secondary infringement) in respect of the rental of infringing copies.

Playing of sound recordings for purposes of club, society, &c.

67.—(1) It is not an infringement of the copyright in a sound recording to play it as part of the activities of, or for the benefit of, a club, society or other organisation if the following conditions are met.

(2) The conditions are—
  (a) that the organisation is not established or conducted for profit and its main objects are charitable or are otherwise concerned with the advancement of religion, education or social welfare, and
  (b) that the proceeds of any charge for admission to the place where the recording is to be heard are applied solely for the purposes of the organisation.

Miscellaneous: broadcasts and cable programmes

Incidental recording for purposes of broadcast or cable programme

68.—(1) This section applies where by virtue of a licence or assignment of copyright a person is authorised to broadcast or include in a cable programme service—

(a) a literary, dramatic or musical work, or an adaptation of such a work,

(b) an artistic work, or

(c) a sound recording or film.

(2) He shall by virtue of this section be treated as licensed by the owner of the copyright in the work to do or authorise any of the following for the purposes of the broadcast or cable programme—

(a) in the case of a literary, dramatic or musical work, or an adaptation of such a work, to make a sound recording or film of the work or adaptation;

(b) in the case of an artistic work, to take a photograph or make a film of the work;

(c) in the case of a sound recording or film, to make a copy of it.

(3) That licence is subject to the condition that the recording, film, photograph or copy in question—

(a) shall not be used for any other purpose, and

(b) shall be destroyed within 28 days of being first used for broadcasting the work or, as the case may be, including it in a cable programme service.

(4) A recording, film, photograph or copy made in accordance with this section shall be treated as an infringing copy—

(a) for the purposes of any use in breach of the condition mentioned in subsection (3)(a), and

(b) for all purposes after that condition or the condition mentioned in subsection (3)(b) is broken.

Recording for purposes of supervision and control of broadcasts and cable programmes

69.—(1) Copyright is not infringed by the making or use by the British Broadcasting Corporation, for the purpose of maintaining supervision and control over programmes broadcast by them, of recordings of those programmes.

(2) Copyright is not infringed by—

(a) the making or use of recordings by the Independent Broadcasting Authority for the purposes mentioned in section 4(7) of the Broadcasting Act 1981 (maintenance of supervision and control over programmes and advertisements); or

(b) anything done under or in pursuance of provision included in a contract between a programme contractor and the Authority in accordance with section 21 of that Act.

(3) Copyright is not infringed by—

(a) the making by or with the authority of the Cable Authority, or the use by that Authority, for the purpose of maintaining supervision and control over programmes included in services licensed under Part I of the Cable and Broadcasting Act 1984, of recordings of those programmes; or

(b) anything done under or in pursuance of—

    (i) a notice or direction given under section 16 of the Cable and Broadcasting Act 1984 (power of Cable Authority to require production of recordings); or

    (ii) a condition included in a licence by virtue of section 35 of that Act (duty of Authority to secure that recordings are available for certain purposes).

Recording for purposes of time shifting

70. The making for private and domestic use of a recording of a broadcast or cable programme solely for the purpose of enabling it to be viewed or listened to at a more convenient time does not infringe any copyright in the broadcast or cable programme or in any work included in it.

Photographs of television broadcasts or cable programmes

71. The making for private and domestic use of a photograph of the whole or any part of an image forming part of a television broadcast or cable programme, or a copy of such a photograph, does not infringe any copyright in the broadcast or cable programme or in any film included in it.

Free public showing or playing of broadcast or cable programme

72.—(1) The showing or playing in public of a broadcast or cable programme to an audience who have not paid for admission to the place where the broadcast or programme is to be seen or heard does not infringe any copyright in—

(a) the broadcast or cable programme, or

(b) any sound recording or film included in it.

(2) The audience shall be treated as having paid for admission to a place—

(a) if they have paid for admission to a place of which that place forms part; or

(b) if goods or services are supplied at that place (or a place of which it forms part)—

    (i) at prices which are substantially attributable to the facilities afforded for seeing or hearing the broadcast or programme, or

    (ii) at prices exceeding those usually charged there and which are partly attributable to those facilities.

(3) The following shall not be regarded as having paid for admission to a place—

(a) persons admitted as residents or inmates of the place;

(b) persons admitted as members of a club or society where the payment is only for membership of the club or society and the provision of facilities for seeing or hearing broadcasts or programmes is only incidental to the main purposes of the club or society.

(4) Where the making of the broadcast or inclusion of the programme in a cable programme service was an infringement of the copyright in a sound recording or film, the fact that it was heard or seen in public by the reception of the broadcast or programme shall be taken into account in assessing the damages for that infringement.

Reception and re-transmission of broadcast in cable programme service

73.—(1) This section applies where a broadcast made from a place in the United Kingdom is, by reception and immediate re-transmission, included in a cable programme service.

(2) The copyright in the broadcast is not infringed—

    (a) if the inclusion is in pursuance of a requirement imposed under section 13(1) of the Cable and Broadcasting Act 1984 (duty of Cable Authority to secure inclusion in cable service of certain programmes), or

    (b) if and to the extent that the broadcast is made for reception in the area in which the cable programme service is provided and is not a satellite transmission or an encrypted transmission.

(3) The copyright in any work included in the broadcast is not infringed—

    (a) if the inclusion is in pursuance of a requirement imposed under section 13(1) of the Cable and Broadcasting Act 1984 (duty of Cable Authority to secure inclusion in cable service of certain programmes), or

    (b) if and to the extent that the broadcast is made for reception in the area in which the cable programme service is provided;

but where the making of the broadcast was an infringement of the copyright in the work, the fact that the broadcast was re-transmitted as a programme in a cable programme service shall be taken into account in assessing the damages for that infringement.

Provision of subtitled copies of broadcast or cable programme

74—(1) A designated body may, for the purpose of providing people who are deaf or hard of hearing, or physically or mentally handicapped in other ways, with copies which are sub-titled or otherwise modified for their special needs, make copies of television broadcasts or cable programmes and issue copies to the public, without infringing any copyright in the broadcasts or cable programmes or works included in them.

(2) A "designated body" means a body designated for the purposes of this section by order of the Secretary of State, who shall not designate a body unless he is satisfied that it is not established or conducted for profit.

(3) An order under this section shall be made by statutory instrument which shall be subject to annulment in pursuance of a resolution of either House of Parliament.

(4) This section does not apply if, or to the extent that, there is a licensing scheme certified for the purposes of this section under section 143 providing for the grant of licences.

Recording for archival purposes

75.—(1) A recording of a broadcast or cable programme of a designated class, or a copy of such a recording, may be made for the purpose of being placed in an archive maintained by a designated body without thereby infringing any copyright in the broadcast or cable programme or in any work included in it.

(2) In subsection (1) "designated" means designated for the purposes of this section by order of the Secretary of State, who shall not designate a body unless he is satisfied that it is not established or conducted for profit.

(3) An order under this section shall be made by statutory instrument which shall be subject to annulment in pursuance of a resolution of either House of Parliament.

Adaptations

76. An act which by virtue of this Chapter may be done without infringing copyright in a literary, dramatic or musical work does not, where that work is an adaptation, infringe any copyright in the work from which the adaptation was made.

CHAPTER IV
MORAL RIGHTS
Rights to be identified as author or director

77.—(1) The author of a copyright literary, dramatic, musical or artistic work, and the director of a copyright film, has the right to be identified as the author or director of the work in the circumstances mentioned in this section; but this right is not infringed unless it has been asserted in accordance with section 78.

(2) The author of a literary work (other than words intended to be sung or spoken with music) or a dramatic work has the right to be identified whenever—

(a) the work is published commercially, performed in public, broadcast or included in a cable programme service; or

(b) copies of a film or sound recording including the work are issued to the public;

and that right includes the right to be identified whenever any of those events occur in relation to an adaptation of the work as the author of the work from which the adaptation was made.

(3) The author of a musical work, or a literary work consisting of words intended to be sung or spoken with music, has the right to be identified whenever—

(a) the work is published commercially;

(b) copies of a sound recording of the work are issued to the public; or

(c) a film of which the sound-track includes the work is shown in public or copies of such a film are issued to the public;

and that right includes the right to be identified whenever any of those events occur in relation to an adaptation of the work as the author of the work from which the adaptation was made.

(4) The author or an artistic work has the right to be identified whenever—

(a) the work is published commercially or exhibited in public, or a visual image of it is broadcast or included in a cable programme service;

(b) a film including a visual image of the work is shown in public or copies of such a film are issued to the public; or

(c) in the case of a work of architecture in the form of a building or a model for a building, a sculpture or a work of artistic craftsmanship, copies of a graphic work representing it, or of a photograph of it, are issued to the public.

(5) The author of a work of architecture in the form of a building also has the right to be identified on the building as constructed or, where more than one building is constructed to the design, on the first to be constructed.

(6) The director of a film has the right to be identified whenever the film is shown in public, broadcast or included in a cable programme service or copies of the film are issued to the public.

(7) The right of the author or director under this section is—

(a) in the case of commercial publication or the issue to the public of copies of a film or sound recording, to be identified in or on each copy or, if that is not appropriate, in some other manner likely to bring his identity to the notice of a person acquiring a copy,

(b) in the case of identification on a building, to be identified by appropriate means visible to persons entering or approaching the building, and

(c) in any other case, to be identified in a manner likely to bring his identity to the attention of a person seeing or hearing the performance, exhibition, showing, broadcast or cable programme in question;

and the identification must in each case be clear and reasonably prominent.

(8) If the author or director in asserting his right to be identified specifies a pseudonym, initials or some other particular form of identification, that form shall be used; otherwise any reasonable form of identification may be used.

(9) This section has effect subject to section 79 (exceptions to right).

Requirement that right be asserted

78.—(1) A person does not infringe the right conferred by section 77 (right to be identified as author or director) by doing any of the acts mentioned in that section unless the right has been asserted in accordance with the following provisions so as to bind him in relation to that act.

(2) The right may be asserted generally, or in relation to any specified act or description of acts—

(a) on an assignment of copyright in the work, by including in the instrument effecting the assignment a statement that the author or director asserts in relation to that work his right to be identified, or

(b) by instrument in writing signed by the author or director.

(3) The right may also be asserted in relation to the public exhibition of an artistic work—

    (a) by securing that when the author or other first owner of copyright parts with possession of the original, or of a copy made by him or under his direction or control, the author is identified on the original or copy, or on a frame, mount or other thing to which it is attached, or

    (b) by including in a licence by which the author or other first owner of copyright authorises the making of copies of the work a statement signed by or on behalf of the person granting the licence that the author asserts his right to be identified in the event of the public exhibition of a copy made in pursuance of the licence.

(4) The persons bound by an assertion of the right under subsection (2) or (3) are—

    (a) in the case of an assertion under subsection (2)(a), the assignee and anyone claiming through him, whether or not he has notice of the assertion;

    (b) in the case of an assertion under subsection (2)(b), anyone to whose notice the assertion is brought;

    (c) in the case of an assertion under subsection (3)(a), anyone into whose hands that original or copy comes, whether or not the identification is still present or visible;

    (d) in the case of an assertion under subsection (3)(b), the licensee and anyone into whose hands a copy made in pursuance of the licence comes, whether or not he has notice of the assertion.

(5) In an action for infringement of the right the court shall, in considering remedies, take into account any delay in asserting the right.

Exceptions to right

79.—(1) The right conferred by section 77 (right to be identified as author or director) is subject to the following exceptions.

(2) The right does not apply in relation to the following descriptions of work—

    (a) a computer program;

    (b) the design of a typeface;

    (c) any computer-generated work.

(3) The right does not apply to anything done by or with the authority of the copyright owner where copyright in the work originally vested—

    (a) in the author's employer by virtue of section 11(2) (works produced in course of employment), or

    (b) in the director's employer by virtue of section 9(2)(a) (person to be treated as author of film).

(4) The right is not infringed by an act which by virtue of any of the following provisions would not infringe copyright in the work—

(a) section 30 (fair dealing for certain purposes), so far as it relates to the reporting of current events by means of a sound recording, film, broadcast or cable programme;

(b) section 31 (incidental inclusion of work in an artistic work, sound recording, film, broadcast or cable programme);

(c) section 32(3) (examination questions);

(d) section 45 (parliamentary and judicial proceedings);

(e) section 46(1) or (2) (Royal Commissions and statutory inquiries);

(f) section 51 (use of design documents and models);

(g) section 52 (effect of exploitation of design derived from artistic work);

(h) section 57 (anonymous or pseudonymous works; acts permitted on assumptions as to expiry of copyright or death of author).

(5) The right does not apply in relation to any work made for the purpose of reporting current events.

(6) The right does not apply in relation to the publication in—

(a) a newspaper, magazine or similar periodical, or

(b) an encyclopaedia, dictionary, yearbook or other collective work of reference,

of a literary, dramatic or artistic work made for the purposes of such publication or made available with the consent of the author for the purposes of such publication.

(7) The right does not apply in relation to—

(a) a work in which Crown copyright or Parliamentary copyright subsists, or

(b) a work in which copyright originally vested in an international organisation by virtue of section 168,

unless the author or director has previously been identified as such in or on published copies of the work.

Right to object to derogatory treatment of work

80.—(1) The author of a copyright literary, dramatic, musical or artistic work, and the director of a copyright film, has the right in the circumstances mentioned in this section not to have his work subjected to derogatory treatment.

(2) For the purposes of this section—

(a) "treatment" of a work means any addition to, deletion from or alteration to or adaptation of the work, other than—

(i) a translation of a literary or dramatic work, or

(ii) an arrangement or transcription of a musical work involving no more than a change of key or register; and

(b) the treatment of a work is derogatory if it amounts to distortion or mutilation of the work of is otherwise prejudicial to the honour or reputation of the author or director;

and in the following provisions of this section references to a derogatory treatment of a work shall be construed accordingly.

(3) In the case of a literary, dramatic or musical work the right is infringed by a person who—

(a) publishes commercially, performs in public, broadcasts or includes in a cable programme service a derogatory treatment of the work; or

(b) issues to the public copies of a film or sound recording of, or including, a derogatory treatment of the work.

(4) In the case of an artistic work the right is infringed by a person who—

(a) publishes commercially or exhibits in public a derogatory treatment of the work, or broadcasts or includes in a cable programme service a visual image of a derogatory treatment of the work,

(b) shows in public a film including a visual image of a derogatory treatment of the work or issues to the public copies of such a film, or

(c) in the case of—

(i) a work of architecture in the form of a model for a building,

(ii) a sculpture, or

(iii) a work of artistic craftsmanship,

issues to the public copies of a graphic work representing, or of a photograph of, a derogatory treatment of the work.

(5) Subsection (4) does not apply to a work of architecture in the form of a building; but where the author of such a work is identified on the building and it is the subject of derogatory treatment he has the right to require the identification to be removed.

(6) In the case of a film, the right is infringed by a person who—

(a) shows in public, broadcasts or includes in a cable programme service a derogatory treatment of the film; or

(b) issues to the public copies of a derogatory treatment of the film,

or who, along with the film, plays in public, broadcasts or includes in a cable programme service, or issues to the public copies of, a derogatory treatment of the film sound-track.

(7) The right conferred by this section extends to the treatment of parts of a work resulting from a previous treatment by a person other than the author or director, if those parts are attributed to, or are likely to be regarded as the work of, the author or director.

(8) This section has effect subject to sections 81 and 82 (exceptions to and qualifications of right).

Exceptions to right

81.—(1) The right conferred by section 80 (right to object to derogatory treatment of work) is subject to the following exceptions.

(2) The right does not apply to a computer program or to any computer-generated work.

(3) The right does not apply in relation to any work made for the purpose of reporting current events.

(4) The right does not apply in relation to the publication in—

(a) a newspaper, magazine or similar periodical, or

(b) an encyclopaedia, dictionary, yearbook or other collective work of reference,

of a literary, dramatic, musical or artistic work made for the purposes of such publication or made available with the consent of the author for the purposes of such publication.

Nor does the right apply in relation to any subsequent exploitation elsewhere of such a work without any modification of the published version.

(5) The right is not infringed by an act which by virtue of section 57 (anonymous or pseudonymous works: acts permitted on assumptions as to expiry of copyright or death of author) would not infringe copyright.

(6) The right is not infringed by anything done for the purpose of—

(a) avoiding the commission of an offence,

(b) complying with a duty imposed by or under an enactment, or

(c) in the case of the British Broadcasting Corporation, avoiding the inclusion in a programme broadcast by them of anything which offends against good taste or decency or which is likely to encourage or incite to crime or to lead to disorder or to be offensive to public feeling,

provided, where the author or director is identified at the time of the relevant act or has previously been identified in or on published copies of the work, that there is a sufficient disclaimer.

Qualification of right in certain cases

82.—(1) This section applies to—

(a) works in which copyright originally vested in the author's employer by virtue of section 11(2) (works produced in course of employment) or in the director's employer by virtue of section 9(2)(a) (person to be treated as author of film),

(b) works in which Crown copyright or Parliamentary copyright subsists, and

(c) works in which copyright originally vested in an international organisation by virtue of section 168.

(2) The right conferred by section 80 (right to object to derogatory treatment of work) does not apply to anything done in relation to such a work by or with the authority of the copyright owner unless the author or director—

(a) is identified at the time of the relevant act, or

(b) has previously been identified in or on published copies of the work;

and where in such a case the right does apply, it is not infringed if there is a sufficient disclaimer.

Infringement of right by possessing or dealing with infringing article

83.—(1) The right conferred by section 80 (right to object to derogatory treatment of work) is also infringed by a person who—

(a) possesses in the course of a business, or

(b) sells or lets for hire, or offers or exposes for sale or hire, or

(c) in the course of a business exhibits in public or distributes, or

(d) distributes otherwise than in the course of a business so as to affect prejudicially the honour or reputation of the author or director,

an article which is, and which he knows or has reason to believe is, an infringing article.

(2) An "infringing article" means a work or a copy of a work which—

(a) has been subjected to derogatory treatment within the meaning of section 80, and

(b) has been or is likely to be the subject of any of the acts mentioned in that section in circumstances infringing that right.

False attribution of work

False attribution of work

84.—(1) A person has the right in the circumstances mentioned in this section—

(a) not to have a literary, dramatic, musical or artistic work falsely attributed to him as author, and

(b) not to have a film falsely attributed to him as director;

and in this section an "attribution", in relation to such a work, means a statement (express or implied) as to who is the author or director.

(2) The right is infringed by a person who—

(a) issues to the public copies of a work of any of those descriptions in or on which there is a false attribution, or

(b) exhibits in public an artistic work, or a copy of an artistic work, in or on which there is a false attribution.

(3) The right is also infringed by a person who—

(a) in the case of a literary, dramatic or musical work, performs the work in public, broadcasts it or includes it in a cable programme service as being the work of a person, or

(b) in the case of a film, shows it in public, broadcasts it or includes it in a cable programme service as being directed by a person,

knowing or having reason to believe that the attribution is false.

(4) The right is also infringed by the issue to the public or public display of material containing a false attribution in connection with any of the acts mentioned in subsection (2) or (3).

(5) The right is also infringed by a person who in the course of a business—

(a) possesses or deals with a copy of a work of any of the descriptions mentioned in subsection (1) in or on which there is a false attribution, or

(b) in the case of an artistic work, possesses or deals with the work itself when there is a false attribution in or on it,

knowing or having reason to believe that there is such an attribution and that it is false.

(6) In the case of an artistic work the right is also infringed by a person who in the course of a business—

(a) deals with a work which has been altered after the author parted with possession of it as being the unaltered work of the author, or

(b) deals with a copy of such a work as being a copy of the unaltered work of the author,

knowing or having reason to believe that that is not the case.

(7) References in this section to dealing are to selling or letting for hire, offering or exposing for sale or hire, exhibiting in public, or distributing.

(8) This section applies where, contrary to the fact—

(a) a literary, dramatic or musical work is falsely represented as being an adaptation of the work of a person, or

(b) a copy of an artistic work is falsely represented as being a copy made by the author of the artistic work,

as it applies where the work is falsely attributed to a person as author.

Right to privacy of certain photographs and films

Right to privacy of certain photographs and films

85.—(1) A person who for private and domestic purposes commissions the taking of a photograph or the making of a film has, where copyright subsists in the resulting work, the right not to have—

(a) copies of the work issued to the public,

(b) the work exhibited or shown in public, or

(c) the work broadcast or included in a cable programme service;

and, except as mentioned in subsection (2), a person who does or authorises the doing of any of those acts infringes that right.

(2) The right is not infringed by an act which by virtue of any of the following provisions would not infringe copyright in the work—

(a) section 31 (incidental inclusion of work in an artistic work, film, broadcast or cable programme);

(b) section 45 (parliamentary and judicial proceedings);

(c) section 46 (Royal Commissions and statutory inquiries);

(d) section 50 (acts done under statutory authority);

(e) section 57 (anonymous or pseudonymous works: acts permitted on assumptions as to expiry of copyright or death of author).

Supplementary

Duration of rights

86.—(1) The rights conferred by section 77 (right to be identified as author or director), section 80 (right to object to derogatory treatment of work) and section 85 (right to privacy of certain photographs and films) continue to subsist so long as copyright subsists in the work.

(2) The right conferred by section 84 (false attribution) continues to subsist until 20 years after a person's death.

Consent and waiver of rights

87.—(1) It is not an infringement of any of the rights conferred by this Chapter to do any act to which the person entitled to the right has consented.

(2) Any of those rights may be waived by instrument in writing signed by the person giving up the right.

(3) A waiver—

   (a) may relate to a specific work, to works of a specified description or to works generally, and may relate to existing or future works, and

   (b) may be conditional or unconditional and may be expressed to be subject to revocation;

and if made in favour of the owner or prospective owner of the copyright in the work or works to which it relates, it shall be presumed to extend to his licensees and successors in title unless a contrary intention is expressed.

(4) Nothing in this Chapter shall be construed as excluding the operation of the general law of contract or estoppel in relation to an informal waiver or other transaction in relation to any of the rights mentioned in subsection (1).

Application of provisions to joint works

88.—(1) The right conferred by section 77 (right to be identified as author or director) is, in the case of a work of joint authorship, a right of each joint author to be identified as a joint author and must be asserted in accordance with section 78 by each joint author in relation to himself.

(2) The right conferred by section 80 (right to object to derogatory treatment of work) is, in the case of a work of joint authorship, a right of each joint author and his right is satisfied if he consents to the treatment in question.

(3) A waiver under section 87 of those rights by one joint author does not affect the rights of the other joint authors.

(4) The right conferred by section 84 (false attribution) is infringed, in the circumstances mentioned in that section—

   (a) by any false statement as to the authorship of a work of joint authorship, and

   (b) by the false attribution of joint authorship in relation to a work of sole authorship;

and such a false attribution infringes the right of every person to whom authorship of any description is, whether rightly or wrongly, attributed.

(5) The above provisions also apply (with any necessary adaptations) in relation to a film which was, or is alleged to have been, jointly directed, as they apply to a work which is, or is alleged to be, a work of joint authorship.

A film is "jointly directed" if it is made by the collaboration of two or more directors and the contribution of each director is not distinct from that of the other director or directors.

(6) The right conferred by section 85 (right to privacy of certain photographs and films) is, in the case of a work made in pursuance of a joint commission, a right of each person who commissioned the making of the work, so that—

(a) the right of each is satisfied if he consents to the act in question, and

(b) a waiver under section 87 by one of them does not affect the rights of the others.

Application of provisions to parts of works

89.—(1) The rights conferred by section 77 (right to be identified as author or director) and section 85 (right to privacy of certain photographs and films) apply in relation to the whole or any substantial part of work.

(2) The rights conferred by section 80 (right to object to derogatory treatment of work) and section 84 (false attribution) apply in relation to the whole or any part of a work.

Chapter V

Dealings with Rights in Copyright Works

Copyright

Assignment and licences

90.—(1) Copyright is transmissible by assignment, by testamentary disposition or by operation of law, as personal or moveable property.

(2) An assignment or other transmission of copyright may be partial, that is, limited so as to apply—

(a) to one or more, but not all, of the things the copyright owner has the exclusive right to do;

(b) to part, but not the whole, of the period for which the copyright is to subsist.

(3) An assignment of copyright is not effective unless it is in writing signed by or on behalf of the assignor.

(4) A licence granted by a copyright owner is binding on every successor in title to his interest in the copyright, except a purchaser in good faith for valuable consideration and without notice (actual or constructive) of the licence or a person deriving title from such a purchaser; and references in this Part to doing anything with, or without, the licence of the copyright owner shall be construed accordingly.

Prospective ownership of copyright

91.—(1) Where by an agreement made in relation to future copyright, and signed by or on behalf of the prospective owner of the copyright, the prospective owner purports to assign the future copyright (wholly or partially) to another person, then if, on the copyright coming into existence, the assignee or another person claiming under him would be entitled as against all other persons to require the copyright to be vested in him, the copyright shall vest in the assignee or his successor in title by virtue of this subsection.

(2) In this Part—

"future copyright" means copyright which will or may come into existence in respect of a future work or class of works or on the occurrence of a future event; and

"prospective owner" shall be construed accordingly, and includes a person who is prospectively entitled to copyright by virtue of such an agreement as is mentioned in subsection (1).

(3) A licence granted by a prospective owner of copyright is binding on every successor in title to his interest (or prospective interest) in the right, except a purchaser in good faith for valuable consideration and without notice (actual or constructive) of the licence or a person deriving title from such a purchaser; and references in this Part to doing anything with, or without, the licence of the copyright owner shall be construed accordingly.

Exclusive licences

92.—(1) In this Part an "exclusive licence" means a licence in writing signed by or on behalf of the copyright owner authorising the licensee to the exclusion of all other persons, including the person granting the licence, to exercise a right which would otherwise be exercisable exclusively by the copyright owner.

(2) The licensee under an exclusive licence has the same rights against a successor in title who is bound by the licence as he has against the person granting the licence.

Copyright to pass under will with unpublished work

93. Where under a bequest (whether specific or general) a person is entitled, beneficially or otherwise, to—

(a) an original document or other material thing recording or embodying a literary, dramatic, musical or artistic work which was not published before the death of the testator, or

(b) an original material thing containing a sound recording or film which was not published before the death of the testator,

the bequest shall, unless a contrary intention is indicated in the testator's will or a codicil to it, be construed as including the copyright in the work in so far as the testator was the owner of the copyright immediately before his death.

Moral rights

Moral rights not assignable

94. The rights conferred by Chapter IV (moral rights) are not assignable.

Transmission of moral rights on death

95—(1) On the death of a person entitled to the right conferred by section 77 (right to identification of author or director), section 80 (right to object to derogatory treatment of work) or section 85 (right to privacy of certain photographs and films)—

    (a) the right passes to such person as he may by testamentary disposition specifically direct,

    (b) if there is no such direction but the copyright in the work in question forms part of his estate, the right passes to the person to whom the copyright passes, and

    (c) if or to the extent that the right does not pass under paragraph (a) or (b) it is exercisable by his personal representatives.

(2) Where copyright forming part of a person's estate passes in part to one person and in part to another, as for example where a bequest is limited so as to apply—

    (a) to one or more, but not all, of the things the copyright owner has the exclusive right to do or authorise, or

    (b) to part, but not the whole, of the period for which the copyright is to subsist.

any right which passes with the copyright by virtue of subsection (1) is correspondingly divided.

(3) Where by virtue of subsection (1)(a) or (b) a right becomes exercisable by more than one person—

    (a) it may, in the case of the right conferred by section 77 (right to identification of author or director), be asserted by any of them;

    (b) it is, in the case of the right conferred by section 80 (right to object to derogatory treatment of work) or section 85 (right to privacy of certain photographs and films), a right exercisable by each of them and is satisfied in relation to any of them if he consents to the treatment or act in question; and

    (c) any waiver of the right in accordance with section 87 by one of them does not affect the rights of the others.

(4) A consent or waiver previously given or made binds any person to whom a right passes by virtue of subsection (1).

(5) Any infringement after a person's death of the right conferred by section 84 (false attribution) is actionable by his personal representatives.

(6) Any damages recovered by personal representatives by virtue of this section in respect of an infringement after a person's death shall devolve as part of his estate as if the right of action had subsisted and been vested in him immediately before his death.

Chapter VI

Remedies for Infringement

Rights and remedies of copyright owner

Infringement actionable by copyright owner

96.—(1) An infringement of copyright is actionable by the copyright owner.

(2) In an action for infringement of copyright all such relief by way of damages, injunctions, accounts or otherwise is available to the plaintiff as is available in respect of the infringement of any other property right.

(3) This section has effect subject to the following provisions of this Chapter.

Provisions as to damages in infringement action

97.—(1) Where in an action for infringement of copyright it is shown that at the time of the infringement the defendant did not know, and had no reason to believe, that copyright subsisted in the work to which the action relates, the plaintiff is not entitled to damages against him, but without prejudice to any other remedy.

(2) The court may in an action for infringement of copyright having regard to all the circumstances, and in particular to—

(a) the flagrancy of the infringement, and

(b) any benefit accruing to the defendant by reason of the infringement,

award such additional damages as the justice of the case may require.

Undertaking to take licence of right in infringement proceedings

98.—(1) If in proceedings for infringement of copyright in respect of which a licence is available as of right under section 44 (powers exercisable in consequence of report of Monopolies and Mergers Commission) the defendant undertakes to take a licence on such terms as may be agreed or, in default of agreement, settled by the Copyright Tribunal under that section—

(a) no injunction shall be granted against him,

(b) no order for delivery up shall be made under section 99, and

(c) the amount recoverable against him by way of damages or on an account of profits shall not exceed double the amount which would have been payable by him as licensee if such a licence on those terms had been granted before the earliest infringement.

(2) An undertaking may be given at any time before final order in the proceedings, without any admission of liability.

(3) Nothing in this section affects the remedies available in respect of an infringement committed before licences of right were available.

Order for delivery up

99.—(1) Where a person—

(a) has an infringing copy of a work in his possession, custody or control in the course of a business, or

(b) has in the possession, custody or control an article specifically designed or adapted for making copies of a particular copyright work, knowing or having reason to believe that it has been or is to be used to make infringing copies,

the owner of the copyright in the work may apply to the court for an order that the infringing copy or article be delivered up to him or to such other person as the court may direct.

(2) An application shall not be made after the end of the period specified in section 113 (period after which remedy of delivery up not available); and no order shall be made unless the court also makes, or it appears to the court that there are grounds for making, an order under section 114 (order as to disposal of infringing copy or other article).

(3) A person to whom an infringing copy or other article is delivered up in pursuance of an order under this section shall, if an order under section 114 is not made, retain it pending the making of an order, or the decision not to make an order, under that section.

(4) Nothing in this section affects any other power of the court.

Right to seize infringing copies and other articles

100.—(1) An infringing copy of a work which is found exposed or otherwise immediately available for sale or hire, and in respect of which the copyright owner would be entitled to apply for an order under section 99, may be seized and detained by him or a person authorised by him.

The right to seize and detain is exercisable subject to the following conditions and is subject to any decision of the court under section 114.

(2) Before anything is seized under this section notice of the time and place of the proposed seizure must be given to a local police station.

(3) A person may for the purpose of exercising the right conferred by this section enter premises to which the public have access but may not seize anything in the possession, custody or control of a person at a permanent or regular place of business of his, and may not use any force.

(4) At the time when anything is seized under this section there shall be left at the place where it was seized a notice in the prescribed form containing the prescribed particulars as to the person by whom or on whose authority the seizure is made and the grounds on which it is made.

(5) In this section—

"premises" includes land, buildings, moveable structures, vehicles, vessels, aircraft and hovercraft; and

"prescribed" means prescribed by order of the Secretary of State.

(6) An order of the Secretary of State under this section shall be made by statutory instrument which shall be subject to annulment in pursuance of a resolution of either House of Parliament.

Rights and remedies of exclusive licensee

Rights and remedies of exclusive licensee

101.—(1) An exclusive licensee has, except against the copyright owner, the same rights and remedies in respect of matters occurring after the grant of the licence as if the licence had been an assignment.

(2) His rights and remedies are concurrent with those of the copyright owner; and references in the relevant provisions of this Part to the copyright owner shall be construed accordingly.

(3) In an action brought by an exclusive licensee by virtue of this section a defendant may avail himself of any defence which would have been available to him if the action had been brought by the copyright owner.

Exercise of concurrent rights

102.—(1) Where an action for infringement of copyright brought by the copyright owner or an exclusive licensee relates (wholly or partly) to an infringement in respect of which they have concurrent rights of action, the copyright owner or, as the case may be, the exclusive licensee may not, without the leave of the court, proceed with the action unless the other is either joined as a plaintiff or added as a defendant.

(2) A copyright owner or exclusive licensee who is added as a defendant in pursuance of subsection (1) is not liable for any costs in the action unless he takes part in the proceedings.

(3) The above provisions do not affect the granting of interlocutory relief on an application by a copyright owner or exclusive licensee alone.

(4) Where an action for infringement of copyright is brought which relates (wholly or partly) to an infringement in respect of which the copyright owner and an exclusive licensee have or had concurrent rights of action—

(a) the court shall in assessing damages take into account—

(i) the terms of the licence, and

(ii) any pecuniary remedy already awarded or available to either of them in respect of the infringement;

(b) no account of profits shall be directed if an award of damages has been made, or an account of profits has been directed, in favour of the other of them in respect of the infringement; and

(c) the court shall if an account of profits is directed apportion the profits between them as the court considers just, subject to any agreement between them;

and these provisions apply whether or not the copyright owner and the exclusive licensee are both parties to the action.

(5) The copyright owner shall notify any exclusive licensee having concurrent rights before applying for an order under section 99 (order for delivery up) or exercising the right conferred by section 100 (right of seizure); and the court may on the application of the licensee make such order under section 99 or, as the case may be, prohibiting or permitting the exercise by the copyright owner of the right conferred by section 100, as it thinks fit having regard to the terms of the licence.

Remedies for infringement of moral rights

Remedies for infringement of moral rights

103.—(1) An infringment of a right conferred by Chapter IV (moral rights) is actionable as a breach of statutory duty owed to the person entitled to the right.

(2) In proceedings for infringement of the right conferred by section 80 (right to object to derogatory treatment of work) the court may, if it thinks it is an adequate remedy in the circumstances, grant an injunction on terms prohibiting the doing of any act unless a disclaimer is made, in such terms and in such manner as may be approved by the court, dissociating the author or director from the treatment of the work.

Presumptions

Presumptions relevant to literary, dramatic, musical and artistic works

104.—(1) The following presumptions apply in proceedings brought by virtue of this Chapter with respect to a literary, dramatic, musical or artistic work.

(2) Where a name purporting to be that of the author appeared on copies of the work as published or on the work when it was made, the person whose name appeared shall be presumed, until the contrary is proved—

    (a) to be the author of the work;

    (b) to have made it in circumstances not falling within section 11(2), 163, 165 or 168 (works produced in course of employment, Crown copyright, Parliamentary copyright or copyright of certain international organisations).

(3) In the case of a work alleged to be a work of joint authorship, subsection (2) applies in relation to each person alleged to be one of the authors.

(4) Where no name purporting to be that of the author appeared as mentioned in subsection (2) but—

    (a) the work qualifies for copyright protection by virtue of section 155 (qualification by reference to country of first publication), and

    (b) a name purporting to be that of the publisher appeared on copies of the work as first published,

the person whose name appeared shall be presumed, until the contrary is proved, to have been the owner of the copyright at the time of publication.

(5) If the author of the work is dead or the identity of the author cannot be ascertained by reasonable inquiry, it shall be presumed, in the absence of evidence to the contrary—

    (a) that the work is an original work, and

    (b) that the plaintiff's allegations as to what was the first publication of the work and as to the country of first publication are correct.

Presumptions relevant to sound recordings and films

105.—(1) In proceedings brought by virtue of this Chapter with respect to a sound recording, where copies of the recording as issued to the public bear a label or other mark stating—

(a) that a named person was the owner of copyright in the recording at the date of issue of the copies, or

(b) that the recording was first published in a specified year or in a specified country,

the label or mark shall be admissible as evidence of the facts stated and shall be presumed to be correct until the contrary is proved.

(2) In proceedings brought by virtue of this Chapter with respect to a film, where copies of the film as issued to the public bear a statement—

(a) that a named person was the author or director of the film,

(b) that a named person was the owner of copyright in the film at the date of issue of the copies, or

(c) that the film was first published in a specified year or in a specified country,

the statement shall be admissible as evidence of the facts stated and shall be presumed to be correct until the contrary is proved.

(3) In proceedings brought by virtue of this Chapter with respect to a computer program, where copies of the program are issued to the public in electronic form bearing a statement—

(a) that a named person was the owner of copyright in the program at the date of issue of the copies, or

(b) that the program was first published in a specified country or that copies of it were first issued to the public in electronic form in a specified year,

the statement shall be admissible as evidence of the facts stated and shall be presumed to be correct until the contrary is proved.

(4) The above presumptions apply equally in proceedings relating to an infringement alleged to have occurred before the date on which the copies were issued to the public.

(5) In proceedings brought by virtue of this Chapter with respect to a film, where the film as shown in public, broadcast or included in a cable programme service bears a statement—

(a) that a named person was the author or director of the film, or

(b) that a named person was the owner of copyright in the film immediately after it was made,

the statement shall be admissible as evidence of the facts stated and shall be presumed to be correct until the contrary is proved.

This presumption applies equally in proceedings relating to an infringement alleged to have occurred before the date on which the film was shown in public, broadcast or included in a cable programme service.

Presumptions relevant to works subject to Crown copyright

106.—(1) In proceedings brought by virtue of this Chapter with respect to a literary, dramatic or musical work in which Crown copyright subsists, where there appears on printed copies of the work a statement of the year in which the work was first published commercially, that statement shall be admissible as evidence of the fact stated and shall be presumed to be correct in the absence of evidence to the contrary.

Offences

Criminal liability for making or dealing with infringing articles, &c

107.—(1) A person commits an offence who, without the licence of the copyright owner—

(a) makes for sale or hire, or

(b) imports into the United kingdom otherwise than for his private and domestic use, or

(c) possesses in the course of a business with a view to committing any act infringing the copyright, or

(d) in the course of a business—

    (i) sells or lets for hire, or

    (ii) offers or exposes for sale or hire, or

    (iii) exhibits in public, or

    (iv) distributes, or

(e) distributes otherwise than in the course of a business to such an extent as to affect prejudicially the owner of the copyright,

an article which is, and which he knows or has reason to believe is, an infringing copy of a copyright work.

(2) A person commits an offence who—

(a) makes an article specifically designed or adapted for making copies of a particular copyright work, or

(b) has such an article in his possession,

knowing or having reason to believe that it is to be used to make infringing copies for sale or hire or for use in the course of a business.

(3) Where copyright is infringed (otherwise than by reception of a broadcast or cable programme)—

(a) by the public performance of a literary, dramatic or musical work, or

(b) by the playing or showing in public of a sound recording or film,

any person who caused the work to be so performed, played or shown is guilty of an offence if he knew or had reason to believe that copyright would be infringed.

(4) A person guilty of an offence under subsection (1)(a), (b), (d)(iv) or (e) is liable—

(a) on summary conviction to imprisonment for a term not exceeding six months or a fine not exceeding the statutory maximum, or both;

(b) on conviction on indictment to a fine or imprisonment for a term not exceeding two years, or both.

(5) A person guilty of any other offence under this section is liable on summary conviction to imprisonment for a term not exceeding six months or a fine not exceeding level 5 on the standard scale, or both.

(6) Sections 104 to 106 (presumptions as to various matters connected with copyright) do not apply to proceedings for an offence under this section; but without prejudice to their application in proceedings for an order under section 108 below.

Order for delivery up in criminal proceedings

108.—(1) The court before which proceedings are brought against a person for an offence under section 107 may, if satisfied that at the time of his arrest or charge—

(a) he had in his possession, custody or control in the course of a business an infringing copy of a copyright work, or

(b) he had in his possession, custody or control an article specifically designed or adapted for making copies of a particular copyright work, knowing or having reason to believe that it had been or was to be used to make infringing copies,

order that the infringing copy or article be delivered up to the copyright owner or to such other person as the court may direct.

(2) For this purpose a person shall be treated as charged with an offence—

(a) in England, Wales and Northern Ireland, when he is orally charged or is served with a summons or indictment;

(b) in Scotland, when he is cautioned, charged or served with a complaint or indictment.

(3) An order may be made by the court of its own motion or on the application of the prosecutor (or, in Scotland, the Lord Advocate or procurator-fiscal), and may be made whether or not the person is convicted of the offence, but shall not be made—

(a) after the end of the period specified in section 113 (period after which remedy of delivery up not available), or

(b) if it appears to the court unlikely that any order will be made under section 114 (order as to disposal of infringing copy or other article).

(4) An appeal lies from an order made under this section by a magistrates' court—

(a) in England and Wales, to the Crown Court, and

(b) in Northern Ireland, to the county court;

and in Scotland, where an order has been made under this section, the person from whose possession, custody or control the infringing copy or article has been removed may, without prejudice to any other form of appeal under any rule of law, appeal against that order in the same manner as against sentence.

(5) A person to whom an infringing copy or other article is delivered up in pursuance of an order under this section shall retain it pending the making of an order, or the decision not to make an order, under section 114.

(6) Nothing in this section affects the powers of the court under section 43 of the Powers of Criminal Courts Act 1973, section 223 or 436 of the Criminal Procedure (Scotland) Act 1975 or Article 7 of the Criminal Justice (Northern Ireland) Order 1980 (general provisions as to forfeiture in criminal proceedings).

Search warrants

109.—(1) Where a justice of the peace (in Scotland, a sheriff or justice of the peace) is satisfied by information on oath given by a constable (in Scotland, by evidence on oath) that there are reasonable grounds for believing—

(a) that an offence under section 107(1)(a), (b), (d)(iv) or (e) has been or is about to be committed in any premises, and

(b) that evidence that such an offence has been or is about to be committed is in those premises,

he may issue a warrant authorising a constable to enter and search the premises, using such reasonable force as is necessary.

(2) The power conferred by subsection (1) does not, in England and Wales, extend to authorising a search for material of the kinds mentioned in section 9(2) of the Police and Criminal Evidence Act 1984 (certain classes of personal or confidential material).

(3) A warrant under this section—

(a) may authorise persons to accompany any constable executing the warrant, and

(b) remains in force for 28 days from the date of its issue.

(4) In executing a warrant issued under this section a constable may seize an article if he reasonably believes that it is evidence that any offence under section 107(1) has been or is about to be committed.

(5) In this section "premises" includes land, buildings, moveable structures, vehicles, vessels, aircraft and hovercraft.

Offence by body corporate: liability of officers

110.—(1) Where an offence under section 107 committed by a body corporate is proved to have been committed with the consent or connivance of a director, manager, secretary or other similar officer of the body, or a person purporting to act in any such capacity, he as well as the body corporate is guilty of the offence and liable to be proceeded against and punished accordingly.

(2) In relation to a body corporate whose affairs are managed by its members "director" means a member of the body corporate.

Provision for preventing importation of infringing copies

Infringing copies may be treated as prohibited goods

111.—(1) The owner of the copyright in a published literary, dramatic or musical work may give notice in writing to the Commissioners of Customs and Excise—

(a) that he is the owner of the copyright in the work, and

(b) that he requests the Commissioners, for a period specified in the notice, to treat as prohibited goods printed copies of the work which are infringing copies.

(2) The period specified in a notice under subsection (1) shall not exceed five years and shall not extend beyond the period for which copyright is to subsist.

(3) The owner of the copyright in a sound recording or film may give notice in writing to the Commissioners of Customs and Excise—

(a) that he is the owner of the copyright in the work,

(b) that infringing copies of the work are expected to arrive in the United Kingdom at a time and a place specified in the notice, and

(c) that he requests the Commissioners to treat the copies as prohibited goods.

(4) When a notice is in force under this section the importation of goods to which the notice relates, otherwise than by a person for his private and domestic use, is prohibited; but a person is not by reason of the prohibition liable to any penalty other than forfeiture of the goods.

Power of Commissioners of Customs and Excise to make regulations

112.—(1) The Commissioners of Customs and Excise may make regulations prescribing the form in which notice is to be given under section 111 and requiring a person giving notice—

(a) to furnish the Commissioners with such evidence as may be specified in the regulations, either on giving notice or when the goods are imported, or at both those times, and

(b) to comply with such other conditions as may be specified in the regulations.

(2) The regulations may, in particular, require a person giving such a notice—

(a) to pay such fees in respect of the notice as may be specified by the regulations;

(b) to give such security as may be so specified in respect of any liability or expense which the Commissioners may incur in consequence of the notice by reason of the detention of any article or anything done to an article detained;

(c) to indemnify the Commissioners against any such liability or expense, whether security has been given or not.

(3) The regulations may make different provision as respects different classes of case to which they apply and may include such incidental and supplementary provisions as the Commissioners consider expedient.

(4) Regulations under this section shall be made by statutory instrument which shall be subject to annulment in pursuance of a resolution of either House of Parliament.

(5) Section 17 of the Customs and Excise Management Act 1979 (general provisions as to Commissioners' receipts) applies to fees paid in pursuance of

regulations under this section as to receipts under the enactments relating to customs and excise.

Supplementary

Period after which remedy of delivery up not available

113.—(1) An application for an order under section 99 (order for delivery up in civil proceedings) may not be made after the end of the period of six years from the date on which the infringing copy or article in question was made, subject to the following provisions.

(2) If during the whole or any part of that period the copyright owner—

    (a) is under a disability, or

    (b) is prevented by fraud or concealment from discovering the facts entitling him to apply for an order.

an application may be made at any time before the end of the period of six years from the date on which he ceased to be under a disability or, as the case may be, could with reasonable diligence have discovered those facts.

(3) In subsection (2) "disability"—

    (a) in England and Wales, has the same meaning as in the Limitation Act 1980;

    (b) in Scotland, means legal disability within the meaning of the Prescription and Limitation (Scotland) Act 1973;

    (c) in Northern Ireland, has the same meaning as in the Statute of Limitations (Northern Ireland) 1958.

(4) An order under section 108 (order for delivery up in criminal proceedings) shall not, in any case, be made after the end of the period of six years from the date on which the infringing copy or article in question was made.

Order as to disposal of infringing copy or other article

114.—(1) An application may be made to the court for an order that an infringing copy or other article delivered up in pursuance of an order under section 99 or 108, or seized and detained in pursuance of the right conferred by section 100, shall be—

    (a) forfeited to the copyright owner, or

    (b) destroyed or otherwise dealt with as the court may think fit, or for a decision that no such order should be made.

(2) In considering what order (if any) should be made, the court shall consider whether other remedies available in an action for infringment of copyright would be adequate to compensate the copyright owner and to protect his interests.

(3) Provision shall be made by rules of court as to the service of notice on persons having an interest in the copy or other articles, and any such person is entitled—

    (a) to appear in proceedings for an order under this section, whether or not he was served with notice, and

(b) to appeal against any order made, whether or not he appeared;

and an order shall not take effect until the end of the period within which notice of an appeal may be given or, if before the end of that period notice of appeal is duly given, until the final determination or abandonment of the proceedings on the appeal.

(4) Where there is more than one person interested in a copy or other article, the court shall make such order as it thinks just and may (in particular) direct that the article be sold, or otherwise dealt with, and the proceeds divided.

(5) If the court decides that no order should be made under this section, the person in whose possession, custody or control the copy of other article was before being delivered up or seized is entitled to its return.

(6) References in this section to a person having an interest in a copy or other article include any person in whose favour an order could be made in respect of it under this section or under section 204 or 231 of this Act or section 58C of the Trade Marks Act 1938 (which make similar provision in relation to infringement of rights in performances, design right and trade marks).

Jurisdiction of county court and sheriff court

115.—(1) In England, Wales and Northern Ireland a county court may entertain proceedings under—

section 99 (order for delivery up of infringing copy or other article),

section 101(5) (order as to exercise of rights by copyright owner where exclusive licensee has concurrent rights), or

section 114 (order as to disposal of infringing copy or other article),

where the value of the infringing copies and other articles in question does not exceed the county court limit for actions in tort.

(2) In Scotland proceedings for an order under any of those provisions may be brought in the sheriff court.

(3) Nothing in this section shall be construed as affecting the jurisdiction of the High Court or, in Scotland, the Court of Session.

CHAPTER VII

COPYRIGHT LICENSING

Licensing schemes and licensing bodies

Licensing schemes and licensing bodies

116.—(1) In this Part a "licensing scheme" means a scheme setting out—

(a) the classes of case in which the operator of the scheme, or the person on whose behalf he acts, is willing to grant copyright licences, and

(b) the terms on which licences would be granted in those classes of case;

and for this purpose a "scheme" includes anything in the nature of a scheme, whether described as a scheme or as a tariff or by any other name.

(2) In this Chapter a "licensing body" means a society or other organisation which has as its main object, or one of its main objects, the negotiation or

granting, either as owner or prospective owner of copyright or as agent for him, of copyright licences, and whose objects include the granting of licences covering works of more than one author.

(3) In this section "copyright licences" means licences to do, or authorise the doing of, any of the acts restricted by copyright.

(4) References in this Chapter to licences or licensing schemes covering works of more than one author do not include licences or schemes covering only—

(a) a single collective work or collective works of which the authors are the same, or

(b) works made by, or by employees of or commissioned by, a single individual, firm, company or group of companies.

For this purpose a group of companies means a holding company and its subsidiaries, within the meaning of section 736 of the Companies Act 1985.

References and applications with respect to licensing schemes

Licensing schemes to which ss. 118 to 123 apply

117. Sections 118 and 123 (references and applications with respect to licensing schemes) apply to—

(a) licensing schemes operated by licensing bodies in relation to the copyright in literary, dramatic, musical or artistic works or films (or film sound-tracks when accompanying a film) which cover works of more than one author, so far as they relate to licences for—

(i) copying the work,

(ii) performing, playing or showing the work in public, or

(iii) broadcasting the work or including it in a cable programme service;

(b) all licensing schemes in relation to the copyright in sound recordings (other than film sound-tracks when accompanying a film), broadcasts or cable programmes, or the typographical arrangement of published editions; and

(c) all licensing schemes in relation to the copyright in sound recordings, films or computer programs so far as they relate to licences for the rental of copies to the public;

and in those sections "licensing scheme" means a licensing scheme of any of those descriptions.

References of proposed licensing scheme to tribunal

118.—(1) The terms of a licensing scheme proposed to be operated by a licensing body may be referred to the Copyright Tribunal by an organisation claiming to be representative of persons claiming that they require licences in cases of a description to which the scheme would apply, either generally or in relation to any description of case.

(2) The Tribunal shall first decide whether to entertain the reference, and may decline to do so on the ground that the reference is premature.

(3) If the Tribunal decides to entertain the reference it shall consider the matter referred and make such order, either confirming or varying the proposed scheme, either generally or so far as it relates to cases of the description to which the reference relates, as the Tribunal may determine to be reasonable in the circumstances.

(4) The order may be made so as to be in force indefinitely or for such period as the Tribunal may determine.

Reference of licensing scheme to tribunal

119.—(1) If while a licensing scheme is in operation a dispute arises between the operator of the scheme and—

    (a) a person claiming that he requires a licence in a case of a description to which the scheme applies, or

    (b) an organisation claiming to be representative of such persons,

that person or organisation may refer the scheme to the Copyright Tribunal in so far as it relates to cases of that description.

(2) A scheme which has been referred to the Tribunal under this section shall remain in operation until proceedings on the reference are concluded.

(3) The Tribunal shall consider the matter in dispute and make such order, either confirming or varying the scheme so far as it relates to cases of the description to which the reference relates, as the Tribunal may determine to be reasonable in the circumstances.

(4) The order may be made so as to be in force indefinitely or for such period as the Tribunal may determine.

Further reference of scheme to tribunal

120.—(1) Where the Copyright Tribunal has on a previous reference of a licensing scheme under section 118 or 119, or under this section, made an order with respect to the scheme, then, while the order remains in force—

    (a) the operator of the scheme,

    (b) a person claiming that he requires a licence in a case of the description to which the order applies, or

    (c) an organisation claiming to be representative of such persons,

may refer the scheme again to the Tribunal so far as it relates to cases of that description.

(2) A licensing scheme shall not, except with the special leave of the Tribunal, be referred again to the Tribunal in respect of the same description of cases—

    (a) within twelve months from the date of the order on the previous reference, or

    (b) if the order was made so as to be in force for 15 months or less, until the last three months before the expiry of the order.

(3) A scheme which has been referred to the Tribunal under this section shall remain in operation until proceedings on the reference are concluded.

(4) The Tribunal shall consider the matter in dispute and make such order, either confirming, varying or further varying the scheme so far as it relates to cases of the description to which the reference relates, as the Tribunal may determine to be reasonable in the circumstances.

(5) The order may be made so as to be in force indefinitely or for such period as the Tribunal may determine.

Application for grant of licence in connection with licensing scheme

121.—(1) A person who claims, in a case covered by a licensing scheme, that the operator of the scheme has refused to grant him or procure the grant to him of a licence in accordance with the scheme, or has failed to do so within a reasonable time after being asked, may apply to the Copyright Tribunal.

(2) A person who claims, in a case excluded from a licensing scheme, that the operator of the scheme either—

    (a) has refused to grant him a licence to procure the grant to him of a licence, or has failed to do so within a reasonable time of being asked, and that in the circumstances it is unreasonable that a licence should not be granted, or

    (b) proposes terms for a licence which are unreasonable,

may apply to the Copyright Tribunal.

(3) A case shall be regarded as excluded from a licensing scheme for the purposes of subsection (2) if—

    (a) the scheme provides for the grant of licences subject to terms excepting matters from the licence and the case falls within such an exception, or

    (b) the case is so similar to those in which licences are granted under the scheme that it is unreasonable that it should not be dealt with in the same way.

(4) If the Tribunal is satisfied that the claim is well-founded, it shall make an order declaring that, in respect of the matters specified in the order, the applicant is entitled to a licence on such terms as the Tribunal may determine to be applicable in accordance with the scheme or, as the case may be, to be reasonable in the circumstances.

(5) The order may be made so as to be in force indefinitely or for such period as the Tribunal may determine.

Application for review of order as to entitlement to licence

122.—(1) Where the Copyright Tribunal has made an order under section 121 that a person is entitled to a licence under a licensing scheme, the operator of the scheme or the original applicant may apply to the Tribunal to review its order.

(2) An application shall not be made, except with the special leave of the Tribunal—

    (a) within twelve months from the date of the order, or of the decision on a previous application under this section, or

(b) if the order was made so as to be in force for 15 months or less, or as a result of the decision on a previous application under this section is due to expire within 15 months of that decision, until the last three months before the expiry date.

(3) The Tribunal shall on an application for review confirm or vary its order as the Tribunal may determine to be reasonable having regard to the terms applicable in accordance with the licensing scheme or, as the case may be, the circumstances of the case.

Effect of order of tribunal as to licensing scheme

123.—(1) A licensing scheme which has been confirmed or varied by the Copyright Tribunal—

(a) under section 118 (reference of terms of proposed scheme), or

(b) under section 119 or 120 (reference of existing scheme to Tribunal),

shall be in force or, as the case may be, remain in operation, so far as it relates to the descriptions of case in respect of which the order was made, so long as the order remains in force.

(2) While the order is in force a person who in a case of a class to which the order applies—

(a) pays to the operator of the scheme any charges payable under the scheme in respect of a licence covering the case in question or, if the amount cannot be ascertained, gives an undertaking to the operator to pay them when ascertained, and

(b) complies with the other terms applicable to such a licence under the scheme,

shall be in the same position as regards infringement of copyright as if he had at all material times been the holder of a licence granted by the owner of the copyright in question in accordance with the scheme.

(3) The Tribunal may direct that the order, so far as it varies the amount of charges payable, has effect from a date before that on which it is made, but not earlier than the date on which the reference was made or, if later, on which the scheme came into operation.

If such a direction is made—

(a) any necessary repayments, or further payments, shall be made in respect of charges already paid, and

(b) the reference in subsection (2)(a) to the charges payable under the scheme shall be construed as a reference to the charges so payable by virtue of the order.

No such direction may be made where subsection (4) below applies.

(4) An order of the Tribunal under section 119 or 120 made with respect to a scheme which is certified for any purpose under section 143 has effect, so far as it varies the scheme by reducing the charges payable for licences, from the date on which the reference was made to the Tribunal.

(5) Where the Tribunal has made an order under section 121 (order as to entitlement to licence under licensing scheme) and the order remains in force, the person in whose favour the order is made shall if he—

    (a) pays to the operator of the scheme any charges payable in accordance with the order or, if the amount cannot be ascertained, gives an undertaking to pay the charges when ascertained, and

    (b) complies with the other terms specified in the order,

be in the same position as regards infringement of copyright as if he had at all material times been the holder of a licence granted by the owner of the copyright in question on the terms specified in the order.

References and applications with respect to licensing by licensing bodies

Licences to which ss. 125 to 128 apply

124. Sections 125 to 128 (references and applications with respect to licensing by licensing bodies) apply to the following descriptions of licence granted by a licensing body otherwise than in pursuance of a licensing scheme—

    (a) licences relating to the copyright in literary, dramatic, musical or artistic works or films (or film sound-tracks when accompanying a film) which cover works of more than one author, so far as they authorise—

        (i) copying the work,

        (ii) performing, playing or showing the work in public, or

        (iii) broadcasting the work or including it in a cable programme service;

    (b) any licence relating to the copyright in a sound recording (other than a film sound-track when accompanying a film), broadcast or cable programme, or the typographical arrangement of a published edition; and

    (c) all licences in relation to the copyright in sound recordings, films or computer programs so far as they relate to the rental of copies to the public;

and in those sections a "licence" means a licence of any of those descriptions.

Reference to tribunal of proposed licence

125.—(1) The terms on which body proposes to grant a licence may be referred to the Copyright Tribunal by the prospective licensee.

(2) The Tribunal shall first decide whether to entertain the reference, and may decline to do so on the ground that the reference is premature.

(3) If the Tribunal decides to entertain the reference it shall consider the terms of the proposed licence and make such order, either confirming or varying the terms, as it may determine to be reasonable in the circumstances.

(4) The order may be made so as to be in force indefinitely or for such period as the Tribunal may determine.

Reference to tribunal of expiring licence

126.—(1) A licensee under a licence which is due to expire, by effluxion of time or as a result of notice given by the licensing body, may apply to the Copyright Tribunal on the ground that it is unreasonable in the circumstances that the licence should cease to be in force.

(2) Such an application may not be made until the last three months before the licence is due to expire.

(3) A licence in respect of which a reference has been made to the Tribunal shall remain in operation until proceedings on the reference are concluded.

(4) If the Tribunal finds the application well-founded, it shall make an order declaring that the licensee shall continue to be entitled to the benefit of the licence on such terms as the Tribunal may determine to be reasonable in the circumstances.

(5) An order of the Tribunal under this section may be made so as to be in force indefinitely or for such period as the Tribunal may determine.

Application for review of order as to licence

127.—(1) Where the Copyright Tribunal has made an order under section 125 or 126, the licensing body or the person entitled to the benefit of the order may apply to the Tribunal to review its order.

(2) An application shall not be made, except with the special leave of the Tribunal—

(a) within twelve months from the date of the order or of the decision on a previous application under this section, or

(b) if the order was made so as to be in force for 15 months of less, or as a result of the decision on a previous application under this section is due to expire within 15 months of that decision, until the last three months before the expiry date.

(3) The Tribunal shall on an application for review confirm or vary its order as the Tribunal may determine to be reasonable in the circumstances.

Effect of order of tribunal as to licence

128.—(1) Where the Copyright Tribunal has made an order under section 125 or 126 and the order remains in force, the person entitled to the benefit of the order shall if he—

(a) pays to the licensing body any charges payable in accordance with the order or, if the amount cannot be ascertained, gives an undertaking to pay the charges when ascertained, and

(b) complies with the other terms specified in the order,

be in the same position as regards infringement of copyright as if he had at all material times been the holder of a licence granted by the owner of the copyright in question on the terms specified in the order.

(2) The benefit of the order may be assigned—

(a) in the case of an order under section 125, if assignment is not prohibited under the terms of the Tribunal's order; and

(b) in the case of an order under section 126, if assignment was not prohibited under the terms of the original licence.

(3) The Tribunal may direct that an order under section 125 or 126, or an order under section 127 varying such an order, so far as it varies the amount of charges payable, has effect from a date before that on which it is made, but not earlier than the date on which the reference or application was made or, if later, on which the licence was granted or, as the case may be, was due to expire.

If such a direction is made—

(a) any necessary repayments, or further repayments, shall be made in respect of charges already paid, and

(b) the reference in subsection (1)(a) to the charges payable in accordance with the order shall be construed, where the order is varied by a later order, as a reference to the charges so payable by virtue of the later order.

Factors to be taken into account in certain classes of case

General considerations: unreasonable discrimination

129. In determining what is reasonable on a reference or application under this Chapter relating to a licensing scheme or licence, the Copyright Tribunal shall have regard to—

(a) the availability of other schemes, or the granting of other licences, to other persons in similar circumstances, and

(b) the terms of those schemes or licences,

and shall exercise its power so as to secure that there is no unreasonable discrimination between licensees, or prospective licensees, under the scheme or licence to which the reference or application relates and licensees under other schemes operated by, or other licences granted by, the same person.

Licences for reprographic copying

130. Where a reference or application is made to the Copyright Tribunal under this Chapter relating to the licensing of reprographic copying of published literary, dramatic, musical or artistic works, or the typographical arrangement of published editions, the Tribunal shall have regard to—

(a) the extent to which published editions of the works in question are otherwise available,

(b) the proportion of the work to be copied, and

(c) the nature of the use to which the copies are likely to be put.

Licences for educational establishments in respect of works included in broadcasts or cable programmes

131.—(1) This section applies to references or applications under this Chapter relating to licences for the recording by or on behalf of educational establishments of broadcasts or cable programmes which include copyright works, or the making of copies of such recordings, for educational purposes.

(2) The Copyright Tribunal shall, in considering what charges (if any) should be paid for a licence, have regard to the extent to which the owners of copyright in the works included in the broadcast or cable programme have already received, or are entitled to receive, payment in respect of their inclusion.

Licences to reflect conditions imposed by promoters of events

132.—(1) This section applies to references or applications under this Chapter in respect of licences relating to sound recordings, films, broadcasts or cable programmes which include, or are to include, any entertainment or other event.

(2) The Copyright Tribunal shall have regard to any conditions imposed by the promoters of the entertainment or other event; and, in particular, the Tribunal shall not hold a refusal or failure to grant a licence to be unreasonable if it could not have been granted consistently with those conditions.

(3) Nothing in this section shall require the Tribunal to have regard to any such conditions in so far as they—

(a) purport to regulate the charges to be imposed in respect of the grant of licences, or

(b) relate to payments to be made to the promoters of any event in consideration of the grant of facilities for making the recording, film, broadcast or cable programmes.

Licences to reflect payments in respect of underlying rights

133.—(1) In considering what charges should be paid for a licence—

(a) on a reference or application under this Chapter relating to licences for the rental to the public of copies of sound recordings, films or computer programs, or

(b) on an application under section 142 (settlement of royalty or other sum payable for deemed licence),

the Copyright Tribunal shall take into account any reasonable payments which the owner of the copyright in the sound recording, film or computer program is liable to make in consequence of the granting of the licence, or of the acts authorised by the licence, to owners of copyright in works included in that work.

(2) On any reference or application under this Chapter relating to licensing in respect of the copyright in sound recordings, films, broadcasts or cable programmes, the Copyright Tribunal shall take into account, in considering what charges should be paid for a licence, any reasonable payments which the copyright owner is liable to make in consequence of the granting of the licence, or of the acts authorised by the licence, in respect of any performance included in the recording, film, broadcast or cable programme.

Licences in respect of works included in re-transmissions

134.—(1) This section applies to references or applications under this Chapter relating to licences to include in a broadcast or cable programme service—

(a) literary, dramatic, musical or artistic works, or,

(b) sound recordings or films,

where one broadcast or cable programme ("the first transmission") is, by reception and immediate re-transmission, to be further broadcast or included in a cable programme service ("the further transmission").

(2) So far as the further transmission is to the same area as the first transmission, the Copyright Tribunal shall, in considering what charges (if any) should be paid for licences for either transmission, have regard to the extent to which the copyright owner has already received, or is entitled to receive, payment for the other transmission which adequately remunerates him in respect of transmissions to that area.

(3) So far as the further transmission is to an area outside that to which the first transmission was made, the Tribunal shall (except where subsection (4) applies) leave the further transmission out of account in considering what charges (if any) should be paid for licences for the first transmission.

(4) If the Tribunal is satisfied that requirements imposed under section 13(1) of the Cable and Broadcasting Act 1984 (duty of Cable Authority to secure inclusion of certain broadcasts in cable programme services) will result in the further transmission being to areas part of which fall outside the area to which the first transmission is made, the Tribunal shall exercise its powers so as to secure that the charges payable for licences for the first transmission adequately reflect that fact.

Mention of specific matters not to exclude other relevant considerations

135. The mention in sections 129 to 134 of specific matters to which the Copyright Tribunal is to have regard in certain classes of case does not affect the Tribunal's general obligation in any case to have regard to all relevant considerations.

Implied indemnity in schemes or licences for reprographic copying

Implied indemnity in certain schemes and licences for reprographic copying

136.—(1) This section applies to—

(a) schemes for licensing reprographic copying of published literary, dramatic, musical or artistic works, or the typographical arrangement of published editions, and

(b) licences granted by licensing bodies for such copying,

where the scheme or licence does not specify the works to which it applies with such particularity as to enable licensees to determine whether a work falls within the scheme or licence by inspection of the scheme or licence and the work.

(2) There is implied—

(a) in every scheme to which this section applies an undertaking by the operator of the scheme to indemnify a person granted a licence under the scheme, and

(b) in every licence to which this section applies an undertaking by the licensing body to indemnify the licensee, against any liability incurred by him by reason of his having infringed copyright by making or authorising the making of reprographic copies of a work in circumstances within the apparent scope of his licence.

(3) The circumstances of a case are within the apparent scope of a licence if—

(a) it is not apparent from inspection of the licence and the work that it does not fall within the description of works to which the licence applies; and

(b) the licence does not expressly provide that it does not extend to copyright of the description infringed.

(4) In this section "liability" includes liability to pay costs; and this section applies in relation to costs reasonably incurred by a licensee in connection with actual or contemplated proceedings against him for infringement of copyright as it applies to sums which he is liable to pay in respect of such infringement.

(5) A scheme or licence to which this section applies may contain reasonable provision—

(a) with respect to the manner in which, and time within which, claims under the undertaking implied by this section are to be made;

(b) enabling the operator of the scheme or, as the case may be, the licensing body to take over the conduct of any proceedings affecting the amount of his liability to indemnify.

Reprographic copying by educational establishments

Power to extend coverage of scheme or licence

137.—(1) This section applies to—

(a) a licensing scheme to which sections 118 to 123 apply (see section 117) and which is operated by a licensing body, or

(b) a licence to which sections 125 to 128 apply (see section 124),

so far as it provides for the grant of licences, or is a licence, authorising the making by or on behalf of educational establishments for the purposes of instruction of reprographic copies of published literary, dramatic, musical or artistic works, or of the typographical arrangement of published editions.

(2) If it appears to the Secretary of State with respect to a scheme or licence to which this section applies that—

(a) works of a description similar to those covered by the scheme or licence are unreasonably excluded from it, and

(b) making them subject to the scheme or licence would not conflict with the normal exploitation of the works or unreasonably prejudice the legitimate interests of the copyright owners,

he may by order provide that the scheme or license shall extend to those works.

(3) Where he proposes to make such an order, the Secretary of State shall give notice of the proposal to—

(a) the copyright owners,

(b) the licensing body in question, and

(c) such persons or organisations representative of educational establishments, and such other persons or organisations, as the Secretary of
State thinks fit.

(4) The notice shall inform those persons of their right to make written or oral
representations to the Secretary of State about the proposal within six months
from the date of the notice; and if any of them wishes to make oral representations, the Secretary of State shall appoint a person to hear the representations and
report to him.

(5) In considering whether to make an order the Secretary of State shall take
into account any representations made to him in accordance with subsection (4),
and such other matters as appears to him to be relevant.

Variation or discharge of order extending scheme or licence

138.—(1) The owner of the copyright in a work in respect of which an order
is the force under section 137 may apply to the Secretary of State for the variation
or discharge of the order, stating his reasons for making the application.

(2) The Secretary of State shall not entertain an application made within two
years of the making of the original order, or of the making of an order on a
previous application under this section, unless it appears to him that the
circumstances are exceptional.

(3) On considering the reasons for the application the Secretary of State may
confirm the order forthwith; if he does not do so, he shall give notice of the
application to—

(a) the licensing body in question, and

(b) such persons or organisations representative of educational establishments, and such other persons or organisations, as he thinks fit.

(4) The notice shall inform those persons of their right to make written or oral
representations to the Secretary of State about the application within the period
of two months from the date of the notice; and if any of them wishes to make
oral representations, the Secretary of State shall appoint a person to hear the
representations and report to him.

(5) In considering the application the Secretary of State shall take into account
the reasons for the application, any representations made to him in accordance
with subsection (4), and such other matters as appear to him to be relevant.

(6) The Secretary of State may make such order as he thinks fit confirming or
discharging the order (or, as the case may be, the order as previously varied), or
varying (or further varying) it so as to exclude works from it.

Appeals against orders

139.—(1) The owner of the copyright in a work which is the subject of an
order under section 137 (order extending coverage of scheme or licence) may
appeal to the Copyright Tribunal which may confirm or discharge the order, or
vary it so as to exclude works from it, as it thinks fit having regard to the
considerations mentioned in subsection (2) of that section.

(2) Where the Secretary of State has made an order under section 138 (order confirming, varying or discharging order extending coverage of scheme or licence) —

(a) the person who applied for the order, or

(b) any person or organisation representative of educational establishments who was given notice of the application for the order and made representations in accordance with subsection (4) of that section,

may appeal to the Tribunal which many confirm or discharge the order or make any other order which the Secretary of State might have made.

(3) An appeal under this section shall be brought within six weeks of the making of the order or such further period as the Tribunal may allow.

(4) An order under section 137 or 138 shall not come into effect until the end of the period of six weeks from the making of the order or, if an appeal is brought before the end of that period, until the appeal proceedings are disposed of or withdrawn.

(5) If an appeal is brought after the end of that period, any decision of the Tribunal on the appeal does not affect the validity of anything done in reliance on the order appealed against before that decision takes effect.

Inquiry whether new scheme or general licence required

140.—(1) The Secretary of State may appoint a person to inquire into the question whether new provision is required (whether by way of a licensing scheme or general licence) to authorise the making by or on behalf of educational establishments for the purposes of instruction of reprographic copies of—

(a) published literary, dramatic, musical or artistic works, or

(b) the typographical arrangement of published editions,

of a description which appears to the Secretary of State not to be covered by an existing licensing scheme or general licence and not to fall within the power conferred by section 137 (power to extend existing schemes and licences to similar works).

(2) The procedure to be followed in relation to an inquiry shall be such as may be prescribed made by the Secretary of State.

(3) The regulations shall, in particular, provide for notice to be given to—

(a) persons or organisations appearing to the Secretary of State to represent the owners of copyright in works of that description, and

(b) persons or organisations appearing to the Secretary of State to represent educational establishments,

and for the making of written or oral representations by such persons; but without prejudice to the giving of notice to, and the making of representations by, other persons and organisations.

(4) The person appointed to hold the inquiry shall not recommend the making of new provision unless he is satisfied—

(a) that it would be of advantage to educational establishments to be authorised to make reprographic copies of the works in question, and

(b) that making those works subject to a licensing scheme or general licence would not conflict with the normal exploitation of the works or unreasonably prejudice the legitimate interests of the copyright owners.

(5) If he does recommend the making of new provision he shall specify any terms, other than terms as to charges payable, on which authorisation under the new provision should be available.

(6) Regulations under this section shall be made by statutory instrument which shall be subject to annulment in pursuance of a resolution of either House of Parliament.

(7) In this section (and section 141) a "general licence" means a licence granted by a licensing body which covers all works of the description to which it applies.

Statutory licence where recommendation not implemented

141.—(1) The Secretary of State may, within one year of the making of a recommendation under section 140 by order provide that if, or to the extent that, provision has not been made in accordance with the recommendation, the making by or on behalf of an educational establishment, for the purposes of instruction, of reprographic copies of the works to which the recommendation relates shall be treated as licensed by the owners of the copyright in the works.

(2) For that purpose provision shall be regarded as having been made in accordance with the recommendation if—

(a) a certified licensing scheme has been established under which a licence is available to the establishment in question, or

(b) a general licence has been—

(i) granted to or for the benefit of that establishment, or

(ii) referred by or on behalf of that establishment to the Copyright Tribunal under section 125 (reference of terms of proposed licence), or

(iii) offered to or for the benefit of that establishment and refused without such a reference,

and the terms of the scheme or licence accord with the recommendation.

(3) The order shall also provide that any existing licence authorising the making of such copies (not being a licence granted under a certified licensing scheme or a general licence) shall cease to have effect to the extent that it is more restricted or more onerous than the licence provided for by the order.

(4) The order shall provide for the licence to be free of royalty but, as respects other matters, subject to any terms specified in the recommendation and to such other terms as the Secretary of State may think fit.

(5) The order may provide that where a copy which would otherwise be an infringing copy is made in accordance with the licence provide by the order but is subsequently dealt with, it shall be treated as an infringing copy for the purposes of that dealing, and if that dealing infringes copyright for all subsequent purposes.

In this subsection "dealt with" means sold or let for hire, offered or exposed for sale or hire, or exhibited in public.

(6) The order shall not come into force until at least six months after it is made.

(7) An order may be varied from time to time, but not so as to exclude works other than those to which the recommendation relates or remove any terms specified in the recommendation, and may be revoked.

(8) An order under this section shall be made by statutory instrument which shall be subject to annulment in pursuance of a resolution of either House of Parliament.

(9) In this section a "certified licensing scheme" means a licensing scheme certified for the purposes of this section under section 143.

Royalty or other sum payable for rental of certain works

Royalty or other sum payable for rental of sound recording,
film or computer program

142.—(1) An application to settle the royalty or other sum payable in pursuance of section 66 (rental of sound recordings, films and computer programs) may be made to the Copyright Tribunal by the copyright owner or the person claiming to be treated as licensed by him.

(2) The Tribunal shall consider the matter and make such order as it may determine to be reasonable in the circumstances.

(3) Either party may subsequently apply to the Tribunal to vary the order, and the Tribunal shall consider the matter and make such order confirming or varying the original order as it may determine to be reasonable in the circumstances.

(4) An application under subsection (3) shall not, except with the special leave of the Tribunal, be made within twelve months from the date of the original order or of the order on a previous application under that subsection.

(5) An order under subsection (3) has effect from the date on which it is made or such later date as may be specified by the Tribunal.

Certification of licensing schemes

Certification of licensing schemes

143.—(1) A person operating or proposing to operate a licensing scheme may apply to the Secretary of State to certify the scheme for the purposes of—

    (a) section 35 (educational recording of broadcasts or cable programmes),

    (b) section 60 (abstracts of scientific or technical articles),

    (c) section 66 (rental of sound recordings, films and computer programs),

    (d) section 74 (sub-titled copies of broadcasts or cable programmes for people who are deaf or hard of hearing), or

    (e) section 141 (reprographic copying of published works by educational establishments).

(2) The Secretary of State shall by order made by statutory instrument certify the scheme if he is satisfied that it—

(a) enables the works to which it relates to be identified with sufficient certainty by persons likely to require licences, and

(b) sets out clearly the charges (if any) payable and the other terms on which licences will be granted.

(3) The scheme shall be scheduled to the order and the certification shall come into operation for the purposes of section 35, 60, 66, 74 and 141, as the case may be—

(a) on such date, not less than eight weeks after the order is made, as may be specified in the order, or

(b) if the scheme is the subject of a reference under section 118 (reference of proposed scheme), any later date on which the order of the Copyright Tribunal under that section comes into force or the reference is withdrawn.

(4) A variation of the scheme is not effective unless a corresponding amendment of the order is made; and the Secretary of State shall make such an amendment in the case of a variation ordered by the Copyright Tribunal on a reference under section 118, 119 or 120, and may do so in any other case if he thinks fit.

(5) The order shall be revoked if the scheme ceases to be operated and may be revoked if it appears to the Secretary of State that it is no longer being operated according to its terms.

Powers exercisable in consequence of competition report

Powers exercisable in consequence of report of
Monopolies and Mergers Commission

144.—(1) Where the matters specified in a report of the Monopolies and Mergers Commission as being those which in the Commission's opinion operate, may be expected to operate or have operated against the public interest include—

(a) conditions in licences granted by the owner of copyright in a work restricting the use of the work by the licensee or the right of the copyright owner to grant other licences, or

(b) a refusal of a copyright owner to grant licences on reasonable terms,

the powers conferred by Part I of Schedule 8 to the Fair Trading Act 1973 (powers exercisable for purpose of remedying or preventing adverse effects specified in report of Commission) include power to cancel or modify those conditions and, instead or in addition, to provide that licences in respect of the copyright shall be available as of right.

(2) The references in sections 56(2) and 73(2) of that Act, and sections 10(2)(b) and 12(5) of the Competition Act 1980, to the powers specified in that Part of that Schedule shall be construed accordingly.

(3) A Minister shall only exercise the powers available by virtue of this section if he is satisfied that to do so does not contravene any Convention relating to copyright to which the United Kingdom is a party.

(4) The terms of a licence available by virtue of this section shall, in default of agreement, be settled by the Copyright Tribunal on an application by the person requiring the licence; and terms so settled shall authorise the licensee to do everything in respect of which a licence is so available.

(5) Where the terms of a licence are settled by the Tribunal, the licence has effect from the date on which the application to the Tribunal was made.

CHAPTER VIII

THE COPYRIGHT TRIBUNAL

The Tribunal

The Copyright Tribunal

145.—(1) The Tribunal established under section 23 of the Copyright Act 1956 is renamed the Copyright Tribunal.

(2) The Tribunal shall consist of a chairman and two deputy chairmen appointed by the Lord Chancellor, after consultation with the Lord Advocate, and not less than two or more than eight ordinary members appointed by the Secretary of State.

(3) A person is not eligible for appointment as chairman or deputy chairman unless he is a barrister, advocate or solicitor of not less than seven years' standing or has held judicial office.

Membership of the Tribunal

146.—(1) The members of the Copyright Tribunal shall hold and vacate office in accordance with their terms of appointment, subject to the following provisions.

(2) A member of the Tribunal may resign his office by notice in writing to the Secretary of State or, in the case of the Chairman or a deputy chairman, to the Lord Chancellor.

(3) The Secretary of State or, in the case of the chairman or a deputy chairman, the Lord Chancellor may by notice in writing to the member concerned remove him from office if—

   (a) he has become bankrupt or made an arrangement with his creditors or, in Scotland, his estate has been sequestrated or he has executed a trust deed for his creditors or entered into a composition contract, or

   (b) he is incapacitated by physical or mental illness,

or if he is in the opinion of the Secretary of State or, as the case may be, the Lord Chancellor otherwise unable or unfit to perform his duties as member.

(4) If a member of the Tribunal is by reason of illness, absence or other reasonable cause for the time being unable to perform the duties of his office, either generally or in relation to particular proceedings, a person may be appointed to discharge his duties for a period not exceeding six months at one time or, as the case may be, in relation to those proceedings.

(5) The appointment shall be made—

(a) in the case of the chairman or deputy chairman, by the Lord Chancellor, who shall appoint a person who would be eligible for appointment to that office, and

(b) in the case of an ordinary member, by the Secretary of State;

and a person so appointed shall have during the period of his appointment, or in relation to the proceedings in question, the same powers as the person in whose place he is appointed.

(6) The Lord Chancellor shall consult the Lord Advocate before exercising his powers under this section.

Financial provisions

147.—(1) There shall be paid to the members of the Copyright Tribunal such remuneration (whether by way of salaries or fees), and such allowances, as the Secretary of State with the approval of the Treasury may determine.

(2) The Secretary of State may appoint such staff for the Tribunal as, with the approval of the Treasury as to numbers and remuneration, he may determine.

(3) The remuneration and allowances of members of the Tribunal, the remuneration of any staff and such other expenses of the Tribunal as the Secretary of State with the approval of the Treasury may determine shall be paid out of money provided by Parliament.

Constitution for purposes of proceedings

148.—(1) For the purposes of any proceedings the Copyright Tribunal shall consist of—

(a) a chairman, who shall be either the chairman or a deputy chairman of the Tribunal, and

(b) two or more ordinary members.

(2) If the members of the Tribunal dealing with any matter are not unanimous, the decision shall be taken by majority vote; and if, in such a case, the votes are equal the chairman shall have a further, casting vote.

(3) Where part of any proceedings before the Tribunal has been heard and one or more members of the Tribunal are unable to continue, the Tribunal shall remain duly constituted for the purpose of those proceedings so long as the number of members is not reduced to less than three.

(4) If the chairman is unable to continue, the chairman of the Tribunal shall—

(a) appoint one of the remaining members to act as chairman, and

(b) appoint a suitably qualified person to attend the proceedings and advise the members on any questions of law arising.

(5) A person is "suitably qualified" for the purposes of subsection (4)(b) if he is, or is eligible for appointment as, a deputy chairman of the Tribunal.

Jurisdiction and procedure

Jurisdiction of the Tribunal

149. The function of the Copyright Tribunal is to hear and determine proceedings under—

(a) section 118, 119, or 120 (reference of licensing scheme);

(b) section 121 or 122 (application with respect to entitlement to licence under licensing scheme);

(c) section 125, 126 or 127 (reference or application with respect to licensing by licensing body);

(d) section 139 (appeal against order as to coverage of licensing scheme or licence);

(e) section 142 (application to settle royalty or other sum payable for rental of sound recording, film or computer program);

(f) section 144(4) (application to settle terms of copyright licence available as of right);

(g) section 190 (application to give consent for purposes of Part II on behalf of performer);

(h) paragraph 5 of Schedule 6 (determination of royalty or other remuneration to be paid to trustees for the Hospital for Sick Children).

General power to make rules

150.—(1) The Lord Chancellor may, after consultation with the Lord Advocate, make rules for regulating proceedings before the Copyright Tribunal and, subject to the approval of the Treasury, as to the fees chargeable in respect of such proceedings.

(2) The rules may apply in relation to the Tribunal—

(a) as respects proceedings in England and Wales, any of the provisions of the Arbitration Act 1950;

(b) as respects proceedings in Northern Ireland, any of the provisions of the Arbitration Act (Northern Ireland) 1937;

and any provisions so applied shall be set out in or scheduled to the rules.

(3) Provision shall be made by the rules—

(a) prohibiting the Tribunal from entertaining a reference under section 118, 119 or 120 by a representative organisation unless the Tribunal is satisfied that the organisation is reasonably representative of the class of persons which it claims to represent:

(b) specifying the parties to any proceedings and enabling the Tribunal to make a party to the proceedings any person or organisation satisfying the Tribunal that they have a substantial interest in the matter; and

(c) requiring the Tribunal to give the parties to proceedings an opportunity to state their case, in writing or orally as the rules may provide.

(4) The rules may make provision for regulating or prescribing any matters incidental to or consequential upon any appeal from the Tribunal under section 152 (appeal to the court on point of law).

(5) Rules under this section shall be made by statutory instrument which shall be subject to annulment in pursuance of a resolution of either House of Parliament.

Costs, proof of orders, &c

151.—(1) The Copyright Tribunal may order that the costs of a party to proceedings before it shall be paid by such other party as the Tribunal may direct; and the Tribunal may tax or settle the amount of the costs, or direct in what manner they are to be taxed.

(2) A document purporting to be a copy of an order of the Tribunal and to be certified by the chairman to be a true copy shall, in any proceedings, be sufficient evidence of the order unless the contrary is proved.

(3) As respect proceedings in Scotland, the Tribunal has the like powers for securing the attendance of witnesses and the production of documents, and with regard to the examination of witnesses on oath, as an arbiter under a submission.

Appeals

Appeal to the court on point of law

152.—(1) An appeal lies on any point of law arising from a decision of the Copyright Tribunal to the High Court or, in the case of proceedings of the Tribunal in Scotland, to the Court of Session.

(2) Provision shall be made by rules under section 150 limiting the time within which an appeal may be brought.

(3) Provision may be made by rules under that section—

    (a) for suspending, or authorising or requiring the Tribunal to suspend, the operation of orders of the Tribunal in cases where its decision is appealed against;

    (b) for modifying in relation to an order of the Tribunal whose operation is suspended the operation of any provision of this Act as to the effect of the order;

    (c) for the publication of notices or the taking of other steps for securing that persons affected by the suspension of an order of the Tribunal will be informed of its suspension.

CHAPTER IX

QUALIFICATION FOR AND EXTENT OF COPYRIGHT PROTECTION

Qualification for copyright protection

Qualification for copyright protection

153.—(1) Copyright does not subsist in a work unless the qualification requirements of this Chapter are satisfied as regards—

    (a) the author (see section 154), or

    (b) the country in which the work was first published (see section 155), or

(c) in the case of a broadcast or cable programme, the country from which the broadcast was made or the cable programme was sent (see section 156).

(2) Subsection (1) does not apply in relation to Crown copyright or Parliamentary copyright (see sections 163 to 166) or to copyright subsisting by virtue of section 168 (copyright of certain international organisations).

(3) If the qualification requirements of this Chapter, or section 163, 165 or 168, are once satisfied in respect of a work, copyright does not cease to subsist by reason of any subsequent event.

Qualification by reference to author

154.—(1) A work qualifies for copyright protection if the author was at the material time a qualifying person, that is—

(a) a British citizen, a British Dependent Territories citizen, a British National (Overseas), a British Overseas citizen, a British subject or a British protected person within the meaning of the British Nationality Act 1981, or

(b) an individual domiciled or resident in the United Kingdom or another country to which the relevant provisions of this Part extend, or

(c) a body incorporated under the law of a part of the United Kingdom or of another country to which the relevant provisions of this Part extend.

(2) Where, or so far as, provision is made by Order under section 159 (application of this Part to countries to which it does not extend), a work also qualifies for copyright protection if at the material time the author was a citizen or subject of, an individual domiciled or resident in, or a body incorporated under the law of, a country to which the Order relates.

(3) A work of joint authorship qualifies for copyright protection if at the material time any of the authors satisfies the requirements of subsection (1) or (2); but where a work qualifies for copyright protection only under this section, only those authors who satisfy those requirements shall be taken into account for the purposes of—

section 11(1) and (2) (first ownership of copyright; entitlement of author or author's employer),

section 12(1) and (2) (duration of copyright; dependent on life of author unless work of unknown authorship), and section 9(4) (meaning of "unknown authorship") so far as it applies for the purposes of section 12(2), and

section 57 (anonymous or pseudonymous works: acts permitted on assumptions as to expiry of copyright or death of author).

(4) The material time in relation to a literary, dramatic, musical or artistic work is—

(a) in the case of an unpublished work, when the work was made or, if the making of the work extended over a period, a substantial part of that period;

(b) in the case of a published work, when the work was first published or, if the author had died before that time, immediately before his death.

(5) The material time in relation to other descriptions of work is as follows—

(a) in the case of a sound recording or film, when it was made;

(b) in the case of a broadcast, when the broadcast was made;

(c) in the case of a cable programme, when the programme was included in a cable programme service;

(d) in the case of the typographical arrangement of a published edition, when the edition was first published.

Qualification by reference to country of first publication

155.—(1) A literary, dramatic, musical or artistic work, a sound recording or film, or the typographical arrangement of a published edition, qualifies for copyright protection if it is first published—

(a) in the United Kingdom, or

(b) in another country to which the relevant provisions of this Part extend.

(2) Where, or so far as, provision is made by Order under section 159 (application of this part to countries to which it does not extend), such a work also qualifies for copyright protection if it is first published in a country to which the Order relates.

(3) For the purposes of this section, publication in one country shall not be regarded as other than the first publication by reason of simultaneous publication elsewhere; and for this purpose publication elsewhere within the previous 30 days shall be treated as simultaneous.

Qualification by reference to place of transmission

156.—(1) A broadcast qualifies for copyright protection if it is made from, and a cable programme qualifies for copyright protection if it is sent from, a place in—

(a) the United Kingdom, or

(b) another country to which the relevant provisions of this Part extend.

(2) Where, or so far as, provision is made by Order under section 159 (application of this Part to countries to which it does not extend), a broadcast or cable programme also qualifies for copyright protection if it is made from or, as the case may be, sent from a place in a country to which the Order relates.

Extent and application of this Part

Countries to which this Part extends

157.—(1) This Part extends to England and Wales, Scotland and Northern Ireland.

(2) Her Majesty may by Order in Council direct that this Part shall extend, subject to such exceptions and modifications as may be specified in the Order, to—

(a) any of the Channel Islands,

(b) the Isle of Man, or

(c) any colony.

(3) That power includes power to extend, subject to such exceptions and modifications as may be specified in the Order, and Order in Council made under the following provisions of this Chapter.

(4) The legislature of a country to which this Part has been extended may modify or add to the provisions of this Part, in their operation as part of the law of that country, as the legislature may consider necessary to adapt the provisions to the circumstances of that country—

(a) as regards procedure and remedies, or

(b) as regards works qualifying for copyright protection by virtue of a connection with that country.

(5) Nothing in this section shall be construed as restricting the extent of paragraph 36 of Schedule 1 (transitional provisions: dependent territories where the Copyright Act 1956 or the Copyright Act 1911 remains in force) in relation to the law of a dependent territory to which this Part does not extend.

Countries ceasing to be colonies

158.—(1) The following provisions apply where a country to which this Part has been extended ceases to be a colony of the United Kingdom.

(2) As from the date on which it ceases to be a colony it shall cease to be regarded as a country to which this Part extends for the purposes of—

(a) section 160(2)(a) (denial of copyright protection to citizens of countries not giving adequate protection to British works), and

(b) sections 163 and 165 (Crown and Parliamentary copyright).

(3) But it shall continue to be treated as a country to which this Part extends for the purposes of sections 154 to 156 (qualification for copyright protection) until—

(a) an Order in Council is made in respect of that country under section 159 (application of this Part to countries to which it does not extend), or

(b) an Order in Council is made declaring that is shall cease to be so treated by reason of the fact that the provisions of this Part as part of the law of that country have been repealed or amended.

(4) A statutory instrument containing an Order in Council under subsection (3)(b) shall be subject to annulment in pursuance of a resolution of either House of Parliament.

Application of this Part to countries to which it does not extend

159.—(1) Her Majesty may by Order in Council make provision for applying in relation to a country to which this Part does not extend any of the provisions of this Part specified in the Order, so as to secure that those provisions—

(a) apply in relation to persons who are citizens or subjects of that country or are domiciled or resident there, as they apply to persons who are British citizens or are domiciled or resident in the United Kingdom, or

(b) apply in relation to bodies incorporated under the law of that country as they apply in relation to bodies incorporated under the law of a part of the United Kingdom, or

(c) apply in relation to works first published in that country as they apply in relation to works first published in the United Kingdom, or

(d) apply in relation to broadcasts made from or cable programmes sent from that country as they apply in relation to broadcasts made from or cable programmes sent from the United Kingdom.

(2) An Order may make provision for all or any of the matters mentioned in subsection (1) and may—

(a) apply any provisions of this Part subject to such exceptions and modifications as are specified in the Order; and

(b) direct that any provisions of this Part apply either generally or in relation to such classes of works, or other classes of case, as are specified in the Order.

(3) Except in the case of a Convention country or another member State of the European Economic Community, Her Majesty shall not make an Order in Council under this section in relation to a country unless satisfied that provision has been or will be made under the law of that country, in respect of the class of works to which the Order relates, giving adequate protection to the owners of copyright under this Part.

(4) In subsection (3) "Convention country" means a country which is a party to a Convention relating to copyright to which the United Kingdom is also a party.

(5) A statutory instrument containing an Order in Council under this section shall be subject to annulment in pursuance of a resolution of either House of Parliament.

Denial of copyright protection to citizens of countries
not giving adequate protection to British works

160.—(1) If it appears to Her Majesty that the law of a country fails to give adequate protection to British works to which this section applies, or to one or more classes of such works, Her Majesty may make provision by Order in Council in accordance with this section restricting the rights conferred by this Part in relation to works of authors connected with that country.

(2) An Order in Council under this section shall designate the country concerned and provide that, for the purposes specified in the Order, works first published after a date specified in the Order shall not be treated as qualifying for copyright protection by virtue of such publication if at that time the authors are—

(a) citizens or subjects of that country (not domiciled or resident in the United Kingdom or another country to which the relevant provisions of this Part extend), or

(b) bodies incorporated under the law of that country;

and the Order may make such provision for all the purposes of this Part or for such purposes as are specified in the Order, and either generally or in relation to such class of cases as are specified in the Order, having regard to the nature and extent of that failure referred to in subsection (1).

(3) This section applies to literary, dramatic, musical and artistic works, sound recordings and films; and "British works" means works of which the author was a qualifying person at the material time within the meaning of section 154.

(4) A statutory instrument containing an Order in Council under this section shall be subject to annulment in pursuance of a resolution of either House of Parliament.

Supplementary

Territorial waters and the continental shelf

161.—(1) For the purposes of this Part the territorial waters of the United Kingdom shall be treated as part of the United Kingdom.

(2) This Part applies to things done in the United Kingdom sector of the continental shelf on a structure or vessel which is present there for purposes directly connected with the exploration of the sea bed or subsoil or the exploitation of their natural resources as it applies to things done in the United Kingdom.

(3) The United Kingdom sector of the continental shelf means the areas designated by order under section 1(7) of the Continental Shelf Act 1964.

British ships, aircraft and hovercraft

162.—(1) This Part applies to things done on a British ship, aircraft or hovercraft as it applies to things done in the United Kingdom.

(2) In this Section—

"British ship" means a ship which is a British ship for the purposes of the Merchant Shipping Acts (see section 2 of the Merchant Shipping Act 1988) otherwise than by virtue of registration in a country outside the United Kingdom; and

"British aircraft" and "British hovercraft" mean an aircraft or hovercraft registered in the United Kingdom.

Chapter X

Miscellaneous and General

Crown and Parliamentary copyright

Crown copyright

163.—(1) Where a work is made by Her Majesty or by an officer or servant of the Crown in the course of his duties—

   (a) the work qualifies for copyright protection notwithstanding section 153(1) (ordinary requirement as to qualification for copyright protection), and

   (b) Her Majesty is the first owner of any copyright in the work.

(2) Copyright in such a work is referred to in this Part as "Crown copyright", nothwithstanding that it may be, or have been, assigned to another person.

(3) Crown copyright in a literary, dramatic, musical or artistic work continues to subsist —

   (a) until the end of the period of 125 years from the end of the calendar year in which the work was made, or

   (b) if the work is published commercially before the end of the period of 75 years from the end of the calendar year in which it was made, until the end of the period of 50 years from the end of the calendar year in which it was first so published.

(4) In the case of a work of joint authorship where one or more but not all of the authors are persons falling within subsection (1), this section applies only in relation to those authors and the copyright subsisting by virtue of their contribution to the work.

(5) Except as mentioned above, and subject to any express exclusion elsewhere in this Part, the provisions of this Part apply in relation to Crown copyright as to other copyright.

(6) This section does not apply to work if, or to the extent that, Parliamentary copyright subsists in the work (see sections 165 and 166).

Copyright in Acts and Measures

164.—(1) Her Majesty is entitled to copyright in every Act of Parliament or Measure of the General Synod of the Church of England.

(2) The copyright subsists from Royal Assent until the end of the period of 50 years from the end of the calendar year in which Royal Assent was given.

(3) References in this Part to Crown copyright (except in section 163) include copyright under this section; and, except as mentioned above, the provisions of this Part apply in relation to copyright under this section as to other Crown copyright.

(4) No other copyright, or right in the nature of copyright, subsists in an Act or Measure.

Parliamentary copyright

165.—(1) Where a work is made by or under the direction or control of the House of Commons or the House of Lords—

   (a) the work qualifies for copyright protection notwithstanding section 153(1) (ordinary requirement as to qualification for copyright protection), and

(b) the House by whom, or under whose direction or control, the work is made is the first owner of any copyright in the work, and if the work is made by or under the direction or control of both Houses, the two Houses are joint first owners of copyright.

(2) Copyright in such a work is referred to in this Part as "Parliamentary copyright", notwithstanding that it may be, or have been, assigned to another person.

(3) Parliamentary copyright in a literary, dramatic, musical or artistic work continues to subsist until the end of the period of 50 years from the end of the calendar year in which the work was made.

(4) For the purposes of this section, works made by or under the direction or control of the House of Commons or the House of Lords include—

(a) any work made by an officer or employee of that House in the course of his duties, and

(b) any sound recording, film, live broadcast or live cable programme of the proceedings of that House;

but a work shall not be regarded as made by or under the direction or control of either House by reason only of its being commissioned by or on behalf of that House.

(5) In the case of a work of joint authorship where one or more but not all of the authors are acting on behalf of, or under the direction or control of, the House of Commons or the House of Lords, this section applies only in relation to those authors and the copyright subsisting by virtue of their contribution to the work.

(6) Except as mentioned above, and subject to any express exclusion elsewhere in this Part, the provisions of this Part apply in relation to Parliamentary copyright as to other copyright.

(7) The provisions of this section also apply, subject to any exceptions or modifications specified by Order in Council, to works made by or under the direction or control of any other legislative body of a country to which this Part extends; and references in this Part to "Parliamentary copyright" shall be construed accordingly.

(8) A statutory instrument containing an Order in Council under subsection (7) shall be subject to annulment in pursuance of a resolution of either House of Parliament.

Copyright in Parliamentary Bills

166.—(1) Copyright in every Bill introduced into Parliament belongs, in accordance with the following provisions, to one or both of the Houses of Parliament.

(2) Copyright in a public Bill belongs in the first instance to the House into which the Bill is introduced, and after the Bill has been carried to the second House to both Houses jointly, and subsists from the time when the text of the Bill is handed in to the House in which it is introduced.

(3) Copyright in a private Bill belongs to both Houses jointly and subsists from the time when a copy of the Bill is first deposited in either House.

(4) Copyright in a personal Bill belongs in the first instance to the House of Lords, and after the Bill has been carried to the House of Commons to both Houses jointly, and subsists from the time when it is given a First Reading in the House of Lords.

(5) Copyright under this section ceases—

    (a) on Royal Assent, or

    (b) if the Bill does not receive Royal Assent, on the withdrawal or rejection of the Bill or the end of the Session:

Provided that, copyright in a Bill continues to subsist notwithstanding its rejection in any Session by the House of Lords if, by virtue of the Parliament Acts 1911 and 1949, it remains possible for it to be presented for Royal Assent in that Session.

(6) References in this Part to Parliamentary copyright (except in section 165) include copyright under this section; and, except as mentioned above, the provisions of this Part apply in relation to copyright under this section as to other Parliamentary copyright.

(7) No other copyright, or right in the nature of copyright, subsists in a Bill after copyright has once subsisted under this section; but without prejudice to the subsequent operation of this section in relation to a Bill which, not having passed in one Session, is reintroduced in a subsequent Session.

Houses of Parliament: supplementary provisions with respect to copyright

167.—(1) For the purposes of holding, dealing with and enforcing copyright, and in connection with all legal proceedings relating to copyright, each House of Parliament shall be treated as having the legal capacities of a body corporate, which shall not be affected by a prorogation or dissolution.

(2) The functions of the House of Commons as owner of copyright shall be exercised by the Speaker on behalf of the House; and if so authorised by the Speaker, or in case of a vacancy in the office of Speaker, those functions may be discharged by the Chairman of Ways and Means or a Deputy Chariman.

(3) For this purpose a person who on the dissolution of Parliament was Speaker of the House of Commons, Chariman of Ways and Means or a Deputy Chairman may continue to act until the corresponding appointment is made in the next Session of Parliament.

(4) The functions of the House of Lords as owner of copyright shall be exercised by the Clerk of the Parliaments on behalf of the House; and if so authorised by him, or in case of a vacancy in the office of Clerk of the Parliaments, those functions may be discharged by the Clerk Assistant or the Reading Clerk.

(5) Legal proceedings relating to copyright—

    (a) shall be brought by or against the House of Commons in the name of "The Speaker of the House of Commons", and

(b) shall be brought by or against the House of Lords in the name of "The Clerk of the Parliaments".

Other miscellaneous provisions

Copyright vesting in certain international organisations

168.—(1) Where an original literary, dramatic, musical or artistic work—

(a) is made by an officer or employee of, or is published by, an international organisation to which this section applies, and

(b) does not qualify for copyright protection under section 154 (qualification by reference to author) or section 155 (qualification by reference to country of first publication),

copyright nevertheless subsists in the work by virtue of this section and the organisation is first owner of that copyright.

(2) The international organisations to which this section applies are those as to which Her Majesty has by Order in Council declared that it is expedient that this section should apply.

(3) Copyright of which an international organisation is first owner by virtue of this section continues to subsist until the end of the period of 50 years from the end of the calendar year in which the work was made or such longer period as may be specified by Her Majesty by Order in Council for the purpose of complying with the international obligations of the United Kingdom.

(4) An international organisation to which this section applies shall be deemed to have, and to have had at all material times, the legal capacities of a body corporate for the purpose of holding, dealing with and enforcing copyright and in connection with all legal proceedings relating to copyright.

(5) A statutory instrument containing an Order in Council under this section shall be subject to annulment in pursuance of a resolution of either House of Parliament.

Folklore, &c: anonymous unpublished works

169.—(1) Where in the case of an unpublished literary, dramatic, musical or artistic work of unknown authorship there is evidence that the author (or, in the case of a joint work, any of the authors) was a qualifying individual by connection with a country outside the United Kingdom, it shall be presumed until the contrary is proved that he was such a qualifying individual and that copyright accordingly subsists in the work, subject to the provisions of this Part.

(2) If under the law of that country a body is appointed to protect and enforce copyright in such works, Her Majesty may by Order in Council designate that body for the purposes of this section.

(3) A body so designated shall be recognised in the United Kingdom as having authority to do in place of the copyright owner anything, other than assign copyright, which it is empowered to do under the law of that country; and it may, in particular, bring proceedings in its own name.

(4) A statutory instrument containing an Order in Council under this section shall be subject to annulment in pursuance of a resolution of either House of Parliament.

(5) In subsection (1) a "qualifying individual" means an individual who at the material time (within the meaning of section 154) was a person whose works qualified under that section for copyright protection.

(6) This section does not apply if there has been an assignment of copyright in the work by the author of which notice has been given to the designated body; and nothing in this section affects the validity of an assignment of copyright made, or licence granted, by the author or a person lawfully claiming under him.

Transitional provisions and savings

Transitional provisions and savings

170. Schedule 1 contains transitional provisions and savings relating to works made, and acts or events occurring, before the commencement of this Part, and otherwise with respect to the operation of the provisions of this Part.

Rights and privileges under other enactments or the common law

171.—(1) Nothing in this Part affects—

    (a) any right or privilege of any person under any enactment (except where the enactment is expressly repealed, amended or modified by this Act);

    (b) any right or privilege of the Crown subsisting otherwise than under an enactment;

    (c) any right or privilege of either House of Parliament;

    (d) the right of the Crown or any person deriving title from the Crown to sell, use or otherwise deal with articles forfeited under the laws relating to customs and excise;

    (e) the operation of any rule of equity relating to breaches of trust or confidence.

(2) Subject to those savings, no copyright or right in the nature of copyright shall subsist otherwise than by virtue of this Part or some other enactment in that behalf.

(3) Nothing in this Part affects any rule of law preventing or restricting the enforcement of copyright, on grounds of public interest or otherwise.

(4) Nothing in this Part affects any right of action or other remedy, whether civil or criminal, available otherwise than under this Part in respect of acts infringing any of the rights conferred by Chapter IV (moral rights).

(5) The savings in subsection (1) have effect subject to section 164(4) and section 166(7) (copyright in Acts, Measures and Bills; exclusion of other rights in the nature of copyright).

Interpretation

General provisions as to construction.

172.—(1) This Part restates and amends the law of copyright, that is, the provisions of the Copyright Act 1956, as amended.

(2) A provision of this Part which corresponds to a provision of the previous law shall not be construed as departing from the previous law merely because of a change of expression.

(3) Decisions under the previous law may be referred to for the purpose of establishing whether a provision of this Part departs from the previous law, or otherwise for establishing the true construction of this Part.

Construction of references to copyright owner

173.—(1) Where different persons are (whether in consequence of a partial assignment or otherwise) entitled to different aspects of copyright in a work, the copyright owner for any purpose of this Part is the person who is entitled to the aspect of copyright relevant for that purpose.

(2) Where copyright (or any aspect of copyright) is owned by more than one person jointly, references in this Part to the copyright owner are to all the owners, so that, in particular, any requirement of the licence of the copyright owner requires the licence of all of them.

Meaning of "educational establishment" and related expressions

174.—(1) The expression "educational establishment" in a provision of this Part means—

    (a) any school, and

    (b) any other description of educational establishment specified for the purposes of this Part, or that provision, by order of the Secretary of State.

(2) The Secretary of State may by order provide that the provisions of this Part relating to educational establishments shall apply, with such modifications and adaptations as may be specified in the order, in relation to teachers who are employed by a local education authority to give instruction elsewhere to pupils who are unable to attend an educational establishment.

(3) In subsection (1)(a) "school"—

    (a) in relation to England and Wales, has the same meaning as in the Education Act 1944;

    (b) in relation to Scotland, has the same meaning as in the Education (Scotland) Act 1962, except that it includes an approved school within the meaning of the Social Work (Scotland) Act 1968; and

    (c) in relation to Northern Ireland, has the same meaning as in the Education and Libraries (Northern Ireland) Order 1986.

(4) An order under subsection (1)(b) may specify a description of educational establishment by reference to the instruments from time to time in force under any enactment specified in the order.

(5) In relation to an educational establishment the expressions "teacher" and "pupil" in this Part include, respectively, any person who gives and any person who receives instruction.

(6) References in this Part to anything being done "on behalf of" an educational establishment are to its being done for the purposes of that establishment by any person.

(7) An order under this section shall be made by statutory instrument which shall be subject to annulment in pursuance of a resolution of either House of Parliament.

Meaning of publication and commercial publication

175.—(1) In this Part "publication", in relation to a work—

  (a) means the issue of copies to the public, and

  (b) includes, in the case of a literary, dramatic, musical or artistic work, making it available to the public by means of an electronic retrieval system;

and related expressions shall be construed accordingly.

(2) In this Part "commercial publication", in relation to a literary, dramatic, musical or artistic work means—

  (a) issuing copies of the work to the public at a time when copies made in advance of the receipt of orders are generally available to the public, or

  (b) making the work available to the public by means of an electronic retrieval system;

and related expressions shall be construed accordingly.

(3) In the case of a work of architecture in the form of a building, or an artistic work incorporated in a building, construction of the building shall be treated as equivalent to publication of the work.

(4) The following do not constitute publication for the purposes of this Part and references to commercial publication shall be construed accordingly—

  (a) in the case of a literary, dramatic or musical work—

      (i) the performance of the work, or

      (ii) the broadcasting of the work or its inclusion in a cable programme service (otherwise than for the purposes of an electronic retrieval system);

  (b) in the case of an artistic work—

      (i) the exhibition of the work,

      (ii) the issue to the public of copies, of a graphic work representing, or of photographs of, a work of architecture in the form of a building or a model for a building, a sculpture or a work of artistic craftsmanship,

      (iii) the issue to the public of copies of a film including the work, or

(iv) the broadcasting of the work or its inclusion in a cable programme service (otherwise than for the purposes of an electronic retrieval system);

(c) in the case of a sound recording or film—

(i) in the work being played or shown in public, or

(ii) the broadcasting of the work or its inclusion in a cable programme service.

(5) References in this Part to publication or commercial publication do not include publication which is merely colourable and not intended to satisfy the reasonable requirements of the public.

(6) No account shall be taken for the purposes of this section of any unauthorised act.

Requirements of signature: application in relation to body corporate

176.—(1) The requirement in the following provisions that an instrument be signed by or on behalf of a person is also satisfied in the case of a body corporate by the affixing of its seal—

section 78(3)(b) (assertion by licensor of right to identification of author in case of public exhibition of copy made in pursuance of the licence),

section 90(3) (assignment of copyright),

section 91(1) (assignment of future copyright),

section 92(1) (grant of exclusive licence).

(2) The requirement in the following provisions that an instrument be signed by a person is satisfied in the case of a body corporate by signature on behalf of the body or by the affixing of its seal—

section 78(2)(b) (assertion by instrument in writing of right to have author identified),

section 87(2) (waiver of moral rights).

Adaptation of expressions for Scotland

177. In the application of this Part to Scotland—

"account of profits" means accounting and payment of profits;

"accounts" means count, reckoning and payment;

"assignment" means assignation;

"costs" means expenses;

"defendant" means defender;

"delivery up" means delivery;

"estoppel" means personal bar;

"injunction" means interdict;

"interlocutory relief" means interim remedy; and

"plaintiff" means pursuer.

Minor definitions

178. In this Part—

"article", in the context of an article in a periodical, includes an item of any description;

"business" includes a trade or profession;

"collective work" means—

    (a) a work of joint authorship, or

    (b) a work in which there are distinct contributions by different authors or in which works or parts of works of different authors are incorporated;

"computer-generated", in relation to a work, means that the work is generated by computer in circumstances such that there is no human author of the work;

"country" includes any territory;

"the Crown" includes the Crown in right of Her Majesty's Government in Northern Ireland or in any country outside the United Kingdom to which this Part extends;

"electronic" means actuated by electric, magnetic, electro-magnetic, electro-chemical or electro-mechanical energy, and "in electronic form" means in a form usable only by electronic means;

"employed", "employee", "employer" and "employment" refer to employment under a contract of service or of apprenticeship;

"facsimile copy" includes a copy which is reduced or enlarged in scale;

"international organisation" means an organisation the members of which include one or more states;

"judicial proceedings" includes proceedings before any court, tribunal or person having authority to decide any matter affecting a person's legal rights or liabilities;

"parliamentary proceedings" includes proceedings of the Northern Ireland Assembly or of the European Parliament;

"rental" means any arrangement under which a copy of a work is made available—

    (a) for payment (in money or money's worth), or

    (b) in the course of a business, as part of services or amenities for which payment is made,

on terms that it will or may be returned;

"reprographic copy" and "reprographic copying" refer to copying by means of a reprographic process;

"reprographic process" means a process—

    (a) for making facsimile copies, or

    (b) involving the use of an appliance for making multiple copies,

and includes, in relation to a work held in electronic form, any copying by electronic means, but does not include the making of a film or sound recording;

"sufficient acknowledgement" means an acknowledgement identifying the work in question by its title or other description, and identifying the author unless—

(a) in the case of a published work, it is published anonymously;

(b) in the case of an unpublished work, it is not possible for a person to ascertain the identity of the author by reasonable inquiry;

"sufficient disclaimer", in relation to an act capable of infringing the right conferred by section 80 (right to object to derogatory treatment of work), means a clear and reasonably prominent indication—

(a) given at the time of the act, and

(b) if the author or director is then identified, appearing along with the identification,

that the work has been subjected to treatment to which the author or director has not consented;

"telecommunications system" means a system for conveying visual images, sounds or other information by electronic means;

"typeface" includes an ornamental motif used in printing;

"unauthorised", as regards anything done in relation to a work, means done otherwise than—

(a) by or with the licence of the copyright owner, or

(b) if copyright does not subsist in the work, by or with the licence of the author or, in a case where section 11(2) would have applied, the author's employer or, in either case, persons lawfully claiming under him, or

(c) in pursuance of section 48 (copying, &c. of certain material by the Crown);

"wireless telegraphy" means the sending of electro-magnetic energy over paths not provided by a material substance constructed or arranged for that purpose;

"writing" inlcudes any form of notation or code, whether by hand or otherwise and regardless of the method by which, or medium in or on which, it is recorded, and "written" shall be construed accordingly.

Index of defined expressions

179. The following Table shows provisions defining or otherwise explaining expressions used in this Part (other than provisions defining or explaining an expression used only in the same section) —

account of profits and accounts (in Scotland)	section 177
acts restricted by copyright	section 16(1)
adaptation	section 21(3)
archivist (in sections 37 to 43)	section 37(6)
article (in a periodical)	section 178
artistic work	section 4(1)
assignment (in Scotland)	section 177

author	sections 9 and 10(3)
broadcast (and related expressions)	section 6
building	section 4(2)
business	section 178
cable programme, cable programme service (and related expressions)	section 7
collective work	section 178
commencement (in Schedule 1)	paragraph 1(2) of that Schedule
commercial publication	section 175
computer-generated	section 178
copy and copying	section 17
copyright (generally)	section 1
copyright (in Schedule 1)	paragraph 2(2) of that Schedule
copyright owner	sections 101(2) and 173
Copyright Tribunal	section 145
copyright work	section 1(2)
costs (in Scotland)	section 177
country	section 178
the Crown	section 178
Crown copyright	sections 163(2) and 164(3)
defendant (in Scotland)	section 177
delivery up (in Scotland)	section 177
dramatic work	section 3(1)
educational establishment	sections 174(1) to (4)
electronic and electronic form	section 178
employed, employee, employer and employment	section 178
exclusive licence	section 92(1)
existing works (in Schedule 1)	paragraph 1(3) of that Schedule
facsimile copy	section 178
film	section 5
future copyright	section 91(2)
general licence (in sections 140 and 141)	section 140(7)
graphic work	section 4(2)
infringing copy	section 27
injunction (in Scotland)	section 177
interlocutory relief (in Scotland)	section 177
international organisation	section 178
issue of copies to the public	section 18(2)
joint authorship (work of)	sections 10(1) and (2)
judicial proceedings	section 178
librarian (in sections 37 to 43)	section 37(6)
licence (in sections 125 to 128)	section 124
licence of copyright owner	sections 90(4), 91(3) and 173
licensing body (in Chapter VII)	section 116(2)

licensing scheme (generally)	section 116(1)
licensing scheme (in sections 118 to 121)	section 117
literary work	section 3(1)
made (in relation to a literary, dramatic or musical work)	section 3(2)
musical work	section 3(1)
the new copyright provisions (in Schedule 1)	paragraph 1(1) of that Schedule
the 1911 Act (in Schedule 1)	paragraph 1(1) of that Schedule
the 1956 Act (in Schedule 1)	paragraph 1(1) of that Schedule
on behalf of (in relation to an educational establishment)	section 174(5)
Parliamentary copyright	sections 165(2) and (7) and 166(6)
parliamentary proceedings	section 178
performance	section 19(2)
photograph	section 4(2)
plaintiff (in Scotland)	section 177
prescribed conditions (in sections 38 to 43)	section 37(1)(b)
prescribed library or archive (in sections 38 to 43)	section 37(1)(a)
programme (in the context of broadcasting)	section 6(3)
prospective owner (of copyright)	section 91(2)
publication and related expressions	section 175
published edition (in the context of copyright in the typographical arrangement)	section 8
pupil	section 174(5)
rental	section 178
reprographic copies and reprographic copying	section 178
reprographic process	section 178
sculpture	section 4(2)
signed	section 176
sound recording	section 5
sufficient acknowledgement	section 178
sufficient disclaimer	section 178
teacher	section 174(5)
telecommunications system	section 178
typeface	section 178
unauthorised (as regards things done in relation to a work)	section 178
unknown (in relation to the author of a work)	section 9(5)
unknown authorship (work of)	section 9(4)
wireless telegraphy	section 178

work (in Schedule 1)	paragraph 2(1) of that Schedule
work of more than one author (in Chapter VII)	section 116(4)
writing and written	section 178

PART II: RIGHTS IN PERFORMANCES

Introductory

Rights conferred on performers and persons having recording rights

180.—(1) This Part confers rights—

(a) on a performer, by requiring his consent to the exploitation of his performances (see sections 181 to 184), and

(b) on a person having recording rights in relation to a performance, in relation to recordings made without his consent or that of the performer (see sections 185 to 188),

and creates offences in relation to dealing with or using illicit recordings and certain other related acts (see sections 198 and 201).

(2) In this Part—

"performance" means—

(a) a dramatic performance (which includes dance and mime),

(b) a musical performance,

(c) a reading or recitation of a literary work, or

(d) a performance of a variety act or any similar presentation,

which is, or so far as it is, a live performance given by one or more individuals; and

"recording", in relation to a performance, means a film or sound recording—

(a) made directly from the live performance,

(b) made from a broadcast of, or cable programme including, the performance, or

(c) made, directly or indirectly, from another recording of the performance.

(3) The rights conferred by this Part apply in relation to performances taking place before the commencement of this Part; but no act done before commencement, or in pursuance of arrangements made before commencement, shall be regarded as infringing those rights.

(4) The rights conferred by this Part are independent of—

(a) any copyright in, or moral rights relating to, any work performed or any film or sound recording of, or broadcast or cable programme including, the performance, and

(b) any other right or obligation arising otherwise than under this Part.

Performers' rights

Qualifying performances

181. A performance is a qualifying performance for the purposes of the provisions of this Part relating to performers' rights if it is given by a qualifying individual (as defined in section 206) or takes place in a qualifying country (as so defined).

Consent required for recording or live transmission of performance

182.—(1) A performer's rights are infringed by a person who, without his consent—

(a) makes, otherwise than for his private and domestic use, a recording of the whole or any substantial part of a qualifying performance, or

(b) broadcasts live, or includes live in a cable programme service, the whole or any substantial part of a qualifying performance.

(2) In an action for infringement of a performer's rights brought by virtue of this section damages shall not be awarded against a defendant who shows that at the time of the infringement he believed on reasonable grounds that consent had been given.

Infringement of performer's rights by use of recording made without consent

183. A performer's rights are infringed by a person who, without his consent—

(a) shows or plays in public the whole or any substantial part of a qualifying performance, or

(b) broadcasts or includes in a cable programme service the whole or any substantial part of a qualifying performance,

by means of a recording which was, and which that person knows or has reason to believe was, made without the performer's consent.

Infringement of performer's rights by importing, possessing or dealing with illicit recording

184.—(1) A performer's rights are infringed by a person who, without his consent—

(a) imports into the United Kingdom otherwise than for his private and domestic use, or

(b) in the course of a business possesses, sells or lets for hire, offers or exposes for sale or hire, or distributes,

a recording of a qualifying performance which is, and which that person knows or has reason to believe is, an illicit recording.

(2) Where in an action for infringement of a performer's rights brought by virtue of this section a defendant shows that the illicit recording was innocently acquired by him or a predecessor in title of his, the only remedy available against him in respect of the infringement is damages not exceeding a reasonable payment in respect of the act complained of.

(3) In subsection (2) "innocently acquired" means that the person acquiring the recording did not know and had no reason to believe that it was an illicit recording.

Rights of person having recording rights

Exclusive recording contracts and persons having recording rights

185.—(1) In this Part an "exclusive recording contract" means a contract between a performer and another person under which that person is entitled to the exclusion of all other persons (including the performer) to make recordings of one or more of his performances with a view to their commercial exploitation.

(2) References in this Part to a "person having recording rights", in relation to a performance, are (subject to subsection (3)) to a person—

(a) who is party to and has the benefit of an exclusive recording contract to which the performance is subject, or

(b) to whom the benefit of such a contract has been assigned,

and who is a qualifying person.

(3) If a performance is subject to an exclusive recording contract but the person mentioned in subsection (2) is not a qualifying person, references in this Part to a "person having recording rights" in relation to the performance are to any person—

(a) who is licensed by such a person to make recordings of the performance with a view to their commercial exploitation, or

(b) to whom the benefit of such a licence has been assigned,

and who is a qualifying person.

(4) In this section "with a view to commercial exploitation" means with a view to the recordings being sold or let for hire, or shown or played in public.

Consent required for recrodings of performance subject to exclusive contract

186.—(1) A person infringes the rights of a person having recording rights in relation to a performance who, without his consent or that of the performer, makes a recording of the whole or any substantial part of the performance, otherwise than for his private and domestic use.

(2) In an action for infringement of those rights brought by virtue of this section damages shall not be awarded against a defendant who shows that at the time of the infringement he believed on reasonable grounds that consent had been given.

Infringement of recording rights by use of recording made without consent

187.—(1) A person infringes the rights of a person having recording rights in relation to a performance who, without his consent or, in the case of a qualifying performance, that of the performer—

(a) shows or plays in public the whole or any substantial part of the performance, or

(b) broadcasts or includes in a cable programme service the whole or any substantial part of the performance,

by means of a recording which was, and which that person knows or has reason to believe was, made without the appropriate consent.

(2) The reference in subsection (1) to "the appropriate consent" is to the consent of—

(a) the performer, or

(b) the person who at the time the consent was given had recording rights in relation to the performance (or, if there was more than one such person, of all of them).

Infringement of recording rights by importing, possessing or dealing with illicit recording

188.—(1) A person infringes the rights of a person having recording rights in relation to a performance who, without his consent or, in the case of a qualifying performance, that of the performer—

(a) imports into the United Kingdom otherwise than for his private and domestic use, or

(b) in the course of a business possesses, sells or lets for hire, offers or exposes for sale or hire, or distributes,

a recording of the performance which is, and which that person knows or has reason to believe is, an illicit recording.

(2) Where in an action for infringement of those rights brought by virtue of this section a defendant shows that the illicit recording was innocently acquired by him or a predecessor in title of his, the only remedy available against him in respect of the infringement is damages not exceeding a reasonable payment in respect of the act complained of.

(3) In subsection (2) "innocently acquired" means that the person acquiring the recording did not know and had no reason to believe that it was an illicit recording.

Exceptions to rights conferred

Acts permitted notwithstanding rights conferred by this Part

189. The provisions of Schedule 2 specify acts which may be done notwithstanding the rights conferred by this Part, being acts which correspond broadly to certain of those specified in Chapter III of Part I (acts permitted notwithstanding copyright).

Power of tribunal to give consent on behalf of performer in certain cases

190.—(1) The Copyright Tribunal may, on the application of a person wishing to make a recording from a previous recording of a performance, give consent in a case where—

(a) the identity or whereabouts of a performer cannot be ascertained by reasonable inquiry, or

(b) a performer unreasonably withholds his consent.

(2) Consent given by the Tribunal has effect as consent of the performer for the purposes of—

(a) the provisions of this Part relating to performers' rights, and

(b) section 198(3)(a) (criminal liability: sufficient consent in relation to qualifying performances),

and may be given subject to any conditions specified in the Tribunal's order.

(3) The Tribunal shall not give consent under subsection (1)(a) except after the service or publication of such notices as may be required by rules made under section 150 (general procedural rules) or as the Tribunal may in any particular case direct.

(4) The Tribunal shall not give consent under subsection (1)(b) unless satisfied that the performer's reasons for withholding consent do not include the protection of any legitimate interest of his; but it shall be for the performer to show what his reasons are for withholding consent, and in default of evidence as to his reasons the Tribunal may draw such inferences as it thinks fit.

(5) In any case the Tribunal shall take into account the following factors—

(a) whether the original recording was made with the performer's consent and is lawfully in the possession or control of the person proposing to make the further recording;

(b) whether the making of the further recording is consistent with the obligations of the parties to the arrangements under which, or is otherwise consistent with the purposes for which, the original recording was made.

(6) Where the Tribunal gives consent under this section it shall, in default of agreement between the applicant and the performer, make such order as it thinks fit as to the payment to be made to the performer in consideration of consent being given.

Duration and transmission of rights; consent

Duration of rights

191. The rights conferred by this Part continue to subsist in relation to a performance until the end of the period of 50 years from the end of the calendar year in which the performance takes place.

Transmission of rights

192.—(1) The rights conferred by this Part are not assignable or transmissible, except to the extent that performers' rights are transmissible in accordance with the following provisions.

(2) On the death of a person entitled to performer's rights—

(a) the rights pass to such person as he may by testamentary disposition specifically direct, and

(b) if or to the extent that there is no such direction, the rights are exercisable by his personal representatives;

and references in this Part to the performer, in the context of the person having performers' rights, shall be construed as references to the person for the time being entitled to exercise those rights.

(3) Where by virtue of subsection (2)(a) a right becomes exercisable by more than one person, it is exercisable by each of them independently of the other or others.

(4) The above provisions do not affect section 185(2)(b) or (3)(b), so far as those provisions confer rights under this Part on a person to whom the benefit of a contract or licence is assigned.

(5) Any damages recovered by personal representatives by virtue of this section in respect of an infringement after a person's death shall devolve as part of his estate as if the right of action had subsisted and been vested in him immediately before his death.

Consent

193.—(1) Consent for the purposes of this Part may be given in relation to a specific performance, a specified description of performances or performances generally, and may relate to past or future performances.

(2) A person having recording rights in a performance is bound by any consent given by a person through whom he derives his rights under the exclusive recording contract or licence in question, in the same way as if the consent had been given by him.

(3) Where a right conferred by this Part passes to another person, any consent binding on the person previously entitled binds the person to whom the right passes in the same way as if the consent had been given by him.

Remedies for infringement

Infringement actionable as breach of statutory duty

194. An infringement of any of the rights conferred by this Part is actionable by the person entitled to the right as a breach of statutory duty.

Order for delivery up

195.—(1) Where a person has in his possession, custody or control in the course of a business an illicit recording of a performance, a person having performer's rights or recording rights in relation to the performance under this Part may apply to the court for an order that the recording be delivered up to him or to such other person as the court may direct.

(2) An application shall not be made after the end of the period specified in section 203; and no order shall be made unless the court also makes, or it appears to the court that there are grounds for making, an order under section 204 (order as to disposal of illicit recording).

(3) A person to whom a recording is delivered up in pursuance of an order under this section shall, if an order under section 204 is not made, retain it pending the making of an order, or the decision not to make an order, under that section.

(4) Nothing in this section affects any other power of the court.

Right to seize illicit recordings

196.—(1) An illicit recording of a performance which is found exposed or otherwise immediately available for sale or hire, and in respect of which a person would be entitled to apply for an order under section 195, may be seized and detained by him or a person authorised by him.

The right to seize and detain is exercisable subject to the following conditions and is subject to any decision of the court under section 204 (order as to disposal of illicit recording).

(2) Before anything is seized under this section notice of the time and place of the proposed seizure must be given to a local police station.

(3) A person may for the purpose of exercising the right conferred by this section enter premises to which the public have access but may not seize anything in the possession, custody or control of a person at a permanent or regular place of business of his and may not use any force.

(4) At the time when anything is seized under this section there shall be left at the place where it was seized a notice in the prescribed form containing the prescribed particulars as to the person by whom or on whose authority the seizure is made and the grounds on which it is made.

(5) In this section—

"premises" includes land, buildings, fixed or moveable structures, vehicles, vessels, aircraft and hovercraft; and

"prescribed" means prescribed by order of the Secretary of State.

(6) An order of the Secretary of State under this section shall be made by statutory instrument which shall be subject to annulment in pursuance of a resolution of either House of Parliament.

Meaning of "illicit recording"

197.—(1) In this Part "illicit recording", in relation to a performance, shall be construed in accordance with this section.

(2) For the purposes of a performer's rights, a recording of the whole or any substantial part of a performance of his is an illicit recording if it is made, otherwise than for private purposes, without his consent.

(3) For the purposes of the rights of a person having recording rights, a recording of the whole or any substantial part of a performace subject to the exclusive recording contract is an illicit recording if it is made, otherwise than for private purposes, without his consent or that of the performer.

(4) For the purposes of sections 198 and 199 (offences and orders for delivery up in criminal proceedings), a recording is an illicit recording if it is an illicit recording for the purposes mentioned in subsection (2) or subsection (3).

(5) In this Part "illicit recording" includes a recording falling to be treated as an illicit recording by virtue of any of the following provisions of Schedule 2—

paragraph 4(3) (recordings made for purposes of instruction or examination),

paragraph 6(2) (recordings made by educational establishments for educational purposes),

paragraph 12(2) (recordings of performance in electronic form retained on transfer of principal recording), or

paragraph 16(3) (recordings made for purposes of broadcast or cable programme),

but otherwise does not include a recording made in accordance with any of the provisions of that Schedule.

(6) It is immaterial for the purposes of this section where the recording was made.

Offences

Criminal liability for making, dealing with or using illicit recordings

198.—(1) A person commits an offence who without sufficient consent—

(a) makes for sale or hire, or

(b) imports into the United Kingdom otherwise than for his private and domestic use, or

(c) possesses in the course of a business with a view to committing any act infringing the rights conferred by this Part, or

(d) in the course of a business—

(i) Sells or lets for hire, or

(ii) offers or exposes for sale or hire, or

(iii) distributes,

a recording which is, and which he knows or has reason to believe is, an illicit recording.

(2) A person commits an offence who causes a recording of a performance made without sufficient consent to be—

(a) shown or played in public, or

(b) broadcast or included in a cable programme service,

thereby infringing any of the rights conferred by this Part, if he knows or has reason to believe that those rights are thereby infringed.

(3) In subsections (1) and (2) "sufficient consent" means—

(a) in the case of a qualifying performance, the consent of the performer, and

(b) in the case of a non-qualifying performance subject to an exclusive recording contract—

(i) for the purposes of subsection (1)(a) (making of recording), the consent of the performer or the person having recording rights, and

(ii) for the purposes of subsection (1)(b), (c) and (d) and subsection (2) (dealing with or using recording), the consent of the person having recording rights.

The references in this subsection to the person having recording rights are to the person having those rights at the time the consent is given or, if there is more than one such person, to all of them.

(4) No offence is committed under subsection (1) or (2) by the commission of an act which by virtue of any provision of Schedule 2 may be done without infringing the rights conferred by this Part.

(5) A person guilty of an offence under subsection (1)(a), (b) or (d)(iii) is liable—

(a) on summary conviction to imprisonment for a term not exceeding six months or a fine not exceeding the statutory maximum, or both;

(b) on conviction on indictment to a fine or imprisonment for a term not exceeding two years, or both.

(6) A person guilty of any other offence under this section is liable on summary conviction to a fine not exceeding level 5 on the standard scale or imprisonment for a term not exceeding six months, or both.

Order for delivery up in criminal proceedings

199.—(1) The court before which proceedings are brought against a person for an offence under section 198 may, if satisfied that at the time of his arrest or charge he had in his possession, custody or control in the course of a business an illicit recording of a performance, order that it be delivered up to a person having performers' rights or recording rights in relation to the performance or to such other person as the court may direct.

(2) For this purpose a person shall be treated as charged with an offence—

(a) in England, Wales and Northern Ireland, when he is orally charged or is served with a summons or indictment;

(b) in Scotland, when he is cautioned, charged or served with a complaint or indictment.

(3) An order may be made by the court of its own motion or on the application of the prosecutor (or, in Scotland, the Lord Advocate or procurator-fiscal), and may be made whether or not the person is convicted of the offence, but shall not be made—

(a) after the end of the period specified in section 203 (period after which remedy of delivery up not available), or

(b) if it appears to the court unlikely that any order will be made under section 204 (order as to disposal of illicit recording).

(4) An appeal lies from an order made under this section by a magistrates' court—

(a) in England and Wales, to the Crown Court, and

(b) in Northern Ireland, to the county court;

and in Scotland, where an order has been made under this section, the person from whose possession, custody or control the illicit recording has been removed may, without prejudice to any other form of appeal under any rule of law, appeal against that order in the same manner as against sentence.

(5) A person to whom an illicit recording is delivered up in pursuance of an order under this section shall retain it pending the making of an order, or the decision not to make an order, under section 204.

(6) Nothing in this section affects the powers of the court under section 43 of the Powers of Criminal Courts Act 1973, section 223 or 436 of the Criminal Procedure (Scotland) Act 1975 or Article 7 of the Criminal Justice (Northern Ireland) Order 1980 (general provisions as to forfeiture in criminal proceedings).

Search warrants

200.—(1) Where a justice of the peace (in Scotland, a sheriff or justice of the peace) is satisfied by information on oath given by a constable (in Scotland, by evidence on oath) that there are reasonable grounds for believing—

(a) that an offence under section 198(1)(a), (b) or (d)(iii) (offences of making, importing or distributing illicit recordings) has been or is about to be committed in any premises, and

(b) that evidence that such an offence has been or is about to be committed is in those premises,

he may issue a warrant authorising a constable to enter and search the premises, using such reasonable force as is necessary.

(2) The power conferred by subsection (1) does not, in England and Wales, extend to authorising a search for material of the kinds mentioned in section 9(2) of the Police and Criminal Evidence Act 1984 (certain classes of personal or confidential material).

(3) A warrant under subsection (1)—

(a) may authorise persons to accompany any constable executing the warrant, and

(b) remains in force for 28 days from the date of its issue.

(4) In this section "premises" includes land, buildings, fixed or moveable structures, vehicles, vessels, aircraft and hovercraft.

False representation of authority to give consent

201.—(1) It is an offence for a person to represent falsely that he is authorised by any person to give consent for the purposes of this Part in relation to a performance, unless he believes on reasonable grounds that he is so authorised.

(2) A person guilty of an offence under this section is liable on summary conviction to imprisonment for a term not exceeding six months or a fine not exceeding level 5 on the standard scale or both.

Offence by body corporate: liability of officers

202.—(1) Where an offence under this Part committed by a body corporate is proved to have been committed with the consent or connivance of a director, manager, secretary or other similar officer of the body, or a person purporting to act in any such capacity, he as well as the body corporate is guilty of the offence and liable to be proceeded against and punished accordingly.

(2) In relation to a body corporate whose affairs are managed by its members "director" means a member of the body corporate.

Supplementary provisions with respect to delivery up and seizure

Period after which remedy of delivery up not available

203.—(1) An application for an order under section 195 (order for delivery up in civil proceedings) may not be made after the end of the period of six years from the date on which the illicit recording in question was made, subject to the following provisions.

(2) If during the whole or any part of that period a person entitled to apply for an order—

    (a) is under a disability, or

    (b) is prevented by fraud or concealment from discovering the facts entitling him to apply,

an application may be made by him at any time before the end of the period of six years from the date on which he ceased to be under a disability or, as the case may be, could with reasonable diligence have discovered those facts.

(3) In subsection (2) "disability"—

    (a) in England and Wales, has the same meaning as in the Limitation Act 1980;

    (b) in Scotland, means legal disability within the meaning of the Prescription and Limitations (Scotland) Act 1973;

    (c) in Northern Ireland, has the same meaning as in the Statute of Limitation (Northern Ireland) 1958.

(4) An order under section 199 (order for delivery up in criminal proceedings) shall not, in any case, be made after the end of the period of six years from the date on which the illicit recording in question was made.

Order as to disposal of illicit recording

204.—(1) An application may be made to the court for an order that an illicit recording of a performance delivered up in pursuance of an order under section 195 or 199, or seized and detained in pursuance of the right conferred by section 196, shall be—

    (a) forfeited to such person having performer's rights or recording rights in relation to the performance as the court may direct, or

    (b) destroyed or otherwise dealt with as the court may think fit,

or for a decision that no such order should be made.

(2) In considering what order (if any) should be made, the court shall consider whether other remedies available in an action for infringement of the rights conferred by this Part would be adequate to compensate the person or persons entitled to the rights and to protect their interests.

(3) Provisons shall be made by rules of court as to the service of notice on persons having an interest in the recording, and any such person is entitled—

(a) to appear in proceedings for an order under this section, whether or not he was served with notice, and

(b) to appeal against any order made, whether or not he appeared;

and an order shall not take effect until the end of the period within which notice of an appeal may be given or, if before the end of that period notice of appeal is duly given, until the final determination or abandonment of the proceedings on the appeal.

(4) Where there is more than one person interested in a recording, the court shall make such order as it thinks just and may (in particular) direct that the recording be sold, or otherwise dealt with, and the proceeds divided.

(5) If the court decides that no order should be made under this section, the person in whose possession, custody or control the recording was before being delivered up or seized is entitled to its return.

(6) References in this section to a person having an interest in a recording include any person in whose favour an order could be made in respect of the recording under this section or under section 114 or 231 of this Act or section 58C of the Trade Marks Act 1938 (which make similar provision in relation to infringement of copyright, design right and trade marks).

Jurisdiction of county court and sheriff court

205.—(1) In England, Wales and Northern Ireland a county court may entertain proceedings under—

section 195 (order for delivery up of illicit recording), or

section 204 (order as to disposal of illicit recording),

where the value of the illicit recordings in question does not exceed the county court limit for actions in tort.

(2) In Scotland proceedings for an order under either of those provisions may be brought in the sheriff court.

(3) Nothing in this section shall be construed as affecting the jurisdiction of the High Court or, in Scotland, the Court of Session.

Qualification for protection and extent

Qualifying countries, individuals and persons

206.—(1) In this Part—

"qualifying country" means—

(a) the United Kingdom,

(b) another member State of the European Economic Community, or

(c) to the extent that an Order under section 208 so provides, a country designated under that section as enjoying reciprocal protection;

"qualifying individual" means a citizen or subject of, or an individual resident in, a qualifying country; and

"qualifying person" means a qualifying individual or a body corporate or other body having legal personality which—

(a) is formed under the law of a part of the United Kingdom or another qualifying country, and

(b) has in any qualifying country a place of business at which substantial business activity is carried on.

(2) The reference in the definition of "qualifying individual" to a person's being a citizen or subject of a qualifying country shall be construed—

(a) in relation to the United Kingdom, as a reference to his being a British citizen, and

(b) in relation to a colony of the United Kingdom, as a reference to his being a British Dependent Territories' citizen by connection with that colony.

(3) In determining for the purpose of the definition of "qualifying person" whether substantial business activity is carried on at a place of business in any country, no account shall be taken of dealings in goods which are at all material times outside that country.

Countries to which this Part extends

207. This Part extends to England and Wales, Scotland and Northern Ireland.

Countries enjoying reciprocal protection

208.—(1) Her Majesty may by Order in Council designate as enjoying reciprocal protection under this Part—

(a) a Convention country, or

(b) a country as to which Her Majesty is satisfied that provision has been or will be made under its law giving adequate protection for British performances.

(2) A "Convention country" means a country which is a party to a Convention relating to performers' rights to which the United Kingdom is also a party.

(3) A "British performance" means a performance—

(a) given by an individual who is a British citizen or resident in the United Kingdom, or

(b) taking place in the United Kingdom.

(4) If the law of that country provides adequate protection only for certain descriptions of performance, an Order under subsection (1)(b) designating that

country shall contain provision limiting to a corresponding extent the protection afforded by this Part in relation to performances connected with that country.

(5) The power conferred by subsection (1)(b) is exercisable in relation to any of the Channel Islands, the Isle of Man or any colony of the United Kingdom, as in relation to a foreign country.

(6) A statutory instrument containing an Order in Council under this section shall be subject to annulment in pursuance of a resolution of either House of Parliament.

Territorial waters and the continental shelf

209.—(1) For the purposes of this Part the territorial waters of the United Kingdom shall be treated as part of the United Kingdom.

(2) This Part applies to things done in the United Kingdom sector of the continental shelf on a structure or vessel which is present there for purposes directly connected with the exploration of the sea bed or subsoil or the exploitation of their natural resources as it applies to things done in the United Kingdom.

(3) The United Kingdom sector of the continental shelf means the areas designated by order under section 1(7) of the Continental Shelf Act 1964.

British ships, aircraft and hovercraft

210.—(1) This Part applies to things done on a British ship, aircraft or hovercraft as it applies to things done in the United Kingdom.

(2) In this section—

"British ship" means a ship which is a British ship for the purposes of the Merchant Shipping Acts (see section 2 of the Merchant Shipping Act 1988) otherwise than by virtue of registration in a country outside the United Kingdom; and

"British aircraft" and "British hovercraft" mean an aircraft or hovercraft registered in the United Kingdom.

Interpretation

Expressions having same meaning as in copyright provisions

211.—(1) The following expressions have the same meaning in this Part as in Part I (copyright)—

> broadcast,
> business,
> cable programme,
> cable programme service,
> country,
> defendant (in Scotland),
> delivery up (in Scotland),
> film,
> literary work,
> published, and
> sound recording.

(2) The provisions of section 6(3) to (5), section 7(5) and 19(4) (supplementary provisions relating to broadcasting and cable programme services) apply for the purposes of this Part, and in relation to an infringement of the rights conferred by this Part, as they apply for the purposes of Part I and in relation to an infringement of copyright.

Index of defined expressions

212. The following Table shows provisions defining or otherwise explaining expressions used in this Part (other than provisions defining or explaining an expression used only in the same section) —

broadcast (and related expressions)	section 211 (and section 6)
business	section 211(1) (and section 178)
cable programme, cable programme service (and related expressions)	section 211 (and section 7)
country	section 211(1) (and section 178)
defendant (in Scotland)	section 211(1) (and section 177)
delivery up (in Scotland)	section 211(1) (and section 177)
exclusive recording contract	section 185(1)
film	section 211(1) (and section 5)
illicit recording	section 197
literary work	section 211(1) (and section 3(1))
performance	section 180(2)
published	section 211(1) (and section 175)
qualifying country	section 206(1)
qualifying individual	section 206(1) and (2)
qualifying performance	section 181
qualifying person	section 206(1) and (3)
recording (of a performance)	section 180(2)
recording rights (person having)	section 185(2) and (3)
sound recording	section 211(1) (and section 5).

PART III: DESIGN RIGHT

CHAPTER I

DESIGN RIGHT IN ORIGINAL DESIGNS

Introductory

Design right

213.—(1) Design right is a property right which subsists in accordance with this Part in an original design.

(2) In this Part "design" means the design of any aspect of the shape or configuration (whether internal or external) of the whole or part of an article.

(3) Design right does not subsist in—

    (a) a method or principle of construction,

    (b) features of shape or configuration of an article which—

(i) enable the article to be connected to, or placed in, around or against, another article so that either article may perform its function, or

(ii) are dependent upon the appearance of another article of which the article is intended by the designer to form an integral part, or

(c) surface decoration.

(4) A design is not "original" for the purposes of this Part if it is commonplace in the design field in question at the time of its creation.

(5) Design right subsists in a design only if the design qualifies for design right protection by reference to—

(a) the designer or the person by whom the design was commissioned or the designer employed (see sections 218 and 219), or

(b) the person by whom and country in which articles made to the design were first marketed (see section 220),

or in accordance with any Order under section 221 (power to make further provision with respect to qualification).

(6) Design right does not subsist unless and until the design has been recorded in a design document or an article has been made to the design.

(7) Design right does not subsist in a design which was so recorded, or to which an article was made, before the commencement of this Part.

The designer

214.—(1) In this Part the "designer", in relation to a design, means the person who creates it.

(2) In the case of a computer-generated design the person by whom the arrangements necessary for the creation of the design are undertaken shall be taken to be the designer.

Ownership of design right

215.—(1) The designer is the first owner of any design right in a design which is not created in pursuance of a commission or in the course of employment.

(2) Where a design is created in pursuance of a commission, the person commissioning the design is the first owner of any design right in it.

(3) Where, in a case not falling within subsection (2) a design is created by an employee in the course of his employment, his employer is the first owner of any design right in the design.

(4) If a design qualifies for design right protection by virtue of section 220 (qualification by reference to first marketing of articles made to the design), the above rules do not apply and the person by whom the articles in question are marketed is the first owner of the design right.

Duration of design right

216.—(1) Design right expires—

(a) fifteen years from the end of the calendar year in which the design was first recorded in a design document or an article was first made to the design, whichever first occurred, or

(b) if articles made to the design are made available for sale or hire within five years from the end of that calendar year, ten years from the end of the calendar year in which that first occurred.

(2) The reference in subsection (1) to articles being made available for sale or hire is to their being made so available anywhere in the world by or with the licence of the design right owner.

Qualification for design right protection

Qualifying individuals and qualifying persons

217.—(1) In this Part—

"qualifying individual" means a citizen or subject of, or an individual habitually resident in, a qualifying country; and

"qualifying person" means a qualifying individual or a body corporate or other body having legal personality which—

(a) is formed under the law of a part of the United Kingdom or another qualifying country, and

(b) has in any qualifying country a place of business at which substantial business activity is carried on.

(2) References in this Part to a qualifying person include the Crown and the government of any other qualifying country.

(3) In this section "qualifying country" means—

(a) the United Kingdom,

(b) a country to which this Part extends by virtue of an Order under section 255,

(c) another member State of the European Economic Community, or

(d) to the extent that an Order under section 256 so provides, a country designated under that section as enjoying reciprocal protection.

(4) The reference in the definition of "qualifying individual" to a person's being a citizen or subject of a qualifying country shall be construed—

(a) in relation to the United Kingdom, as a reference to his being a British citizen, and

(b) in relation to a colony of the United Kingdom, as a reference to his being a British Dependent Territories' citizen by connection with that colony.

(5) In determining for the purpose of the definition of "qualifying person" whether substantial business activity is carried on at a place of business in any country, no account shall be taken of dealings in goods which are at all material times outside that country.

Qualification by reference to designer

218.—(1) This section applies to a design which is not created in pursuance of a commission or in the course of employment.

(2) A design to which this section applies qualifies for design right protection if the designer is a qualifying individual or, in the case of a computer-generated design, a qualifying person.

(3) A joint design to which this section applies qualifies for design right protection if any of the designers is a qualifying individual or, as the case may be, a qualifying person.

(4) Where a joint design qualifies for design right protection under this section, only those designers who are qualifying individuals or qualifying persons are entitled to design right under section 215(1) (first ownership of design right: entitlement of designer).

Qualification by reference to commissioner or employer

219.—(1) A design qualifies for design right protection if it is created in pursuance of a commission from, or in the course of employment with, a qualifying person.

(2) In the case of a joint commission or joint employment a design qualifies for design right protection if any of the commissioners or employers is a qualifying person.

(3) Where a design which is jointly commissioned or created in the course of joint employment qualifies for design right protection under this section, only those commissioners or employers who are qualifying persons are entitled to design right under section 215(2) or (3) (first ownership of design right: entitlement of commissioner or employer).

Qualification by reference to first marketing

220.—(1) A design which does not qualify for design right protection under section 218 or 219 (qualification by reference to designer, commissioner or employer) qualifies for design right protection if the first marketing of articles made to the design—

  (a) is by a qualifying person who is exclusively authorised to put such articles on the market in the United Kingdom, and

  (b) takes place in the United Kingdom, another country to which this Part extends by virtue of an Order under section 255, or another member State of the European Economic Community.

(2) If the first marketing of articles made to the design is done jointly by two or more persons, the design qualifies for design right protection if any of those persons meets the requirements specified in subsection (1)(a).

(3) In such a case only the persons who meet those requirements are entitled to design right under section 215(4) (first ownership of design right: entitlement of first marketer of articles made to the design).

(4) In subsection (1)(a) "exclusively authorised" refers—

(a) to authorisation by the persons who would have been first owner of design right as designer, commissioner of the designs or employer of the designer if he had been a qualifying person, or by a person lawfully claiming under such a person, and

(b) to exclusivity capable of being enforced by legal proceedings in the United Kingdom.

Power to make further provision as to qualification

221.—(1) Her Majesty may, with a view to fulfilling an international obligation of the United Kingdom, by Order in Council provide that a design qualifies for design right protection if such requirements as are specified in the Order are met.

(2) An Order may make different provision for different descriptions of design or article; and may make such consequential modifications of the operation of sections 215 (ownership of design right) and sections 218 to 220 (other means of qualification) as appear to Her Majesty to be appropriate.

(3) A statutory instrument containing an Order in Council under this section shall be subject to annulment in pursuance of a resolution of either House of Parliament.

Dealings with design right

Assignment and licences

222.—(1) Design right is transmissible by assignment, by testamentary disposition or by operation of law, as personal or moveable property.

(2) An assignment or other transmission of design right may be partial, that is, limited so as to apply—

(a) to one or more, but not all, of the things the design right owner has the exclusive right to do;

(b) to part, but not the whole, of the period for which the right is to subsist.

(3) An assignment of design right is not effective unless it is in writing signed by or on behalf of the assignor.

(4) A licence granted by the owner of design right is binding on every successor in title to his interest in the right, except a purchaser in good faith for valuable consideration and without notice (actual or constructive) of the licence or a person deriving title from such a purchaser; and references in this Part to doing anything with, or without, the licence of the design right owner shall be construed accordingly.

Prospective ownership of design right

223.—(1) Where by an agreement made in relation to future design right, and signed by or on behalf of the prospective owner of the design right, the prospective owner purports to assign the future design right (wholly or partially) to another person, then if, on the right coming into existence, the assignee or another person claiming under him would be entitled as against all other persons to require the right to be vested in him, the right shall vest in him by virtue of this section.

(2) In this section—

"future design right" means design right which will or may come into existence in respect of a future design or class of designs or on the occurrence of a future event; and

"prospective owner" shall be construed accordingly, and includes a person who is prospectively entitled to design right by virtue of such an agreement as is mentioned in subsection (1).

(3) A licence granted by a prospective owner of design right is binding on every successor in title to his interest (or prospective interest) in the right, except a purchaser in good faith for valuable consideration and without notice (actual or constructive) of the licence or a person deriving title from such a purchaser; and references in this Part to doing anything with, or without, the licence of the design right owner shall be construed accordingly.

*Assignment of right in registered design presumed
to carry with it design right*

224. Where a design consisting of a design in which design rights subsists is registered under the Registered Designs Act 1949 and the proprietor of the registered design is also the design right owner, an assignment of the right in the registered design shall be taken to be also an assignment of the design right, unless a contrary intention appears.

Exclusive licences

225.—(1) In this Part an "exclusive licence" means a licence in writing signed by or on behalf of the design right owner authorising the licensee to the exclusion of all other persons, including the person granting the licence, to exercise a right which would otherwise be exercisable exclusively by the design right owner.

(2) The licensee under an exclusive licence has the same rights against any successor in title who is bound by the licence as he has against the person granting the licence.

Chapter II

Rights of Design Right Owner and Remedies

Infringement of design right

Primary infringement of design right

226.—(1) The owner of design right in a design has the exclusive right to reproduce the design for commercial purposes—

(a) by making articles to that design, or

(b) by making a design document recording the design for the purpose of enabling such articles to be made.

(2) Reproduction of a design by making articles to the design means copying the design so as to produce articles exactly or substantially to that design, and references in this Part to making articles to a design shall be construed accordingly.

(3) Design right is infringed by a person who without the licence of the design right owner does, or authorises another to do, anything which by virtue of this section is the exclusive right of the design right owner.

(4) For the purposes of this section reproduction may be direct or indirect, and it is immaterial whether any intervening acts themselves infringe the design right.

(5) This section has effect subject to the provisions of Chapter III (exceptions to rights of design right owner).

Secondary infringement: importing or dealing with infringing article

227.—(1) Design right is infringed by a person who, without the licence of the design right owner—

    (a) imports into the United Kingdom for commercial purposes, or

    (b) has in his possession for commercial purposes, or

    (c) sells, lets for hire, or offers or exposes for sale or hire, in the course of a business,

an article which is, and which he knows or has reason to believe is, an infringing article.

(2) This section has effect subject to the provisions of Chapter III (exceptions to rights of design right owner).

Meaning of "infringing article"

228.—(1) In this Part "infringing article", in relation to a design, shall be construed in accordance with this section.

(2) An article is an infringing article if its making to that design was an infringement of design right in the design.

(3) An article is also an infringing article if—

    (a) it has been or is proposed to be imported into the United Kingdom, and

    (b) its making to that design in the United Kingdom would have been an infringement of design right in the design or a breach of an exclusive licence agreement relating to the design.

(4) Where it is shown that an article is made to a design in which design right subsists or has subsisted at any time, it shall be presumed until the contrary is proved that the article was made at a time when design right subsisted.

(5) Nothing in subsection (3) shall be construed as applying to an article which may lawfully be imported into the United Kingdom by virtue of any enforceable Community right within the meaning of section 2(1) of the European Communities Act 1972.

(6) The expression "infringing article" does not include a design document, notwithstanding that its making was or would have been an infringement of design right.

Remedies for infringement

Rights and remedies of design right owner

229.—(1) An infringement of design right is actionable by the design right owner.

(2) In an action for infringement of design right all such relief by way of damages, injunctions, accounts or otherwise is available to the plantiff as is available in respect of the infringement of any other property right.

(3) The court may in an action for infringement of design right, having regard to all the circumstances and in particular to—

(a) the flagrancy of the infringement, and

(b) any benefit accruing to the defendant by reason of the infringement,

award such additional damages as the justice of the case may require.

(4) This section has effect subject to section 233 (innocent infringement).

Order for delivery up

230.—(1) Where a person—

(a) has in his possession, custody or control for commercial purposes an infringing article, or

(b) has in his possession, custody or control anything specifically designed or adapted for making articles to a particular design, knowing or having reason to believe that it has been or is to be used to make an infringing article,

the owner of the design right in the design in question may apply to the court for an order that the infringing article or other thing be delivered up to him or to such other person as the court may direct.

(2) An application shall not be made after the end of the period specified in the following provisions of this section; and no order shall be made unless the court also makes, or it appears to the court that there are grounds for making, an order under section 231 (order as to disposal of infringing article, &c.).

(3) An application for an order under this section may not be made after the end of the period of six years from the date on which the article or thing in question was made, subject to subsection (4).

(4) If during the whole or any part of that period the design right owner—

(a) is under a disability, or

(b) is prevented by fraud or concealment from discovering the facts entitling him to apply for an order,

an application may be made at any time before the end of the period of six years from the date on which he ceased to be under a disability or, as the case may be, could with reasonable diligence have discovered those facts.

(5) In subsection (4) "disability"—

(a) in England and Wales, has the same meaning as in the Limitation Act 1980;

(b) in Scotland, means legal disability within the meaning of the Prescription and Limitation (Scotland) Act 1973;

(c) in Northern Ireland, has the same meaning as in the Statute of Limitations (Northern Ireland) 1958.

(6) A person to whom an infringing article or other thing is delivered up in pursuance of an order under this section shall, if an order under section 231 is not made, retain it pending the making of an order, or the decision not to make an order, under that section.

(7) Nothing in this section affects any other power of the court.

Orders as to disposal of infringing articles, &c.

231.—(1) An application may be made to the court for an order that an infringing article or other thing delivered up in pursuance of an order under section 230 shall be—

(a) forfeited to the design right owner, or

(b) destroyed or otherwise dealt with as the court may think fit,

or for a decision that no such order should be made.

(2) In considering what order (if any) should be made, the court shall consider whether other remedies available in an action for infringement of design right would be adequate to compensate the design right owner and to protect his interests.

(3) Provision shall be made by rules of court as to the service of notice on persons having an interest in the article or other thing, and any such person is entitled—

(a) to appear in proceedings for an order under this section, whether or not he was served with notice, and

(b) to appeal against any order made, whether or not he appeared;

and an order shall not take effect until the end of the period within which notice of an appeal may be given or, if before the end of that period notice of appeal is duly given, until the final determination or abandonment of the proceedings on the appeal.

(4) Where there is more than one person interested in an article or other thing, the court shall make such order as it thinks just and may (in particular) direct that the thing be sold, or otherwise dealt with, and the proceeds divided.

(5) If the court decides that no order should be made under this section, the person in whose possession, custody or control the article or other thing was before being delivered up or seized is entitled to its return.

(6) References in this section to a person having an interest in an article or other thing include any person in whose favour an order could be made in respect of it under this section or under section 114 or 204 of this Act or section 58C of the Trade Marks Act 1938 (which make similar provision in relation to infringement of copyright, right in performances and trade marks).

Jurisdiction of county court and sheriff court

232.—(1) In England, Wales and Northern Ireland a county court may entertain proceedings under—

section 230 (order for delivery up of infringing article, &c.),

section 231 (order as to disposal of infringing article, &c.),

section 235(5) (application by exclusive licensee having concurrent rights),

where the value of the infringing articles and other things in question does not exceed the county court limit for actions in tort.

(2) In Scotland proceedings for an order under any of those provisions may be brought in the sheriff court.

(3) Nothing in this section shall be construed as affecting the jurisdiction of the High Court or, in Scotland, the Court of Session.

Innocent infringement

233.—(1) Where in an action for infringement of design right brought by virtue of section 226 (primary infringement) it is shown that at the time of the infringement the defendant did not know, and had no reason to believe, that design right subsisted in the design to which the action relates, the plantiff is not entitled to damages against him, but without prejudice to any other remedy.

(2) Where in an action for infringement of design right brought by virtue of section 227 (secondary infringement) a defendant shows that the infringing article was innocently acquired by him or a predecessor in title of his, the only remedy available against him in respect of the infringement is damages not exceeding a reasonable royalty in respect of the act complained of.

(3) In subsection (2) "innocently acquired" means that the person acquiring the article did not know and had no reason to believe that it was an infringing article.

Rights and remedies of exclusive licensee

234.—(1) An exclusive licensee has, except against the design right owner, the same rights and remedies in respect of matters occurring after the grant of the licence as if the licence had been an assignment.

(2) His rights and remedies are concurrent with those of the design right owner; and relevant provisions of this Part to the design right owner shall be construed accordingly.

(3) In an action brought by an exclusive licensee by virtue of this section a defendant may avail himself of any defence which would have been available to him if the action had been brought by the design right owner.

Exercise of concurrent rights

235.—(1) Where an action for infringement of design right brought by the design right owner or an exclusive licensee relates (wholly or partly) to an infringement in respect of which they have concurrent rights of action, the design right owner or, as the case may be, the exclusive licensee may not, without the leave of the court, proceed with the action unless the other is either joined as a plaintiff or added as a defendant.

(2) A design right owner or exclusive licensee who is added as a defendant in pursuance of subsection (1) is not liable for any costs in the action unless he takes part in the proceedings.

(3) The above provisions do not affect the granting of interlocutory relief on the application of the design right owner or an exclusive licensee.

(4) Where an action for infringement of design right is brought which relates (wholly or partly) to an infringement in respect of which the design right owner and an exclusive licensee have concurrent rights of action—

(a) the court shall, in assessing damages, take into account—

(i) the terms of the licence, and

(ii) any pecuniary remedy already awarded or available to either of them in respect of the infringement;

(b) no account of profits shall be directed if an award of damages has been made, or an account of profits has been directed, in favour of the other of them in respect of the infringement; and

(c) the court shall if an account of profits is directed apportion the profits between them as the court considers just, subject to any agreement between them;

and these provisions apply whether or not the design right owner and the exclusive licensee are both parties to the action.

(5) The design right owner shall notify any exclusive licensee having concurrent rights before applying for an order under section 230 (order for delivery up of infringing article, &c.); and the court may on the application of the licensee make such order under that section as it thinks fit having regard to the terms of the licence.

CHAPTER III

EXCEPTIONS TO RIGHTS OF DESIGN RIGHT OWNERS

Infringement of copyright

Infringement of copyright

236. Where copyright subsists in a work which consists of or includes a design in which design right subsists, it is not an infringement of design right in the design to do anything which is an infringement of the copyright in that work.

Availability of licences of right

Licences available in last five years of design right

237.—(1) Any person is entitled as of right to a licence to do in the last five years of the design right term anything which would otherwise infringe the design right.

(2) The terms of the licence shall, in default of agreement, be settled by the comptroller.

(3) The Secretary of State may if it appears to him necessary in order to—

(a) comply with an international obligation of the United Kingdom, or

(b) secure or maintain reciprocal protection for British designs in other countries,

by order exclude from the operation of subsection (1) designs of a description specified in the order or designs applied to articles of a description so specified.

(4) An order shall be made by statutory instrument; and no order shall be made unless a draft of it has been laid before and approved by a resolution of each House of Parliament.

Powers exercisable for protection of the public interest

238.—(1) Where the matters specified in a report of the Monopolies and Mergers Commission as being those which in the Commission's opinion operate, may be expected to operate or have operated against the public interest include—

(a) conditions in licences granted by a design right owner restricting the use of the design by the licensee or the right of the design right owner to grant other licences, or

(b) a refusal of a design right owner to grant licences on reasonable terms,

the powers conferred by Part I of Schedule 8 to the Fair Trading Act 1973 (powers exercisable for purpose of remedying or preventing adverse effects specified in report of Commission) include power to cancel or modify those conditions and, instead or in addition, to provide that licences in respect of the design right shall be available as of right.

(2) The references in sections 56(2) and 73(2) of the Act, and sections 10(2)(b) and 12(5) of the Competition Act 1980, to the powers specified in that Part of that Schedule shall be construed accordingly.

(3) The terms of a licence available by virtue of this section shall, in default of agreement, be settled by the comptroller.

Undertaking to take licence of right in infringement proceedings

239.—(1) If in proceedings for infringement of design right in a design in respect of which a licence is available as of right under section 237 or 238 the defendant undertakes to take a licence on such terms as may be agreed or, in default of agreement, settled by the comptroller under that section—

(a) no injunction shall be granted against him,

(b) no order for delivery up shall be made under section 230, and

(c) the amount recoverable against him by way of damages or on an account of profits shall not exceed double the amount which would have been payable by him as licensee if such a licence on those terms had been granted before the earliest infringement.

(2) An undertaking may be given at any time before final order in the proceedings, without any admission of liability.

(3) Nothing in this section affects the remedies available in respect of an infringement committed before licences of right were available.

Crown use of designs

Crown use of designs

240.—(1) A government department, or a person authorised in writing by a government department, may without the licence of the design right owner—

(a) do anything for the purpose of supplying articles for the services of the Crown, or

(b) dispose of articles no longer required for the services of the Crown;

and nothing done by virtue of this section infringes the design right.

(2) References in this Part to "the services of the Crown" are to—

(a) the defence of the realm,

(b) foreign defence purposes, and

(c) health service purposes.

(3) The reference to the supply of articles for "foreign defence purposes" is to their supply—

(a) for the defence of a country outside the realm in pursuance of an agreement to which the government of that country and Her Majesty's Government in the United Kingdom are parties; or

(b) for use by armed forces operating in pursuance of a resolution of the United Nations or one of its organs.

(4) The references to the supply of articles for "health service purposes" are to their supply for the purpose of providing—

(a) pharmaceutical services,

(b) general medical services, or

(c) general dental services,

that is, services of those kinds under Part II of the National Health Service Act 1977, Part II of the National Health Service (Scotland) Act 1978 or the corresponding provisions of the law in force in Northern Ireland.

(5) In this Part—

"Crown use", in relation to a design, means the doing of anything by virtue of this section which would otherwise be an infringement of design right in the design; and

"the government department concerned", in relation to such use, means the government department by whom or on whose authority the act was done.

(6) The authority of a government department in respect of Crown use of a design may be given to a person either before or after the use and whether or not he is authorised, directly or indirectly, by the design right owner to do anything in relation to the design.

(7) A person acquiring anything sold in the exercise of powers conferred by this section, and any person claiming under him, may deal with it in the same manner as if the design right were held on behalf of the Crown.

Settlement of terms for Crown use

241.—(1) Where Crown use is made of a design, the government department concerned shall—

    (a) notify the design right owner as soon as practicable, and

    (b) give him such information as to the extent of the use as he may from time to time require,

unless it appears to the department that it would be contrary to the public interest to do so or the identity of the design right owner cannot be ascertained on reasonable inquiry.

(2) Crown use of a design shall be on such terms as, either before or after the use, are agreed between the government department concerned and the design right owner with the approval of the Treasury or, in default of agreement, are determined by the court.

In the application of this subsection to Northern Ireland the reference to the Treasury shall, where the government department referred to in that subsection is a Northern Ireland department, be construed as a reference to the Department of Finance and Personnel.

(3) Where the identity of the design right owner cannot be ascertained on reasonable inquiry, the government department concerned may apply to the court who may order that no royalty or other sum shall be payable in respect of Crown use of the design until the owner agrees terms with the department or refers the matter to the court for determination.

Rights of third parties in case of Crown use

242.—(1) The provisions of any licence, assignment or agreement made between the design right owner (or anyone deriving title from him or from whom he derives title) and any person other than a government department are of no effect in relation to Crown use of a design, or any act incidental to Crown use, so far as they—

    (a) restrict or regulate anything done in relation to the design, or the use of any model, document or other information relating to it, or

    (b) provide for the making of payments in respect of, or calculated by reference to such use;

and the copying or issuing to the public of copies of any such model or document in connection with the thing done, or any such use, shall be deemed not to be an infringement of any copyright in the model or document.

(2) Subsection (1) shall not be construed as authorising the disclosure of any such model, document or information in contravention of the licence, assignment or agreement.

(3) Where an exclusive licence is in force in respect of the design—

(a) if the licence was granted for royalties—

> (i) any agreement between the design right owner and a government department under section 241 (settlement of terms for Crown use) requires the consent of the licensee, and

> (ii) the licensee is entitled to recover from the design right owner such part of the payment for Crown use as may be agreed between them or, in default of agreement, determined by the court;

(b) if the licence was granted otherwise than for royalties—

> (i) section 241 applies in relation to anything done which but for section 240 (Crown use) and subsection (1) above would be an infringement of the rights of the licensee with the substitution for references to the design right owner of references to the licensee, and

> (ii) section 241 does not apply in relation to anything done by the licensee by virtue of an authority given under section 240.

(4) Where the design right has been assigned to the design right owner in consideration of royalties—

(a) section 241 applies in relation to Crown use of the design as if the references to the design right owner included the assignor, and any payment for Crown use shall be divided between them in such proportion as may be agreed or, in default of agreement, determined by the court, and

(b) section 241 applies in relation to any act incidental to Crown use as it applies in relation to Crown use of the design.

(5) Where any model, document or other information relating to a design is used in connection with Crown use of the design, or any act incidental to Crown use, section 241 applies to the use of the model, document or other information with the substitution for the references to the design right owner of references to the person entitled to the benefit of any provision of an agreement rendered inoperative by subsection (1) above.

(6) In this section—

"act incidental to Crown use" means anything done for the services of the Crown to the order of a government department by the design right owner in respect of a design;

"payment for Crown use" means such amount as is payable by the government department concerned by virtue of section 241; and

"royalties" includes any benefit determined by reference to the use of the design.

Crown use: compensation for loss of profit

243.—(1) Where Crown use is made of a design, the government department concerned shall pay—

(a) to the design right owner, or

(b) if there is an exclusive licence in force in respect of the design, to the exclusive licensee, compensation for any loss resulting from his not being awarded a contract to supply the articles made to the design.

(2) Compensation is payable only to the extent that such a contract could have been fulfilled from his existing manufacturing capacity; but is payable notwithstanding the existence of circumstances rendering him ineligible for the award of such a contract.

(3) In determining the loss, regard shall be had to the profit which would have been made on such a contract and to the extent to which any manufacturing capacity was under-used.

(4) No compensation is payable in respect of any failure to secure contracts for the supply of articles made to the design otherwise than for the services of the Crown.

(5) The amount payable shall, if not agreed between the design right owner or licensee and the government concerned with the approval of the Treasury, be determined by the court on a reference under section 252; and it is in addition to any amount payable under section 241 or 242.

(6) In the application of this section to Northern Ireland, the reference in subsection (5) to the Treasury shall, where the government department concerned is a Northern Ireland department, be construed as a reference to the Department of Finance and Personnel.

Special provision for Crown use during emergency

244.—(1) During a period of emergency the powers exercisable in relation to a design by virtue of section 240 (Crown use) include power to do any act which would otherwise be an infringement of design right for any purpose which appears to the government department concerned necessary or expedient—

(a) for the efficient prosecution of any war in which Her Majesty may be engaged;

(b) for the maintenance of supplies and services essential to the life of the community;

(c) for securing a sufficiency of supplies and services essential to the well-being of the community;

(d) for promoting the productivity of industry, commerce and agriculture;

(e) for fostering and directing exports and reducing imports, or imports of any classes, from all or any countries and for redressing the balance of trade;

(f) generally for ensuring that the whole resources of the community are available for use, and are used, in a manner best calculated to serve the interests of the community; or

(g) for assisting the relief of suffering and the restoration and distribution of essential supplies and services in any country outside the United Kingdom which is in grave distress as the result of war.

(2) References in this part to the services of the Crown include, as respects a period of emergency, those purposes; and references to "Crown use" include any act which would apart from this section be an infringement of design right.

(3) In this section "period of emergency" means a period beginning with such date as may be declared by Order in Council to be the beginning, and ending with such date as may be so declared to be the end, of a period of emergency for the purposes of this section.

(4) No Order in Council under this section shall be submitted to Her Majesty unless a draft of it has been laid before and approved by a resolution of each House of Parliament.

General

Power to provide for further exceptions

245.—(1) The Secretary of State may if it appears to him necessary in order to—

(a) comply with an international obligation of the United Kingdom, or

(b) secure or maintain reciprocal protection for British designs in other countries,

by order provide that acts of a description specified in the order do not infringe design right.

(2) An order may make different provision for different descriptions of design or article.

(3) An order shall be made by statutory instrument and no order shall be made unless a draft of it has been laid before and approved by a resolution of each House of Parliament.

Chapter IV

Jurisdiction of the Comptroller and the Court

Jurisdiction of the comptroller

Jurisdiction to decide matters relating to design right

246.—(1) A party to a dispute as to any of the following matters may refer the dispute to the comptroller for his decision—

(a) the subsistence of design right,

(b) the term of design right, or

(c) the identity of the person in whom design right first vested;

and the comptroller's decision on the reference is binding on the parties to the dispute.

(2) No other court or tribunal shall decide any such matter except—

(a) on a reference or appeal from the comptroller,

(b) in infringement or other proceedings in which the issue arises incidentally, or

(c) in proceedings brought with the agreement of the parties or the leave of the comptroller.

(3) The comptroller has jurisdiction to decide any incidental question of fact or law arising in the course of a reference under this section.

Application to settle terms of licence of right

247.—(1) A person requiring a licence which is available as of right by virtue of—

    (a) section 237 (licences available in last five years of design right), or

    (b) an order under section 238 (licences made available in the public interest),

may apply to the comptroller to settle the terms of the licence.

(2) No application for the settlement of the terms of a licence available by virtue of section 237 may be made earlier than one year before the earliest date on which the licence may take effect under that section.

(3) The terms of a licence settled by the comptroller shall authorise the licensee to do—

    (a) in the case of licence available by virtue of section 237, everything which would be an infringement of the design right in the absence of a licence;

    (b) in the case of a licence available by virtue of section 238, everything in respect of which a licence is so available.

(4) In settling the terms of a licence the comptroller shall have regard to such factors as may be prescribed by the Secretary of State by order made by statutory instrument.

(5) No such order shall be made unless a draft of it has been laid before and approved by a resolution of each House of Parliament.

(6) Where the terms of a licence are settled by the comptroller, the licence has effect—

    (a) in the case of an application in respect of a licence available by virtue of section 237 made before the earliest date on which the licence may take effect under that section, from that date;

    (b) in any other case, from the date on which the application to the comptroller was made.

Settlement of terms where design right owner unknown

248.—(1) This section applies where a person making an application under section 247 (settlement of terms of licence of right) is unable on reasonable inquiry to discover the identity of the design right owner.

(2) The comptroller may in settling the terms of the licence order that the licence shall be free of any obligation as to royalties or other payments.

(3) If such an order is made the design right owner may apply to the comptroller to vary the terms of the licence with effect from the date on which his application is made.

(4) If the terms of a licence are settled by the comptroller and it is subsequently established that a licence was not available as of right, the licensee shall not be liable in damages for, or for an account of profits in respect of, anything done before he was aware of any claim by the design right owner that a licence was not available.

Appeals as to terms of licence of right

249.—(1) An appeal lies from any decision of the comptroller under section 247 or 248 (settlement of terms of licence of right) to the Appeal Tribunal constituted under section 28 of the Registered Designs Act 1949.

(2) Section 28 of that Act applies to appeals from the comptroller under this section as it applies to appeals from the registrar under that Act; but rules made under that section may make different provision for appeals under this section.

Rules

250.—(1) The Secretary of State may make rules for regulating the procedure to be followed in connection with any proceeding before the comptroller under this Part.

(2) Rules may, in particular, make provision—

(a) prescribing forms;

(b) requiring fees to be paid;

(c) authorising the rectification of irregularities of procedure;

(d) regulating the mode of giving evidence and empowering the comptroller to compel the attendance of witnesses and the discovery of and production of documents;

(e) providing for the appointment of advisers to assist the comptroller in proceedings before him;

(f) prescribing time limits for doing anything required to be done (and providing for the alteration of any such limit); and

(g) empowering the comptroller to award costs and to direct how, to what party and from what parties, costs are to be paid.

(3) Rules prescribing fees require the consent of the Treasury.

(4) The remuneration of an adviser appointed to assist the comptroller shall be determined by the Secretary of State with the consent of the Treasury and shall be defrayed out of money provided by Parliament.

(5) Rules shall be made by statutory instrument which shall be subject to annulment in pursuance of a resolution of either House of Parliament.

Jurisdiction of the court

References and appeals on design right matters

251.—(1) In any proceedings before him under section 246 (reference of matter relating to design right), the comptroller may at any time order the whole proceedings or any question or issue (whether of fact or law) to be referred, on such terms as he may direct, to the High Court or, in Scotland, the Court of Session.

(2) The comptroller shall make such an order if the parties to the proceedings agree that he should do so.

(3) On a reference under this section the court may exercise any power available to the comptroller by virtue of this Part as respects the matter referred

to it and, following its determination, may refer any matter back to the comptroller.

(4) An appeal lies from any decision of the comptroller in proceedings before him under section 246 (decisions on matters relating to design right) to the High Court or, in Scotland, the Court of Session.

Reference of disputes relating to Crown use

252.—(1) A dispute as to any matter which falls to be determined by the court in default of agreement under—

    (a) section 241 (settlement of terms for Crown use),

    (b) section 242 (rights of third parties in case of Crown use), or

    (c) section 243 (Crown use: compensation for loss of profit),

may be referred to the court by any party to the dispute.

(2) In determining a dispute between a government department and any person as to the terms for Crown use of a design the court shall have regard to—

    (a) any sums which that person or a person from whom he derives title has received or is entitled to receive, directly or indirectly, from any government department in respect of the design; and

    (b) whether that person or a person from whom he derives title has in the court's opinion without reasonable cause failed to comply with a request of the department for the use of the design on reasonable terms.

(3) One of two or more joint owners of design right may, without the concurrence of the others, refer a dispute to the court under this section, but shall not do so unless the others are made parties; and none of those others is liable for any costs unless he takes part in the proceedings.

(4) Where the consent of an exclusive licensee is required by section 242(3)(a)(i) to the settlement by agreement of the terms for Crown use of a design, a determination by the court of the amount of any payment to be made for such use is of no effect unless the licensee has been notified of the reference and given an opportunity to be heard.

(5) On the reference of a dispute as to the amount recoverable as mentioned in section 242(3)(a)(ii) (right of exclusive licensee to recover part of amount payable to design right owner) the court shall determine what is just having regard to any expenditure incurred by the licensee—

    (a) in developing the design, or

    (b) in making payments to the design right owner in consideration of the licence (other than royalties or other payments determined by reference to the use of the design).

(6) In this section "the court" means—

    (a) in England and Wales, the High Court or any patents county court having jurisdiction by virtue of an order under section 287 of this Act,

    (b) in Scotland, the Court of Session, and

    (c) in Northern Ireland, the High Court.

CHAPTER V

MISCELLANEOUS AND GENERAL

Miscellaneous

Remedy for groundless threats of infringement proceedings

253.—(1) Where a person threatens another person with proceedings for infringement of design right, a person aggrieved by the threats may bring an action against him claiming—

(a) a declaration to the effect that the threats are unjustifiable;

(b) an injunction against the continuance of the threats;

(c) damages in respect of any loss which he has sustained by the threats.

(2) If the plaintiff proves that the threats were made and that he is a person aggrieved by them, he is entitled to the relief claimed unless the defendant shows that the acts in respect of which proceedings were threatened did constitute, or if done would have constituted, an infringement of the design right concerned.

(3) Proceedings may not be brought under this section in respect of a threat to bring proceedings for an infringement alleged to consist of making or importing anything.

(4) Mere notification that a design is protected by design right does not constitute a threat of proceedings for the purposes of this section.

Licensee under licence of right not to claim connection with design right owner

254.—(1) A person who has a licence in respect of a design by virtue of section 237 or 238 (licences of right) shall not, without the consent of the design right owner—

(a) apply to goods which he is marketing, or proposes to market, in reliance on that licence a trade description indicating that he is the licensee of the design right owner, or

(b) use any such trade description in an advertisement in relation to such goods.

(2) A contravention of subsection (1) is actionable by the design right owner.

(3) In this section "trade description", the reference to applying a trade description to goods and "advertisement" have the same meaning as in the Trade Descriptions Act 1968.

Extent of operation of this Part

Countries to which this Part extends

255.—(1) This Part extends to England and Wales, Scotland and Northern Ireland.

(2) Her Majesty may by Order in Council direct that this Part shall extend, subject to such exceptions and modifications as may be specified in the order, to—

(a) any of the Channel Islands,

(b) the Isle of Man, or

(c) any colony.

(3) That power includes power to extend, subject to such exceptions and modifications as may be specified in the Order, any Order in Council made under section 221 (further provision as to qualification for design right protection) or section 256 (countries enjoying reciprocal protection).

(4) The legislature of a country to which this Part has been extended may modify or add to the provisions of this Part, in their operation as part of the law of the country, as the legislature may consider necessary to adapt the provisions to the circumstances of that country; but not so as to deny design right protection in a case where it would otherwise exist.

(5) Where a country to which this Part extends ceases to be a colony of the United Kingdom, it shall continue to be treated as such a country for the purposes of this Part until—

(a) an Order in Council is made under section 256 designating it as a country enjoying reciprocal protection, or

(b) an Order in Council is made declaring that it shall cease to be so treated by reason of the fact that the provisions of this Part as part of the law of that country have been amended or repealed.

(6) A statutory instrument containing an Order in Council under subsection (5)(b) shall be subject to annulment in pursuance of a resolution of either House of Parliament.

Countries enjoying reciprocal protection

256.—(1) Her Majesty may, if it appears to Her that the law of a country provides adequate protection for British designs, by Order in Council designate that country as one enjoying reciprocal protection under this Part.

(2) If the law of a country provides adequate protection only for certain classes of British design, or only for designs applied to certain classes of article, any Order designating that country shall contain provision limiting, to a corresponding extent, the protection afforded by this Part in relation to designs connected with that country.

(3) An order under this section shall be subject to annulment in pursuance of a resolution of either House of Parliament.

Territorial waters and the continental shelf

257.—(1) For the purposes of this Part the territorial waters of the United Kingdom shall be treated as part of the United Kingdom.

(2) This Part applies to things done in the United Kingdom sector of the continental shelf on a structure or vessel which is present there for purposes directly connected with the exploration of the sea bed or subsoil or the exploitation of their natural resources as it applies to things done in the United Kingdom.

(3) The United Kingdom sector of the continental shelf means the areas designated by order under section 1(7) of the Continental Shelf Act 1964.

Interpretation

Construction of references to design right owner

258.—(1) Where different persons are (whether in consequence of a partial assignment or otherwise) entitled to different aspects of design right in a work, the design right owner for any purpose of this Part is the person who is entitled to the right in the respect relevant for that purpose.

(2) Where design right (or any aspect of design right) is owned by more than one person jointly, references in this Part to the design right owner are to all the owners, so that, in particular, any requirement of the licence of the design right owner requires the licence of all of them.

Joint designs

259.—(1) In this Part a "joint design" means a design produced by the collaboration of two or more designers in which the contribution of each is not distinct from that of the other or others.

(2) References in this Part to the designer of a design shall, except as otherwise provided, be construed in relation to a joint design as references to all the designers of the design.

Application of provisions to articles in kit form

260.—(1) The provisions of this Part apply in relation to a kit, that is, a complete or substantially complete set of components intended to be assembled into an article, as they apply in relation to the assembled article.

(2) Subsection (1) does not affect the question whether design right subsists in any aspect of the design of the components of a kit as opposed to the design of the assembled article.

Requirement of signature: application in relation to body corporate

261. The requirement in the following provisions that an instrument be signed by or on behalf of a person is also satisfied in the case of a body corporate by the affixing of its seal—

    section 222(3) (assignment of design right),

    section 223(1) (assignment of future design right),

    section 225(1) (grant of exclusive licence).

Adaptation of expressions in relation to Scotland

262. In the application of this Part to Scotland—

    "account of profits" means accounting and payment of profits;

    "accounts" means count, reckoning and payment;

    "assignment" means assignation;

"costs" means expenses;

"defendant" means defender;

"delivery up" means delivery;

"injunction" means interdict;

"interlocutory relief" means interim remedy; and

"plaintiff" means pursuer.

Minor definitions

263.—(1) In this Part—

"British design" means a design which qualifies for design right protection by reason of a connection with the United Kingdom of the designer or the person by whom the design is commissioned or the designer is employed;

"business" includes a trade or profession;

"commission" means a commission for money or money's worth;

"the comptroller" means the Comptroller-General of Patents, Designs and Trade Marks;

"computer-generated", in relation to a design, means that the design is generated by computer in circumstances such that there is no human designer,

"country" includes any territory;

"the Crown" includes the Crown in right of Her Majesty's Government in Northern Ireland;

"design document" means any record of a design, whether in the form of a drawing, a written description, a photograph, data stored in a computer or otherwise;

"employee, "employment" and "employer" refer to employment under a contract of service or of apprenticeship;

"government department" includes a Northern Ireland department.

(2) References in this Part to "marketing", in relation to an article, are to its being sold or let for hire, or offered or exposed for sale or hire, in the course of a business, and related expressions shall be construed accordingly; but no account shall be taken for the purposes of this Part of marketing which is merely colourable and not intended to satisfy the reasonable requirements of the public.

(3) References in this Part to an act being done in relation to an article for "commercial purposes" are to its being done with a view to the article in question being sold or hired in the course of a business.

Index of defined expressions

264. The following Table shows provisions defining or otherwise explaining expressions used in this Part (other than provisions defining or explaining an expression used only in the same section)—

account of profits and accounts (in Scotland)	section 262
assignment (in Scotland)	section 262
British designs	section 263(1)
business	section 263(1)
commercial purposes	section 263(3)
commission	section 263(1)
the comptroller	section 263(1)
computer-generated	section 263(1)
costs (in Scotland)	section 262
country	section 263(1)
the Crown	section 263(1)
Crown use	sections 240(5) and 244(2)
defendant (in Scotland)	section 262
delivery up (in Scotland)	section 262
design	section 213(2)
design document	section 263(1)
designer	sections 214 and 259(2)
design right	section 213(1)
design right owner	sections 234(2) and 258
employee, employment and employer	section 263(1)
exclusive licence	section 225(1)
government department	section 263(1)
government department concerned (in relation to Crown use)	section 240(5)
infringing article	section 228
injunction (in Scotland)	section 262
interlocutory relief (in Scotland)	section 262
joint design	section 259(1)
licence (of the design right owner)	sections 222(4), 223(3) and 258
making articles to a design	section 226(2)
marketing (and related expressions)	section 263(2)
original	section 213(4)
plaintiff (in Scotland)	section 262
qualifying individual	section 217(1)
qualifying person	sections 217(1) and (2)
signed	section 261

PART IV: REGISTERED DESIGNS

Amendments of the Registered Designs Act 1949

Registrable designs

265.—(1) For section 1 of the Registered Designs Act 1949 (designs registrable under that Act) substitute—

"*Designs registrable under Act*

1.—(1) In this Act 'design' means features of shape, configuration, pattern or ornament applied to an article by any industrial process, being features which in the finished article appeal to and are judged by the eye, but does not include—

(a) a method or principle of construction, or

(b) features of shape or configuration of an article which—

(i) are dictated solely by the function which the article has to perform, or

(ii) are dependent upon the appearance of another article of which the article is intended by the author of the design to form an integral part.

(2) A design which is new may, upon application by the person claiming to be the proprietor, be registered under this Act in respect of any article, or set of articles, specified in the application.

(3) A design shall not be registered in respect of an article if the appearance of the article is not material, that is, if aesthetic considerations are not normally taken into account to a material extent by persons acquiring or using articles of that description, and would not be so taken into account if the design were to be applied to the article.

(4) A design shall not be regarded as new for the purposes of this Act if it is the same as a design—

(a) registered in respect of the same of any other article in pursuance of a prior application, or

(b) published in the United Kingdom in respect of the same or any other article before the date of the application,

or if it differs from such a design only in immaterial details or in features which are variants commonly used in the trade.

This subsection has effect subject to the provisions of sections 4, 6 and 16 of this Act.

(5) The Secretary of State may by rules provide for excluding from registration under this Act designs for such articles of a primarily literary or artistic character as the Secretary of State thinks fit".

(2) The above amendment does not apply in relation to applications for registration made before the commencement of this Part; but the provisions of section 266 apply with respect to the right in certain designs registered in pursuance of such an application.

Provisions with respect to certain designs registered in pursuance of application made before commencement

266.—(1) Where a design is registered under the Registered Designs Act 1949 in pursuance of an application made after 12th January 1988 and before the commencement of this Part which could not have been registered under section 1 of that Act as substituted by section 265 above—

(a) the right in the registered design expires ten years after the commencement of this Part, if it does not expire earlier in accordance with the 1949 Act, and

(b) any person is, after the commencement of this Part, entitled as of right to a licence to do anything which would otherwise infringe the right in the registered design.

(2) The terms of a licence available by virtue of this section shall, in default of agreement, be settled by the registrar on an application by the person requiring the licence; and the terms so settled shall authorise the licensee to do everything which would be an infringement of the right in the registered design in the absence of a licence.

(3) In settling the terms of a licence the registrar shall have regard to such factors as may be prescribed by the Secretary of State by order made by statutory instrument.

No such order shall be made unless a draft of it has been laid before and approved by a resolution of each House of Parliament.

(4) Where the terms of a licence are settled by the registrar, the licence has effect from the date on which the application to the registrar was made.

(5) Section 11B of the 1949 Act (undertaking to take licence of right in infringement proceedings), as inserted by section 270 below, applies where a licence is available as of right under this section, as it applies where a licence is available as of right under section 11A of that Act.

(6) Where a licence is available as of right under this section, a person to whom a licence was granted before the commencement of this Part may apply to the registrar for an order adjusting the terms of that licence.

(7) An appeal lies from any decision of the registrar under this section.

(8) This section shall be construed as one with the Registered Designs Act 1949.

Authorship and first ownership of designs

267.—(1) Section 2 of the Registered Designs Act 1949 (proprietorship of designs) is amended as follows.

(2) For subsection (1) substitute—

"(1) The author of a design shall be treated for the purposes of this Act as the original proprietor of the design, subject to the following provisions.

(1A) Where a design is created in pursuance of a commission for money or money's worth, the person commissioning the design shall be treated as the original proprietor of the design.

(1B) Where, in a case not falling within subsection (1A), a design is created by an employee in the course of his employment, his employer shall be treated as the original proprietor of the design".

(3) After subsection (2) insert—

"(3) In this Act the 'author' of a design means the person who creates it.

(4) In the case of a design generated by computer in circumstances such that there is no human author, the person by whom the arrangements necessary for the creation of the design are made shall be taken to be the author".

(4) The amendments made by this section do not apply in relation to an application for registration made before the commencement of this Part.

Right given by registration of design

268.—(1) For section 7 of the Registered Designs Act 1949 (right given by registration) substitute—

"*Right given by registration*

7.—(1) The registration of a design under this Act gives the registered proprietor the exclusive right—

    (a) to make or import—

        (i) for sale or hire, or

        (ii) for use for the purposes of a trade or business, or

    (b) to sell, hire or offer or expose for sale or hire,

an article in respect of which the design is registered and to which that design or a design not substantially different from it has been applied.

(2) The right in the registered design is infringed by a person who without the licence of the registered proprietor does anything which by virtue of subsection (1) is the exclusive right of the proprietor.

(3) The right in the registered design is also infringed by a person who without the licence of the registered proprietor makes anything for enabling any such article to be made, in the United Kingdom or elsewhere, as mentioned in subsection (1).

(4) The right in the registered design is also infringed by a person who without the licence of the registered proprietor—

    (a) does anything in relation to a kit that would be an infringement if done in relation to the assembled article (see subsection (1)), or

    (b) makes anything for enabling a kit to be made or assembled, in the United Kingdom or elsewhere, if the assembled article would be such an article as is mentioned in subsection (1);

and for this purpose a 'kit' means a complete or substantially complete set of components intended to be assembled into an article.

(5) No proceedings shall be taken in respect of an infringement committed before the date on which the certificate of registration of the design under this Act is granted.

(6) The right in a registered design is not infringed by the reproduction of a feature of the design which, by virtue of section 1(1)(b), is left out of account in determining whether the design is registrable".

(2) The above amendment does not apply in relation to a design registered in pursuance of an application made before the commencement of this Part.

Duration of right in registered design

269.—(1) For section 8 of the Registered Act 1949 (period of right) substitute—

"*Duration of right in registered design*

8.—(1) The right in a registered design subsists in the first instance for a period of five years from the date of the registration of the design.

(2) The period for which the right subsists may be extended for a second, third, fourth, and fifth period of five years, by applying to the registrar for an extension and paying the prescribed renewal fee.

(3) If the first, second, third or fourth period expires without such application and payment being made, the right shall cease to have effect; and the registrar shall, in accordance with rules made by the Secretary of State, notify the proprietor of that fact.

(4) If during the period of six months immediately following the end of that period an application for extension is made and the prescribed renewal fee and any prescribed additional fee is paid, the right shall be treated as if it had never expired, with the result that—

   (a) anything done under or in relation to the right during that further period shall be treated as valid,

   (b) an act which would have constituted an infringement of the right if it had not expired shall be treated as an infringement, and

   (c) an act which would have constituted use of the design for the services of the Crown if the right had not expired shall be treated as such use.

(5) Where it is shown that a registered design—

   (a) was at the time it was registered a corresponding design in relation to an artistic work in which copyright subsists, and

   (b) by reason of a previous use of that work would not have been registrable but for section 6(4) of this Act (registration despite certain prior applications of design),

the right in the registered design expires when the copyright in that work expires, if that is earlier than the time at which it would otherwise expire, and it may not thereafter be renewed.

(6) The above provisions have effect subject to the proviso to section 4(1) (registration of same design in respect of other articles, &c.).

Restoration of lapsed right in design

8A.—(1) Where the right in a registered design has expired by reason of a failure to extend, in accordance with section 8(2) or (4), the period for which the right subsists, an application for the restoration of the right in the design may be made to the registrar within the prescribed period.

(2) The application may be made by the person who was the registered proprietor of the design or by any other person who would have been entitled to the right in the design if it had not expired; and where the design was held by two or more persons jointly, the application may, with the leave of the registrar, be made by one of more of them without joining the others.

(3) Notice of the application shall be published by the registrar in the prescribed manner.

(4) If the registrar is satisfied that the proprietor took reasonable care to see that the period for which the right subsisted was extended in accordance with section 8(2) or (4), he shall, on payment of any unpaid renewal fee and any prescribed additional fee, order the restoration of the right in the design.

(5) The order may be made subject to such conditions as the registrar thinks fit, and if the proprietor of the design does not comply with any condition the registrar may revoke the order and give such consequential directions as he thinks fit.

(6) Rules altering the period prescribed for the purposes of subsection (1) may contain such transitional provisions and savings as appear to the Secretary of State to be necessary or expedient.

Effect of order for restoration of right

8B.—(1) The effect of an order under section 8A for the restoration of the right in a registered design is as follows.

(2) Anything done under or in relation to the right during the period between expiry and restoration shall be treated as valid.

(3) Anything done during that period which would have constituted an infringement if the right had not expired shall be treated as an infringement—

(a) if done at a time when it was possible for an application for extension to be made under section 8(4); or

(b) if it was a continuation or repetition of an earlier infringing act.

(4) If, after it was no longer possible for such an application for extension to be made and before publication of notice of the application for restoration, a person—

(a) began in good faith to do an act which would have constituted an infringement of the right in the design if it had not expired, or

(b) made in good faith effective and serious preparations to do such an act,

he has the right to continue to do the act or, as the case may be, to do the act, notwithstanding the restoration of the right in the design; but this does not extend to granting a licence to another person to do the act.

(5) If the act was done, or the preparations were made, in the course of a business, the person entitled to the right conferred by subsection (4) may—

(a) authorise the doing of that act by any partners of his for the time being in that business, and

(b) assign that right, or transmit it on death (or in the case of a body corporate on its dissolution), to any person who acquires that part of the business in the course of which the act was done or the preparations were made.

(6) Where an article is disposed of to another in exercise of the rights conferred by subsection (4) or subsection (5), that other and any person claiming through him may deal with the article in the same way as if it had been disposed of by the registered proprietor of the design.

(7) The above provisions apply in relation to the use of a registered design for the services of the Crown as they apply in relation to infringement of the right in the design".

(2) The above amendment does not apply in relation to the right in a design registered in pursuance of an application made before the commencement of this Part.

Powers exercisable for protection of the public interest

270. In the Registered Designs Act 1949 after section 11 insert—

"Powers exercisable for protection of the public interest

11A.—(1) Where a report of the Monopolies and Mergers Commission has been laid before Parliament containing conclusions to the effect—

(a) on a monopoly reference, that a monopoly situation exists and facts found by the Commission operate or may be expected to operate against the public interest,

(b) on a merger reference, that a merger situation qualifying for investigation has been created and the creation of the situation, or particular elements in or consequences of it specified in the report, operate or may be expected to operate against the public interest,

(c) on a competition reference, that a person was engaged in an anti-competitive practice which operated or may be expected to operate against the public interest, or

(d) on a reference under section 11 of the Competition Act 1980 (reference of public bodies and certain other persons), that a person is pursuing a course of conduct which operates against the public interest,

the appropriate Minister or Ministers may apply to the registrar to take action under this section.

(2) Before making an application the appropriate Minister or Ministers shall publish, in such a manner as he or they think appropriate, a notice describing the nature of the proposed application and shall consider any representations which may be made within 30 days of such publication by persons whose interests appear to him or them to be affected.

(3) If on an application under this section it appears to the registrar that the matters specified in the Commission's report as being those which in the Commission's opinion operate or operated or may be expected to operate against the public interest include—

(a) conditions in licences granted in respect of a registered design by its proprietor restricting the use of the design by the licensee or the right of the proprietor to grant other licences, or

(b) a refusal by the proprietor of a registered design to grant licences on reasonable terms,

he may by order cancel or modify any such condition or may, instead or in addition, make an entry in the register to the effect that licences in respect of the design are to be available as of right.

(4) The terms of a licence available by virtue of this section shall, in default of agreement, be settled by the registrar on an application by the person requiring the licence; and terms so settled shall authorise the licensee to do everything which would be an infringement of the right in the registered design in the absence of a licence.

(5) Where the terms of a licence are settled by the registrar the licence has effect from the date on which the application to him was made.

(6) An appeal lies from any order of the registrar under this section.

(7) In this section 'the appropriate Minister or Ministers' means the Minister or Ministers to whom the report of the Monopolies and Mergers Commission was made.

Undertaking to take licence of right in infringement proceedings

11B.—(1) If in proceedings for infringement of the right in a registered design in respect of which a licence is available as of right under section 11A of this Act the defendant undertakes to take a licence on such terms as may be agreed or, in default of agreement, settled by the registrar under that section—

(a) no injunction shall be granted against him, and

(b) the amount recoverable against him by way of damages or on an account of profits shall not exceed double the amount which would have been payable by him as licensee if such a licence on those terms had been granted before the earliest infringement.

(2) An undertaking may the given at any time before final order in the proceedings, without any admission of liability.

(3) Nothing in this section affects the remedies available in respect of an infringement committed before licences of right were available".

Crown use: compensation for loss of profit

271.—(1) In Schedule 1 to the Registered Designs Act 1949 (Crown use), after paragraph 2 insert—

"*Compensation for loss of profit*

2A.—(1) Where Crown use is made of a registered design, the government department concerned shall pay—

(a) to the registered proprietor, or

(b) if there is an exclusive licence in force in respect of the design, to the exclusive licensee,

compensation for any loss resulting from his not being awarded a contract to supply the articles to which the design is applied.

(2) Compensation is payable only to the extent that such a contract could have been fulfilled from his existing manufacturing capacity; but is payable notwithstanding the existence of circumstances rendering him ineligible for the award of such a contract.

(3) In determining the loss, regard shall be had to the profit which would have been made on such a contract and to the extent to which any manufacturing capacity was underused.

(4) No compensation is payable in respect of any failure to secure contracts for the supply of articles to which the design is applied otherwise than for the services of the Crown.

(5) The amount payable under this paragraph shall, if not agreed between the registered proprietor or licensee and the government department concerned with the approval of the Treasury, be determined by the court on a reference under paragraph 3; and it is in addition to any amount

payable under paragraph 1 or 2 of this Schedule.

(6) In this paragraph—

'Crown use', in relation to a design, means the doing of anything by virtue of paragraph 1 which would otherwise be an infringement of the right in the design; and

'the government department concerned', in relation to such use, means the government department by whom or on whose authority the act was done."

(2) In paragraph 3 of that Schedule (reference of disputes as to Crown use), for sub-paragraph (1) substitute—

"(1) Any dispute as to—

(a) the exercise by a Government department, or a person authorised by a Government department, of the powers conferred by paragraph 1 of this Schedure,

(b) terms for the use of a design for the services of the Crown under that paragraph,

(c) the right of any person to receive any part of a payment made under paragraph 1(3), or

(d) the right of any person to receive a payment under paragraph 2A,

may be referred to the court by either party to the dispute.".

(3) The above amendments apply in relation to any Crown use of a registered design after the commencement of this section, even if the terms for such use were settled before commencement.

Minor and consequential amendments

272. The Registered Designs Act 1949 is further amended in accordance with Schedule 3 which contains minor amendments and amendments consequential upon the provisions of this Act.

Supplementary

Text of Registered Designs Act 1949 as amended

273. Schedule 4 contains the text of the Registered Designs Act 1949 as amended.

PART V: PATENT AGENTS AND TRADE MARK AGENTS

Patent agents

Persons permitted to carry on business of a patent agent

274.—(1) Any individual, partnership or body corporate may, subject to the following provisions of this Part, carry on the business of acting as agent for others for the purpose of—

(a) applying for or obtaining patents, in the United Kingdom or elsewhere, or

(b) conducting proceedings before the comptroller relating to applications for, or otherwise in connection with, patents.

(2) This does not affect any restriction under the European Patent Convention as to who may act on behalf of another for any purpose relating to European patents.

The register of patent agents

275.—(1) The Secretary of State may make rules requiring the keeping of a register of persons who act as agent for others for the purposes of applying for or obtaining patents; and in this Part a "registered patent agent" means a person whose name is entered in the register kept under this section.

(2) The rules may contain such provision as the Secretary of State thinks fit regulating the registration of persons, and may in particular—

     (a) require the payment of such fees as may be prescribed, and

     (b) authorise in prescribed cases the erasure from the register of the name of any person registered in it, or the suspension of a person's registration.

(3) The rules may delegate the keeping of the register to another person, and may confer on that person—

     (a) power to make regulations—

         (i) with respect to the payment of fees, in the cases and subject to the limits prescribed by rules, and

         (ii) with respect to any other matter which could be regulated by rules, and

     (b) such other functions, including disciplinary functions, as may be prescribed by rules.

(4) Rules under this section shall be made by statutory instrument which shall be subject to annulment in pursuance of a resolution of either House of Parliament.

Persons entitled to describe themselves as patent agents

276.—(1) An individual who is not a registered patent agent shall not—

     (a) carry on a business (otherwise than in partnership) under any name or other description which contains the words "patent agent" or "patent attorney"; or

     (b) in the course of a business otherwise describe himself, or permit himself to be described, as a "patent agent" or "patent attorney".

(2) A partnership shall not—

     (a) carry on business under any name or other description which contains the words "patent agent" or "patent attorney"; or

     (b) in the course of a business otherwise describe itself, or permit itself to be described as, a firm of "patent agents" or "patent attorneys",

unless all the partners are registered patent agents or the partnership satisfies such conditions as may be prescribed for the purposes of this section.

(3) A body corporate shall not—

(a) carry on a business (otherwise than in partnership) under any name or other description which contains the words "patent agent" or "patent attorney"; or

(b) in the course of a business otherwise describe itself, or permit itself to be described as, a "patent agent" or "patent attorney",

unless all the directors of the body corporate are registered patent agents or the body satisfies such conditions as may be prescribed for the purposes of this section.

(4) Subsection (3) does not apply to a company which began to carry on business as a patent agent before 17th November 1917 if the name of a director or the manager of the company who is a registered patent agent is mentioned as being so registered in all professional advertisements, circulars or letters issued by or with the company's consent on which its name appears.

(5) Where this section would be contravened by the use of the words "patent agent" or "patent attorney" in reference to an individual, partnership or body corporate, it is equally contravened by the use of other expressions in reference to that person, or his business or place of business, which are likely to be understood as indicating that he is entitled to be described as a "patent agent" or "patent attorney".

(6) A person who contravenes this section commits an offence and is liable on summary conviction to a fine not exceeding level 5 on the standard scale; and proceedings for such an offence may be begun at any time within a year from the date of the offence.

(7) This section has effect subject to—

(a) section 277 (persons entitled to describe themselves as European patent attorneys, &c.), and

(b) section 278(1) (use of term "patent attorney" in reference to solicitors).

Persons entitled to describe themselves as European patent attorney, &c

277.—(1) The term "European patent attorney" or "European patent agent" may be used in the following cases without any contravention of section 276.

(2) An individual who is on the European list may—

(a) carry on business under a name or other description which contains the words "European patent attorney" or "European patent agent", or

(b) otherwise describe himself, or permit himself to be described, as a "European patent attorney" or "European patent agent".

(3) A partnership of which not less than the prescribed number or proportion of partners is on the European list may—

(a) carry on a business under a name or other description which contains the words "European patent attorneys" or "European patent agents", or

(b) otherwise describe itself, or permit itself to be described, as a firm which carries on the business of a "European patent attorney" or "European patent agent".

(4) A body corporate of which not less than the prescribed number or proportion of directors is on the European list may—

    (a) carry on a business under a name or other description which contains the words "European patent attorney" or "European patent agent", or

    (b) otherwise describe itself, or permit itself to be described as, a company which carries on the business of a "European patent attorney" or "European patent agent".

(5) Where the term "European patent attorney" or "European patent agent" may, in accordance with this section, be used in reference to an individual, partnership or body corporate, it is equally permissible to use other expressions in reference to that person, or to his business or place of business, which are likely to be understood as indicating that he is entitled to be described as a "European patent attorney" or "European patent agent".

Use of the term "patent attorney": supplementary provisions

278.—(1) The term "patent attorney" may be used in reference to a solicitor, and a firm of solicitors may be described as a firm of "patent attorneys", without any contravention of section 276.

(2) No offence is committed under the enactments restricting the use of certain expressions in reference to persons not qualified to act as solicitors—

    (a) by the use of the term "patent attorney" in reference to a registered patent agent, or

    (b) by the use of the term "European patent attorney" in reference to a person on the European list.

(3) The enactments referred to in subsection (2) are section 21 of the Solicitors Act 1974, section 31 of the Solicitors (Scotland) Act 1980 and Article 22 of the Solicitors (Northern Ireland) Order 1976.

Power to prescribe conditions, &c. for mixed partnerships and bodies corporate

279.—(1) The Secretary of State may make rules—

    (a) prescribing the conditions to be satisfied for the purposes of section 276 (persons entitled to describe themselves as patent agents) in relation to a partnership where not all the partners are qualified persons or a body corporate where not all the directors are qualified persons, and

    (b) imposing requirements to be complied with by such partnerships and bodies corporate.

(2) The rules may, in particular—

    (a) prescribe conditions as to the number or proportion or partners or directors who must be qualified persons;

    (b) impose requirements as to—

        (i) the identification of qualified and unqualified persons in professional advertisements, circulars or letters issued by or with

the consent of the partnership or body corporate and which relate
to it or to its business; and

    (ii) the manner in which a partnership or body corporate is
to organise its affairs so as to secure that qualified persons exercise
a sufficient degree of control over the activities of unqualified
persons.

(3) Contravention of a requirement imposed by the rules is an offence for
which a person is liable on summary conviction to a fine not exceeding level 5
on the standard scale.

(4) The Secretary of State may make rules prescribing for the purposes of
section 277 the number or proportion of partners of a partnership or directors
of a body corporate who must be qualified persons in order for the partnership
or body to take advantage of that section.

(5) In this section "qualified person"—

    (a) in subsections (1) and (2), means a person who is a registered patent
agent, and

    (b) in subsection (4), means a person who is on the European list.

(6) Rules under this section shall be made by statutory instrument which shall
be subject to annulment in pursuance of a resolution of either House of
Parliament.

Privilege for communications with patent agents

280.—(1) This section applies to communications as to any matter relating to
the protection of any invention, design, technical information, trade mark or
service mark, or as to any matter involving passing off.

(2) Any such communication—

    (a) between a person and his patent agent, or

    (b) for the purpose of obtaining, or in response to a request for, informa-
tion which a person is seeking for the purpose of instructing his patent
agent,

is privileged from disclosure in legal proceedings in England, Wales or Northern
Ireland in the same way as a communication between a person and his solicitor
or, as the case may be, a communication for the purpose of obtaining, or in
response to a request for, information which a person seeks for the purpose of
instructing his solicitor.

(3) In subsection (2) "patent agent" means—

    (a) a registered patent agent or a person who is on the European list,

    (b) a partnership entitled to describe itself as a firm of patent agents or as
a firm carrying on the business of a European patent attorney, or

    (c) a body corporate entitled to describe itself as a patent agent or as a
company carrying on the business of a European patent attorney.

(4) It is hereby declared that in Scotland the rules of law which confer
privilege from disclosure in legal proceedings in respect of communications
extend to such communications as are mentioned in this section.

Power of comptroller to refuse to deal with certain agents

281.—(1) This section applies to business under the Patents Act 1949, the Registered Designs Act 1949 or the Patents Act 1977.

(2) The Secretary of State may make rules authorising the comptroller to refuse to recognise as agent in respect of any business to which this section applies—

(a) a person who has been convicted of an offence under section 88 of the Patents Act 1949, section 114 of the Patents Act 1977 or section 276 of this Act;

(b) an individual whose name has been erased from and not restored to, or who is suspended from, the register of patent agents on the ground of misconduct;

(c) a person who is found by the Secretary of State to have been guilty of such conduct as would, in the case of an individual registered in the register of patent agents, render him liable to have his name erased from the register on the ground of misconduct;

(d) a partnership or body corporate of which one of the partners or directors is a person whom the comptroller could refuse to recognise under paragraph (a), (b) or (c) above.

(3) The rules may contain such incidental and supplementary provisions as appear to the Secretary of State to be appropriate and may, in particular, prescribe circumstances in which a person is or is not to be taken to have been guilty of misconduct.

(4) Rules made under this section shall be made by statutory instrument which shall be subject to annulment in pursuance of a resolution of either House of Parliament.

(5) The comptroller shall refuse to recognise as agent in respect of any business to which this section applies a person who neither resides nor has a place of business in the United Kingdom, the Isle of Man or another member State of the European Economic Community.

Trade mark agents

The register of trade mark agents

282.—(1) The Secretary of State may make rules requiring the keeping of a register of persons who act as agent for others for the purpose of applying for or obtaining the registration of trade marks; and in this Part a "registered trade mark agent" means a person whose name is entered in the register kept under this section.

(2) The rules may contain such provision as the Secretary of State thinks fit regulating the registration of persons, and may in particular—

(a) require the payment of such fees as may be prescribed, and

(b) authorise in prescribed cases the erasure from the register of the name of any person registered in it, or the suspension of a person's registration.

(3) The rules may delegate the keeping of the register to another person, and may confer on that person—

(a) power to make regulations—

(i) with respect to the payment of fees, in the cases and subject to the limits prescribed by rules, and

(ii) with respect to any other matter which could be regulated by rules, and

(b) such other functions, including disciplinary functions, as may be prescribed by rules.

(4) Rules under this section shall be made by statutory instrument which shall be subject to annulment in pursuance of a resolution of either House of Parliament.

Unregistered persons not to be described as registered trade mark agents

283.—(1) An individual who is not a registered trade mark agent shall not—

(a) carry on a business (otherwise than in partnership) under any name or other description which contains the words "registered trade mark agent"; or

(b) in the course of a business otherwise describe or hold himself out, or permit himself to be described or held out, as a registered trade mark agent.

(2) A partnership shall not—

(a) carry on a business under any name or other description which contains the words "registered trade mark agent"; or

(b) in the course of a business otherwise describe or hold itself out, or permit itself to be described or held out, as a firm of registered trade mark agents,

unless all the partners are registered trade mark agents or the partnership satisfies such conditions as may be prescribed for the purposes of this section.

(3) A body corporate shall not—

(a) carry on a business (otherwise than in partnership) under any name or other description which contains the words "registered trade mark agent"; or

(b) in the course of a business otherwise describe or hold itself out, or permit itself to be described or held out, as a registered trade mark agent,

unless all the directors of the body corporate are registered trade mark agents or the body satisfies such conditions as may be prescribed for the purposes of this section.

(4) The Secretary of State may make rules prescribing the conditions to be satisfied for the purposes of this section in relation to a partnership where not all the partners are registered trade mark agents or a body corporate where not all the directors are registered trade mark agents; and the rules may, in particular, prescribe conditions as to the number or proportion of partners or directors who must be registered trade mark agents.

(5) Rules under this section shall be made by statutory instrument which shall be subject to annulment in pursuance of a resolution of either House of Parliament.

(6) A person who contravenes this section commits an offence and is liable on summary conviction to a fine not exceeding level 5 on the standard scale; and proceedings for such an offence may be begun at any time within a year from the date of the offence.

Privilege for communications with registered trade mark agents

284.—(1) This section applies to communications as to any matter relating to the protection of any design, trade mark or service mark, or as to any matter involving passing off.

(2) Any such communication—

(a) between a person and his trade mark agent, or

(b) for the purpose of obtaining, or in response to a request for, information which a person is seeking for the purpose of instructing his trade mark agent,

is privileged from disclosure in legal proceedings in England, Wales or Northern Ireland in the same way as a communication between a person and his solicitor or, as the case may be, a communication for the purpose of obtaining, or in purpose to a request for, information which a person seeks for the purpose of instructing his solicitor.

(3) In subsection (1) "trade mark agent" means—

(a) a registered trade mark agent, or

(b) a partnership entitled to describe itself as a firm of registered trade mark agents, or

(c) a body corporate entitled to describe itself as a registered trade mark agent.

(4) It is hereby declared that in Scotland the rules of law which confer privilege from disclosure in legal proceedings in respect of communications extend to such communications as are mentioned in subsection (1).

Offences committed by partnerships and bodies corporate

285.—(1) Proceedings for an offence under this Part alleged to have been committed by a partnership shall be brought in the name of the partnership and not in that of the partners; but without prejudice to any liability of theirs under subsection (4) below.

(2) The following provisions apply for the purposes of such proceedings as in relation to a body corporate—

(a) any rules of court relating to the service of documents;

(b) in England, Wales or Northern Ireland, Schedule 3 to the Magistrates' Courts Act 1980 or Schedule 4 to the Magistrates' Courts (Northern Ireland) Order 1981 (procedure on charge of offence).

(3) A fine imposed on a partnership on its conviction in such proceedings shall be paid out of the partnership assets.

(4) Where a partnership is guilty of an offence under this Part, every partner, other than a partner who is proved to have been ignorant of or to have attempted to prevent the commission of the offence, is also guilty of the offence and liable to be proceeded against and punished accordingly.

(5) Where an offence under this Part committed by a body corporate is proved to have been committed with the consent or connivance of a director, manager, secretary or other similar officer of the body, or a person purporting to act in any such capacity, he as well as the body corporate is guilty of the offence and liable to be proceeded against and punished accordingly.

Interpretation

286. In this Part—

"the comptroller" means the Comptroller-General of Patents, Designs and Trade Marks;

"director", in relation to a body corporate whose affairs are managed by its members, means any member of the body corporate;

"the European list" means the list of professional representatives maintained by the European Patent Office in pursuance of the European Patent Convention;

"registered patent agent" has the meaning given by section 275(1);

"registered trade mark agent" has the meaning given by section 282(1).

PART VI: PATENTS

Patents county courts

Patents county courts: special jurisdiction

287.—(1) The Lord Chancellor may by order made by statutory instrument designate any county court as a patents county court and confer on it jurisdiction (its "special jurisdiction") to hear and determine such descriptions of proceedings—

(a) relating to patents or designs, or

(b) ancillary to, or arising out of the same subject matter as, proceedings relating to patents or designs,

as may be specified in the order.

(2) The special jurisdiction of a patents county court is exercisable throughout England and Wales, but rules of court may provide for a matter pending in one such court to be heard and determined in another or partly in that and partly in another.

(3) A patents county court may entertain proceedings within its special jurisdiction notwithstanding that no pecuniary remedy is sought.

(4) An order under this section providing for the discontinuance of any of the special jurisdiction of a patents county court may make provision as to proceedings pending in the court when the order comes into operation.

(5) Nothing in this section shall be construed as affecting the ordinary jurisdiction of a county court.

*Financial limits in relation to proceedings within
special jurisdiction of patents county court*

288.—(1) Her Majesty may by Order in Council provide for limits of amount or value in relation to any description of proceedings within the special jurisdiction of a patents county court.

(2) If a limit is imposed on the amount of a claim of any description and the plaintiff has a cause of action for more than that amount, he may abandon the excess; in which case a patents county court shall have jurisdiction to hear and determine the action, but the plaintiff may not recover more than that amount.

(3) Where the court has jurisdiction to hear and determine an action by virtue of subsection (2), the judgement of the court in the action is in full discharge of all demands in respect of the cause of action, and entry of the judgement shall be made accordingly.

(4) If the parties agree, by a memorandum signed by them or by their respective solicitors or other agents, that a patents county court shall have jurisdiction in any proceedings, that court shall have jurisdiction to hear and determine the proceedings notwithstanding any limit imposed under this section.

(5) No recommendation shall be made to Her Majesty to make an Order under this section unless a draft of the Order has been laid before and approved by a resolution of each House of Parliament.

Transfer of proceedings between High Court and patents county court

289.—(1) No order shall be made under section 41 of the County Courts Act 1984 (power of High Court to order proceedings to be transferred from the county court) in respect of proceedings within the special jurisdiction of a patents county court.

(2) In considering in relation to proceedings within the special jurisdiction of a patents county court whether an order should be made under section 40 or 42 of the County Courts Act 1984 (transfer of proceedings from or to the High Court), the court shall have regard to the financial position of the parties and may order the transfer of the proceedings to a patents county court or, as the case may be, refrain from ordering their transfer to the High Court notwithstanding that the proceedings are likely to raise an important question of fact or law.

*Limitation of costs where pecuniary claim could have
been brought in patents county court*

290.—(1) Where an action is commenced in the High Court which could have been commenced in a patents county court and in which a claim for a pecuniary remedy is made, then, subject to the provisions of this section, if the plaintiff recovers less than the prescribed amount, he is not entitled to recover any more costs than those to which he would have been entitled if the action had been brought in the county court.

(2) For this purpose a plaintiff shall be treated as recovering the full amount recoverable in respect of his claim without regard to any deduction made in respect of matters not falling to be taken into account in determining whether the action could have been commenced in a patents county court.

(3) This section does not affect any question as to costs if it appears to the High Court that there was reasonable ground for supposing the amount recoverable in respect of the plaintiff's claim to be in excess of the prescribed amount.

(4) The High Court, if satisfied that there was sufficient reason for bringing the action in the High Court, may make an order allowing the costs or any part of the costs on the High Court scale or on such one of the county court scales as it may direct.

(5) This section does not apply to proceedings brought by the Crown.

(6) In this section "the prescribed amount" means such amount as may be prescribed by Her Majesty for the purposes of this section by Order in Council.

(7) No recommendation shall be made to Her Majesty to make an Order under this section unless a draft of the Order has been laid before and approved by a resolution of each House of Parliament.

Proceedings in patents county court

291.—(1) Where a county court is designated a patents county court, the Lord Chancellor shall nominate a person entitled to sit as a judge of that court as the patents judge.

(2) County court rules shall make provision for securing that, so far as is practicable and appropriate—

(a) proceedings within the special jurisdiction of a patents county court are dealt with by the patents judge, and

(b) the judge, rather than a registrar or other officer of the court, deals with interlocutory matters in the proceedings.

(3) County court rules shall make provision empowering a patents county court in proceedings within its special jurisdiction, on or without the application of any party—

(a) to appoint scientific advisers or assessors to assist the court, or

(b) to order the Patent Office to inquire into and report on any question of fact or opinion.

(4) Where the court exercises either of those powers on the application of a party, the remuneration or fees payable to the Patent Office shall be at such rate as may be determined in accordance with county court rules and shall be costs of the proceedings unless otherwise ordered by the judge.

(5) Where the court exercises either of those powers of its own motion, the remuneration or fees payable to the Patent Office shall be at such rate as may be determined by the Lord Chancellor with the approval of the Treasury and shall be paid out of money provided by Parliament.

*Rights and duties of registered patent agents in relation
to proceedings in patents county court*

292.—(1) A registered patent agent may do, in or in connection with proceedings in a patents county court which are within the special jurisdiction of that court, anything which a solicitor of the Supreme Court might do, other than prepare a deed.

(2) The Lord Chancellor may by regulations provide that the right conferred by subsection (1) shall be subject to such conditions and restrictions as appear to the Lord Chancellor to be necessary or expedient; and different provision may be made for different descriptions of proceedings.

(3) A patents county court has the same power to enforce an undertaking by a registered patent agent acting in pursuance of this section as it has, by virtue of section 142 of the County Courts Act 1984, in relation to a solicitor.

(4) Nothing in section 143 of the County Courts Act 1984 (prohibition on persons other than solicitors receiving remuneration) applies to a registered patent agent acting in pursuance of this section.

(5) The provisions of county court rules prescribing scales of costs to be paid to solicitors apply in relation to registered patent agents acting in pursuance of this section.

(6) Regulations under this section shall be made by statutory instrument which shall be subject to annulment in pursuance of a resolution of either House of Parliament.

Licences of right in respect of certain patents

Restriction of acts authorised by certain licences

293. In paragraph 4(2)(c) of Schedule 1 to the Patents Act 1977 (licences to be available as of right where term of existing patent extended), at the end insert ", but subject to paragraph 4A below", and after that paragraph insert—

"**4A.**—(1) If the proprietor of a patent for an invention which is a product files a declaration with the Patent Office in accordance with this paragraph, the licences to which persons are entitled by virtue of paragraph 4(2)(c) above shall not extend to a use of the product which is excepted by or under this paragraph.

(2) Pharmaceutical use is excepted, that is—

  (a) use as a medicinal product within the meaning of the Medicines Act 1968, and

  (b) the doing of any other act mentioned in section 60(1)(a) above with a view to such use.

(3) The Secretary of State may by order except such other uses as he thinks fit; and an order may—

  (a) specify as an excepted use any act mentioned in section 60(1)(a) above, and

  (b) make different provision with respect to acts done in different circumstances or for different purposes.

(4) For the purposes of this paragraph the question what uses are excepted, so far as that depends on—

    (a) orders under section 130 of the Medicines Act 1968 (meaning of "medicinal product"), or

    (b) orders under sub-paragraph (3) above,

shall be determined in relation to a patent at the beginning of the sixteenth year of the patent.

(5) A declaration under this paragraph shall be in the prescribed form and shall be filed in the prescribed manner and within the prescribed time limits.

(6) A declaration may not be filed—

    (a) in respect of a patent which has at the commencement of section 293 of the Copyright, Designs and Patents Act 1988 passed the end of its fifteenth year; or

    (b) if at the date of filing there is—

        (i) an existing licence for any description of excepted use of the product, or

        (ii) an outstanding application under section 46(3)(a) or (b) above for the settlement by the comptroller of the terms of a licence for any description of excepted use of the product,

    and, in either case, the licence took or is to take effect at or after the end of the sixteenth year of the patent.

(7) Where a declaration has been filed under this paragraph in respect of a patent—

    (a) section 46(3)(c) above (restriction of remedies for infringement where licences available as of right) does not apply to an infringement of the patent in so far as it consists of the excepted use of the product after the filing of the declaration; and

    (b) section 46(3)(d) above (abatement of renewal fee if licences available as of right) does not apply to the patent".

When application may be made for settlement of terms of licence

294. In Schedule 1 to the Patents Act 1977, after the paragraph inserted by section 293 above, insert—

"4B.—(1) An application under section 46(3)(a) or (b) above for the settlement by the comptroller of the terms on which a person is entitled to a licence by virtue of paragraph 4(2)(c) above is ineffective if made before the beginning of the sixteenth year of the patent.

(2) This paragraph applies to applications made after the commencement of section 294 of the Copyright, Designs and Patents Act 1988 and to any application made before the commencement of that section in respect of a patent which has not at the commencement of that section passed the end of its fifteenth year".

Patents: miscellaneous amendments

Patents: miscellaneous amendments

295. The Patents Act 1949 and the Patents Act 1977 are amended in accordance with Schedule 5.

PART VII: MISCELLANEOUS AND GENERAL

Devices designed to circumvent copy-protection

Devices designed to circumvent copy-protection

296.—(1) This section applies where copies of a copyright work are issued to the public, by or with the licence of the copyright owner, in an electronic form which is copy-protected.

(2) The person issuing the copies to the public has the same rights against a person who, knowing or having reason to believe that it will be used to make infringing copies—

(a) makes, imports, sells or lets for hire, offers or exposes for sale or hire, or advertises for sale or hire, any device or means specifically designed or adapted to circumvent the form of copy-protection employed, or

(b) publishes information intended to enable or assist persons to circumvent that form of copy-protection,

as a copyright owner has in respect of an infringement of copyright.

(3) Further, he has the same rights under section 99 or 100 (delivery up or seizure of certain articles) in relation to any such device or means which a person has in his possession, custody or control with the intention that it should be used to make infringing copies of copyright works, as a copyright owner has in relation to an infringing copy.

(4) References in this section to copy-protection include any device or means intended to prevent or restrict copying of a work or to impair the quality of copies made.

(5) Expressions used in this session which are defined for the purposes of Part I of this Act (copyright) have the same meaning as in that Part.

(6) The following provisions apply in relation to proceedings under this section as in relation to proceedings under Part I (copyright)—

(a) sections 104 to 106 of this Act (presumptions as to certain matters relating to copyright), and

(b) section 72 of the Supreme Court Act 1981, section 15 of the Law Reform (Miscellaneous Provisions) (Scotland) Act 1985 and section 94A of the Judicature (Northern Ireland) Act 1978 (withdrawal of privilege against self-incrimination in certain proceedings relating to intellectual property);

and section 114 of this Act applies, with the necessary modifications, in relation to the disposal of anything delivered up or seized by virtue of subsection (3) above.

Fraudulent reception of transmissions

Offences of fraudulently receiving programmes

297.—(1) A person who dishonestly receives a programme included in a broadcasting or cable programme service provided from a place in the United Kingdom with intent to avoid payment of any charge applicable to the reception of the programme commits an offence and is liable on summary conviction to a fine not exceeding level 5 on the standard scale.

(2) Where an offence under this section committed by a body corporate is proved to have been committed with the consent or connivance of a director, manager, secretary or other similar officer of the body, or a person purporting to act in any such capacity, he as well as the body corporate is guilty of the offence and liable to be proceeded against and punished accordingly.

In relation to a body corporate whose affairs are managed by its members "director" means a member of the body corporate.

Rights and remedies in respect of apparatus, &c.
for unauthorised reception of transmission

298.—(1) A person who—

(a) makes charges for the reception of programmes included in a broadcasting or cable programme service provided from a place in the United Kingdom, or

(b) sends encrypted transmissions of any other description from a place in the United Kingdom,

is entitled to the following rights and remedies.

(2) He has the same right and remedies against a person who—

(a) makes, imports or sells or lets for hire any apparatus or device designed or adapted to enable or assist persons to receive the programmes or other transmissions when they are not entitled to do so, or

(b) publishes any information which is calculated to enable or assist persons to receive the programmes or other transmissions when they are not entitled to do so,

as a copyright owner has in respect of an infringement of copyright.

(3) Further, he has the same rights under section 99 or 100 (delivery up or seizure of certain articles) in relation to any such apparatus or device as a copyright owner has in relation to an infringing copy.

(4) Section 72 of the Supreme Court Act 1981, section 15 of the Law Reform (Miscellaneous Provisions) (Scotland) Act 1985 and section 95A of the Judicature (Northern Ireland) Act 1978 (withdrawal of privilege against self-incrimination in certain proceedings relating to intellectual property) apply to proceedings under this section as to proceedings under Part I of this Act (copyright).

(5) In section 97(1) (innocent infringement of copyright) as it applies to proceedings for infringement of the rights conferred by this section, the reference to the defendant not knowing or having reason to believe that copyright subsisted in the work shall be construed as a reference to his not knowing or having reason to believe that his acts infringed the rights conferred by this section.

(6) Section 114 of this Act applies, with the necessary modifications, in relation to the disposal of anything delivered up or seized by virtue of subsection (3) above.

Supplementary provisions as to fraudulent reception

299.—(1) Her Majesty may by Order in Council—

(a) provide that section 297 applies in relation to programmes included in services provided from a country or territory outside the United Kingdom, and

(b) provide that section 298 applies in relation to such programmes and to encrypted transmissions sent from such a country or territory.

(2) No such Order shall be made unless it appears to Her Majesty that provision has been or will be made under the laws of that country or territory giving adequate protection to persons making charges for programmes included in broadcasting or cable programme services provided from the United Kingdom or, as the case may be, for encrypted transmissions sent from the United Kingdom.

(3) A statutory instrument containing an Order in Council under subsection (1) shall be subject to annulment in pursuance of a resolution of either House of Parliament.

(4) Where sections 297 and 298 apply in relation to a broadcasting service or cable programme service, they also apply to any service run for the person providing that service, or a person providing programmes for that service, which consists wholly or mainly in the sending by means of a telecommunications system of sounds or visual images, or both.

(5) In sections 297 and 298, and this section, "programme", "broadcasting" and "cable programme service", and related expressions, have the same meaning as in Part I (copyright).

Fraudulent application or use of trade mark

Fraudulent application or use of trade mark an offence

300. In the Trade Marks Act 1938 the following sections are inserted before section 59, after the heading "Offences and restraint of use of Royal Arms"—

"*Fraudulent application of use of trade mark an offence*

58A.—(1) It is an offence, subject to subsection (3) below, for a person—

(a) to apply a mark identical to or nearly resembling a registered trade mark to goods, or to material used or intended to be used for labelling, packaging or advertising goods, or

(b) to sell, let for hire, or offer or expose for sale or hire, or distribute—

(i) goods bearing such a mark, or

(ii) material bearing such a mark which is used or intended to be used for labelling, packaging or advertising goods, or

   (c) to use material bearing such a mark in the course of a business for labelling, packaging or advertising goods, or

   (d) to possess in the course of a business goods or material bearing such a mark with a view to doing any of the things mentioned in paragraphs (a) to (c),

when he is not entitled to use the mark in relation to the goods in question and the goods are not connected in the course of trade with a person who is so entitled.

   (2) It is also an offence, subject to subsection (3) below, for a person to possess in the course of a business goods or material bearing a mark identical to or nearly resembling a registered trade mark with a view to enabling or assisting another person to do any of the things mentioned in subsection (1)(a) to (c), knowing or having reason to believe that the other person is not entitled to use the mark in relation to the goods in question and that the goods are not connected in the course of trade with a person who is so entitled.

   (3) A person commits an offence under subsection (1) or (2) only if—

   (a) he acts with a view to gain for himself or another, or with intent to cause loss to another, and

   (b) he intends that the goods in question should be accepted as connected in the course of trade with a person entitled to use the mark in question;

and it is a defence for a person charged with an offence under subsection (1) to show that he believed on reasonable grounds that he was entitled to use the mark in relation to the goods in question.

   (4) A person guilty of an offence under this section is liable—

   (a) on summary conviction to imprisonment for a term not exceeding six months or a fine not exceeding the statutory maximum, or both;

   (b) on conviction on indictment to a fine or imprisonment for a term not exceeding ten years, or both.

   (5) Where an offence under this section committed by a body corporate is proved to have been committed with the consent or connivance of a director, manager, secretary or other similar officer of the body, or a person purporting to act in any such capacity, he as well as the body corporate is guilty of the offence and liable to be proceeded against and punished accordingly.

In relation to a body corporate whose affairs are managed by its members 'director' means a member of the body corporate.

   (6) In this section 'business' includes a trade or profession."

Delivery up of offending goods and material

58B.—(1) The court by which a person is convicted of an offence under section 58A may, if satisfied that at the time of his arrest or charge he had in his possession, custody or control—

   (a) goods or material in respect of which the offence was committed, or

(b) goods of the same description as those in respect of which the offence was committed, or material similar to that in respect of which the offence was committed, bearing a mark identical to or nearly resembling that in relation to which the offence was committed,

order that the goods or material be delivered up to such person as the court may direct.

(2) For this purpose a person shall be treated as charged with an offence—

(a) in England, Wales and Northern Ireland, when he is orally charged or is served with a summons or indictment;

(b) in Scotland, when he is cautioned, charged or served with a complaint or indictment.

(3) An order may be made by the court of its own motion or on the application of the prosecutor (or, in Scotland, the Lord Advocate or procurator-fiscal), but shall not be made if it appears to the court unlikely that any order will be made under section 58C (order as to disposal of offending goods or material).

(4) An appeal lies from an order made under this section by a magistrates' court—

(a) in England and Wales, to the Crown Court, and

(b) in Northern Ireland, to the county court;

and in Scotland, where an order has been made under this section, the person from whose possession, custody or control the goods or material have been removed may, without prejudice to any other form of appeal under any rule of law, appeal against that order in the same manner as against sentence.

(5) A person to whom goods or material are delivered up in pursuance of an order under this section shall retain it pending the making of an order under section 58C.

(6) Nothing in this section affects the powers of the court under section 43 of the Powers of Criminal Courts Act 1973, section 223 or 436 of the Criminal Procedure (Scotland) Act 1975 or Article 7 of the Criminal Justice (Northern Ireland) Order 1980 (general provisions as to forfeiture in criminal proceedings).

Order as to disposal of offending goods or material

58C.—(1) Where goods or material have been delivered up in pursuance of an order under section 58B, an application may be made to the court for an order that they be destroyed or forfeited to such person as the court may think fit.

(2) Provision shall be made by rules of court as to the service of notice on persons having an interest in the goods or material, and any such person is entitled—

(a) to appear in proceedings for an order under this section, whether or not he was served with notice, and

(b) to appeal against any order made, whether or not he appeared;

and an order shall not take effect until the end of the period within which notice of an appeal may be given or, if before the end of that period notice of appeal is duly given, until the final determination or abandonment of the proceedings on the appeal.

(3) Where there is more than one person interested in goods or material, the court shall make such order as it thinks fit.

(4) References in this section to a person having an interest in goods or material include any person in whose favour an order could be made under this section or under sections 114, 204 or 231 of the Copyright, Designs and Patents Act 1988 (which make similar provision in relation to infringement of copyright, rights in performances and design right).

(5) Proceedings for an order under this section may be brought—

(a) in a county court in England, Wales and Northern Ireland, provided the value of the goods or material in question does not exceed the county court limit for actions in tort, and

(b) in a sheriff court in Scotland;

but this shall not be construed as affecting the jurisdiction of the High Court or, in Scotland, the Court of Session.

Enforcement of section 58A

58D.—(1) The functions of a local weights and measures authority include the enforcement in their area of section 58A.

(2) The following provisions of the Trade Descriptions Act 1968 apply in relation to the enforcement of that section as in relation to the enforcement of that Act—

section 27 (power to make test purchases),

section 28 (power to enter premises and inspect and seize goods and documents),

section 29 (obstruction of authorised officers), and

section 33 (compensation for loss, &c. of goods seized under s.28).

(3) Subsection (1) above does not apply in relation to the enforcement of section 58A in Northern Ireland, but the functions of the Department of Economic Development include the enforcement of that section in Northern Ireland.

For that purpose the provisions of the Trade Descriptions Act 1968 specified in subsection (2) apply as if for the references to a local weights and measures authority and any officer of such an authority there were substituted references to that Department and any of its officers.

(4) Any enactment which authorises the disclosure of information for the purpose of facilitating the enforcement of the Trade Descriptions Act 1968 shall apply as if section 58A above were contained in that Act and as if the functions of any person in relation to the enforcement of that section were functions under that Act."

Provisions for the benefit of the Hospital for Sick Children

Provisions for the benefit of the Hosptial for Sick Children

301. The provisions of Schedule 6 have effect for conferring on trustees for the benefit of the Hospital for Sick Children, Great Ormond Street, London, a right to a royalty in respect of the public performance, commercial publication, broadcasting or inclusion in a cable programme service of the play "Peter Pan" by Sir James Matthew Barrie, or of any adaptation of that work, notwithstanding that copyright in the work expired on 31st December 1987.

Financial assistance for certain international bodies

Financial assistance for certain international bodies

302.—(1) The Secretary of State may give financial assistance, in the form of grants, loans or guarantees to—

(a) any international organisation having functions relating to trade marks or other intellectual property, or

(b) any Community institution or other body established under any of the Community Treaties having any such functions,

with a view to the establishment or maintenance by that organisation, institution or body of premises in the United Kingdom.

(2) Any expenditure of the Secretary of State under this section shall be defrayed out of money provided by Parliament; and any sums received by the Secretary of State in consequence of this section shall be paid into the Consolidated Fund.

General

Consequential amendments and repeals

303.—(1) The enactments specified in Schedule 7 are amended in accordance with that Schedule, the amendments being consequential on the provisions of this Act.

(2) The enactments specified in Schedule 8 are repealed to the extent specified.

Extent

304.—(1) Provision as to the extent of Part I (copyright), Part II (rights in performances) and Part III (design right) is to be found in sections 157, 207 and 255 respectively; the extent of the other provisions of this Act is as follows.

(2) Parts IV to VII extend to England and Wales, Scotland and Northern Ireland, except that—

(a) sections 287 to 292 (patents county courts) extend to England and Wales only,

(b) the proper law of the trust created by Schedule 6 (provisions for the benefit of the Hospital for Sick Children) is the law of England and Wales, and

(c) the amendments and repeals in Schedules 7 and 8 have the same extent as the enactments amended or repealed.

(3) The following provisions extend to the Isle of Man subject to any modifications contained in an Order made by Her Majesty in Council—

(a) sections 293 and 294 (patents: licences of right), and

(b) paragraphs 24 and 29 of Schedule 5 (patents: effect of filing international application for patent and power to extend time limits).

(4) Her Majesty may by Order in Council direct that the following provisions extend to the Isle of Man, with such exceptions and modifications as may be specified in the Order—

(a) Part IV (registered designs),

(b) Part V (patent agents),

(c) the provisions of Schedule 5 (patents: miscellaneous amendments) not mentioned in subsection (3) above,

(d) sections 297 to 299 (fraudulent reception of transmissions), and

(e) section 300 (fraudulent application or use of trade mark).

(5) Her Majesty may by Order in Council direct that sections 297 to 299 (fraudulent reception of transmissions) extend to any of the Channel Islands, with such exceptions and modifications as may be specified in the Order.

(6) Any power conferred by this Act to make provision by Order in Council for or in connection with the extent of provisions of this Act to a country outside the United Kingdom includes power to extend to that country, subject to any modifications specified in the Order, any provision of this Act which amends or repeals an enactment extending to that country.

Commencement

305.—(1) The following provisions of this Act come into force on Royal Assent—

paragraphs 24 and 29 of Schedule 5 (patents: effect of filing international application for patent and power to extend time limits);

section 301 and Schedule 6 (provisions for the benefit of the Hospital for Sick Children).

(2) Sections 293 and 294 (licences of right) come into force at the end of the period of two months beginning with the passing of this Act.

(3) The other provisions of this Act come into force on such day as the Secretary of State may appoint by order made by statutory instrument, and different days may be appointed for different provisions and different purposes.

Short title

306. This Act may be cited as the Copyright, Designs and Patents Act 1988.

Note on commencement

Section 301, Schedule 5 paras 24 and 29 and Schedule 6 came into force on 15 November 1988 (section 305(1)).

Sections 293 and 294 came into force on 15 January 1989 (section 305(2)).

Part I (copyright), Part II (rights in performances), Part III (design right), Part IV (registered designs) (except section 272 so far as it relates to para 21 of Schedule 3, and section 273), Part VI (patents) (except sections 293 and 294 and section 295 so far as it relates to paras 1–11 and 17–30 of Schedule 5), Part VII (miscellaneous) (except section 301 (already in force) and section 303(1) so far as it relates to the references in Schedule 8 to section 32 of the Registered Designs Act 1949 and to the provisions of the Patents Act 1977, other than section 49(3) of, and paras 1 and 3 of Schedule 5 to, that Act) and Schedules 1, 2, 3 (other than para 21), 5 (other than paras 1–11 and 17–30), 7 (other than paras 15, 18(2) and 21) and 8 (except in so far as it relates to section 32 of the Registered Designs Act 1949 and the provisions of the Patents Act 1977, other than section 49(3) of, and paras 1 and 3 of Schedule 5 to, that Act) came into force on 1 August 1989 (Copyright, Designs and Patents Act 1988 (Commencement No. 1) order 1989, SI 1989/816).

Sections 37(1), (2) and (4), 38–43, 47(4) and (5), 52(4), 61, 74, 75, 100(4) and (5), 112(1), (2) and (3), 150, 152(2) and (3), 159, 168(2), 174(1)(b) and (2), 196(4) and (5), 208(1)(a), 250, 256(1) and Schedule 1 para 34 came into force on 9 June 1989 for the purpose of making subordinate legislation thereunder (Copyright, Designs and Patents Act 1988 (Commencement No. 2) Order 1989, SI 1989/955).

SCHEDULES

SCHEDULE 1

(Section 170)

COPYRIGHT: TRANSITIONAL PROVISIONS AND SAVINGS

Introductory

1.—(1) In this Schedule—

"the 1911 Act" means the Copyright Act 1911,

"the 1956 Act" means the Copyright Act 1956, and

"the new copyright provisions" means the provisions of this Act relating to copyright, that is, Part I (including this Schedule) and Schedules 3, 7 and 8 so far as they make amendments or repeals consequential on the provisions of Part I.

(2) References in this Schedule to "commencement", without more, are to the date on which the new copyright provisions come into force.

(3) References in this Schedule to "existing works" are to works made before commencement; and for this purpose a work of which the making extended over a period shall be taken to have been made when its making was completed.

2.—(1) In relation to the 1956 Act, references in this Schedule to a work include any work or other subject-matter within the meaning of that Act.

(2) In relation to the 1911 Act—

    (a) references in this Schedule to copyright included the right conferred by section 24 of that Act in substitution for a right subsisting immediately before the commencement of that Act;

    (b) references in this Schedule to copyright in a sound recording are to the copyright under that Act in records embodying the recording; and

    (c) references in this Schedule to copyright in a film are to any copyright under that Act in the film (so far as it constituted a dramatic work for the purposes of that Act) or in photographs forming part of the film.

General principles: continuity of the law

3. The new copyright provisions apply in relation to things existing at commencement as they apply in relation to things coming into existence after commencement, subject to any express provision to the contrary.

4.—(1) The provisions of this paragraph have effect for securing the continuity of the law so far as the copyright provisions re-enact (with or without modification) earlier provisions.

(2) A reference in an enactment, instrument or other document to copyright, or to a work or other subject-matter in which copyright subsists, which apart from this Act would be construed as referring to copyright under the 1956 Act shall be construed, so far as may be required for continuing its effect, as being, or as the case may require, including, a

reference to copyright under this Act or to works in which copyright subsists under this Act.

(3) Anything done (including subordinate legislation made), or having effect as done, under or for the purposes of a provision repealed by this Act has effect as if done under or for the purposes of the corresponding provision of the new copyright provisions.

(4) References (expressed or implied) in this Act or any other enactment, instrument or document to any of the new copyright provisions shall, so far as the context permits, be construed as including, in relation to times, circumstances and purposes before commencement, a reference to corresponding earlier provisions.

(5) A reference (express or implied) in an enactment, instrument or other document to a provision repealed by this Act shall be construed, so far as may be required for continuing its effect, as a reference to the corresponding provision of this Act.

(6) The provisions of this paragraph have effect subject to any specific transitional provision or saving and to any express amendment made by this Act.

Subsistence of copyright

5.—(1) Copyright subsists in an existing work after commencement only if copyright subsisted in it immediately before commencement.

(2) Sub-paragraph (1) does not prevent an existing work qualifying for copyright protection after commencement—

(a) under section 155 (qualification by virtue of first publication), or

(b) by virtue of an Order under section 159 (application of Part I to countries to which it does not extend).

6.—(1) Copyright shall not subsist by virtue of this Act in an artistic work made before 1st June 1957 which at the time when the work was made constituted a design capable of registration under the Registered Designs Act 1949 or under the enactments repealed by that Act, and was used, or intended to be used, as a model or pattern to be multiplied by an industrial process.

(2) For this purpose a design shall be deemed to be used as a model or pattern to be multiplied by any industrial process—

(a) when the design is reproduced or is intended to be reproduced on more than 50 single articles, unless all the articles in which the design is reproduced or is intended to be reproduced together form only a single set of articles as defined in section 44(1) of the Registered Designs Act 1949, or

(b) when the design is to be applied to—

(i) printed paper hangings,

(ii) carpets, floor cloths or oil cloths, manufactured or sold in lengths or pieces,

(iii) textile piece goods, or textile goods manufactured or sold in lengths or pieces, or

(iv) lace, not made by hand.

7.—(1) No copyright subsists in a film, as such, made before 1st June 1957.

(2) Where a film made before that date was an original dramatic work within the meaning of the 1911 Act, the new copyright provisions have effect in relation to photographs forming part of a film made from 1st June 1957 as they have effect in relation to photographs not forming part of a film.

8.—(1) A film sound-track to which section 13(9) of the 1956 Act applied before commencement (film to be taken to include sounds in associated sound-track) shall be treated for the purposes of the new copyright provisions not as part of the film, but as a sound recording.

(2) However—

   (a) copyright subsists in the sound recording only if copyright subsisted in the film immediately before commencement, and it continues to subsist until copyright in the film expires;

   (b) the author and first owner of copyright in the film shall be treated as having been author and first owner of the copyright in the sound recording; and

   (c) anything done before commencement under or in relation to the copyright in the film continues to have effect in relation to the sound recording as in relation to the film.

9. No copyright subsists in—

   (a) a broadcast made before 1st June 1957, or

   (b) a cable programme included in a cable programme service before 1st January 1985;

and any such broadcast or cable programme shall be disregarded for the purposes of section 14(2) (duration of copyright in repeats).

Authorship of work

10. The question who was the author of an existing work shall be determined in accordance with the new copyright provisions for the purposes of the rights conferred by Chapter IV of Part I (moral rights), and for all other purposes shall be determined in accordance with the law in force at the time the work was made.

First ownership of copyright

11.—(1) The question who was first owner of copyright in an existing work shall be determined in accordance with the law in force at the time the work was made.

(2) Where before commencement a person commissioned the making of a work in circumstances falling within—

   (a) section 4(3) of the 1956 Act or paragraph (a) of the proviso to section 5(1) of the 1911 Act (photographs, portraits and engravings), or

   (b) the proviso to section 12(4) of the 1956 Act (sound recordings),

those provisions apply to determine first ownership of copyright in any work made in pursuance of the commission after commencement.

Duration of copyright in existing works

12.—(1) The following provisions have effect with respect to the duration of copyright in existing works.

The question which provision applies to a work shall be determined by reference to the facts immediately before commencement; and expressions used in this paragraph which were defined for the purposes of the 1956 Act have the same meaning as in that Act.

(2) Copyright in the following descriptions of work continues to subsist until the date on which it would have expired under the 1956 Act—

(a) literary, dramatic or musical works in relation to which the period of 50 years mentioned in the proviso to section 2(3) of the 1956 Act (duration of copyright in works made available to the public after the death of the author) has begun to run;

(b) engravings in relation to which the period of 50 years mentioned in the proviso to section 3(4) of the 1956 Act (duration of copyright in works published after the death of the author) has begun to run;

(c) published photographs and photographs taken before 1st June 1957;

(d) published sound recordings and sound recordings made before 1st June 1957;

(e) published films and films falling within section 13(3) of the 1956 Act (films registered under former enactments relating to registration of films).

(3) Copyright in anonymous or pseudonymous literary, dramatic, musical or artistic works (other than photographs) continues to subsist—

(a) if the work is published, until the date on which it would have expired in accordance with the 1956 Act, and

(b) if the work is unpublished, until the end of the period of 50 years from the end of the calendar year in which the new copyright provisions come into force or, if during that period the work is first made available to the public within the meaning of section 12(2) (duration of copyright in works of unknown authorship), the date on which copyright expires in accordance with that provision;

unless, in any case, the identity of the author becomes known before that date, in which case section 12(1) applies (general rule: life of the author plus 50 years).

(4) Copyright in the following descriptions of work continues to subsist until the end of the period of 50 years from the end of the calendar year in which the new copyright provisions come into force—

(a) literary, dramatic and musical works of which the author has died and in relation to which none of the acts mentioned in paragraphs (a) to (e) of the proviso to section 2(3) of the 1956 Act has been done;

(b) unpublished engravings of which the author has died;

(c) unpublished photographs taken on or after 1st June 1957.

(5) Copyright in the following descriptions of work continues to subsist until the end of the period of 50 years from the end of the calendar year in which the new copyright provisions come into force—

(a) unpublished sound recordings made on or after 1st June 1957;

(b) films not falling within sub-paragraph (2)(e) above,

unless the recording or film is published before the end of that period in which case copyright in it shall continue until the end of the period of 50 years from the end of the calendar year in which the recording or film is published.

(6) Copyright in any other description of existing work continues to subsist until the date on which copyright in that description of work expires in accordance with sections 12 to 15 of this Act.

(7) The above provisions do not apply to works subject to Crown or Parliamentary copyright (see paragraphs 41 to 43 below).

Perpetual copyright under the Copyright Act 1775

13.—(1) The rights conferred on universities and colleges by the Copyright Act 1775 shall continue to subsist until the end of the period of 50 years from the end of the calendar year in which the new copyright provisions come into force and shall then expire.

(2) The provisions of the following Chapters of Part I—

Chapter III (acts permitted in relation to copyright works),

Chapter VI (remedies for infringement),

Chapter VII (provisions with respect to copyright licensing), and

Chapter VIII (the Copyright Tribunal),

apply in relation to those rights as they apply in relation to copyright under this Act.

Acts infringing copyright

14.—(1) The provisions of Chapters II and III of Part I as to the acts constituting an infringement of copyright apply only in relation to acts done after commencement; the provisions of the 1956 Act continue to apply in relation to acts done before commencement.

(2) So much of section 18(2) as extends the restricted act of issuing copies to the public to include the rental to the public of copies of sound recordings, films or computer programs does not apply in relation to a copy of a sound recording, film or computer program acquired by any person before commencement for the purpose of renting it to the public.

(3) For the purposes of section 27 (meaning of "infringing copy") the question whether the making of an article constituted an infringement of copyright, or would have done if the article had been made in the United Kingdom, shall be determined—

(a) in relation to an article made on or after 1st June 1957 and before commencement, by reference to the 1956 Act, and

(b) in relation to an article made before 1st June 1957, by reference to the 1911 Act.

(4) For the purposes of the application of sections 31(2), 51(2) and 62(3) (subsequent exploitation of things whose making was, by virtue of an earlier provision of the section, not an infringement of copyright) to things made before commencement, it shall be assumed that the new copyright provisions were in force at all material times.

(5) Section 55 (articles for producing material in a particular typeface) applies where articles have been marketed as mentioned in subsection (1) before commencement with the substitution for the period mentioned in subsection (3) of the period of 25 years from the end of the calendar year in which the new copyright provisions come into force.

(6) Section 56 (transfer of copies, adaptations, &c. of work in electronic form) does not apply in relation to a copy purchased before commencement.

(7) In section 65 (reconstruction of buildings) the reference to the owner of the copyright in the drawings or plans is, in relation to buildings constructed before commencement, to the person who at the time of the construction was the owner of the copyright in the drawings or plans under the 1956 Act, the 1911 Act or any enactment repealed by the 1911 Act.

15.—(1) Section 57 (anonymous or pseudonymous works: acts permitted on assumptions as to expiry of copyright or death of author) has effect in relation to existing works subject to the following provisions.

(2) Subsection (1)(b)(i) (assumption as to expiry of copyright) does not apply in relation to—

(a) photographs, or

(b) the rights mentioned in paragraph 13 above (rights conferred by the Copyright Act 1775).

(3) Subsection (1)(b)(ii) (assumption as to death of author) applies only—

   (a) where paragraph 12(3)(b) above applies (unpublished anonymous or pseudonymous works), after the end of the period of 50 years from the end of the
calendar year in which the new copyright provisions come into force, or

   (b) where paragraph 12(6) above applies (cases in which the duration of copyright is
the same under the new copyright provisions as under the previous law).

16. The following provisions of section 7 of the 1956 Act continue to apply in relation
to existing works—

   (a) subsection (6) (copying of unpublished works from manuscript or copy in library,
museum or other institution);

   (b) subsection (7) (publication of work containing material to which subsection (6)
applies), except paragraph (a) (duty to give notice of intended publication);

   (c) subsection (8) (subsequent broadcasting, performance, &c. of material published
in accordance with subsection (7));

and subsection (9)(d) (illustrations) continues to apply for the purposes of those provisions.

17. Where in the case of a dramatic or musical work made before 1st July 1912, the
right conferred by the 1911 Act did not include the sole right to perform the work in
public, the acts restricted by the copyright shall be treated as not including—

   (a) performing the work in public,

   (b) broadcasting the work or including it in a cable programme service, or

   (c) doing any of the above in relation to an adaptation of the work;

and where the right conferred by the 1911 Act consisted only of the sole right to perform
the work in public, the acts restricted by the copyright shall be treated as consisting only
of those acts.

18. Where a work made before 1st July 1912 consists of an essay, article or portion
forming part of and first published in a review, magazine or other periodical or work of
a like nature, the copyright is subject to any right of publishing the essay, article, or
portion in a separate form to which the author was entitled at the commencement of the
1911 Act, or would if that Act had not been passed, have become entitled under section
18 of the Copyright Act 1842.

Designs

19.—(1) Section 51 (exclusion of copyright protection in relation to works recorded or
embodied in design document or models) does not apply for ten years after commencement
in relation to a design recorded or embodied in a design document or model before
commencement.

(2) During those ten years the following provisions of Part III (design right) apply to
any relevant copyright as in relation to design right—

   (a) sections 237 to 239 (availability of licences of right), and

   (b) sections 247 and 248 (application to comptroller to settle terms of licence of
right).

(3) In section 237 as it applies by virtue of this paragraph, for the reference in
subsection (1) to the last five years of the design right term there shall be substituted a
reference to the last five years of the period of ten years referred to in sub-paragraph (1)
above, or to so much of those last five years during which copyright subsists.

(4) In section 239 as it applies by virtue of this paragraph, for the reference in
subsection (1)(b) to section 230 there shall be substituted a reference to section 99.

(5) Where a licence of right is available by virtue of this paragraph, a person to whom a licence was granted before commencement may apply to the comptroller for an order adjusting the terms of that licence.

(6) The provisions of sections 249 and 250 (appeals and rules) apply in relation to proceedings brought under or by virtue of this paragraph as to proceedings under Part III.

(7) A licence granted by virtue of this paragraph shall relate only to acts which would be permitted by section 51 if the design document or model had been made after commencement.

(8) Section 100 (right to seize infringing copies, &c.) does not apply during the period of ten years referred to in sub-paragraph (1) in relation to anything to which it would not apply if the design in question had been first recorded or embodied in a design document or model after commencement.

(9) Nothing in this paragraph affects the operation of any rule of law preventing or restricting the enforcement of copyright in relation to a design.

20.—(1) Where section 10 of the 1956 Act (effect of industrial application of design corresponding to artistic work) applied in relation to an artistic work at any time before commencement, section 52(2) of this Act applies with the substitution for the period of 25 years mentioned there of the relevant period of 15 years as defined in section 10(3) of the 1956 Act.

(2) Except as provided in sub-paragraph (1), section 52 applies only where articles are marketed as mentioned in subsection (1)(b) after commencement.

Abolition of statutory recording licence

21. Section 8 of the 1956 Act (statutory licence to copy records sold by retail) continues to apply where notice under subsection (1)(b) of that section was given before the repeal of that section by this Act, but only in respect of the making of records—

(a) within one year of the repeal coming into force, and

(b) up to the number stated in the notice as intended to be sold.

Moral rights

22.—(1) No act done before commencement is actionable by virtue of any provision of Chapter IV of Part I (moral rights).

(2) Section 43 of the 1956 Act (false attribution of authorship) continues to apply in relation to acts done before commencement).

23.—(1) The following provisions have effect with respect to the rights conferred by—

(a) section 77 (right to be identified as author or director), and

(b) section 80 (right to object to derogatory treatment of work).

(2) The rights do not apply—

(a) in relation to a literary, dramatic, musical and artistic work of which the author died before commencement; or

(b) in relation to a film made before commencement.

(3) The rights in relation to an existing literary, dramatic, musical or artistic work do not apply—

(a) where copyright first vested in the author, to anything which by virtue of an assignment of copyright made or licence granted before commencement may be done without infringing copyright;

(b) where copyright first vested in a person other than the author, to anything done by or with the licence of the copyright owner.

(4) The rights do not apply to anything done in relation to a record made in pursuance of section 8 of the 1956 Act (statutory recording licence).

24. The right conferred by section 85 (right to privacy of certain photographs and films) does not apply to photographs taken or films made before commencement.

Assignments and licences

25.—(1) Any document made or event occurring before commencement which had any operation—

(a) affecting the ownership of the copyright in an existing work, or

(b) creating, transferring or terminating an interest, right or licence in respect of the copyright in an existing work,

has the corresponding operation in relation to copyright in the work under this Act.

(2) Expressions used in such a document shall be construed in accordance with their effect immediately before commencement.

26.—(1) Section 91(1) of this Act (assignment of future copyright: statutory vesting of legal interest on copyright coming into existence) does not apply in relation to an agreement made before 1st June 1957.

(2) The repeal by this Act of section 37(2) of the 1956 Act (assignment of future copyright: devolution of right where assignee dies before copyright comes into existence) does not affect the operation of that provision in relation to an agreement made before commencement.

27.—(1) Where the author of a literary, dramatic, musical or artistic work was the first owner of the copyright in it, no assignment of the copyright and no grant of any interest in it, made by him (otherwise than by will) after the passing of the 1911 Act and before 1st June 1957, shall be operative to vest in the assignee or grantee any rights with respect to the copyright in the work beyond the expiration of 25 years from the death of the author.

(2) The reversionary interest in the copyright expectant on the termination of that period may after commencement be assigned by the author during his life but in the absence of any assignment shall, on his death, devolve on his legal personal representatives as part of his estate.

(3) Nothing in this paragraph affects—

(a) an assignment of the reversionary interest by a person to whom it has been assigned,

(b) an assignment of the reversionary interest after the death of the author by his personal representatives or any person becoming entitled to it, or

(c) any assignment of the copyright after the reversionary interest has fallen in.

(4) Nothing in this paragraph applies to the assignment of the copyright in a collective work or a licence to publish a work or part of a work as part of a collective work.

(5) In sub-paragraph (4) "collective work" means—

(a) any encyclopaedia, dictionary, yearbook, or similar work;

(b) a newspaper, review, magazine, or similar periodical; and

(c) any work written in distinct parts by different authors, or in which works or parts of works of different authors are incorporated.

28.—(1) This paragraph applies where copyright subsists in a literary, dramatic, musical or artistic work made before 1st July 1912 in relation to which the author, before the commencement of the 1911 Act, made such an assignment or grant as was mentioned in paragraph (a) of the proviso to section 24(1) of that Act (assignment or grant of copyright or performing right for full term of the right under the previous law).

(2) If before commencement any event has occured or notice has been given which by virtue of paragraph 38 of Schedule 7 to the 1956 Act had any operation in relation to copyright in the work under that Act, the event or notice has the corresponding operation in relation to copyright under this Act.

(3) Any right which immediately before commencement would by virtue of paragraph 38(3) of that Schedule have been exercisable in relation to the work, or copyright in it, is exercisable in relation to the work or copyright in it under this Act.

(4) If in accordance with paragraph 38(4) of that Schedule copyright would, on a date after the commencement of the 1956 Act, have reverted to the author or his personal representatives and that date falls after the commencement of the new copyright provisions—

  (a) the copyright in the work shall revert to the author or his personal representatives, as the case may be, and

  (b) any interest of any other person in the copyright which subsists on that date by virtue of any document made before the commencement of the 1911 Act shall thereupon determine.

29. Section 92(2) of this Act (rights of exclusive licensee against successors in title of person granting licence) does not apply in relation to an exclusive licence granted before commencement.

Bequests

30.—(1) Section 93 of this Act (copyright to pass under will with original document or other material thing embodying unpublished work)—

  (a) does not apply where the testator died before 1st June 1957, and

  (b) where the testator died on or after that date and before commencement, applies only in relation to an original document embodying a work.

(2) In the case of an author who died 1st June 1957, the ownership after his death of a manuscript of his, where such ownership has been acquired under a testamentary disposition made by him and the manuscript is of a work which has not been published or performed in public, is prima facie proof of the copyright being with the owner of the manuscript.

Remedies for infringement

31.—(1) Sections 96 and 97 of this Act (remedies for infringement) apply only in relation to an infringement of copyright committed after commencement; section 17 of the 1956 Act continues to apply in relation to infringements committed before commencement.

(2) Sections 99 and 100 of this Act (delivery up or seizure of infringing copies, &c.) apply to infringing copies and other articles made before or after commencement; section 18 of the 1956 Act, and section 7 of the 1911 Act, (conversion damages, &c.), do not apply after commencement except for the purposes of proceedings begun before commencement.

(3) Section 101 to 102 of this Act (rights and remedies of exclusive licensee) apply where sections 96 to 100 of this Act apply; section 19 of the 1956 Act continues to apply where section 17 or 18 of that Act applies.

(4) Sections 104 to 106 of this Act (presumptions) apply only to proceedings brought by virtue of this Act; section 20 of the 1956 Act continues to apply in proceedings brought by virtue of that Act.

32. Sections 101 and 102 of this Act (rights and remedies of exclusive licensee) do not apply to a licence granted before 1st June 1957.

33.—(1) The provisions of section 107 of this Act (criminal liability for making or dealing with infringing articles, &c.) apply only in relation to acts done after commencement; section 21 of the 1956 Act (penalites and summary proceedings in respect of dealings which infringe copyright) continues to apply in relation to acts done before commencement.

(2) Section 109 of this Act (search warrants) applies in relation to offences committed before commencement in relation to which section 21A or 21B of the 1956 Act applied; sections 21A and 21B continue to apply in relation to warrants issued before commencement.

Copyright Tribunal: proceedings pending on commencement

34.—(1) The Lord Chancellor may, after consultation with the Lord Advocate, by rules make such provision as he considers necessary or expedient with respect to proceedings pending under Part IV of the 1956 Act immediately before commencement.

(2) Rules under this paragraph shall be made by statutory instrument which shall be subject to annulment in pursuance of a resolution of either House of Parliament.

Qualification for copyright protection

35. Every work in which copyright subsisted under the 1956 Act immediately before commencement shall be deemed to satisfy the requirements of Part I of this Act as to qualification for copyright protection.

Dependent territories

36.—(1) The 1911 Act shall remain in force as part of the law of any dependent territory in which it was in force immediately before commencement until—

(a) the new copyright provisions come into force in that territory by virtue of an Order under section 157 of this Act (power to extend new copyright provisions), or

(b) in the case of any of the Channel Islands, the Act is repealed by Order under sub-paragraph (3) below.

(2) An order in Council in force immediately before commencement which extends to any dependent territory any provisions of the 1956 Act shall remain in force as part of the law of that territory until—

(a) the new copyright provisions come into force in that territory by virtue of an Order under section 157 of this Act (power to extend new copyright provisions), or

(b) in the case of the Isle of Man, the Order is revoked by Order under sub-paragraph (3) below;

and while it remains in force such an Order may be varied under the provisions of the 1956 Act under which it was made.

(3) If it appears to Her Majesty that provision with respect to copyright has been made in the law of any of the Channel Islands or the Isle of Man otherwise than by extending

the provisions of Part I of this Act, Her Majesty may by Order in Council repeal the 1911 Act as it has effect as part of the law of that territory or, as the case may be, revoke the Order extending the 1956 Act there.

(4) A dependent territory in which the 1911 of 1956 Act remains in force shall be treated, in the law of the countries to which Part I extends, as a country to which that Part extends; and those countries shall be treated in the law of such a territory as countries to which the 1911 Act or, as the case may be, the 1956 Act extends.

(5) If a country in which the 1911 or 1956 Act is in force ceases to be a colony of the United Kingdom, section 158 of this Act (consequences of country ceasing to be colony) applies with the substitution for the reference in subsection (3)(b) to the provisions of Part I of this Act of a reference to the provisions of the 1911 or 1956 Act, as the case may be.

(6) In this paragraph "dependent territory" means any of the Channel Islands, the Isle of Man or any colony.

37.—(1) This paragraph applies to a country which immediately before commencement was not a dependent territory within the meaning of paragraph 36 above but—

(a) was a country to which the 1956 Act extended, or

(b) was treated as such a country by virtue of paragraph 39(2) of Schedule 7 to that Act (countries to which the 1911 Act extended or was treated as extending);

and Her Majesty may by Order in Council conclusively declare for the purposes of this paragraph whether a country was such a country or was so treated.

(2) A country to which this paragraph applies shall be treated as a country to which Part I extends for the purposes of sections 154 to 156 (qualification for copyright protection) until—

(a) an Order in Council is made in respect of that country under section 159 (application of Part I to countries to which it does not extend), or

(b) an Order in Council is made declaring that it shall cease to be so treated by reason of the fact that the provisions of the 1956 Act or, as the case may be, the 1911 Act, which extended there as part of the law of that country have been repealed or amended.

(3) A statutory instrument containing an Order in Council under this paragraph shall be subject to annulment in pursuance of a resolution of either House of Parliament.

Territorial waters and the continental shelf

38. Section 161 of this Act (application of Part I to things done in territorial waters or the United Kingdom sector of the continental shelf) does not apply in relation to anything done before commencement.

British ships, aircraft and hovercraft

39. Section 162 (British ships, aircraft and hovercraft) does not apply in relation to anything done before commencement.

Crown copyright

40.—(1) Section 163 of this Act (general provisions as to Crown copyright) applies to an existing work if—

(a) section 39 of the 1956 Act applied to the work immediately before commencement, and

(b) the work is not one to which section 164, 165 or 166 applies (copyright in Acts, Measures and Bills and Parliamentary copyright: see paragraphs 42 and 43 below).

(2) Section 163 (1)(b) (first ownership of copyright) has effect subject to any agreement entered into before commencement under section 39(6) of the 1956 Act.

41.—(1) The following provisions have effect with respect to the duration of copyright in existing works to which section 163 (Crown copyright) applies.

The question which provision applies to a work shall be determined by reference to the facts immediately before commencement; and expressions used in this paragraph which were defined for the purposes of the 1956 Act have the same meaning as in that Act.

(2) Copyright in the following descriptions of work continues to subsist until the date on which it would have expired in accordance with the 1956 Act—

(a) published literary, dramatic or musical works;

(b) artistic works other than engravings or photographs;

(c) published engravings;

(d) published photographs and photographs taken before 1st June 1957;

(e) published sound recordings and sound recordings made before 1st June 1957;

(f) published films and films falling within section 13(3)(a) of the 1956 Act (films registered under former enactments relating to registration of films).

(3) Copyright in unpublished literary, dramatic or musical works continues to subsist until—

(a) the date on which copyright expires in accordance with section 163(3), or

(b) the end of the period of 50 years from the end of the calendar year in which the new copyright provisions come into force,

whichever is the later.

(4) Copyright in the following descriptions of work continues to subsist until the end of the period of 50 years from the end of the calendar year in which the new copyright provisions come into force—

(a) unpublished engravings;

(b) unpublished photographs taken on or after 1st June 1957.

(5) Copyright in a film or sound recording not falling within sub-paragraph (2) above continues to subsist until the end of the period of 50 years from the end of the calendar year in which the new copyright provisions come into force, unless the film or recording is published before the end of that period, in which case copyright expires 50 years from the end of the calendar year in which it is published.

42.—(1) Section 164 (copyright in Acts and Measures) applies to existing Acts of Parliament and Measures of the General Synod of the Church of England.

(2) References in that section to Measures of the General Synod of the Church of England include Church Assembly Measures.

Parliamentary copyright

43.—(1) Section 165 of this Act (general provisions as to Parliamentary copyright) applies to existing unpublished literary, dramatic, musical or artistic works, but does not otherwise apply to existing works.

(2) Section 166 (copyright in Parliamentary Bills) does not apply—

(a) to a public Bill which was introduced into Parliament and published before commencement,

(b) to a private Bill of which a copy was deposited in either House before commencement, or

(c) to a personal Bill which was given a First Reading in the House of Lords before commencement.

Copyright vesting in certain international organisations

44.—(1) Any work in which immediately before commencement copyright subsisted by virtue of section 33 of the 1956 Act shall be deemed to satisfy the requirements of section 168(1); but otherwise section 168 does not apply to works made or, as the case may be, published before commencement.

(2) Copyright in any such work which is unpublished continues to subsist until the date on which it would have expired in accordance with the 1956 Act, or the end of the period of 50 years from the end of the calendar year in which the new copyright provisions come into force, whichever is the earlier.

Meaning of "publication"

45. Section 175(3) (construction of building treated as equivalent to publication) applies only where the construction of the building began after commencement.

Meaning of "unauthorised"

46. For the purposes of the application of the definition in section 178 (minor definitions) of the expression "unauthorised" in relation to things done before commencement—

(a) paragraph (a) applies in relation to things done before 1st June 1957 as if the reference to the licence of the copyright owner were a reference to his consent or acquiescence;

(b) paragraph (b) applies with the substitution for the words from "or, in a case" to the end of the words "or any person lawfully claiming under him"; and

(c) paragraph (c) shall be registered.

SCHEDULE 2

(Section 189)

RIGHTS IN PERFORMANCES: PERMITTED ACTS

Introductory

1.—(1) The provisions of this Schedule specify acts which may be done in relation to a performance or recording notwithstanding the rights conferred by Part II; they relate only to the question of infringement of those rights and do not affect any other right or obligation restricting the doing of any of the specified acts.

(2) No reference shall be drawn from the description of any act which may by virtue of this Schedule be done without infringing the rights conferred by Part II as to the scope of those rights.

(3) The provisions of this Schedule are to be construed independently of each other, so that the fact that an act does not fall within one provision does not mean that it is covered by another provision.

Criticism, reviews and news reporting

2.—(1) Fair dealing with a performance or recording—

(a) for the purpose of criticism or review, of that or another performance or recording, or of a work, or

(b) for the purpose of reporting current events,

does not infringe any of the rights conferred by Part II.

(2) Expressions used in this paragraph have the same meaning as in section 30.

Incidental inclusion of performance or recording

3.—(1) The rights conferred by Part II are not infringed by the incidental inclusion of a performance or recording in a sound recording, film, broadcast or cable programme.

(2) Nor are those rights infringed by anything done in relation to copies of, or the playing, showing, broadcasting or inclusion in a cable programme service of, anything whose making was, by virtue of sub-paragraph (1), not an infringement of those rights.

(3) A performance or recording so far as it consists of music, or words spoken or sung with music, shall not be regarded as incidentally included in a sound recording, broadcast or cable programme if it is deliberately included.

(4) Expressions used in this paragraph have the same meaning as in section 31.

Things done for purposes of instruction or examination

4.—(1) The rights conferred by Part II are not infringed by the copying of a recording of a performance in the course of instruction, or of preparation for instruction, in the making of films or film sound-tracks, provided the copying is done by a person giving or receiving instruction.

(2) The rights conferred by Part II are not infringed—

(a) by the copying of a recording of a performance for the purposes of setting or answering the questions in an examination, or

(b) by anything done for the purposes of an examination by way of communicating the questions to the candidates.

(3) Where a recording which would otherwise be an illicit recording is made in accordance with this paragraph but is subsequently dealt with, it shall be treated as an illicit recording for the purposes of that dealing, and if that dealing infringes any right conferred by Part II for all subsequent purposes.

For this purpose "dealt with" means sold or let for hire, or offered or exposed for sale or hire.

(4) Expressions used in this paragraph have the same meaning as in section 32.

Playing or showing sound recording, film, broadcast or cable programme at educational establishment

5.—(1) The playing or showing of a sound recording, film, broadcast or cable programme at an educational establishment for the purposes of instruction before an audience consisting of teachers and pupils at the establishment and other persons directly connected with the activities of the establishment is not a playing or showing of a performance in public for the purposes of infringement or the rights conferred by Part II.

(2) A person is not for this purpose directly connected with the activities of the educational establishment simply because he is the parent of a pupil at the establishment.

(3) Expressions used in this paragraph have the same meaning as in section 34 and any provision made under section 174(2) with respect to the application of that section also applies for the purposes of this paragraph.

Recording of broadcasts and cable programmes by educational establishments

6.—(1) A recording of a broadcast or cable programme, or a copy of such a recording, may be made by or on behalf of an educational establishment for the educational purposes of that establishment without thereby infringing any of the rights conferred by Part II in relation to any performance or recording included in it.

(2) Where a recording which would otherwise be an illicit recording is made in accordance with this paragraph but is subsequently dealt with, it shall be treated as an illicit recording for the purposes of that dealing, and if that dealing infringes any right conferred by Part II for all subsequent purposes.

For this purpose "dealt with" means sold or let for hire, or offered or exposed for sale or hire.

(3) Expressions used in this paragraph have the same meaning as in section 35 and any provision made under section 174(2) with respect to the application of that section also applies for the purposes of this paragraph.

Copy of work required to be made as condition of export

7.—(1) If an article of cultural or historical importance or interest cannot lawfully be exported from the United Kingdom unless a copy of it is made and deposited in an appropriate library or archive, it is not an infringement of any right conferred by Part II to make that copy.

(2) Expressions used in this paragraph have the same meaning as in section 144.

Parliamentary and judicial proceedings

8.—(1) The rights conferred by Part II are not infringed by anything done for the purposes of parliamentary or judicial proceedings or for the purpose of reporting such proceedings.

(2) Expressions used in this paragraph have the same meaning as in section 45.

Royal Commissions and statutory inquiries

9.—(1) The rights conferred by Part II are not infringed by anything done for the purposes of the proceedings of a Royal Commission or statutory inquiry or for the purpose of reporting any such proceedings held in public.

(2) Expressions used in this paragraph have the same meaning as in section 46.

Public records

10.—(1) Material which is comprised in public records within the meaning of the Public Records Act 1958, the Public Records (Scotland) Act 1937 or the Public Records Act (Northern Ireland) 1923 which are open to public inspection in pursuance of that Act, may be copied, and a copy may be supplied to any person, by or with the authority of any officer appointed under that Act, without infringing any right conferred by Part II.

(2) Expressions used in this paragraph have the same meaning as in section 49.

Acts done under statutory authority

11.—(1) Where the doing of a particular act is specifically authorised by an Act of Parliament, whenever passed, then, unless the Act provides otherwise, the doing of that Act does not infringe the rights conferred by Part II.

(2) Sub-paragraph (1) applies in relation to an enactment contained in Northern Ireland legislation as it applies to an Act of Parliament.

(3) Nothing in this paragraph shall be construed as excluding any defence of statutory authority otherwise available under or by virtue of any enactment.

(4) Expressions used in this paragraph have the same meaning as in section 50.

Transfer of copies of works in electronic form

12.—(1) This paragraph applies where a recording of a performance in electronic form has been purchased on terms which, expressly or impliedly or by virtue of any rule of law, allow the purchaser to make further recordings in connection with his use of the recording.

(2) If there are no express terms—

(a) prohibiting the transfer of the recording by the purchaser, imposing obligations which continue after a transfer, prohibiting the assignment or any consent or terminating any consent on a transfer, or

(b) providing for the terms on which a transferee may do the things which the purchaser was permitted to do,

anything which the purchaser was allowed to do may also be done by a transferee without infringement of the rights conferred by this Part, but any recording made by the purchaser which is not also transferred shall be treated as an illicit recording for all purposes after the transfer.

(3) The same applies where the original purchased recording is no longer usable and what is transferred is a further copy used in its place.

(4) The above provisions also apply on a subsequent transfer, with the substitution for references in sub-paragraph (2) to the purchaser of references to the subsequent transferor.

(5) This paragraph does not apply in relation to a recording purchased before the commencement of Part II.

(6) Expressions used in this paragraph have the same meaning as in section 56.

Use of recordings of spoken works in certain cases

13.—(1) Where a recording of the reading or recitation of a literary work is made for the purpose—

(a) of reporting current events, or

(b) of broadcasting or including in a cable programme service the whole or part of the reading or recitation,

it is not an infringement of the rights conferred by Part II to use the recording (or to copy the recording and use the copy) for that purpose, provided the following conditions are met.

(2) The conditions are that—

(a) the recording is a direct recording of the reading or recitation and is not taken from a previous recording or from a broadcast or cable programme;

(b) the making of the recording was not prohibited by or on behalf of the person giving the reading or recitation,

(c) the use made of the recording is not of a kind prohibited by or on behalf of that person before the recording was made; and

(d) the use is by or with the authority of a person who is lawfully in possession of the recording.

(3) Expressions used in this paragraph have the same meaning as in section 58.

Recordings of folksongs

14.—(1) A recording of a performance of a song may be made for the purpose of including it in an archive maintained by a designated body without infringing any of the rights conferred by Part II, provided the conditions in sub-paragraph (2) below are met.

(2) The conditions are that—

(a) the words are unpublished and of unknown authorship at the time the recording is made,

(b) the making of the recording does not infringe any copyright, and

(c) its making is not prohibited by any performer.

(3) Copies of a recording made in reliance on sub-paragraph (1) and included in an archive maintained by a designated body may, if the prescribed conditions are met, be made and supplied by the archivist without infringing any of the rights conferred by Part II.

(4) In this paragraph—

"designated body" means a body designated for the purposes of section 61, and

"the prescribed conditions" means the conditions prescribed for the purposes of subsection (3) of that section;

and other expressions used in this paragraph have the same meaning as in that section.

Playing of sound recordings for purposes of club, society, &c

15.—(1) It is not an infringement of any right conferred by Part II to play a sound recording as part of the activities of, or for the benefit of, a club, society or other organisation if the following conditions are met.

(2) The conditions are—

(a) that the organisation is not established or conducted for profit and its main objects are charitable or are otherwise concerned with the advancement of religion, education, or social welfare, and

(b) that the proceeds of any charge for admission to the place where the recording is to be heard are applied solely for the purposes of the organisation.

(3) Expressions used in this paragraph have the same meaning as in section 67.

Incidental recording for purposes of broadcast or cable programme

16.—(1) A person who purposes to broadcast a recording of a performance, or include a recording of a performance in a cable programme service, in circumstances not infringing the rights conferred by Part II shall be treated as having consent for the purposes of that Part for the making of a further recording for the purposes of the broadcast or cable programme.

(2) That consent is subject to the condition that the further recording—

(a) shall not be used for any other purpose, and

(b) shall be destroyed within 28 days of being first used for broadcasting the performance or including it in a cable programme service.

(3) A recording made in accordance with this paragraph shall be treated as an illicit recording—

(a) for the purposes of any use in breach of the condition mentioned in sub-paragraph (2)(a), and

(b) for all purposes after that condition or the condition mentioned in sub-paragraph (2)(b) is broken.

(4) Expressions used in this paragraph have the same meaning as in section 68.

Recordings for purposes of supervision and control of broadcasts and cable programmes

17.—(1) The rights conferred by Part II are not infringed by the making or use by the British Broadcasting Corporation, for the purpose of maintaining supervision and control over programmes broadcast by them, of recordings of those programmes.

(2) The rights conferred by Part II are not infringed by—

(a) the making or use of recordings by the Independent Broadcasting Authority for the purposes mentioned in section 4(7) of the Broadcasting Act 1981 (maintenance of supervision and control over programmes and advertisements); or

(b) anything done under or in pursuance of provision included in a contract between a programme contractor and the Authority in accordance with section 21 of that Act.

(3) The rights conferred by Part II are not infringed by—

(a) the making by or with the authority of the Cable Authority, or the use by that Authority, for the purpose of maintaining supervision and control over programmes included in services licensed under Part I of the Cable and Broadcasting Act 1984, of recordings of those programmes; or

(b) anything done under or in pursuance of—

(i) a notice or direction given under section 16 of the Cable and Broadcasting Act 1984 (power of Cable Authority to require production of recordings); or

(ii) a condition included in a licence by virtue of section 35 of that Act (duty of Authority to secure that recordings are available for certain purposes).

(4) Expressions used in this paragraph have the same meaning as in section 69.

Free public showing or playing of broadcast or cable programme

18.—(1) The showing or playing in public of a broadcast or cable programme to an audience who have not paid for admission to the place where the broadcast or programme is to be seen or heard does not infringe any right conferred by Part II in relation to a performance or recording included in—

(a) the broadcast or cable programme, or

(b) any sound recording or film which is played or shown in public by reception of the broadcast or cable programme.

(2) The audience shall be treated as having paid for admission to a place—

(a) if they have paid for admission to a place of which that place forms part; or

(b) if goods or services are supplied at that place (or a place of which it forms part)—

(i) at prices which are substantially attributable to the facilities afforded for seeing or hearing the broadcast or programme, or

(ii) at prices exceeding those usually charged there and which are partly attributable to those facilities.

(3) The following shall not be regarded as having paid for admission to a place—

(a) persons admitted as residents or inmates of the place;

(b) persons admitted as members of a club or society where the payment is only for membership of the club or society and the provision of facilities for seeing or hearing broadcasts or programmes is only incidental to the main purposes of the club or society.

(4) Where the making of the broadcast or inclusion of the programme in a cable programme service was an infringement of the rights conferred by Part II in relation to a performance or recording, the fact that it was heard or seen in public by the reception of the broadcast or programme shall be taken into account in assessing the damages for that infringement.

(5) Expressions used in this paragraph have the same meaning as in section 72.

Reception and re-transmission of broadcast in cable programme service

19.—(1) This paragraph applies where a broadcast made from a place in the United Kingdom is, by reception and immediate re-transmission, included in a cable programme service.

(2) The rights conferred in Part II in relation to a performance or recording included in the broadcast are not infringed—

(a) if the inclusion of the broadcast in the cable programme service is in pursuance of a requirement imposed under section 13(1) of the Cable and Broadcasting Act 1984 (duty of Cable Authority to secure inclusion in cable service of certain programmes), or

(b) if and to the extent that the broadcast is made for reception in the area in which the cable programme service is provided;

but where the making of the broadcast was an infringement of those rights, the fact that the broadcast was re-transmitted as a programme in a cable programme service shall be taken into account in assessing the damages for that infringement.

(3) Expressions used in this paragraph have the same meaning as in section 73.

Provision of sub-titled copies of broadcast or cable programme

20.—(1) A designated body may, for the purpose of providing people who are deaf or hard of hearing, or physically or mentally handicapped in other ways, with copies which are sub-titled or otherwise modified for their special needs, make recordings of television broadcasts or cable programmes without infringing any right conferred by Part II in relation to a performance or recording included in the broadcast or cable programme.

(2) In this paragraph "designated body" means a body designated for the purposes of section 74 and other expressions used in this paragraph have the same meaning as in that section.

Recording of broadcast or cable programme for archival purposes

21.—(1) A recording of a broadcast or cable programme of a designated class, or a copy of such a recording, may be made for the purpose of being placed in an archive maintained by a designated body without thereby infringing any right conferred by Part II in relation to a performance or recording included in the broadcast or cable programme.

(2) In this paragraph "designated class" and "designated body" means a class or body designated for the purposes of section 75 and other expressions used in this paragraph have the same meaning as in that section.

SCHEDULE 3

(Section 272)

REGISTERED DESIGNS: MINOR AND CONSEQUENTIAL AMENDMENTS OF 1949 ACT

Section 3: proceedings for registration

1. In section 3 of the Registered Designs Act 1949 (proceedings for registration) for subsections (2) to (6) substitute—

"(2) An application for the registration of a design in which design right subsists shall not be entertained unless made by the person claiming to be the design right owner.

(3) For the purpose of deciding whether a design is new, the registrar may make such searches, if any, as he thinks fit.

(4) The registrar may, in such cases as may be prescribed, direct that for the purpose of deciding whether a design is new an application shall be treated as made on a date earlier or later than that on which it was in fact made.

(5) The registrar may refuse an application for the registration of a design or may register the design in pursuance of the application subject to such modifications, if any, as he thinks fit; and a design when registered shall be registered as of the date on which the application was made or is treated as having been made.

(6) An application which, owing to any default or neglect on the part of the applicant, has not been completed so as to enable registration to be effected within such time as may be prescribed shall be deemed to be abandoned.

(7) An appeal lies from any decision of the registrar under this section.".

Section 4: registration of same design in respect of other articles, etc.

2. In section 4 of the Registered Designs Act 1949 (registration of same design in respect of other articles, etc.), in subsection (1), for the proviso substitute—

"Provided that the right in a design registered by virtue of this section shall not extend beyond the end of the period, and any extended period, for which the right subsists in the original registered design.".

Section 5: provision for secrecy of certain designs

3.—(1) Section 5 of the Registered Designs Act 1949 is amended as follows.

(2) For "a competent authority" or "the competent authority", wherever occurring, substitute "the Secretary of State"; and in subsection (3)(c) for "that authority" substitute "he".

(3) For subsection (2) substitute—

"(2) The Secretary of State shall by rules make provision for securing that where such directions are given—

(a) the representation or specimen of the design, and

(b) any evidence filed in support of the applicant's contention that the appearance of an article is material (for the purposes of section 1(3) of this Act),

shall not be open to public inspection at the Patent Office during the continuance in force of the directions."

(4) In subsection (3)(b) after "representation or specimen of the design" insert ", or any such evidence as is mentioned in subsection (2)(b) above.".

(5) Omit subsection (5).

Section 6: provisions as to confidential disclosure, etc.

4.—(1) Section 6 of the Registered Designs Act 1949 (provisions as to confidential disclosure, etc.) is amended as follows.

(2) In subsection (2) (display of design at certified exhibition), in paragraph (a) for "certified by the Board of Trade" substitute "certified by the Secretary of State".

(3) For subsections (4) and (5) (registration of designs corresponding to copyright artistic works) substitute—

"(4) Where an application is made by or with the consent of the owner of copyright in an artistic work for the registration of a corresponding design, the design shall not be treated for the purposes of this Act as being other than new by reason only of any use previously made of the artistic work, subject to subsection (5).

(5) Subsection (4) does not apply if the previous use consisted of or included the sale, letting for hire or offer or exposure for sale or hire of articles to which had been applied industrially—

(a) the design in question, or

(b) a design differing from it only in immaterial details or in features which are variants commonly used in the trade,

and that previous use was made by or with the consent of the copyright owner.

(6) The Secretary of State may make provision by rules as to the circumstances in which a design is to be regarded for the purposes of this section as 'applied industrially' to articles, or any description of articles.".

Section 9: exemption of innocent infringer from liability for damages

5. In section 9 of the Registered Designs Act 1949 (exemption of innocent infringer from liability for damages), in subsections (1) and (2) for "copyright in a registered design" substitute "the right in a registered design".

Section 11: cancellation of registration

6.—(1) Section 11 of the Registered Designs Act 1949 (cancellation of registration) is amended as follows.

(2) In subsection (2) omit "or original".

(3) For subsections (2A) and (3) substitute—

"(3) At any time after a design has been registered, any person interested may apply to the registrar for the cancellation of the registration on the gound that—

(a) the design was at the time it was registered a corresponding design in relation to an artistic work in which copyright subsisted, and

(b) the right in the registered design has expired in accordance with section 8(4) of this Act (expiry of right in registered design on expiry of copyright in artistic work);

and the registrar may make such order on the application as he thinks fit.

(4) A cancellation under this section takes effect—

(a) in the case of cancellation under subsection (1), from the date of the registrar's decision,

(b) in the case of cancellation under subsection (2), from the date of registration,

(c) in the case of cancellation under subsection (3), from the date on which the right in the registered design expired,

or, in any case, from such other date as the registrar may direct.

(5) An appeal lies from any order of the registrar under this section.".

Section 14: registration where application has been made in convention country

7. In section 14 of the Registered Designs Act 1949 (registration where application has been made in convention country), for subsections (2) and (3) substitute—

"(2) Where an application for registration of a design is made by virtue of this section, the application shall be treated, for the purpose of determining whether that or any other design is new, as made on the date of the application for protection in the convention country or, if more than one such application was made, on the date of the first such application.

(3) Subsection (2) shall not be construed as excluding the power to give directions under section 3(4) of this Act in relation to an application made by virtue of this section.".

Section 15: extension of time for application under s.14 in certain cases

8. In section 15(1) of the Registered Designs Act 1949 (power to make rules empowering registrar to extend time for applications under s.14) for "the Board of Trade are satisfied" substitute "the Secretary of State is satisfied" and for "they" substitute "he".

Section 16: protection of designs communicated under international agreements

9. In section 16 of the Registered Designs Act 1949 (protection of designs communicated under international agreements)—

(a) in subsection (1) for "the Board of Trade" substitute "the Secretary of State", and

(b) in subsection (3) for "the Board of Trade" substitute "the Secretary of State" and for "the Board are satisfied" substitute "the Secretary of State is satisfied".

Section 19: registration of assignments, &c.

10. In section 19 of the Registered Designs Act 1949 (registration of assignments, &c.), after subsection (3) insert—

"(3A) Where design right subsists in a registered design, the registrar shall not register an interest under subsection (3) unless he is satisfied that the person entitled to that interest is also entitled to a corresponding interest in the design right.

"(3B) Where design right subsists in a registered design and the proprietor of the registered design is also the design right owner, an assignment of the design right shall be taken to be also an assignment of the right in the registered design, unless a contrary intention appears.".

Section 20: rectification of the register

11. In section 20 of the Registered Designs Act 1949 (rectification of the register), after subsection (4) add—

"(5) A rectification of the register under this section has effect as follows—

(a) an entry made has effect from the date on which it should have been made,

(b) an entry varied has effect as if it had originally been made in its varied form, and

(c) an entry deleted shall be deemed never to have had effect,

unless, in any case, the court directs otherwise.".

Section 22: inspection of registered designs

12.—(1) Section 22 of the Registered Designs Act 1949 (inspection of registered designs) is amended as follows.

(2) For subsection (1) substitute–

"(1) Where a design has been registered under this Act, there shall be open to inspection at the Patent Office on and after the day on which the certificate of registration is issued—

(a) the representation or specimen of the design, and

(b) any evidence filed in support of the applicant's contention that the appearance of an article is material (for the purposes of section 1(3) of this Act).

This subsection has effect subject to the following provisions of this section and to any rules made under section 5(2) of this Act."

(3) In subsection (2), subsection (3) (twice) and subsection (4) for "representation or specimen of the design" substitute "representation, specimen or evidence".

Section 23: information as to existence of right in registered design

13. For section 23 of the Registered Design Act 1949 (information as to existence of right in registered design) substitute—

"*Information as to existence of right in registered design*
23. On the request of a person furnishing such information as may enable the registrar to identify the design, and on payment of the prescribed fee, the registrar shall inform him—

(a) whether the design is registered and, if so, in respect of what articles, and

(b) whether any extension of the period of the right in the registered design has been granted,

and shall state the date of registration and the name and address of the registered proprietor.".

Section 25: certificate of contested validity of registration

14. In section 25 of the Registered Designs Act 1949 (certificate of contested validity of registration), in subsection (2) for "the copyright in the registered design" substitute "the right in the registered design".

Section 26: remedy for groundless threats of infringement proceedings

15.—(1) Section 26 of the Registered Designs Act 1949 (remedy for groundless threats of infringement proceedings) is amended as follows.

(2) In subsections (1) and (2) for "the copyright in a registered design" substitute "the right in a registered design".

(3) After subsection (2) insert—

"(2A) Proceedings may not be brought under this section in respect of a threat to bring proceedings for an infringement alleged to consist of the making or importing of anything.".

Section 27: the court

16. For section 27 of the Registered Designs Act 1949 (the court) substitute—

"The court

27.—(1) In this Act 'the court' means—

(a) in England and Wales the High Court or any patents county court having jurisdiction by virtue of an order under section 287 of the Copyright, Designs and Patents Act 1988,

(b) in Scotland, the Court of Session, and

(c) in Northern Ireland, the High Court.

(2) Provision may be made by rules of court with respect to proceedings in the High Court in England and Wales for references and applications under this Act to be dealt with by such judge of that court as the Lord Chancellor may select for the purpose.".

Section 28: the Appeal Tribunal

17.—(1) Section 28 of the Registered Designs Act 1949 (the Appeal Tribunal) is amended as follows.

(2) For subsection (2) (members of Tribunal) substitute—

"(2) The Appeal Tribunal shall consist of—

(a) one or more judges of the High Court nominated by the Lord Chancellor, and

(b) one judge of the Court of Session nominated by the Lord President of that Court."

(3) In subsection (5) (costs), after "costs" (twice) insert "or expenses", and for the words from "and any such order" to the end substitute—

"and any such order may be enforced—

(a) in England and Wales or Northern Ireland, in the same way as an order of the High Court;

(b) in Scotland, in the same way as a decree for expenses granted by the Court of Session.".

(4) For subsection (10) (seniority of judges) substitute—

"(10) In this section 'the High Court' means the High Court in England and Wales; and for the purposes of this section the seniority of judges shall be reckoned by reference to the dates on which they were appointed judges of that court or the Court of Session.".

(5) The amendments to section 28 made by section 10(5) of the Administration of Justice Act 1970 (power to make rules as to right of audience) shall be deemed always to have extended to Northern Ireland.

Section 29: exercise of discretionary powers of registrar

18. In section 29 of the Registered Designs Act 1949 (exercise of discretionary powers of registrar) for "the registrar shall give" substitute "rules made by the Secretary of State under this Act shall require the registrar to give".

Section 30: costs and security for costs

19. For section 30 of the Registered Designs Act 1949 (costs and security for costs) substitute—

Costs and security for costs

30.—(1) Rules made by the Secretary of State under this Act may make provision empowering the registrar, in any proceedings before him under this Act—

  (a) to award any part such costs as he may consider reasonable, and

  (b) to direct how and by what parties they are to be paid.

(2) Any such order of the registrar may be enforced—

  (a) in England and Wales or Northern Ireland, in the same way as an order of the High Court;

  (b) in Scotland, in the same way as a decree for expenses granted by the Court of Session.

(3) Rules made by the Secretary of State under this Act may make provision empowering the registrar to require a person, in such cases as may be prescribed, to give security for the costs of—

  (a) an application for cancellation of the registration of a design,

  (b) an application for the grant of a licence in respect of a registered design, or

  (c) an appeal from any decision of the registrar under this Act,

and enabling the application or appeal to be treated as abandoned in default of such security being given.".

Section 31: evidence before registrar

20. For section 31 of the Registered Designs Act 1949 (evidence before registrar) substitute—

"Evidence before registrar

31. Rules made by the Secretary of State under this Act may make provision—

  (a) as to the giving of evidence in proceedings before the registrar under this Act by affidavit or statutory declaration;

  (b) conferring on the registrar the powers of an official referee of the Supreme Court as regards the examination of witnesses on oath and the discovery and production of documents; and

  (c) applying in relation to the attendance of witnesses in proceedings before the registrar the rules applicable to the attendance of witnesses in proceedings before such a referee.".

Section 32: power of registrar to refuse to deal with certain agents

21. Section 32 of the Registered Designs Act 1949 (power of registrar to refuse to deal with certain agents) is repealed.

Section 33: offences under s.5 (secrecy of certain designs)

22.—(1) Section 33 of the Registered Designs Act 1949 (offences under s.5 (secrecy of certain designs)) is amended as follows.

(2) In subsection (1), for paragraphs (a) and (b) substitute—

"(a) on conviction on indictment to imprisonment for a term not exceeding two years or a fine, or both;

(b) on summary conviction to imprisonment for a term not exceeding six months or a fine not exceeding the statutory maximum, or both.".

(3) Omit subsection (2).

(4) The above amendments do not apply in relation to offences committed before the commencement of Part IV.

Section 34: falsification of register, &c.

23.—(1) In section 34 of the Registered Designs Act 1949 (falsification of register, &c.) for "shall be guilty of a misdemeanour" substitute—

"shall be guilty of an offence and liable—

(a) on conviction on indictment to imprisonment for a term not exceeding two years or a fine, or both;

(b) on summary conviction to imprisonment for a term not exceeding six months or a fine not exceeding the statutory maximum, or both.".

(2) The above amendment does not apply in relation to offences committed before the commencement of Part IV.

Section 35: fine for falsely representing a design as registered

24.—(1) Section 35 of the Registered Designs Act 1949 (fine for falsely representing a design as registered) is amended as follows.

(2) In subsection (1) for the words from "a fine not exceeding £50" substitute "a fine not exceeding level 3 on the standard scale".

(3) In subsection (2)—

(a) for "the copyright in a registered design" substitute "the right in a registered design";

(b) for "subsisting copyright in the design" substitute "subsisting right in the design under this Act"; and

(c) for the words from "a fine" to the end substitute "a fine not exceeding level 1 on the standard scale".

(4) The amendment in sub-paragraph (2) does not apply in relation to offences committed before the commencement of Part IV.

Section 35A: offence by body corporate – liability of officers

25.—(1) In the Registered Designs Act 1949 after section 35 insert—

"Offence by body corporate liability of officers

35A.—(1) Where an offence under this Act committed by a body corporate is proved to have been committed with the consent or connivance of a director, manager, secretary or other similar officer of the body, or a person purporting to act in any such capacity, he as well as the body corporate is guilty of the offence and liable to be proceeded against and punished accordingly.

(2) In relation to a body corporate whose affairs are managed by its members "director" means a member of the body corporate.".

(2) The above amendment does not apply in relation to offences committed before the commencement of Part IV.

Section 36: general power to make rules, &c.

26.—(1) Section 36 of the Registered Designs Act 1949 (general power to make rules, &c.) is amended as follows.

(2) In subsection (1) for "the Board of Trade" and "the Board" substitute "the Secretary of State", and for "as they think expedient" substitute "as he thinks expedient".

(3) For the words in subsection (1) from "and in particular" to the end substitute the following subsections—

"(1A) Rules may, in particular, make provision—

(a) prescribing the form of applications for registration of designs and of any representations or specimens of designs or other documents which may be filed at the Patent Office, and requiring copies to be furnished of any such representations, specimens or documents;

(b) regulating the procedure to be followed in connection with any application or request to the registrar or in connection with any proceeding before him, and authorising the rectification of irregularities of procedure;

(c) providing for the appointment of advisers to assist the registrar in proceedings before him;

(d) regulating the keeping of the register of designs;

(e) authorising the publication and sale of copies of representations of designs and other documents in the Patent Office;

(f) prescribing anything authorised or required by this Act to be prescribed by rules.

(1B) The remuneration of an adviser appointed to assist the registrar shall be determined by the Secretary of State with the consent of the Treasury and shall be defrayed out of money provided by Parliament.".

Section 37: provisions as to rules and Orders

27.—(1) Section 37 of the Registered Designs Act 1949 (provisions as to rules and orders) is amended as follows.

(2) Omit subsection (1) (duty to advertise making of rules).

(3) In subsections (2), (3) and (4) for "the Board of Trade" substitute "the Secretary of State".

Section 38: proceedings of the Board of Trade

28. Section 38 of the Registered Designs Act 1949 (proceedings of the Board of Trade) is repealed.

Section 39: hours of business and excluded days

29. In section 39 of the Registered Designs Act 1949 (hours of business and excluded days), in subsection (1) for "the Board of Trade" substitute "the Secretary of State".

Section 40: fees

30. In section 40 of the Registered Designs Act 1949 (fees) for "the Board of Trade" substitute "the Secretary of State".

Section 44: interpretation

31.—(1) In section 44 of the Registered Designs Act 1949 (interpretation) subsection (1) is amended as follows.

(2) In the definition of "artistic work" for "the Copyright Act 1956" substitute "Part I of the Copyright, Designs and Patents Act 1988".

(3) At the appropriate place insert—

"'author' in relation to a design, has the meaning given by section 2(3) and (4);".

(4) Omit the definition of "copyright".

(5) In the definition of "corresponding design", for the words from "has the same meaning" to the end substitute ", in relation to an artistic work, means a design which if applied to an article would produce something which would be treated for the purposes of Part I of the Copyright, Designs and Patents Act 1988 as a copy of that work;".

(6) For the definition of "court" substitute—

"'the court' shall be construed in accordance with section 27 of this Act;".

(7) In the definition of "design" for "subsection (3) of section one of this Act" substitute "section 1(1) of this Act".

(8) At the appropriate place insert—

"'employee', 'employment' and 'employer' refer to employment under a contract of service or of apprenticeship,".

(9) Omit the definition of "Journal".

(10) In the definition of "prescribed" for "the Board of Trade" substitute "the Secretary of State".

Section 45: application to Scotland

32. In section 45 of the Registered Designs Act 1949 (application to Scotland), omit paragraphs (1) and (2).

Section 46: application to Northern Ireland

33.—(1) Section 46 of the Registered Designs Act 1949 (application to Northern Ireland) is amended as follows.

(2) Omit paragraphs (1) and (2).

(3) For paragraph (3) substitute—

"(3) References to enactments include enactments comprised in Northern Irelandlegislation:".

(4) After paragraph (3) insert—

"(3A) References to the Crown include the Crown in right of Her Majesty's Government in Northern Ireland:".

(5) In paragraph (4) for "a department of the Government of Northern Ireland" substitute "a Northern Ireland department", and at the end add "and in relation to a Northern Ireland department references to the Treasury shall be construed as references to the Department of Finance and Personnel".

Section 47: application to Isle of Man

34. For section 47 of the Registered Designs Act 1949 (application to Isle of Man) substitute—

"*Application to Isle of Man*

47. This Act extends to the Isle of Man, subject to any modifications contained in an Order made by Her Majesty in Council, and accordingly, subject to any such Order, references in this Act to the United Kingdom shall be construed as including the Isle of Man.".

Section 47A: territorial waters and the continental shelf

35. In the Registered Designs Act 1949, after section 47 insert—

"*Territorial waters and the continental shelf*

47A.—(1) For the purposes of this Act the territorial waters of the United Kingdom shall be treated as part of the United Kingdom.

(2) This Act applies to things done in the United Kingdom sector of the continental shelf on a structure or vessel which is present there for purposes directly connected with the exploration of the sea bed or subsoil or the exploitation of their natural resources as it applies to things done in the United Kingdom.

(3) The United Kingdom sector of the continental shelf means the areas designated by order under section 1(7) of the Continental Shelf Act 1964.".

Section 48: repeals, savings and transitional provisions

36. In section 48 of the Registered Designs Act 1949 (repeals, savings and transitional provisions), omit subsection (1) (repeals).

Schedule 1: provisions as to Crown use of registered designs

37.—(1) The First Schedule to the Registered Designs Act 1949 (provisions as to Crown use of registered designs) is amended as follows.

(2) In paragraph 2(1) after "copyright" insert "or design right".

(3) In paragraph 3(1) omit "in such manner as may be prescribed by rules of court".

(4) In paragraph 4(2) (definition of "period of emergency") for the words from "the period ending" to "any other period" substitute "a period".

(5) For paragraph 4(3) substitute—

"(3) No Order in Council under this paragraph shall be submitted to Her Majesty unless a draft of it has been laid before and approved by a resolution of each House of Parliament.".

Schedule 2: enactments repealed

38. Schedule 2 to the Registered Designs Act 1949 (enactments repealed) is repealed.

SCHEDULE 4

(Section 273).

An Act to consolidate certain enactments relating to registered designs.

[16th December 1949]

Registrable designs and proceedings for registration

Designs registrable under Act

1.—(1) In this Act "design" means features of shape, configuration, pattern or ornament applied to an article by any industrial process, being features which in the finished article appeal to and are judged by the eye, but does not include—

(a) a method or principle of construction, or

(b) features of shape or configuration of an article which—

(i) are dictated solely by the function which the article has to perform, or

(ii) are dependent upon the appearance of another article of which the article is intended by the author of the design to form an integral part.

(2) A design which is new may, upon application by the person claiming to be the proprietor, be registered under this Act in respect of any article, or set of articles, specified in the application.

(3) A design shall not be registered in respect of an article if the appearance of the article is not material, that is, if aesthetic considerations are not normally taken into account to a material extent by persons acquiring or using articles of that description, and would not be so taken into account if the design were to be applied to the article.

(4) A design shall not be regarded as new for the purposes of this Act if it is the same as a design—

(a) registered in respect of the same or any other article in pursuance of a prior application, or

(b) published in the United Kingdom in respect of the same or any other article before the date of the application,

of if it differs from such a design only in immaterial details or in features which are variants commonly used in the trade.

This subsection has effect subject to the provisions of sections 4, 6 and 16 of this Act.

(5) The Secretary of State may by rules provide for excluding from registration under this Act designs for such articles of a primarily literary or artistic character as the Secretary of State thinks fit.

Proprietorship of designs

2.—(1) The author of a design shall be treated for the purposes of this Act as the original proprietor of the design, subject to the following provisions.

(1A) Where a design is created in pursuance of a commission for money or money's worth, the person commissioning the design shall be treated as the original proprietor of the design.

(1B) Where, in a case not falling within subsection (1A), a design is created by an employee in the course of his employment, his employer shall be treated as the original proprietor of the design.

(2) Where a design, or the right to apply a design to any article, becomes vested, whether by assignment, transmission or operation of law, in any person other than the original proprietor, either alone or jointly with the original proprietor, that other person, or as the case may be the original proprietor and that other person, shall be treated for the purposes of this Act as the proprietor of the design or as the proprietor of the design in relation to that article.

(3) In this Act the "author" of a design means the person who creates it.

(4) In the case of a design generated by computer in circumstances such that there is no human author, the person by whom the arrangements necessary for the creation of the design are made shall be taken to be the author.

Proceedings for registration

3.—(1) An application for the registration of a design shall be made in the prescribed form and shall be filed at the Patent Office in the prescribed manner.

(2) An application for the registration of a design in which design right subsists shall not be entertained unless made by the person claiming to be the design right owner.

(3) For the purpose of deciding whether a design is new, the registrar may make such searches, if any, as he thinks fit.

(4) The registrar may, in such cases as may be prescribed, direct that for the purpose of deciding whether a design is new an application shall be treated as made on a date earlier or later than that on which it was in fact made.

(5) The registrar may refuse an application for the registration of a design or may register the design in pursuance of the application subject to such modifications, if any, as he thinks fit; and a design when registered shall be registered as of the date on which the application was made or is treated as having been made.

(6) An application which, owing to any default or neglect on the part of the applicant, has not been completed so as to enable registration to be effected within such time as may be prescribed shall be deemed to be abandoned.

(7) An appeal lies from any decision of the registrar under this section.

Registration of same design in respect of other articles, etc.

4.—(1) Where the registered proprietor of a design registered in respect of any article makes an application—

    (a) for registration in respect of one or more other articles, of the registered design, or

    (b) for registration in respect of the same or one or more other articles, of a design consisting of the registered design with modifications or variations not sufficient to alter the character or substantially to affect the identity thereof,

the application shall not be refused and the registration made on that application shall not be invalidated by reason only of the previous registration or publication of the registered design:

Provided that the right in a design registered by virtue of this section shall not extend beyond the end of the period, and any extended period, for which the right subsists in the original registered design.

(2) Where any person makes an application for the registration of a design in respect of any article and either—

    (a) that design has been previously registered by another person in respect of some other article; or

    (b) the design to which the application relates consists of a design previously registered by another person in respect of the same or some other article with modifications or variations not sufficient to alter the character or substantially to affect the identity thereof,

then, if at any time while the application is pending the applicant becomes the registered proprietor of the design previously registered, the foregoing provisions of this section shall apply as if at the time of making the application the applicant had been the registered proprietor of that design.

Provisions for secrecy of certain designs

5.—(1) Where, either before or after the commencement of this Act, an application for the registration of a design has been made, and it appears to the registrar that the design is one of a class notified to him by the Secretary of State as relevant for defence purposes, he may give directions for prohibiting or restricting the publication of information with respect to the design, or the communication of such information to any person or class of persons specified in the directions.

(2) The Secretary of State shall by rules make provision for securing that where such directions are given—

    (a) the representation or specimen of the design, and

    (b) any evidence filed in support of the applicant's contention that the appearance of an article is material (for the purposes of section 1(3) of this Act),

shall not be open to public inspection at the Patent Office during the continuance in force of the directions.

(3) Where the registrar gives any such directions as aforesaid, he shall give notice of the application and of the directions to the Secretary of State, and thereupon the following provisions shall have effect, that is to say:—

(a) the Secretary of State shall, upon receipt of such notice, consider whether the publication of the design would be prejudicial to the defence of the realm and unless a notice under paragraph (c) of this subsection has previously been given by that authority to the registrar, shall reconsider that question before the expiration of nine months from the date of filing of the application for registration of the design and at least once in every subsequent year;

(b) for the purpose aforesaid, the Secretary of State may, at any time after the design has been registered or, with the consent of the applicant, at any time before the design has been registered, inspect the representation or specimen of the design, or any such evidence as is mentioned in subsection (2)(b) above, filed in pursuance of the application;

(c) if upon consideration of the design at any time it appears to the Secretary of State that the publication of the design would not, or would no longer, be prejudicial to the defence of the realm, he shall give notice to the registrar to that effect;

(d) on the receipt of any such notice the registrar shall revoke the directions and may, subject to such conditions, if any, as he thinks fit, extend the time for doing anything required or authorised to be done by or under this Act in connection with the application or registration, whether or not that time has previously expired.

(4) No person resident in the United Kingdom shall, except under the authority of a written permit granted by or on behalf of the registrar, make or cause to be made any application outside the United Kingdom for the registration of a design of any class prescribed for the purposes of this subsection unless—

(a) an application for registration of the same design has been made in the United Kingdom not less than six weeks before the application outside the United Kingdom; and

(b) either no directions have been given under subsection (1) of this section in relation to the application in the United Kingdom or all such directions have been revoked.

Provided that this subsection shall not apply in relation to a design for which an application for protection has first been filed in a country outside the United Kingdom by a person resident outside the United Kingdom.

Provisions as to confidential disclosure, etc.

6.—(1) An application for the registration of a design shall not be refused, and the registration of a design shall not be invalidated, by reason only of—

(a) the disclosure of the design by the proprietor to any other person in such circumstances as would make it contrary to good faith for that other person to use or publish the design;

(b) the disclosure of the design in breach of good faith by any person other than the proprietor of the design; or

(c) in the case of a new or original textile design intended for registration, the acceptance of a first and confidential order for goods bearing the design.

(2) An application for the registration of a design shall not be refused and the registration of a design shall not be invalidated by reason only—

(a) that a representation of the design, or any article to which the design has been applied, has been displayed, with the consent of the proprietor of the design, at an exhibition certified by the Secretary of State for the purposes of this subsection;

(b) that after any such display as aforesaid, and during the period of the exhibition, a representation of the design or any such article as aforesaid has been displayed by any person without the consent of the proprietor; or

(c) that a representation of the design has been published in consequence of any such display as is mentioned in paragraph (a) of this subsection,

if the application for registration of the design is made not later than six months after the opening of the exhibition.

(3) An application for the registration of a design shall not be refused, and the registration of a design shall not be invalidated, by reason only of the communication of the design by the proprietor thereof to a government department of to any person authorised by a government department to consider the merits of the design, or of anything done in consequence of such a communication.

(4) Where an application is made by or with the consent of the owner of copyright in an artistic work for the registration of a corresponding design, the design shall not be treated for the purposes of this Act as being other than new by reason only of any use previously made of the artistic work, subject to subsection (5).

(5) Subsection (4) does not apply if the previous use consisted of or included the sale, letting for hire or offer or exposure for sale or hire of articles to which had been applied industrially—

(a) the design in question, or

(b) a design differing from it only in immaterial details or in features which are variants commonly used in the trade,

and that previous use was made by or with the consent of the copyright owner.

(6) The Secretary of State may make provision by rules as to the circumstances in which a design is to be regarded for the purposes of this section as "applied industrially" to articles, or any description of articles.

Effect of registration, &c.

Right given by registration

7.—(1) The registration of a design under this Act gives the registered proprietor the exclusive right—

(a) to make or import—

(i) for sale or hire, or

(ii) for use for the purpose of a trade or business, or

(b) to sell, hire or offer or expose for sale or hire,

an article in respect of which the design is registered and to which that design or a design not substantially different from it has been applied.

(2) The right in the registered design is infringed by a person who without the licence of the registered proprietor does anything which by virtue of subsection (1) is the exclusive right of the proprietor.

(3) The right in the registered design is also infringed by a person who, without the licence of the registered proprietor makes anything for enabling any such article to be made, in the United Kingdom or elsewhere, as mentioned in subsection (1).

(4) The right in the registered design is also infringed by a person who without the licence of the registered proprietor—

(a) does anything in relation to a kit that would be an infringement if done in relation to the assembled article (see subsection (1)), or

(b) makes anything for enabling a kit to be made or assembled, in the United Kingdom or elsewhere, if the assembled article would be such an article as is mentioned in subsection (1);

and for this purpose a "kit" means a complete or substantially complete set of components intended to be assembled into an article.

(5) No proceedings shall be taken in respect of an infringement committed before the date on which the certificate of registration of the design under this Act is granted.

(6) The right in a registered design is not infringed by the reproduction of a feature of the design which, by virtue of section 1(1)(b), is left out of account in determining whether the design is registrable.

Duration of right in registered design

8.—(1) The right in a registered design subsists in the first instance for a periods of five years from the date of the registration of the design.

(2) The period for which the right subsists may be extended for a second, third, fourth and fifth period of five years, by applying to the registrar for an extension and paying the prescribed renewal fee.

(3) If the first, second, third or fourth period expires without such application and payment being made, the right shall cease to have effect; and the registrar shall, in accordance with rules made by the Secretary of State, notify the proprietor of that fact.

(4) If during the period of six months immediately following the end of that period an application for extension is made and the prescribed renewal fee and any prescribed additional fee is paid, the right shall be treated as if it had never expired, with the result that—

(a) anything done under or in relation to the right during that further period shall be treated as valid,

(b) an act which would have constituted an infringement of the right if it had not expired shall be treated as an infringement, and

(c) an act which would have constituted use of the design for the services of the Crown if the right had not expired shall be treated as such use.

(5) Where it is shown that a registered design—

(a) was at the time it was registered a corresponding design in relation to an artistic work in which copyright subsists, and

(b) by reason of a previous use of that work would not have registrable but for section 6(4) of this Act (registration despite certain prior applications of design),

the right in the registered design expires when the copyright in that work expires, if that is earlier than the time at which it would otherwise expire, and it may not thereafter be renewed.

(6) The above provisions have effect subject to the proviso to section 4(1) (registration of same design in respect of other articles, &c.).

Restoration of lapsed right in design

8A.—(1) Where the right in a registered design has expired by reason of a failure to extend, in accordance with section 8(2) or (4), the period for which the right subsists, an application for the restoration of the right in the design may be made to the registrar within the prescribed period.

(2) The application may be made by the person who was the registered proprietor of the design or by any other person who would have been entitled to the right in the design if

it had not expired; and where the design was held by two or more persons jointly, the application may, with the leave of the registrar, be made by one or more of them without joining the others.

(3) Notice of the application shall be published by the registrar in the prescribed manner.

(4) If the registrar is satisfied that the proprietor took reasonable care to see that the period for which the right subsisted was extended in accordance with section 8(2) or (4), he shall, on payment of any unpaid renewal fee and any prescribed additional fee, order the restoration of the right in the design.

(5) The order may be made subject to such conditions as the registrar thinks fit, and if the proprietor of the design does not comply with any condition the registrar may revoke the order and give such consequential directions as he thinks fit.

(6) Rules altering the period prescribed for the purposes of subsection (1) may contain such transitional provisions and savings as appear to the Secretary of State to be necessary or expedient.

Effect of order for restoration of right

8B.—(1) The effect of an order under section 8A for the restoration of the right in a registered design is as follows.

(2) Anything done under or in relation to the right during the period between expiry and restoration shall be treated as valid.

(3) Anything done during that period which would have constituted an infringement if the right had not expired shall be treated as an infringement—

(a) if done at a time when it was possible for an application for extension to be made under section 8(4); or

(b) if it was a continuation or repetition of an earlier infringing act.

(4) If after it was no longer possible for such an application for extension to be made, and before publication of notice of the application for restoration, a person—

(a) began in good faith to do an act which would have constituted an infringement of the right in the design if it had not expired, or

(b) made in good faith effective and serious preparations to do such an act,

he has the right to continue to do the act or, as the case may be, to do the act, notwithstanding the restoration of the right in the design; but this does not extend to granting a licence to another person to do the act.

(5) If the act was done, or the preparations were made, in the course of a business, the person entitled to the right conferred by subsection (4) may—

(a) authorise the doing of that act by any partners of his for the time being in that business, and

(b) assign that right, or transmit it on death (or in the case of a body corporate on its dissolution), to any person who acquires that part of the business in the course of which the act was done or the preparatoins were made.

(6) Where an article is disposed of to another in exercise of the rights conferred by subsection (4) or subsection (5), that other and any person claiming through him may deal with the article in the same way as if it had been disposed of by the registered proprietor of the design.

(7) The above provisions apply in relation to the use of a registered design for the services of the Crown as they apply in relation to infringement of the right in the design.

Exemption of innocent infringer from liability for damages

9.—(1) In proceedings for the infringement of the right in a registered design damages shall not be awarded against a defendant who proves that at the date of the infringement he was not aware, and had no reasonable ground for supposing, that the design was registered; and a person shall not be deemed to have been aware or to have had reasonable grounds for supposing as aforesaid by reason only of the marking of an article with the word "registered" or any abbreviation thereof, or any word or words expressing or implying that the design applied to the article has been registered, unless the number of the design accompanied the word or words or the abbreviation in question.

(2) Nothing inthis section shall affect the power of the court to grant an injunction in any proceedings for infringement of the right in a registered design.

Compulsory licence in respect of registered design

10.—(1) At any time after a design has been registered any person interested may apply to the registrar for the grant of a compulsory licence in respect of the design on the ground that the design is not applied in the United Kingdom by any industrial process or means to the article in respect of which it is registered to such an extent as is reasonable in the circumstances of the case; and the registrar may make such order on the application as he thinks fit.

(2) An order for the grant of a licence shall, without prejudice to any other method of enforcement, have effect as if it were a deed executed by the registered proprietor and all other necessary parties, granting a licence in accordance with the order.

(3) No order shall be made under this section which would be at variance with any treaty, convention, arrangement or engagement applying to the United Kingdom and any convention country.

(4) An appeal shall lie from any order of the registrar under this section.

Cancellation of registration

11.—(1) The registrar may, upon a request made in the prescribed manner by the registered proprietor, cancel the registration of a design.

(2) At any time after a design has been registered any person interested may apply to the registrar for the cancellation of the registration of the design on the ground that the design was not, at the date of the registration thereof, new..., or on any other ground on which the registrar could have refused to register the design; and the registrar may make such order on the application as he thinks fit.

(3) At any time after a design has been registered, any person interested may apply to the registrar for the cancellation of the registration on the ground that—

    (a) the design was at the time it was registered a corresponding design in relation to an artistic work in which copyright subsisted, and

    (b) the right in the registered design has expired in accordance with section 8(4) of this Act (expiry of right in registered design on expiry of copyright in artistic work);

and the registrar may make such order on the application as he thinks fit.

(4) A cancellation under this section takes effect—

    (a) in the case of cancellation under subsection (1), from the date of the registrar's decision,

    (b) in the case of cancellation under subsection (2), from the date of registration,

    (c) in the case of cancellation under subsection (3), from the date on which the right in the registered design expired,

or, in any case, from such other date as the registrar may direct.

(5) An appeal lies from any order of the registrar under this section.

Powers exercisable for protection of the public interest

11A.—(1) Where a report of the Monopolies and Mergers Commission has been laid before Parliament containing conclusions to the effect—

(a) on a monopoly reference, that a monopoly situation exists and facts found by the Commission operate or may be expected to operate against the public interest,

(b) on a merger reference, that a merger situation qualifying for investigation has been created and the creation of the situation, or particular elements in or consequences of it specified in the report, operate or may be expected to operate against the public interest,

(c) on a competition reference, that a person was engaged in an anti-competitive practice which operated or may be expected to operate against the public interest, or

(d) on a reference under section 11 of the Competition Act 1980 (reference of public bodies and certain other persons), that a person is pursuing a course of conduct which operates against the public interest,

the appropriate Minister or Ministers may apply to the registrar to take action under this section.

(2) Before making an application the appropriate Minister or Ministers shall publish, in such manner as he or they think appropriate, a notice describing the nature of the proposed application and shall consider any representations which may be made within 30 days of such publication by persons whose interests appear to him or them to be affected.

(3) If on an application under this section it appears to the registrar that the matters specified in the Commission's report as being those which in the Commission's opinion operate, or operate or may be expected to operate, against the public interest include—

(a) conditions in licences granted in respect of a registered design by its proprietor restricting the use of the design by the licensee or the right of the proprietor to grant other licences, or

(b) a refusal by the proprietor of a registered design to grant licences on reasonable terms,

he may by order cancel or modify any such condition or may, instead or in addition, make an entry in the register to the effect that licences in respect of the design are to be available as of right.

(4) The terms of a licence available by virtue of this section shall, in default of agreement, be settled by the registrar on an application by the person requiring the licence; and terms so settled shall authorise the licensee to do everything which would be an infringement of the right in the registered design in the absence of a licence.

(5) Where the terms of a licence are settled by the registrar, the licence has effect from the date on which the application to him was made.

(6) An appeal lies from any order of the registrar under this section.

(7) In this section "the appropriate Minister or Ministers" means the Minister or Ministers to whom the report of the Monopolies and Mergers Commission was made.

Undertaking to take licence of right in infringement proceedings

11B.—(1) If in proceedings for infringement of the right in a registered design in respect of which a licence is available as of right under section 11A of this Act the defendant undertakes to take a licence on such terms as may be agreed or, in default of agreement, settled by the registrar under that section—

(a) no injunction shall be granted against him, and

(b) the amount recoverable against him by way of damages or on an account of profits shall not exceed double the amount which would have been payable by him as licensee if such a licence on those terms had been granted before the earliest infringement.

(2) An undertaking may be given at any time before final order in the proceedings, without any admission of liability.

(3) Nothing in this section affects the remedies available in respect of an infringement committed before licences of right were available.

Use for services of the Crown

12. The provisions of the First Schedule to this Act shall have effect with respect to the use of registered designs for the services of the Crown and the rights of third parties in respect of such use.

International Arrangements

Orders in Council as to convention countries

13.—(1) His Majesty may, with a view to the fulfilment of a treaty, convention, arrangement or engagement, by Order in Council declare that any country specified in the Order is a convention country for the purposes of this Act.

Provided that a declaration may be made as aforesaid for the purposes either of all or of some only of the provisions of this Act, and a country in the case of which a declaration made for the purposes of some only of the provisions of this Act is in force shall be deemed to be a convention country for the purposes of those provisions only.

(2) His Majesty may by Order in Council direct that any of the Channel Islands, any colony,... shall be deemed to be a convention country for the purposes of all or any of the provisions of this Act; and an Order made under this subsection may direct that any such provisions shall have effect, in relation to the territory in question, subject to such conditions or limitations, if any, as may be specified in the Order.

(3) For the purposes of subsection (1) of this section, every colony, protectorate, territory subject to the authority or under the suzerainty of another country, and territory administered by another country... under the trusteeship system of the United Nations, shall be deemed to be a country in the case of which a declaration may be made under that subsection.

Registration of design where application for protection in convention country has been made

14.—(1) An application for registration of a design in respect of which protection has been applied for in a convention country may be made in accordance with the provisions of this Act by the person by whom the application for protection was made or his personal representative or assignee:

Provided that no application shall be made by virtue of this section after the expiration of six months from the date of the application for protection in a convention country or, where more than one such application for protection has been made, from the date of the first application.

(2) Where an application for registration of a design is made by virtue of this section, the application shall be treated, for the purpose of determining whether that or any other design is new, as made on the date of the application for protection in the convention country or, if more that one such application was made, on the date of the first such application.

(3) Subsection (2) shall not be construed as excluding the power to give directions under section 3(4) of this Act in relation to an application made by virtue of this section.

(4) Where a person has applied for protection for a design by an application which—

(a) in accordance with the terms of a treaty subsisting between two or more convention countries, is equivalent to an application duly made in any one of those convention countries; or

(b) in accordance with the law of any convention country, is equivalent to an application duly made in that convention country,

he shall be deemed for the purposes of this section to have applied in that convention country.

Extension of time for applications under s.14 in certain cases

15.—(1) If the Secretary of State is satisfied that provision substantially equivalent to the provisions to be made by or under this section has been or will be made under the law of any convention country, he may make rules empowering the registrar to extend the time for making application under subsection (1) of section 14 of this Act for registration of a design in respect of which protection has been applied for in that country in any case where the period specified in the proviso to that subsection expires during a period prescribed by the rules.

(2) Rules made under this section—

(a) may, where any agreement or arrangement has been made between His Majesty's Government in the United Kingdom and the government of the convention country for the supply or mutual exchange of information or articles, provide, either generally or in any class of case specified in the rules, that an extension of time shall not be granted under this section unless the design has been communicated in accordance with the agreement or arrangement;

(b) may, either generally or in any class of case specified in the rules, fix the maximum extension which may be granted under this section;

(c) may prescribe or allow any special procedure in connection with applications made by virtue of this section;

(d) may empower the registrar to extend, in relation to an application made by virtue of ths section, the time limited by or under the foregoing provisions of this Act for doing any act, subject to such conditions, if any, as may be imposed by or under the rules;

(e) may provide for securing that the rights conferred by registration on an application made by virtue of this section shall be subject to such restrictions or conditions as may be specified by or under the rules and in particular to restrictions and conditions for the protection of persons (including persons acting on behalf of His Majesty) who, otherwise than as the result of a communication made in accordance with such an agreement or arrangement as is mentioned in paragraph (a) of this subsection, and before the date of the application in question or such later date as may be allowed by the rules, may have imported or made articles to which the design is applied or may have made any application for registration of the design.

Protection of designs communicated under international agreements

16.—(1) Subject to the provisions of this section, the Secretary of State may make rules for securing that, where a design has been communicated in accordance with an agreement or arrangement made between His Majesty's Government in the United Kingdom and the government of any other country for the supply or mutual exchange of information or articles,—

(a) an application for the registration of the design made by the person from whom the design was communicated or his personal representative or assignee shall not be prejudiced, and the registration of the design in pursuance of such an application shall not be invalidated, by reason only that the design has been communicated as aforesaid or that in consequence thereof—

(i) the design has been published or applied, or

(ii) an application for registration of the design has been made by any other person, or the design has been registered on such an application;

(b) any application for the registration of a design made in consequence of such a communication as aforesaid may be refused and any registration of a design made on such an application may be cancelled.

(2) Rules made under subsection (1) of this section may provide that the publication or application of a design, or the making of any application for registration thereof shall, in such circumstances and subject to such conditions or exceptions as may be prescribed by the rules, be presumed to have been in consequence of such a communication as is mentioned in that subsection.

(3) The powers of the Secretary of State under this section, so far as they are exercisable of the benefit of persons from whom designs have been communicated to His Majesty's Government in the United Kingdom by the government of any other country, shall only be exercised if and to the extent that the Secretary of State is satisfied that substantially equivalent provision has been or will be made under the law of that country for the benefit of persons from whom designs have been communicated by His Majesty's Government in the United Kingdom to the government of that country.

(4) References in the last foregoing subsection to the communication of a design to or by His Majesty's Government or the government of any other country shall be construed as including references to the communication of the design by or to any person authorised in that behalf by the government in question.

Register of designs etc.

Register of designs

17.—(1) The register shall maintain the register of designs, in which shall be entered—

(a) the names and addresses of proprietors of registered designs;

(b) notices of assignments and of transmission of registered designs; and

(c) such other matters as may be prescribed or as the registrar may think fit.

(2) No notice of any trust, whether express, implied or constructive , shall be entered in the register of designs, and the registrar shall not be affected by any such notice.

(3) The register need not be kept in documentary form.

(4) Subject to the provisions of this Act and to rules made by the Secretary of State under it, the public shall have a right to inspect the register at the Patent Office at all convenient times.

(5) Any person who applies for a certified copy of an entry in the register or a certified extract from the register shall be entitled to obtain such a copy or extract on payment of a fee prescribed in relation to certified copies and extracts; and rules made by the Secretary of State under this Act may provide that any person who applies for an uncertified copy or extract shall be entitled to such a copy or extract on payment of a fee prescribed in relation to uncertified copies and extracts.

(6) Applications under subsection (5) above or rules made by virtue of that subsection shall be made in such manner as may be prescribed.

(7) In relation to any portion of the register kept otherwise than in documentary form—

    (a) the right of inspection conferred by subsection (4) above is a right to inspect the material on the register; and

    (b) the right to a copy or extract conferred by subsection (5) above or rules is a right to a copy or extract in a form in which it can be taken away and in which it is visible and legible.

(8) Subject to subsection (11) below, the register shall be prima facie evidence of anything required or authorised to be entered in it and in Scotland shall be sufficient evidence of any such thing.

(9) A certificate purporting to be signed by the registrar and certifying that any entry which he is authorised by or under this Act to make has or has not been made, or that any other thing which he is so authorised to do has or has not been done, shall be prima facie evidence, and in Scotland shall be sufficient evidence, of the matters so certified.

(10) Each of the following—

    (a) a copy of an entry in the register or an extract from the register which is supplied under subsection (5) above;

    (b) a copy or any representation, specimen or document kept in the Patent Office or an extract from any such document,

which purports to be a certified copy or certified extract shall, subject to subsection (11) below, be admitted in evidence without further proof and without production of any original; and in Scotland such evidence shall be sufficient evidence.

11. In the application of this section to England and Wales nothing in it shall be taken as detracting from section 69 or 70 of the Police and Criminal Act 1984 or any provision made by virtue of either of them.

12. In this section "certified copy" and "certified extract" means a copy and extract certified by the registrar and sealed with the seal of the Patent Office.

Certificate of registration

18.—(1) The registrar shall grant a certificate of registration in the prescribed form to the registered proprietor of a design when the design is registered.

(2) The registrar may, in a case where he is satisfied that the certificate of registration has been lost or destroyed, or in any other case in which he thinks it expedient, furnish one or more copies of the certificate.

Registration of assignments, etc.

19.—(1) Where any person becomes entitled by assignment, transmission or operation of law to a registered design or to a share in a registered design, or becomes entitled as mortgagee, licensee or otherwise to any other interest in a registered design, he shall apply to the registrar in the prescribed manner for the registration of his title as proprietor or co-proprietor or, as the case may be, of notice of his interest, in the register of designs.

(2) Without prejudice to the provisions of the foregoing subsection, an application for the registration of the title of any person becoming entitled by assignment to a registered design or a share in a registered design, or becoming entitled by virtue of a mortgage, licence or other instrument to any other interest in a registered design, may be made in the prescribed manner by the assignor, mortgagor, licensor or other party to that instrument, as the case may be.

(3) Where application is made under this section for the registration of the title of any person, the registrar shall, upon proof of title to his satisfaction—

(a) where that person is entitled to a registered design or a share in a registered design, register him in the register of designs as proprietor or co-proprietor of the design, and enter in that register particulars of the instrument or event by which he derives title; or

(b) where that person is entitled to any other interest in the registered design, enter in that register notice of his interest, with particulars of the instrument (if any) creating it.

(3A) Where a design right subsists in a registered design, the registrar shall not register an interest under subsection (3) unless he is satisfied that the person entitled to that interest is also entitled to a corresponding interest in the design right.

(3B) Where design right subsists in a registered design and the proprietor of the registered design is also the design right owner, an assignment of the design right shall be taken to be also an assignment of the right in the registered design, unless a contrary intention appears.

(4) Subject to any rights vested in any other person of which notice is entered in the register of designs, the person or persons registered as proprietor of a registered design shall have power to assign, grant licences under, or otherwise deal with the design, and to give effectual receipts for any consideration for any such assignment, licence or dealing.

Provided that any equities in respect of the design may be enforced in like manner as in respect of any other personal property.

(5) Except for the purposes of an application to rectify the register under the following provisions of this Act, a document in respect of which no entry has been made in the register of designs under subsection (3) of this section shall not be admitted in any court as evidence of the title of any person to a registered design or share of or interest in a registered design unless the court otherwise directs.

Rectification of register

20.—(1) The court may, on the application of any person aggrieved, order the register of designs to be rectified by the making of any entry therein or the variation or deletion of any entry therein.

(2) In proceedings under this section the court may determine any question which it may be necessary or expedient to decide in connection with the rectification of the register.

(3) Notice of any application to the court under this section shall be given in the prescribed manner to the registrar, who shall be entitled to appear and be heard on the application, and shall appear if so directed by the court.

(4) Any order made by the court under this section shall direct that notice of the order shall be served on the registrar in the prescribed manner; and the registrar shall, on receipt of the notice, rectify the register accordingly.

(5) A rectification of the register under this section has effect as follows—

(a) an entry made has effect from the date on which it should have been made,

(b) an entry varied has effect as if it had originally been made in its varied form, and

(c) an entry deleted shall be deemed never to have had effect,

unless, in any case, the court directs otherwise.

Power to correct clerical errors.

21.—(1) The registrar may, in accordance with the provisions of this section, correct any error in an application for the registration or in the representation of a design, or any error in the register of designs.

(2) A correction may be made in pursuance of this section either upon a request in writing made by any person interested and accompanied by the prescribed fee, or without such a request.

(3) Where the registrar proposes to make any such correction as aforesaid otherwise than in pursuance of a request made under this section, he shall give notice of the proposal to the registered proprietor or the applicant for registration of the design, as the case may be, and to any other person who appears to him to be concerned, and shall give them an opportunity to be heard before making the correction.

Inspection of registered designs

22.—(1) Where a design has been registered under this Act, there shall be open to inspection at the Patent Office on and after the day on which the certificate of registration is issued—

(a) the representation or specimen of the design, and

(b) any evidence filed in support of the applicant's contention that the appearance of an article is material (for the purposes of section 1(3) of this Act).

This subsection has effect subject to the following provisions of this section and to any rules made under section 5(2) of this Act.

(2) In the case of a design registered in respect of an article of any class prescribed for the purposes of this subsection, no representation, specimen or evidence filed in pursuance of the application shall, until the expiration of such period after the day on which the certificate of registration is issued as may be prescribed in relation to articles of that class, be open to inspection at the Patent Office except by the registered proprietor, a person authorised in writing by the registered proprietor, or a person authorised by the registrar or by the court:

Provided that where the registrar proposes to refuse an application for the registration of any other design on the ground that it is the same as the first-mentioned design or differs from that design only in immaterial details or in features which are variants commonly used in the trade, the applicant shall be entitled to inspect the representation or specimen of the first-mentioned design filed in pursuance of the application for registration of that design.

(3) In the case of a design registered in respect of an article of any class prescribed for the purposes of the last foregoing subsection, the representation, specimen or evidence shall not, during the period prescribed as aforesaid, be inspected by any person by virtue of this section except in the presence of the registrar or of an officer acting under him; and except in the case of an inspection authorised by the proviso to that subsection, the person making the inspection shall not be entitled to take a copy of the representation, specimen or evidence or any part thereof.

(4) Where an application for the registration of a design has been abandoned or refused, neither the application for registration nor any representation, specimen or evidence filed in pursuance thereof shall at any time be open to inspection at the Patent Office or be published by the registrar.

Information as to existence of right in registered design

23. On the request of a person furnishing such information as may enable the registrar to identify the design, and on payment of the prescribed fee, the registrar shall inform him—

(a) whether the design is registered and, if so, in respect of what articles, and

(b) whether any extension of the period of the right in the registered design has been granted, and shall state the date of registration and the name and address of the registered proprietor.

Legal proceedings and appeals

Certificate of contested validity of registration

25.—(1) If in any proceedings before the court the validity of the registration of a design is contested, and it is found by the court that the design is validly registered, the court may certify that the validity of the registration of the design was contested in those proceedings.

(2) Where any such certificate has been granted, then if in any subsequent proceedings before the court for infringement of the right in the registered design or for cancellation of the registration of the design, a final order or judgment is made or given in favour of the registered proprietor, he shall, unless the court otherwise directs, be entitled to his costs as between solicitor and client:

Provided that this subsection shall not apply to the costs of any appeal in any such proceedings as aforesaid.

Remedy for groundless threats of infringement proceedings

26.—(1) Where any person (whether entitled to or interested in a registered design or an application for registration of a design or not) by circulars, advertisements or otherwise threatens any other person with proceedings for infringement of the right in a registered design, any person aggrieved thereby may bring an action against him for any such relief as is mentioned in the next following subsection.

(2) Unless in any action brought by virtue of this section the defendant proves that the acts in respect of which proceedings were threatened constitute or, if done, would constitute, an infringement of the right in a registered design the registration of which is not shown by the plaintiff to be invalid, the plaintiff shall be entitled to the following relief, that is to say:—

(a) a declaration to the effect that the threats are unjustifiable;

(b) an injunction against the continuance of the threats; and

(c) such damages, if any, as he has sustained thereby.

(2A) Proceedings may not be brought under this section in respect of a threat to bring proceedings for an infringement alleged to consist of the making or importing of anything.

(3) For the aviodance of doubt it is hereby declared that a mere notification that a design is registered does not constitute a threat of proceedings within the meaning of this section.

The court

27.—(1) In this Act "the court" means—

(a) in England and Wales, the High Court or any patents county court having jurisdiction by virtue of an order under section 287 of the Copyright, Designs and Patents Act 1988,

(b) in Scotland, the Court of Session, and

(c) in Northern Ireland, the High Court.

(2) Provision may be made by rules of court with respect to proceedings in the High Court in England and Wales for references and applications under this Act to be dealt with by such judge of that court as the Lord Chancellor may select for the purpose.

The Appeal Tribunal

28.—(1) Any appeal from the registrar under this Act shall lie to the Appeal Tribunal.

(2) The Appeal Tribunal shall consist of—

(a) one or more judges of the High Court nominated by the Lord Chancellor, and

(b) one judge of the Court of Session nominated by the Lord President of that Court.

(2A) At any time when it consists of two or more judges, the jurisdiction of the Appeal Tribunal—

(a) where in the case of any particular appeal the senior of those judges so directs, shall be exercised in relation to that appeal by both of the judges, or (if there are more than two) by two of them, sitting together, and

(b) inrelation to any appeal in respect of which no such direction is given, may be exercised by any one of the judges;

and, in the exercise of that jurisdiction, different appeals may be heard at the same time by different judges.

(3) The expenses of the Appeal Tribunal shall be defrayed and the fees to be taken therein may be fixed as if the Tribunal were a court of the High Court.

(4) The Appeal Tribunal may examine witnesses on oath and administer oaths for that purpose.

(5) Upon any appeal under this Act the Appeal Tribunal may by order award to any party such costs or expenses as the Tribunal may consider reasonable and direct how and by what parties the costs or expenses are to be paid; and any such order may be enforced—

(a) in England and Wales or Northern Ireland, in the same way as an order of the High Court;

(b) in Scotland, in the same way as a decree for expenses granted by the Court of Session.

(7) Upon any appeal under this Act the Appeal Tribunal may exercise any power which could have been exercised by the registrar in the proceeding from which the appeal is brought.

(8) Subject to the foregoing provisions of this section the Appeal Tribunal may make rules for regulating all matters relating to proceedings before it under this Act, including right of audience.

(8A) At any time when the Appeal Tribunal consists of two or more judges, the power to make rules under subsection (8) of this section shall be exercisable by the senior of those judges:

Provided that another of those judges may exercise that power if it appears to him that it is necessary for rules to be made and that the judge (or, if more than one, each of the judges) senior to him is for the time being prevented by illness, absence or otherwise from making them.

(9) An appeal to the Appeal Tribunal under this Act shall not be deemed to be a proceeding in the High Court.

(10) In this section "the High Court" means the High Court in England and Wales; and for the purposes of this section the seniority of judges shall be reckoned by reference to the dates on which they were appointed judges of that court or the Court of Session.

Powers and duties of Registrar

Exercise of discretionary powers of registrar

29. Without prejudice to any provisions of this Act requiring the registrar to hear any party to proceedings thereunder, or to give to any such party an opportunity to be heard, rules made by the Secretary of State under this Act shall require the registrar to give to any applicant for registration of a design an opportunity to be heard before exercising adversely to the applicant any discretion vested in the registrar by or under this Act.

Costs and security for costs

30.—(1) Rules made by the Secretary of State under this Act may make provision empowering the registrar, in any proceedings before him under this Act—

    (a) to award any party such costs as he may consider reasonable, and

    (b) to direct how and by what parties they are to be paid.

(2) Any such order of the registrar may be enforced—

    (a) in England and Wales or Northern Ireland, in the same way as an order of the High Court;

    (b) in Scotland, in the same way as a decree for expenses granted by the Court of Session.

(3) Rules made by the Secretary of State under this Act may make provision empowering the registrar to require a person, in such cases as may be prescribed, to give security for the costs of—

    (a) an application for cancellation of the registration of a design,

    (b) an application for the grant of a licence in respect of a registered design, or

    (c) an appeal from any decision of the registrar under this Act,

and enabling the application or appeal to be treated as abandoned in default of such security being given.

Evidence before registrar

31. Rules made by the Secretary of State under this Act may make provision—

    (a) as to the giving of evidence in proceedings before the registrar under this Act by affidavit or statutory declaration;

    (b) conferring on the registrar the powers of an official referee of the Supreme Court as regards the examination of witnesses on oath and the discovery and production of documents; and

    (c) applying in relation to the attendance of witnesses in proceedings before the registrar the rules applicable to the attendance of witnesses in proceedings before such a referee.

Offences

Offences under s.5

33.—(1) If any person fails to comply with any direction given under section five of this Act or makes or causes to be made an application for the registration of a design in contravention of that section, he shall be guilty of an offence and liable—

    (a) on conviction on indictment to imprisonment for a term not exceeding two years or a fine, or both;

    (b) on summary conviction to imprisonment for a term not exceeding six months or a fine not exceeding the statutory maximum, or both.

Falsification of register, etc.

34. If any person makes or causes to be made a false entry in the register of designs, or a writing falsely purporting to be a copy of an entry in that register, or produces or tenders or causes to be produced or tendered in evidence any such writing, knowing the entry or writing to be false, he shall be guilty of an offence and liable—

(a) on conviction on indictment to imprisonment for a term not exceeding two years or a fine, or both;

(b) on summary conviction to imprisonment for a term not exceeding six months or a fine not exceeding the statutory maximum, or both.

Fine for falsely representing a design as registered

35.—(1) If any person falsely represents that a design applied to any article sold by him is registered in respect of that article, he shall be liable on summary conviction to a fine not exceeding level 3 on the standard scale; and for the purposes of this provision a person who sells an article having stamped, engraved or impressed thereon or otherwise applied thereto the word "registered", or any other word expressing or implying that the design applied to the article is registered, shall be deemed to represent that the design applied to the article is registered in respect of that article.

(2) If any person, after the right in a registered design has expired, marks any article to which the design has been applied with the word "registered", or any word or words implying that there is a subsisting right in the design under this Act, or causes any such article to be so marked, he shall be liable on summary conviction to a fine not exceeding level 1 on the standard scale.

Offence by body corporate: liability of officers

35A.—(1) Where an offence under this Act committed by a body corporate is proved to have been committed with the consent or connivance of a director, manager, secretary of other similar officer of the body, or a person purporting to act in any such capacity, he as well as the body corporate is guilty of the offence and liable to be proceeded against and punished accordingly.

(2) In relation to a body corporate whose affairs are managed by its members "director" means a member of the body corporate.

Rules, etc.

General power of Secretary of State to make rules, etc.

36.—(1) Subject to the provisions of this Act, the Secretary of State may make such rules as he thinks expedient for regulating the business of the Patent Office in relation to designs and for regulating all matters by this Act placed under the direction or control of the registrar or the Secretary of State.

(1A) Rules may, in particular, make provision—

(a) prescribing the form of applications for registration of designs and of any representations or specimens of designs or other documents which may be filed at the Patent Office, and requiring copies to be furnished of any such representations, specimens or documents;

(b) regulating the procedure to be followed in connection with any application or request to the registrar or in connection with any proceeding before him, and authorising the rectification of irregularities of procedure;

(c) providing for the appointment of advisers to assist the registrar in proceedings before him;

(d) regulating the keeping of the register of designs;

(e) authorising the publication and sale of copies of representations of designs and other documents in the Patent Office;

(f) prescribing anything authorised or required by this Act to be prescribed by rules.

(1B) The remuneration of an adviser appointed to assist the registrar shall be determined by the Secretary of State with the consent of the Treasury and shall be defrayed out of money provided by Parliament.

(2) Rules made under this section may provide for the establishment of branch offices for designs and may authorise any document or thing required by or under this Act to be filed or done at the Patent Office to be filed or done at the branch office at Manchester or any other branch office established in pursuance of the rules.

Provisions as to rules and Orders

37.—(1)

(2) Any rules made by the Secretary of State in pursuance of section 15 or section 16 of this Act, and any other made, direction given, or other action taken under the rules by the registrar, may be made, given or taken so as to have effect as respects things done or omitted to be done on or after such date, whether before or after the coming into operation of the rules or of this Act, as may be specified in the rules.

(3) Any power to make rules conferred by this Act on the Secretary of State or on the Appeal Tribunal shall be exercisable by statutory instrument; and the Statutory Instruments Act 1946 shall apply to a statutory instrument containing rules made by the Appeal Tribunal in like manner as if the rules had been made by a Minister of the Crown.

(4) Any statutory instrument containing rules made by the Secretary of State under this Act shall be subject to annulment in pursuance of a resolution of either House of Parliament.

(5) Any Order in Council made under this Act may be revoked or varied by a subsequent Order in Council.

Supplemental

Hours of business and excluded days

39.—(1) Rules made by the Secretary of State under this Act may specify the hour at which the Patent Office shall be deemed to be closed on any day for purposes of the transaction by the public of business under this Act or of any class of such business, and may specify days as excluded days for any such purposes.

(2) Any business done under this Act on any day after the hour specified as aforesaid in relation to business of that class, or on a day which is an excluded day in relation to business of that class, shall be deemed to have been done on the next following day not being an excluded day; and where the time for doing anything under this Act expires on an excluded day, that time shall be extended to the next following day not being an excluded day.

Fees

40. There shall be paid in respect of the registration of designs and applications thereof, and in respect of other matters relating to designs arising under this Act, such fees as may be prescribed by rules made by the Secretary of State with the consent of the Treasury.

Service of notices, &c., by post

41. Any notice required or authorised to be given by or under this Act, and any application or other document so authorised or required to be made or filed, may be given, made or filed by post.

Annual report of registrar

42. The Comptroller-General of Patents, Designs and Trade Marks shall, in his annual report with respect to the execution of the Patents Act 1977, include a report with respect to the execution of this Act as if it formed a part of or was included in that Act.

Savings

43.—(1) Nothing in this Act shall be construed as authorising or requiring the registrar to register a design the use of which would, in his opinion, be contrary to law or morality.

(2) Nothing in this Act shall affect the right of the Crown or of any person deriving title directly or indirectly from the Crown to sell or use articles forfeited under the laws relating to customs or excise.

Interpretation

44.—(1) In this Act, except where the context otherwise requires, the following expressions have the meanings hereby respectively assigned by them, that is to say—

"Appeal Tribunal" means the Appeal Tribunal constituted and acting in accordance with section 28 of this Act as amended by the Administration of Justice Act 1969;

"article" means any article of manufacture and includes any part of an article if that part is made and sold separately;

"artistic work" has the same meaning as in Part I of the Copyright, Designs and Patents Act 1988,

"assignee" includes the personal representative of a deceased assignee, and references to the assignee of any person include references to the assignee of the personal representative or assignee of that person;

"author", in relation to a design, has the meaning given by section 2(3) and (4);

"corresponding design", in relation to an artistic work, means a design which if applied to an article would produce something which would be treated for the purposes of Part I of the Copyright, Designs and Patents Act 1988 as a copy of that work;

"the court" shall be construed in accordance with section 27 of this Act;

"design" has the meaning assigned to it by section 1(1) of this Act;

"employee", "employment" and "employer" refer to employment under a contract of service or of apprenticeship;

"prescribed" means prescribed by rules made by the Secretary of State under this Act;

"proprietor" has the meaning assigned to it by section two of this Act;

"registered proprietor" means the person or persons for the time being entered in the register of designs as proprietor of the design;

"registrar" means the Comptroller-General of Patents Designs and Trade Marks;

"set of articles" means a number of articles of the same general character ordinarily on sale or intended to be used together, to each of which the same design, or the same design with modifications or variations not sufficient to alter the character or substantially to affect the identity thereof, is applied.

(2) Any reference in this Act to an article in respect of which a design is registered shall, in the case of a design registered in respect of a set of articles, be construed as a reference to any article of that set.

(3) Any question arising under this Act whether a number of articles constitute a set of articles shall be determined by the registrar; and notwithstanding anything in this Act any determination of the registrar under this subsection shall be final.

(4) For the purposes of subsection (1) of section 14 and of section 16 of this Act, the expression "personal representative", in relation to a deceased person, includes the legal representative of the deceased appointed to any country outside the United Kingdom.

Application to Scotland

45. In the application of this Act to Scotland—

(3) The expression "injuction" means "interdict"; the expression "arbitrator" means "arbiter"; the expression "plaintiff" means "pursuer", the expression "defendant" means "defender".

Application to Northern Ireland

46. In the application of this Act to Northern Ireland—

(3) References to enactments include enactments comprised in Northern Ireland legislation:

(3A) References to the Crown include the Crown in right of Her Majesty's Government in Northern Ireland:

(4) References to a government department shall be construed as including references to a Northern Ireland department, and in relation to a Northern Ireland department references to the Treasury shall be construed as references to the Department of Finance and Personnel.

Application to Isle of Man

47. This Act extends to the Isle of Man, subject to any modifications contained in an Order made by Her Majesty in Council, and accordingly, subject to any such Order, references in this Act to the United Kingdom shall be construed as including the Isle of Man.

Territorial waters and the continental shelf

47A.—(1) For the purposes of this Act the territorial waters of the United Kingdom shall be treated as part of the United Kingdom.

(2) This Act applies to things done in the United Kingdom sector of the continental shelf on a structure or vessel which is present there for purposes directly connected with the exploration of the sea bed or subsoil or the exploitation of their natural resources as it applies to things done in the United Kingdom.

(3) The United Kingdom sector of the continental shelf means the areas designated by order under section 1(7) of the Continental Shelf Act 1964.

Repeals, savings, and transitional provisions

48.—(1) ...   .

(2) Subject to the provisions of this section, any Order in Council, rule, order, requirement, certificate, notice, decision, direction, authorisation, consent, application, request or thing made, issued, given or done under any enactment repealed by this Act shall, if in force at the commencement of this Act, and so far as it could have been made, issued, given or done under this Act, continue in force and have effect as if made, issued, given or done under the corresponding enactment of this Act.

(3) Any register kept under the Patents and Designs Act 1907 shall be deemed to form part of the corresponding register under this Act.

(4) Any design registered before the commencement of this Act shall be deemed to be registered under this Act in respect of articles of the class in which it is registered.

(5) Where, in relation to any design, the time for giving notice to the registrar under section 59 of the Patents and Designs Act 1907 expired before the commencement of this Act and the notice was not given, subsection (2) of section 6 of this Act shall not apply in relation to that design or any registration of that design.

(6) Any document referring to any enactment repealed by this Act shall be construed as referring to the corresponding enactment of this Act.

(7) Nothing in the foregoing provisions of this section shall be taken as prejudicing the operation of section 38 of the Interpretation Act 1889 (which relates to the effect of repeals).

Short title and commencement

49.—(1) This Act may be cited as the Registered Designs Act 1949.

(2) This Act shall come into operation on the first day of January, nineteen hundred and fifty, immediately after the coming into operation of the Patents and Designs Act 1949.

FIRST SCHEDULE

PROVISIONS AS TO THE USE OF REGISTERED DESIGNS FOR THE SERVICES OF THE CROWN AND AS TO THE RIGHTS OF THIRD PARTIES IN RESPECT OF SUCH USE

Use of registered designs for services of the Crown

1.—(1) Notwithstanding anything in this Act, any Government department, and any person authorised in writing by a Government department, may use any registered design for the services of the Crown in accordance with the following provisions of this paragraph.

(2) If and so far as the design has before the date of registration thereof been duly recorded by or applied by or on behalf of a Government department otherwise than in consequence of the communication of the design directly or indirectly by the registered proprietor or any person from whom he derives title, any use of the design by virtue of this paragraph may be made free of any royalty or other payment to the registered proprietor.

(3) If and so far as the design has not been so recorded or applied as aforesaid, any use of the design made by virtue of this paragraph at any time after the date of registration thereof, or in consequence of any such communication as aforesaid, shall be made upon such terms as may be agreed upon, either before or after the use, between the Government department and the registered proprietor with the approval of the Treasury, or as may in default of agreement be determined by the court on a reference under paragraph 3 of this Schedule.

(4) The authority of a Government department in respect of a design may be given under this paragraph either before or after the design is registered and either before or after the acts in respect of which the authority is given are done, and may be given to any person

whether or not he is authorised directly or indirectly by the registered proprietor to use the design.

(5) Where any use of a design is made by or with the authority of a Government department under this paragraph, then, unless it appears to the department that it would be contrary to the public interest so to do, the department shall notify the registered proprietor as soon as practicable after the use is begun, and furnish him with such information as to the extent of the use as he may from time to time require.

(6) For the purposes of this and the next following paragraph "the services of the Crown" shall be deemed to include—

(a) the supply to the government of any country outside the United Kingdom, in pursuance of an agreement or arrangement between Her Majesty's Government in the United Kingdom and the goverment of that country, of articles required—

(i) for the defence of that country; or

(ii) for the defence of any other country whose government is party to any agreement or arrangement with Her Majesty's said Government in respect of defence matters;

(b) the supply to the United Nations, or the government of any country belonging to that organisation, in pursuance or an agreement or arrangement between Her Majesty's Government and that organisation or government, of articles required for any armed forces operating in pursuance of a resolution of that organisation or any organ of that organisation;

and the power of a Government department or a person authorised by a Government department under this paragraph to use a design shall include power to sell to any such government or to the said organisation any articles the supply of which is authorised by this sub-paragraph, and to sell to any person any articles made in the exercise of the powers conferred by this paragraph which are no longer required for the purpose for which they were made.

(7) The purchaser of any articles sold in the exercise of powers conferred by this paragraph, and any person claiming through him, shall have power to deal with them in the same manner as if the rights in the registered design were held on behalf of His Majesty.

Rights of third parties in respect of Crown use

2.—(1) In relation to any use of a registered design, or a design of which an application for registration is pending, made for the services of the Crown—

(a) by a Government department or a person authorised by a Government department under the last foregoing paragraph; or

(b) by the registered proprietor or applicant for registration to the order of a Government department;

the provisions of any licence, assignment or agreement made, whether before or after the commencement of this Act, between the registered proprietor or applicant for registration or any person who derives title from him or from whom he derives title and any person other than a Government department shall be of no effect so far as those provisions restrict or regulate the use of the design, or any model, document or information relating thereto, or provide for the making of payments in respect of any such use, or calculated by reference thereto; and the reproduction or publication of any model or document in connection with the said use shall not be deemed to be an infringement of any copyright or design right subsisting in the model or document.

(2) Where an exclusive licence granted otherwise than for royalties or other benefits determined by reference to the use of the design is in force under the registered design then—

(a) in relation to any use of the design which, but for the provisions of this and the last foregoing paragraph, would constitute an infringement of the rights of the licensee, sub-paragraph (3) of the last foregoing paragraph shall have effect as if for the reference to the registered proprietor there were substituted a reference to the licensee; and

(b) in relation to any use of the design by the licensee by virtue of an authority given under the last foregoing paragraph, that paragraph shall have effect as if the said sub-paragraph (3) were omitted.

(3) Subject to the provisions of the last foregoing sub-paragraph, where the registered design or the right to apply for or obtain registration of the design has been assigned to the registered proprietor in consideration of royalties or other benefits determined by reference to the use of the design, then—

(a) in relation to any use of the design by virtue of paragraph 1 of thie Schedule, sub-paragraph (3) of that paragraph shall have effect as if the reference to the registered proprietor included a reference to the assignor, and any sum payable by virtue of that sub-paragraph shall be divided between the registered proprietor and the assignor in such proportion as may be agreed upon between or as may in default of agreement be determined by the court on a reference under the next following paragraph; and

(b) in relation to any use of the design made for the services of the Crown by the registered proprietor to the order of a Government department, sub-paragraph (3) of paragraph 1 of this Schedule shall have effect as if that use were made by virtue of an authority given under that paragraph.

(4) Where, under sub-paragraph (3) of paragraph 1 of this Schedule, payments are required to be made by a Government department to a registered proprietor in respect of any use of a design, any person being the holder of an exclusive licence under the registered design (not being such a licence as is mentioned in sub-paragraphs (2) of this paragraph) authorising him to make that use of the design shall be entitled to recover from the registered proprietor such part (if any) of those payments as may be agreed upon between that person and the registered proprietor, or as may in default of agreement be determined by the court under the next following paragraph to be just having regard to any expenditure incurred by that person—

(a) in developing the said design; or

(b) in making payments to the registered proprietor, other than royalties or other payments determined by referenece to the use of the design, in consideration of the licence;

and if, at any time before the amount of any such payment has been agreed upon between the Government department and the registered proprietor, that person gives notice in writing of his interest to the department, any agreement as to the amount of that payment shall be of no effect unless it is made with his consent.

(5) In this paragraph "exclusive licence" means a licence from a registered proprietor which confers on the licensee, or on the licensee and persons authorised by him, to the exclusion of all other persons (including the registered proprietor), any right in respect of the registered design.

Compensation for loss of profit

2A.—(1) Where Crown use is made of a registered design, the government department concerned shall pay—

(a) to the registered proprietor, or

(b) if there is an exclusive licence in force in respect of the design, to the exclusive licensee, compensation for any loss resulting from his not being awarded a contract to supply the articles to which the design is applied.

(2) Compensation is payable only to the extent that such a contract could have been fulfilled from his existing manufacturing capacity; but is payable notwithstanding the existence of circumstances rendering him ineligible for the award of such a contract.

(3) In determining the loss, regard shall be had to the profit which would have been made on such a contract and to the extent to which any manufacturing capacity was under-used.

(4) No compensation is payable in respect of any failure to secure contracts for the supply of articles to which the design is applied otherwise than for the services of the Crown.

(5) The amount payable under this paragraph shall, if not agreed between the registered proprietor or licensee and the government department concerned with the approval of the Treasury, be determined by the court on a reference under paragraph 3; and it is in addition to any amount payable under paragraph 1 or 2 of this Schedule.

(6) In this paragraph—

"Crown use", in relation to a design, means the doing of anything by virtue of paragraph 1 which would otherwise be an infringement of the right in the design; and

"the government department concerned", in relation to such use, means the government department by whom or on whose authority the act was done.

Reference of disputes as to Crown use

3.—(1) Any dispute as to—

(a) the exercise by a Government department, or a person authorised by a Government department, of the powers conferred by paragraph 1 of this Schedule,

(b) terms for the use of a design for the services of the Crown under that paragraph

(c) the right of any person to receive any part of a payment made under paragraph 1(3), or

(d) the right of any person to receive a payment under paragraph 2A,

may be referred to the court by either party to the dispute.

(2) In any proceedings under this paragraph to which a Government department are a party, the department may—

(a) if the registered proprietor is a party to the proceedings, apply for cancellation of the registration of the design upon any ground upon which the registration of a design may be cancelled on an application to the court under section twenty of this Act;

(b) in any case, put in issue the validity of the registration of the design without applying for its cancellation.

(3) If in such proceedings as aforesaid any question arises whether a design has been recorded or applied as mentioned in paragraph 1 of this Schedule, and the disclosure of any document recording the design, or of any evidence of the application thereof, would in the opinion of the department be prejudicial to the public interest, the disclosure may be made confidentially to counsel for the other party or to an independent expert mutually agreed upon.

(4) In determining under this paragraph any dispute between a Government department and any person as to terms for the use of a design for the services of the Crown, the court shall have regard to any benefit or compensation which that person or any person from whom he derives title may have received, or may be entitled to receive, directly or indirectly from any Government department in respect of the design in question.

(5) In any proceedings under this paragraph the court may at any time order the whole proceedings or any question or issue of fact arising therein to be referred to a special or official referee to an arbitrator on such terms as the court may direct; and references to the court in the foregoing provisions of this paragraph shall be construed accordingly.

Special provisions as to Crown use during emergency

4.—(1) During any period of emergency within the meaning of this paragraph, the powers exercisable in relation to a design by a Government department, or a person authorised by a Government department under paragraph 1 of this Schedule shall include power to use the design for any purpose which appears to the department necessary or expedient—

    (a) for the efficient prosecution of any war in which His Majesty may be engaged;

    (b) for the maintenance of supplies and services essential to the life of the community;

    (c) for securing a sufficiency of supplies and services essential to the well-being of the community;

    (d) for promoting the productivity of industry, commerce and agriculture;

    (e) for fostering and directing exports and reducing imports, or imports of any classes, from all or any countries and for redressing the balance of trade;

    (f) generally for ensuring that the whole resources of the community are available for use, and are used, in a manner best calculated to serve the interests of the community; or

    (g) for assisting the relief of suffering and the restoration and distribution of essential supplies and services in any part of His Majesty's dominions or any foreign countries that are in grave distress as the result of war;

and any reference in this Schedule to the services of the Crown shall be construed as including a reference to the purposes aforesaid.

(2) In this paragraph the expression "period of emergency" means a period beginning on such date as may be declared by Order in Council to be the commencement, and ending on such date as may be so declared to be the termination, of a period of emergency for the purposes of this paragraph.

(3) No Order in Council under this paragraph shall be submitted to Her Majesty unless a draft of it has been laid before and approved by a resolution of each House of Parliament.

SCHEDULE 5

(Section 295)

PATENTS: MISCELLANEOUS AMENDMENTS

Withdrawal of application before publication of specification

1. In section 13(2) of the Patents Act 1949 (duty of comptroller to advertise acceptance of and publish complete specification) after the word "and", in the first place where it occurs, insert ", unless the application is withdrawn,".

Correction of clerical errors

2.—(1) In section 15 of the Patents Act 1977 (filing of application), after subsection (3) insert—

"(3A) Nothing in subsection (2) or (3) above shall be construed as affecting the power of the comptroller under section 117(1) below to correct errors or mistakes with respect to the filing of drawings.".

(2) The above amendment applies only in relation to applications filed after the commencement of this paragraph.

Supplementary searches

3.—(1) Section 17 of the Patents Act 1977 (preliminary examination and search) is amended as follows.

(2) In subsection (7) (supplementary searches) for "subsection (4) above" substitute "subsections (4) and (5) above" and for "it applies" substitute "they apply".

(3) After the subsection add—

"(8) A reference for a supplementary search in consequence of—

(a) an amendment of the application made by the applicant under section 18(3) or 19(1) below, or

(b) a correction of the application, or of a document filed in connection with the application, under section 117 below,

shall be made only on payment of the prescribed fee, unless the comptroller directs otherwise.".

4. In section 18 of the Patents Act 1977 (substantive examination and grant or refusal of patent), after subsection (1) insert—

"(1A) If the examiner forms the view that a supplementary search under section 17 above is required for which a fee is payable, he shall inform the comptroller, who may decide that the substantive examinations should not proceed until the fee is paid; and if he so decides, then unless within such period as he may allow—

(a) the fee is paid, or

(b) the application is amended so as to render the supplementary search unnecessary,

he may refuse the application.".

5. In section 130(1) of the Patents Act 1977 (interpretation), in the definition of "search fee", for "section 17 above" substitute "section 17(1) above".

Application for restoration of lapsed patent

6.—(1) Section 28 of the Patents Act 1977 (restoration of lapsed patents) is amended as follows.

(2) For subsection (1) (application for restoration within period of one year) substitute—

"(1) Where a patent has ceased to have effect by reason of a failure to pay any renewal fee, an application for the restoration of the patent may be made to the comptroller within the prescribed period.

(1A) Rules prescribing that period may contain such transitional provisions and savings as appear to the Secretary of State to be necessary or expedient".

(3) After subsection (2) insert—

"(2A) Notice of the application shall be published by the comptroller in the prescribed manner".

(4) In subsection (3), omit paragraph (b) (requirement that failure to renew is due to circumstances beyond proprietor's control) and the word "and" preceding it.

This amendment does not apply to a patent which has ceased to have effect in accordance with section 25(3) of the Patents Act 1977 (failure to renew within prescribed period) and in respect of which the period referred to in subsection (4) of that section (six months' period of grace for renewal) has expired before commencement.

(5) Omit subsections (5) to (9) (effect of order for restoration).

7. After that section insert—

"*Effect of order for restoration of patent*

28A.—(1) The effect of an order for the restoration of a patent is as follows.

(2) Anything done under or in relation to the patent during the period between expiry and restoration shall be treated as valid.

(3) Anything done during that period which would have constituted an infringement if the patent had not expired shall be treated as an infringement—

(a) if done at a time when it was possible for the patent to be renewed under section 25(4), or

(b) if it was a continuation or repetition of an earlier infringing act.

(4) If after it was no longer possible for the patent to be so renewed, and before publication of notice of the application for restoration, a person—

(a) began in good faith to do an act which would have constituted an infringement of the patent if it had not expired, or

(b) made in good faith effective and serious preparations to do such an act,

he has the right to continue to do the act or, as the case may be, to do the act, notwithstanding the restoration of the patent; but this right does not extend to granting a licence to another person to do the act.

(5) If the act was done, or the preparations were made, in the course of a business, the person entitled to the right conferred by subsection (4) may—

(a) authorise the doing of that act by any partners of his for the time being in that business, and

(b) assign that right, or transmit it on death (or in the case of a body corporate on its dissolution), to any person who acquires that part of the business in the course of which the act was done or the preparations were made.

(6) Where a product is disposed of to another in exercise of the rights conferred by subsection (4) or (5), that other and any person claiming through him may deal with the product in the same way as if it had been disposed of by the registered proprietor of the patent.

(7) The above provisions apply in relation to the use of a patent for the services of the Crown as they apply in relation to infringement of the patent."

8. In consequence of the above amendments—

(a) in section 60(6)(b) of the Patents Act 1977, for "section 28(6)" substitute "section 28A(4) or (5)"; and

(b) in sections 77(5), 78(6) and 80(4) of that Act, for the words from "section 28(6)" to the end substitute "section 28A(4) and (5) above, and subsections (6) and (7) of that section shall apply accordingly."

Determination of right to patent after grant

9.—(1) Section 37 of the Patents Act 1977 (determination of right to patent after grant) is amended as follows.

(2) For subsection (1) substitute—

"(1) After a patent has been granted for an invention any person having or claiming a proprietary interest in or under the patent may refer to the comptroller the question—

(a) who is or are the true proprietor or proprietors of the patent,

(b) whether the patent should have been granted to the person or persons to whom it was granted, or

(c) whether any right in or under the patent should be transferred or granted to any other person or persons;

and the comptroller shall determine the question and make such order as he thinks fit to give effect to the determination".

(3) Substitute "this section"—

(a) in subsections (4) and (7) for "subsection (1)(a) above", and

(b) in subsection (8) for "subsection (1) above".

10. In section 74(6) (meaning of "entitlement proceedings"), for "section 37(1)(a) above" substitute "section 37(1) above".

Employees' inventions

11.—(1) In section 39 of the Patents Act 1977 (right to employees' inventions), after subsection (2) add—

"(3) Where by virtue of this section an invention belongs, as between him and his employer, to an employee, nothing done—

(a) by or on behalf of the employee of any person claiming under him for the purposes of pursuing an application for a patent, or

(b) by any person for the purpose of performing or working the invention,

shall be taken to infringe any copyright or design right to which, as between him and his employer, his employer is entitled in any model or document relating to the invention".

(2) In section 43 of the Patents Act 1977 (supplementary provisions with respect to employees' inventions), in subsection (4) (references to patents to include other forms of protection, whether in UK or elsewhere) for "in sections 40 to 42" substitute "in sections 39 to 42."

Undertaking to take licence in infringement proceedings

12.—(1) Section 46 of the Patents Act 1977 (licences of right) is amended as follows.

(2) In subsection (3)(c) (undertaking to take licence in infringement proceedings) after the words "(otherwise than by the importation of any article" insert "from a country which is not a member State of the European Economic Community".

(3) After subsection (3) insert—

"(3A) An undertaking under subsection (3)(c) above may be given at any time before final order in the proceedings, without any admission of liability".

Power of comptroller on grant of compulsory licence

13. In section 49 of the Patents Act 1977 (supplementary provisions with respect to compulsory licences), omit subsection (3) (power to order that licence has effect to revoke existing licences and deprive proprietor of power to work invention or grant licences).

Powers exercisable in consequence of report of Monopolies and Mergers Commission

14. For section 51 of the Patents Act 1977 (licences of right: application by Crown in consequence of report of Monopolies and Mergers Commission) substitute—

"Powers exercisable in consequence of report of Monopolies and Mergers Commission

51.—(1) Where a report of the Monopolies and Mergers Commission has been laid before parliament containing conclusions to the effect—

(a) on a monopoly reference, that a monopoly situation exists and facts found by the Commission operate or may be expected to operate against the public interest,

(b) on a merger reference, that a merger situation qualifying for investigation has been created and the creation of the situation, or particular elements in or consequences of it specified in the report, operate or may be expected to operate against the public interest,

(c) on a competition reference, that a person was engaged in an anti-competitive practice which operated or may be expected to operate against the public interest, or

(d) on a reference under section 11 of the Competition Act 1980 (reference of public bodies and certain other persons), that a person is pursuing a course of conduct which operates against the public interest,

the appropriate Minister or Ministers may apply to the comptroller to take action under this section.

(2) Before making an application the appropriate Minister or Ministers shall publish, in such manner as he or they think appropriate, a notice describing the nature of the proposed application and shall consider any representations which may be made within 30 days of such publication by persons whose interests appear to him or them to be affected.

(3) If on an application under this section it appears to the comptroller that the matters specified in the Commission's report as being those which in the Commission's opinion operate, or operated or may be expected to operate, against the public interest include—

(a) conditions in licences granted under a patent by its proprietor restricting the use of the invention by the licensee or the right of the proprietor to grant other licences, or

(b) a refusal by the proprietor of a patent to grant licences on reasonable terms

he may by order cancel or modify any such condition or may, instead or in addition, make an entry in the register to the effect that licences under the patent are to be available as of right.

(4) In this section "the appropriate Minister or Ministers" means the Minister or Ministers to whom the report of the Commission was made."

Compulsory licensing: reliance on statements in competition report

15. In section 53(2) of the Patents Act 1977 (compulsory licensing: reliance on statements in reports of Monopolies and Mergers Commission)—

(a) for "application made in relation to a patent under sections 48 to 51 above" substitute "application made under section 48 above in respect of a patent"; and

(b) after "Part VIII of the Fair Trading Act 1973" insert "or section 17 of the Competition Act 1980".

Crown use: compensation for loss of profit

16.—(1) In the Patents Act 1977, after section 57 insert—

"Compensation for loss of profit

57A.—(1) Where use is made of an invention for the services of the Crown, the government department concerned shall pay—

(a) to the proprietor of the patent, or

(b) if there is an exclusive licence in force in respect of the patent, to the exclusive licensee,

compensation for any loss resulting from his not being awarded a contract to supply the patented product or, as the case may be, to perform the patented process or supply a thing made by means of the patented process.

(2) Compensation is payable only to the extent that such a contract could have been fulfilled from his existing manufacturing or other capacity; but is payable notwithstanding the existence of circumstances rendering him ineligible for the award of such a contract.

(3) In determining the loss, regard shall be had to the profit which would have been made on such a contract and to the extent to which any manufacturing or other capacity was under-used.

(4) No compensation is payable in respect of any failure to secure contracts to supply the patented product or, as the case may be, to perform the patented process or supply a thing made by means of the patented process, otherwise than for the services of the Crown.

(5) The amount payable shall, if not agreed between the proprietor or licensee and the government department concerned with the approval of the Treasury, be determined by the court on a reference under section 58, and is in addition to any amount payable under section 55 or 57.

(6) In this section 'the government department concerned', in relation to any use of an invention for the services of the Crown, means the government department by whom or on whose authority the use was made.

(7) In the application of this section to Northern Ireland, the reference in subsection (5) above to the Treasury shall, where the government department concerned is a department of the Government of Northern Ireland, be construed as a reference to the Department of Finance and Personnel".

(2) In section 58 of the Patents Act 1977 (reference of disputes as to Crown use), for subsection (1) substitute—

"(1) Any dispute as to—

(a) the exercise by a government department, or a person authorised by a government department, of the powers conferred by section 55 above,

(b) terms for the use of an invention for the services of the Crown under that section,

(c) the right of any person to receive any part of a payment made in pursuance of subsection (4) of that section, or

(d) the right of any person to receive a payment under section 57A,

may be referred to the court by either party to the dispute after a patent has been granted for the invention".

and in subsection (4) for "under this section" substitute "under subsection (1)(a), (b) or (c) above".

(3) In section 58(11) of the Patents Act 1977 (exclusion of right to compensation for Crown use if relevant transaction, instrument or event not registered), after "section 57(3) above)" insert ", or to any compensation under section 57A above".

(4) The above amendments apply in relation to any use of an invention for the services of the Crown after the commencement of this section, even if the terms for such use were settled before commencement.

Right to continue use begun before priority date

17. For section 64 of the Patents Act 1977 (right to continue use begun before priority date) substitute—

"*Right to continue use begun before priority date*

64.—(1) Where a patent is granted for an invention, a person who in the United Kingdom before the priority date of the invention—

    (a) does in good faith an act which would constitute an infringement of the patent if it were in force, or

    (b) makes in good faith effective and serious preparations to do such an act,

has the right to continue to do the act or, as the case may be, to do the act, notwithstanding the grant of the patent; but this right does not extend to granting a licence to another person to do the act.

(2) If the act was done, or the preparations were made, in the course of a business, the person entitled to the right conferred by subsection (1) may—

    (a) authorise the doing of that act by any partners of his for the time being in that business, and

    (b) assign that right, or transmit it on death (or in the case of a body corporate on its dissolution), to any person who acquires that part of the business in the course of which the act was done or the preparations were made.

(3) Where a product is disposed of to another in exercise of the rights conferred by subsection (1) or (2), that other and any person claiming through him may deal with the product in the same way as if it had been disposed of by the registered proprietor of the patent."

Revocation on grounds of grant to wrong person

18. In section 72(1) of the Patents Act 1977 (grounds for revocation of patent), for paragraph (b) substitute—

    "(b) that the patent was granted to a person who was not entitled to be granted that patent;".

Revocation where two patents granted for same invention

19. In section 73 of the Patents Act 1977 (revocation on initiative of comptroller), for subsections (2) and (3) (revocation of patent where European patent (UK) granted in respect of same invention) substitute—

"(2) If it appears to the comptroller that a patent under this Act and a European patent (UK) have been granted for the same invention having the same priority date, and that the applications for the patents were filed by the same applicant or his successor in title, he shall give the proprietor of the patent under this Act an opportunity of making observations and of amending the specification of the patent, and if the proprietor fails to satisfy the comptroller that there are not two patents in respect of the same invention, or to amend the specification so as to prevent there being two patents in respect of the same invention, the comptroller shall revoke the patent.

(3) The comptroller shall not take action under subsection (2) above before—

(a) the end of the period for filing an opposition to the European patent (UK) under the European Patent Convention, or

(b) if later, the date on which opposition proceedings are finally disposed of;

and he shall not then take any action if the decision is not to maintain the European patent or if it is amended so that there are not two patents in respect of the same invention.

(4) The comptroller shall not take action under subsection (2) above if the European patent (UK) has been surrendered under section 29(1) above before the date on which by virtue of section 25(1) above the patent under this Act is to be treated as having been granted or, if proceedings for the surrender of the European patent (UK) have been begun before that date, until those proceedings are finally disposed of; and he shall not then take any action if the decision is to accept the surrender of the European patent".

Applications and amendments not to include additional matter

20. For section 76 of the Patents Act 1977 (amendments of applications and patents not to include added matter) substitute—

"Amendments of applications and patents not to include added matter

76.—(1) An application for a patent which—

(a) is made in respect of matter disclosed in an earlier application, or in the specification of a patent which has been granted, and

(b) discloses additional matter, that is, matter extending beyond that disclosed in the earlier application, as filed, or the application for the patent, as filed,

may be filed under section 8(3), 12 37(4) above, or as mentioned in section 15(4) above, but shall not be allowed to proceed unless it is amended so as to exclude the additional matter.

(2) No amendment of an application for a patent shall be allowed under section 17(3), 18(3) or 19(1) if it results in the application disclosing matter extending beyond that disclosed in the application as filed.

(3) No amendment of the specification of a patent shall be allowed under section 27(1), 73 or 75 if it—

(a) results in the specification disclosing additional matter, or

(b) extends the protection conferred by the patent."

Effect of European patent (UK)

21.—(1) Section 77 of the Patents Act 1977 (effect of European patent (UK)) is amended as follows.

(2) For subsection (3) (effect of finding of partial validity on pending proceedings) substitute—

"(3) Where in the case of a European patent (UK)—

(a) proceedings for infringement, or proceedings under section 58 above, have been commenced before the court or the comptroller and have not been finally disposed of, and

(b) it is established in proceedings before the European Patent Office that the patent is only partially valid,

the provisions of section 63 or, as the case may be, of subsections (7) to (9) of section 58 apply as they apply to proceedings in which the validity of a patent is put in issue and in which it is found that the patent is only partially valid".

(3) For subsection (4) (effect of amendment or revocation under European Patent Convention) substitute—

"(4) Where a European patent (UK) is amended in accordance with the European Patent Convention, the amendment shall have effect for the purposes of Parts I and III of this Act as if the specification of the patent had been amended under this Act; but subject to subsection (6)(b) below.

(4A) Where a European patent (UK) is revoked in accordance with the European Patent Convention, the patent shall be treated for the purposes of Parts I and III of this Act as having been revoked under this Act."

(4) In subsection (6) (filing of English translation), in paragraph (b) (amendments) for "a translation of the amendment into English" substitute "a translation into English of the specification as amended".

(5) In subsection (7) (effect of failure to file translation) for the words from "a translation" to "above" substitute "such a translation is not filed".

The state of the art: material contained in patent applications

22. In section 78 of the Patents Act 1977 (effect of filing an application for a European patent (UK)), for subsection (5) (effect of withdrawal of application, &c.) substitute—

"(5) Subsections (1) to (3) above shall cease to apply to an application for a European patent (UK), except as mentioned in subsection (5A) below, if—

(a) the application is refused or withdrawn or deemed to be withdrawn, or

(b) the designation of the United Kingdom in the application is withdrawn or deemed to be withdrawn,

but shall apply again if the rights of the applicant are re-established under the European Patent Convention, as from their re-establishment.

(5A) The occurrence of any of the events mentioned in subsection (5)(a) or (b) shall not affect the continued operation of section 2(3) above in relation to matter contained in an application for a European patent (UK) which by virtue of that provision has become part of the state of the art as regards other inventions".

Jurisdiction in certain proceedings

23. Section 88 of the Patents Act 1977 (jurisdiction in legal proceedings in connection with Community Patent Convention) is repealed.

Effect of filing international application for patent

24.—(1) Section 89 of the Patents Act 1977 (effect of filing international application for patent) is amended as follows.

(2) After subsection (3) insert—

"(3A) If the relevant conditions are satisfied with respect to an application which is amended in accordance with the Treaty and the relevant conditions are not satisfied with respect to any amendment, that amendment shall be disregarded".

(3) After subsection (4) insert—

"(4A) In subsection (4)(a) 'a copy of the application' includes a copy of the application published in accordance with the Treaty in a language other than that in which it was filed".

(4) For subsection (10) (exclusion of certain applications subject to European Patent Convention) substitute—

"(10) The foregoing provisions of this section do not apply to an application which falls to be treated as an international application for a patent (UK) by reason only of its containing an indication that the applicant wishes to obtain a European patent (UK); but without prejudice to the application of those provisions to an application which also separately designates the United Kingdom".

(5) The amendments in this paragraph shall be deemed always to have had effect.

(6) This paragraph shall be repealed by the order bringing the following paragraph into force.

25. For section 89 of the Patents Act 1977 (effect of filing international application for patent) substitute—

"Effect of international application for patent

89.—(1) An international application for a patent (UK) for which a date of filing has been accorded under the Patent Co-operation Treaty shall, subject to—

section 89A (international and national phases of application), and

section 89B (adaptation of provisions in relation to international application),

be treated for the purposes of Parts I and III of this Act as an application for a patent under this Act.

(2) If the application, or the designation of the United Kingdom in it, is withdrawn or (except as mentioned in subsection (3)) deemed to be withdrawn under the Treaty, it shall be treated as withdrawn under this Act.

(3) An application shall not be treated as withdrawn under this Act if it, or the designation of the United Kingdom in it, is deemed to be withdrawn under the Treaty—

(a) because of an error or omission in an institution having functions under the Treaty, or

(b) because, owing to circumstances outside the applicant's control, a copy of the application was not received by the International Bureau before the end of the time limited for that purpose under the Treaty,

or in such other circumstances as may be prescribed.

(4) For the purposes of the above provisions an application shall not be treated as an international application for a patent (UK) by reason only of its containing an indication that the applicant wishes to obtain a European patent (UK), but an application shall be so treated if it is also separately designates the United Kingdom.

(5) If an international application for a patent which designates the United Kingdom is refused a filing date under the Treaty and the comptroller determines that the refusal was caused by an error or omission in an institution having functions under the Treaty, he may direct that the application shall be treated as an application under this Act, having such date of filing as he may direct.

International and national phases of application

89A.—(1) The provisions of the Patent Co-operation Treaty relating to publication, search, examination and amendment, and not those of this Act, apply to an international application for a patent (UK) during the international phase of the application.

(2) The international phase of the application means the period from the filing of the application in accordance with the Treaty until the national phase of the application begins.

(3) The national phase of the application begins—

(a) when the prescribed period expires, provided any necessary translation of the application into English has been filed at the Patent Office and the prescribed fee has been paid by the applicant; or

(b) on the applicant expressly requesting the comptroller to proceed earlier with the national phase of the application, filing at the Patent Office—

(i) a copy of the application, if none has yet been sent to the Patent Office in accordance with the Treaty, and

(ii) any necessary translation of the application into English,

and paying the prescribed fee.

For this purpose a "copy of the application" includes a copy published in accordance with the Treaty in a language other than that in which it was originally filed.

(4) If the prescribed period expires without the conditions mentioned in subsection (3)(a) being satisfied, the application shall be taken to be withdrawn.

(5) Where during the international phase the application is amended in accordance with the Treaty, the amendment shall be treated as made under this Act if—

(a) when the prescribed period expires, any necessary translation of the amendment into English has been filed at the Patent Office, or

(b) where the applicant expressly requests the comptroller to proceed earlier with the national phase of the application, there is then filed at the Patent Office—

(i) a copy of the amendment, if none has yet been sent to the Patent Office in accordance with the Treaty, and

(ii) any necessary translation of the amendment into English;

otherwise the amendment shall be disregarded.

(6) The comptroller shall on payment of the prescribed fee publish any translation filed at the Patent Office under subsection (3) or (5) above.

Adaptation of provisions in relation to international application

89B.—(1) Where an international application for a patent (UK) is accorded a filing date under the Patent Co-operation Treaty—

(a) that date, or if the application is re-dated under the Treaty to a later date that later date, shall be treated as the date of filing the application under this Act,

(b) any declaration of priority made under the Treaty shall be treated as made under section 5(2) above, and where in accordance with the Treaty any extra days are allowed, the period of 12 months specified in section 5(2) shall be treated as altered accordingly, and

(c) any statement of the name of the inventor under the Treaty shall be treated as a statement filed under section 13(2) above.

(2) If the application, not having been published under this Act, is published in accordance with the Treaty it shall be treated, for purposes other than those mentioned

in subsection (3), as published under section 16 above when the conditions mentioned in section 89A(3)(a) are complied with.

(3) For the purposes of section 55 (use of invention for service of the Crown) and section 69 (infringement of rights conferred by publication) the application, not having been published under this Act, shall be treated as published under section 16 above—

(a) if it is published in accordance with the Treaty in English, on its being so published; and

(b) if it is so published in a language other than English—

(i) on the publication of a translation of the application in accordance with section 89A(6) above, or

(ii) on the service by the applicant of a translation into English of the specification of the application on the government department concerned or, as the case may be, on the person committing the infringing act.

The reference in paragraph (b)(ii) to the service of a translation on a government department or other person is to its being sent by post or delivered to that department or person.

(4) During the international phase of the application, section 8 above does not apply (determination of questions of entitlement in relation to application under this Act) and section 12 above (determination of entitlement in relation to foreign and convention patents) applies notwithstanding the application; but after the end of the international phase, section 8 applies and section 12 does not.

(5) Where the national phase begins the comptroller shall refer the application for so much of the examination and search under section 17 and 18 above as he considers appropriate in view of any examination or search carried out under the Treaty".

Proceedings before the court or the comptroller

26. In the Patents Act 1977, after section 99 (general powers of the court) insert—

"Powers of Patents Court to order report

99A.—(1) Rules of court shall make provision empowering the Patents Court in any proceedings before it under this Act, on or without the application of any party, to order the Patent Office to inquire into and report on any question of fact or opinion.

(2) Where the court makes such an order on the application of a party, the fee payable to the Patent Office shall be at such rate as may be determined in accoradance with rules of court and shall be costs of the proceedings unless otherwise ordered by the court.

(3) Where the court makes such an order of its own motion, the fee payable to the Patent Office shall be at such rate as may be determined by the Lord Chancellor with the approval of the Treasury and shall be paid out of money provided by Parliament.

Power of Court of Session to order report

99B.—(1) In any proceedings before the Court of Session under this Act the court may, either of its own volition or on the application of any party, order the Patent Office to inquire into and report on any question of fact or opinion.

(2) Where the court makes an order under subsection (1) above of its own volition the fee payable to the Patent Office shall be at such rate as may be determined by the Lord President of the Court of Session with the consent of the Treasury and shall be defrayed out of moneys provided by Parliament.

(3) Where the court makes an order under subsection (1) above on the application of a party, the fee payable to the Patent Office shall be at such rate as may be provided for in rules of court and shall be treated as expenses in the cause."

27. For section 102 of the Patents Act 1977 (right of audience in patent proceedings) substitute—

"*Right of audience, &c. in proceedings before comptroller*

102.—(1) A party to proceedings before the comptroller under this Act, or under any treaty or international convention to which the United Kingdom is a party, may appear before the comptroller in person or be represented by any person whom he desires to represent him.

(2) No offence is committed under the enactments relating to the preparation of documents by persons not legally qualified by reason only of the preparation by any person of a document, other than a deed, for use in such proceedings.

(3) Subsection (1) has effect subject to rules made under section 281 of the Copyright, Designs and Patents Act 1988 (power of comptroller to refuse to recognise certain agents).

(4) In its application to proceedings in relation to applications for, or otherwise in connection with, European patents, this section has effect subject to any restrictions imposed by or under the European Patent Convention.

Right of audience, &c. in proceedings on appeal from the comptroller

102A.—(1) A solicitor of the Supreme Court may appear and be heard on behalf of any party to an appeal under this Act from the comptroller to the Patents Court.

(2) A registered patent agent or a member of the Bar not in actual practice may do, in or in connection with proceedings on an appeal under this Act from the comptroller to the Patents Court, anything which a solicitor of the Supreme Court might do, other than prepare a deed.

(3) The Lord Chancellor may by regulations—

(a) provide that the right conferred by subsection (2) shall be subject to such conditions and restrictions as appear to the Lord Chancellor to be necessary or expedient, and

(b) apply to persons exercising that right such statutory provisions, rules of court and other rules of law and practice applying to solicitors as may be specified in the regulations;

and different provision may be made for different descriptions of proceedings.

(4) Regulations under this section shall be made by statutory instrument which shall be subject to annulment in pursuance of a resolution of either House of Parliament.

(5) This section is without prejudice to the right of counsel to appear before the High Court".

Provision of information

28. In section 118 of the Patents Act 1977 (information about patent applications, &c.), in subsection (3) (restriction on disclosure before publication of application: exceptions) for "section 22(6)(a) above" substitute "section 22(6) above".

Power to extend time limits

29. In section 123 of the Patents Act 1977 (rules), after subsection (3) insert—

"(3A) It is hereby declared that rules—

(a) authorising the rectification of irregularities of procedure, or

(b) providing for the alteration of any period of time,

may authorise the comptroller to extend or further extend any period notwithstanding that the period has already expired."

Availability of samples of micro-organisms

30. In the Patents Act 1977 after section 125 insert—

"*Disclosure of invention by specification: availability of samples of micro-organisms*

125A.—(1) Provision may be made by rules prescribing the circumstances in which the specification of an application for a patent, or of a patent, for an invention which requires for its performance the use of a micro-organism is to be treated as disclosing the invention in a manner which is clear enough and complete enough for the invention to be performed by a person skilled in the art.

(2) The rules may in particular require the applicant or patentee—

(a) to take such steps as may be prescribed for the purposes of making available to the public samples of the micro-organism, and

(b) not to impose or maintain restrictions on the uses to which such samples may be put, except as may be prescribed.

(3) The rules may provide that, in such cases as may be prescribed, samples need only be made available to such persons or descriptions of persons as may be prescribed; and the rules may identity a description of persons by reference to whether the comptroller has given his certificate as to any matter.

(4) An application for revocation of the patent under section 72(1)(c) above may be made if any of the requirements of the rules cease to be complied with".

SCHEDULE 6

(Section 301)

PROVISIONS FOR THE BENEFIT OF THE HOSPITAL FOR SICK CHILDREN

Interpretation

1.—(1) In this Schedule—

"the Hospital" means The Hospital for Sick Children, Great Ormond Street, London,

"the trustees" means the special trustees appointed for the Hospital under the National Health Service Act 1977; and

"the work" means the play "Peter Pan" by Sir James Matthew Barrie.

(2) Expressions used in this Schedule which are defined for the purposes of Part I of this Act (copyright) have the same meaning as in that Part.

Entitlement to royalty

2.—(1) The trustees are entitled, subject to the following provisions of this Schedule, to a royalty in respect of any public performance, commercial publication, broadcasting or inclusion in a cable programme service of the whole or any substantial part of the work or an adaptation of it.

(2) Where the trustees are or would be entitled to a royalty, another form of remuneration may be agreed.

Exceptions

3. No royalty is payable in respect of—

(a) anything which immediately before copyright in the work expired on 31st December 1987 could lawfully have been done without the licence, or further licence, of the trustees as copyright owners; or

(b) anything which if copyright still subsisted in the work could, by virtue of any provision of Chapter III of Part I of this Act (acts permitted notwithstanding copyright), be done without infringing copyright.

Saving

4. No royalty is payable in respect of anything done in pursuance of arrangements made before the passing of this Act.

Procedure for determining amount payable

5.—(1) In default of agreement application may be made to the Copyright Tribunal which shall consider the matter and make such order regarding the royalty or other remuneration to be paid as it may determine to be reasonable in the circumstances.

(2) Application may subsequently be made to the Tribunal to vary its order, and the Tribunal shall consider the matter and make such order confirming or varying the original order as it may determine to be reasonable in the circumstances.

(3) An application for variation shall not, except with the special leave of the Tribunal, be made within twelve months from the date of the original order or of the order on a previous application for variation.

(4) A variation order has effect from the date on which it is made or such later date as may be specified by the Tribunal.

Sums received to be held on trust

6. The sums received by the trustees by virtue of this Schedule, after deduction of any relevant expenses, shall be held by them on trust for the purposes of the Hospital.

Right only for the benefit of the Hospital

7.—(1) The right of the trustees under this Schedule may not be assigned and shall cease if the trustees purport to assign or charge it.

(2) The right may not be the subject of an order under section 92 of the National Health Service Act 1977 (transfers of trust property by order of the Secretary of State) and shall cease if the Hospital ceases to have a separate identity or ceases to have purposes which include the care of sick children.

(3) Any power of Her Majesty, the court (within the meaning of the Charities Act 1960) or any other person to alter the trusts of a charity is not exercisable in relation to the trust created by this Schedule.

SCHEDULE 7

(Section 303(1))

British Mercantile Marine Uniform Act 1919 (c.62)

1. For section 2 of the British Mercantile Marine Uniform Act 1919 (copyright in distinctive marks of uniform) substitute—

"Right in registered design of distinctive marks of uniform

2. The right of the Secretary of State in any design forming part of the British mercantile marine uniform which is registered under the Registered Designs Act 1949 is not limited to the period prescribed by section 8 of that Act but shall continue to subsist so long as the design remains on the register.".

Chartered Associations (Protection of Names and Uniforms) Act 1926 (c.26)

2. In section 1(5) of the Chartered Associations (Protection of Names and Uniforms) Act 1926 for "the copyright in respect thereof" substitute "the right in the registered design".

Patents, Designs, Copyright and Trade Marks (Emergency) Act 1939 (c.107)

3.—(1) The Patents, Designs, Copyright and Trade Marks (Emergency) Act 1939 is amended as follows.

(2) In section 1 (effect of licence where owner is enemy or enemy subject)—

 (a) in subsection (1) after "a copyright" and "the copyright" insert "or design right";

 (b) in subsection (2) after "the copyright" insert "or design right" and for "or copyright" substitute ", copyright or design right".

(3) In section 2 (power of comptroller to grant licences)—

 (a) in subsection (1) after a "copyright", "the copyright" (twice) and "the said copyright" insert "or design right" and for "or copyright" (twice) substitute ", copyright or design right";

 (b) in subsections (2) and (3) for ", or copyright" substitute ", copyright or design right";

 (c) in subsection (4) and in subsection (5) (twice), after "the copyright" insert "or design right".

 (d) in subsection (8)(c) for "or work in which copyright subsists" substitute "work in which copyright subsists or design in which design right subsists".

(4) In section 5 (effect of war on international arrangements)—

 (a) in subsection (1) for "section twenty-nine of the Copyright Act 1911" substitute "section 159 or 256 of the Copyright, Designs and Patents Act 1988 (countries enjoying reciprocal copyright or design right protection)";

 (b) in subsection (2) after "copyright" (four times) insert "or design right" and for "the Copyright Act 1911" (twice) substitute "Part I or III of the Copyright, Designs and Patents Act 1988".

(5) In section 10(1) (interpretation) omit the definition of "copyright", and for the definitions of "design", "invention", "patent" and "patentee" substitute—

"'design has in reference to a registered design the same meaning as in the Registered Designs Act 1949, and in reference to design right the same meaning as in Part III of the Copyright, Designs and Patents Act 1988;

'invention' and 'patent' have the same meaning as in the Patents Act 1977.".

Crown Proceedings Act 1947 (c.44)

4.—(1) In the Crown Proceedings Act 1947 for section 3 (provisions as to industrial property) substitute—

"*Infringement of intellectual property rights*

3.—(1) Civil proceedings lie against the Crown for an infringement committed by a servant or agent of the Crown, with the authority of the Crown, or—

(a) a patent,

(b) a registered trade mark or registered service mark,

(c) the right in a registered design,

(d) design right, or

(e) copyright;

but save as provided by this subsection no proceedings lie against the Crown by virtue of this Act in respect of an infringement of any of those rights.

(2) Nothing in this section, or any other provision of this Act, shall be construed as affecting—

(a) the rights of a government department under section 55 of the Patents Act 1977, Schedule 1 to the Registered Designs Act 1949 or section 240 of the Copyright, Designs and Patents Act 1988 (Crown use of patents and designs), or

(b) the rights of the Secretary of State under section 22 of the Patents Act 1977 or section 5 of the Registered Designs Act 1949 (security of information prejudicial to defence or public safety).".

(2) In the application of sub-paragraph (1) to Northern Ireland—

(a) the reference of the Crown Proceedings Act 1947 is to that Act as it applies to the Crown in right of Her Majesty's Government in Northern Ireland, as well as to the Crown in right of Her Majesty's Government in the United Kingdom, and

(b) in the substituted section 3 as it applies in relation to the Crown in right of Her Majesty's Government in Northern Ireland, subsection (2)(b) shall be omitted.

Patents Act 1949 (c.87)

5. In section 47 of the Patents Act 1949 (rights of third parties in respect of Crown use of patent), in the closing words of subsection (1) (which relate to the use of models or documents), after "copyright" insert "or design right".

Public Libraries (Scotland) Act 1955 (c.27)

6. In section 4 of the Public Libraries (Scotland) Act 1955 (extension of lending power of public libraries), make the existing provision subsection (1) and after it add—

"(2) The provisions of Part I of the Copyright, Designs and Patents Act 1988 (copyright) relating to the rental of copies of sound recordings, films and computer programs apply to any lending by a statutory library authority of copies of such works, whether or not a charge is made for that facility.".

London County Council (General Powers) Act 1958 (c.xxi)

7. In section 36 of the London County Council (General Powers) Act 1958 (power as to libraries: provision and repair of things other than books) for subsection (5) substitute—

"(5) Nothing in this section shall be construed as authorising an infringement of copyright.".

Public Libraries and Museums Act 1964 (c.75)

8. In section 8 of the Public Libraries and Museums Act 1964 (restrictions on charges for library facilities), after subsection (5) add—

"(6) The provisions of Part I of the Copyright, Designs and Patents Act 1988 (copyright) relating to the rental of copies of sound recordings, films and computer programs apply to any lending by a library authority of copies of such works, whether or not a charge is made for that facility.".

Marine, &c., Broadcasting (Offences) Act 1967 (c.41)

9. In section 5 of the Marine, &c., Broadcasting (Offences) Act 1967 (provision of material for broadcasting by pirate radio stations)—

(a) in subsection (3)(a) for the words from "cinematograph film" to "in the record" substitute "film or sound recording with intent that a broadcast of it"; and

(b) in subsection (6) for the words from "and references" to the end substitute "and "film", "sound recording", "literary, dramatic or musical work" and "artistic work" have the same meaning as in Part I of the Copyright, Designs and Patents Act 1988 (copyright)".

Medicines Act 1968 (c.67)

10.—(1) Section 92 of the Medicines Act 1968 (scope of provisions restricting promotion of sales of medicinal products) is amended as follows.

(2) In subsection (1) (meaning of "advertisement") for the words from "or by the exhibition" to "service" substitute "or by means of a photograph, film, sound recording, broadcast or cable programme,".

(3) In subsection (2) (exception for the spoken word)—

(a) in paragraph (a) omit the words from "or embodied" to "film"; and

(b) in paragraph (b) for the words from "by way of" to the end substitute "or included in a cable programme service".

(4) For subsection (6) substitute—

"(6) In this section 'film', 'sound recording', 'broadcast', 'cable programme', 'cable programme service', and related expressions, have the same meaning as in Part I of the Copyright, Designs and Patents Act 1988 (copyright).".

Post Office Act 1969 (c.48)

11. In Schedule 10 to the Post Office Act 1969 (special transitional provisions relating to use of patents and registered designs), in the closing words of paragraph 8(1) and 18(1) (which relate to the use of models and documents), after "copyright" insert "or design right".

Merchant Shipping Act 1970 (c.36)

12. In section 87 of the Merchant Shipping Act 1970 (merchant navy uniform), for subsection (4) substitute—

"(4) Where any design forming part of the merchant navy uniform has been registered under the Registered Designs Act 1949 and the Secretary of State is the proprietor of the design, his right in the design is not limited to the period prescribed by section 8 of that Act but shall continue to subsist so long as the design remains registered.".

Taxes Management Act 1970 (c.9)

13. In section 16 of the Taxes Management Act 1970 (returns to be made in respect of certain payments) —

(a) in subsection (1)(c), and

(b) in subsection (2)(b),

for "or public lending right" substitute ", public lending right, right in a registered design or design right".

Tribunals and Inquiries Act 1971 (c.62)

14. In Part I of Schedule 1 to the Tribunals and Inquiries Act 1971 (tribunals under direct supervision of Council on Tribunals) renumber the entry inserted by the Data Protection Act 1984 as "5B" and before it insert—

"Copyright.   5A. The Copyright Tribunal."

Fair Trading Act 1973 (c.41)

15. In Schedule 4 to the Fair Trading Act 1973 (excluded services), for paragraph 10 (services of patent agents) substitute—

"(10) The services of registered patent agents (within the meaning of Part V of the Copyright, Designs and Patents Act 1988) in their capacity as such.".

and in paragraph 10A (services of European patent attorneys) for "section 84(7) of the Patents Act 1977" substitute "Part V of the Copyright, Designs and Patents Act 1988".

House of Commons Disqualification Act 1975 (c.24)

16. In Part II of Schedule 1 to the House of Commons Disqualification Act 1975 (bodies of which all members are disqualified), at the appropriate place insert "The Copyright Tribunal".

Northern Ireland Assembly Disqualification Act 1975 (c.25)

17. In Part II of Schedule 1 to the Northern Ireland Assembly Disqualification Act 1975 (bodies of which all members are disqualified), at the appropriate place insert "The Copyright Tribunal".

Restrictive Trade Practices Act 1976 (c.34)

18.—(1) The Restrictive Trade Practices Act 1976 is amended as follows.

(2) In Schedule 1 (excluded services) for paragraph 10 (services of patent agents) substitute—

"(10) The services of registered patent agents (within the meaning of Part V of the Copyright, Designs and Patents Act 1988) in their capacity as such.".

and in paragraph 10A (services of European patent attorneys) for "section 84(7) of the Patents Act 1977" substitute "Part V of the Copyright, Designs and Patents Act 1988".

(3) In Schedule 3 (expected agreements), after paragraph 5A insert—

Design right

5B.—(1) This Act does not apply to—

(a) a licence granted by the owner or a licensee of any design right,

(b) an assignment of design right, or

(c) an agreement for such a licence or assignment,

if the licence, assignment or agreement is one under which no such restrictions as are described in section 6(1) above are accepted, or no such information provisions as are described in section 7(1) above are made, except in respect of articles made to the design; but subject to the following provisions.

(2) Sub-paragraph (1) does not exclude a licence, assignment or agreement which is a design pooling agreement or is granted or made (directly or indirectly) in pursuance of a design pooling agreement.

(3) In this paragraph a 'design pooling agreement' means an agreement—

(a) to which the parties are or include at least three persons (the "principal parties") each of whom has an interest in one or more design rights; and

(b) by which each principal party agrees, in respect of design right in which he has, or may during the currency of the agreement acquire, an interest to grant an interest (directly or indirectly) to one or more of the other principal parties, or to one or more of those parties and to other persons.

(4) In this paragraph—

'assignment', in Scotland, means assignation; and

'interest' means an interest as owner or licensee of design right.

(5) This paragraph applies to an interest held by or granted to more than one person jointly as if they were one person.

(6) References in this paragraph to the granting of an interest to a person indirectly are to its being granted to a third person for the purpose of enabling him to make a grant to the person in question.

Resale Prices Act 1976 (c. 53)

19. In section 10(4) of the Resale Prices Act 1976 (patented articles: articles to be treated in same way), in paragraph (a) after "protected" insert "by design right or".

Patents Act 1977 (c. 37)

20. In section 57 of the Patents Act 1977 (rights of third parties in respect of Crown use of patent), in the closing words of subsection (1) (which relate to the use of models or documents), after "copyright" insert "or design right".

21. In section 105 of the Patents Act 1977 (privilege in Scotland for communications relating to patent proceedings), omit "within the meaning of section 104 above", make the existing text subsection (1) and after it insert—

"(2) In this section—

"patent proceedings" means proceedings under this Act or any of the relevant conventions, before the court, the comptroller or the relevant convention court, whether contested or uncontested and including an application for a patent; and

"the relevant conventions" means the European Patent Convention, the Community Patent Convention and the Patent Co-operation Treaty.".

22. In section 123(7) of the Patents Act 1977 (publication of case reports by the comptroller) —

(a) for "and registered designs" substitute "registered designs or design right",

(b) for "and copyright" substitute ", copyright and design right".

23. In section 130(1) of the Patents Act 1977 (interpretation), in the definition of "court", for paragraph (a) substitute —

"(a) as respects England and Wales, the High Court or any patents county court having jurisdiction by virtue of an order under section 287 of the Copyright, Designs and Patents Act 1988;".

Unfair Contract Terms Act 1977 (c.50)

24. In paragraph 1 of Schedule 1 to the Unfair Contract Terms Act 1977 (scope of main provisions: excluded contracts), in paragraph (c) (contracts relating to grant or transfer of interest in intellectual property) after "copyright" insert "or design right".

Judicature (Northern Ireland) Act 1978 (c.23)

25. In section 94A of the Judicature (Northern Ireland) Act 1978 (withdrawal of privilege against self-incrimination in certain proceedings relating to intellectual property), in subsection (5) (meaning of "intellectual property") after "copyright" insert "or design right".

Capital Gains Tax Act 1979 (c.14)

26. In section 18(4) of the Capital Gains Tax Act 1979 (situation of certain assets for purposes of Act), for paragraph (h) (intellectual property) substitute —

"(ha) patents, trade marks, service marks and registered designs are situated where they are registered, and if registered in more than one register, where each register is situated, and rights or licences to use a patent, trade mark, service mark or registered design are situated in the United Kingdom if they or any right derived from them are exercisable in the United Kingdom,

"(hb) copyright, design right and franchises, and rights or licences to use any copyright work or design in which design right subsists, are situated in the United Kingdom if they or any right derived from them are exercisable in the United Kingdom,".

British Telecommunications Act 1981 (c.38)

27. In Schedule 5 to the British Telecommunications Act 1981 (special transitional provisions relating to use of patents and registered designs), in the closing words of paragraphs 9(1) and 19(1) (which relate to the use of models and documents), after "copyright" insert "or design right".

Supreme Court Act 1981 (c.54)

28.—(1) The Supreme Court Act 1981 is amended as follows.

(2) In section 72 (withdrawal of privilege against self-incrimination in certain proceedings relating to intellectual property), in subsection (5) (meaning of "intellectual property") after "copyright" insert ", design right".

(3) In Schedule 1 (distribution of business in the High Court), in paragraph 1(i) (business assigned to the Chancery Division: causes and matters relating to certain intellectual property) for "or copyright" substitute ", copyright or design right".

Broadcasting Act 1981 (c.68)

29.—(1) The Broadcasing Act 1981 is amended as follows.

(2) In section 4 (general duties of IBA as regards programmes) for subsection (7) substitute—

"(7) For the purpose of maintaining supervision and control over the programmes (including advertisements) broadcast by them the Authority may make and use recordings of those programmes or any part of them.".

(3) In section 20(9), omit paragraph (a).

Cable and Broadcasting Act 1984 (c.46)

30.—(1) The Cable and Broadcasting Act 1984 is amended as follows.

(2) In section 8, omit subsection (8).

(3) In section 49 (power of Secretary of State to give directions in the public interest), for subsection (7) substitute—

"(7) For the purposes of this section the place from which a broadcast is made is, in the case of a satellite transmission, the place from which the signals carrying the broadcast are transmitted to the satellite.".

(4) In section 56(2) (interpretation) omit the definition of "the 1956 Act".

Companies Act 1985 (c.6)

31.—(1) Part XII of the Companies Act 1985 (registration of charges) is amended as follows.

(2) In section 396 (registration of charges in England and Wales: charges which must be registered), in subsection (1)(j) for the words "on a patent" to the end substitute "or on any intellectual property", and after subsection (3) insert—

"(3A) The following are 'intellectual property' for the purposes of this section—

(a) any patent, trade mark, service mark, registered design, copyright or design right;

(b) any licence under or in respect of any such right.".

(3) In section 410 (registration of charges in Scotland: charges which must be registered), in subsection (3)(c) (incorporeal moveable property) after subparagraph (vi) insert—

"(vii) a registered design or a licence in respect of such a design,

(viii) a design right or a licence under a design right,".

Law Reform (Miscellaneous Provisions) (Scotland) Act 1985 (c.73)

32. In section 15 of the Law Reform (Miscellaneous Provisions) (Scotland) Act 1985 (withdrawal of privilege against self-incrimination in certain proceedings relating to intellectual property), in subsection (5) (meaning of "intellectual property") after "copyright" insert "or design right".

Atomic Energy Authority Act 1986 (c.3)

33. In section 8(2) of the Atomic Energy Authority Act 1986 (powers of Authority as to exploitation of research: meaning of "intellectual property"), after "copyrights" insert ", design rights".

Education and Libraries (Northern Ireland) Order 1986 (S.I. 1986/594 (N.I.3.))

34. In Article 77 of the Education and Libraries (Northern Ireland) Order 1986 (charges for library services), after paragraph (2) add—

"(3) The provisions of Part I of the Copyright, Designs and Patents Act 1988 (copyright) relating to the rental of copies of sound recordings, films and computer programs apply to any lending by a board of copies of such works, whether or not a charge is made for that facility.".

Companies (Northern Ireland) Order 1986 (S.I. 1986/1032(N.I.6))

35. In Article 403 of the Companies (Northern Ireland) Order 1986 (registration of charges: charges which must be registered), in paragraph (1)(j) for the words from "on a patent" to the end substitute "or on any intellectual property", and after paragraph (3) insert—

"(3A) The following are "intellectual property" for the purposes of this Article—

(a) any patent, trade mark, service mark, registered design, copyright or design right;

(b) any licence under or in respect of any such right.".

Income and Corporation Taxes Act 1988 (c.1)

36.—(1) The Income and Corporation Taxes Act 1988 is amended as follows.

(2) In section 83 (fees and expenses deductible in computing profits and gains of trade) for "the extension of the period of copyright in a design" substitute "an extension of the period for which the right in a registered design subsists".

(3) In section 103 (charge on receipts after discontinuance of trade, profession or vocation), in subsection (3) (sums to which the section does not apply), after paragraph (b) insert—

"(bb) a lump sum paid to the personal representatives of the designer of a design in which design right subsists as consideration for the assignment by them, wholly or partially, of that right,"

(4) In section 378 (carry forward as losses of certain payments made under deduction of tax), in subsection (3) (payments to which the section does not apply), in paragraph (e) (copyright royalties) after "applies" insert "or royalties in respect of a right in a design to which section 537B applies".

(5) In section 536 (taxation of copyright royalties where owner abroad) for the definition of "copyright" in subsection (2) substitute—

"'copyright' does not include copyright in—

(i) a cinematograph film or video recording, or

(ii) the sound-track of such a film or recording, so far as it is not separately exploited; and".

(6) In Chapter I of Part XIII (miscellaneous special provisions: intellectual property), after section 537 insert—

Designs

Relief for payments in respect of designs

537A.—(1) Where the designer of a design in which design right subsists assigns that right, or the author of a registered design assigns the right in the design, wholly or partially, or grants an interest in it by licence, and—

(a) the consideration for the assignment or grant consists, in whole or in part, of a payment to which this section applies, the whole amount of which would otherwise be included in computing the amount of his profits or gains for a single year of assessment, and

(b) he was engaged in the creation of the design for a period of more than 12 months,

he may, on making a claim, require that effect shall be given to the following provisions in connection with that payment.

(2) If the period for which he was engaged in the creation of the design does not exceed 24 months, then, for all income tax purposes, one-half only of the amount of the payment shall be treated as having become receivable on the date on which it actually became receivable and the remaining half shall be treated as having become receivable 12 months before that date.

(3) If the period for which he was engaged in the creation of the design exceeds 24 months, then, for all income tax purposes, one-third only of the amount of the payment shall be treated as having become receivable on the date on which it actually became receivable, and one-third shall be treated as having become receivable 12 months, and one-third 24 months, before that date.

(4) This section applies to—

(a) a lump sum payment, including an advance on account of royalties which is not returnable, and

(b) any other payment of or on account of royalties or sums payable periodically which does not only become receivable more than two years after articles made to the design or, as the case may be, articles to which the design is applied are first made available for sale or hire.

(5) A claim under this section with respect to any payment to which it applies by virtue only of subsection (4)(b) above shall have effect as a claim with respect to all such payments in respect of rights in the design in question which are receivable by the claimant, whether before or after the claim; and such a claim may be made at any time not later than 5th April next following the expiration of eight years after articles made to the design or, as the case may be, articles to which the design is applied were first made available for sale or hire.

(6) In this section—

(a) "designer" includes a joint designer, and

(b) any reference to articles being made available for sale or hire is to their being so made available anywhere in the world by or with the licence of the design right owner or, as the case may be, the proprietor of the registered design.

Taxation of design royalties where owner abroad

537B.—(1) Where the usual place of abode of the owner of a right in a design is not within the United Kingdom, section 349(1) shall apply to any payment of or on account of any royalties or sums paid periodically for or in respect of that right as it applies to annual payments not payable out of profits or gains brought into charge to income tax.

(2) In subsection (1) above—

    (a) "right in a design" means design right or the right in a registered design,

    (b) the reference to the owner of a right includes a person who, notwithstanding that he has assigned the right to some other person, is entitled to receive periodical payments in respect of the right, and

    (c) the reference to royalties or other sums paid periodically for or in respect of a right does not include royalties or sums paid in respect of articles which are shown on a claim to have been exported from the United Kingdom for distribution outside the United Kingdom.

(3) Where a payment to which subsection (1) above applies is made through an agent resident in the United Kingdom and that agent is entitled as against the owner of the right to deduct any sum by way of commission in respect of services rendered, the amount of the payment shall for the purposes of section 349(1) be taken to be diminished by the sum which the agent is entitled to deduct.

(4) Where the person by or through whom the payment is made does not know that any such commission is payable or does not know the amount of any such commission, any income tax deducted by or assessed and charged on him shall be computed in the first instance on, and the account to be delivered of the payment shall be an account of, the total amount of the payment without regard being had to any diminution thereof, and in that case, on proof of the facts on a claim, there shall be made to the agent on behalf of the owner of the right such repayment of income tax as is proper in respect of the sum deducted by way of commission.

(5) The time of the making of a payment to which subsection (1) above applies shall, for all tax purposes, be taken to be the time when it is made by the person by whom it is first made and not the time when it is made by or through any other person.

(6) Any agreement for the making of any payment to which subsection (1) above applies in full and without deduction of income tax shall be void.".

(7) In section 821 (payments made under deduction of tax before passing of Act imposing income tax for that year), in subsection (3) (payments subject to adjustment) after (a) insert—

    "(aa) any payment for or in respect of a right in a design to which section 537B applies; and".

(8) In Schedule 19 (apportionment of income of close companies), in paragraph 10(4) (cessation or liquidation: debts taken into account although creditor is participator or associate), in paragraph (c) (payments for use of certain property) for the words from "tangible property" to "extend)" substitute—

    "—

        (i) tangible property,

        (ii) copyright in a literary, dramatic, musical or artistic work within the meaning of Part I of the Copyright, Designs and Patents Act 1988 (or any similar right under the law of a country to which that Part does not extend), or

        (iii) design right,".

(9) In Schedule 25 (taxation of UK-controlled foreign companies: exempt activities), in paragraph 9(1)(a) (investment business: holding of property) for "patents or copyrights" substitute "or intellectual property" and after that subparagraph insert—

    "(1A) In sub-paragraph (1)(a) above 'intellectual property' means patents, registered designs, copyright and design right (or any similar rights under the law of a country outside the United Kingdom).".

SCHEDULE 8

(Section 303(2).)

REPEALS

Chapter	Short title	Extent of repeal
1939 c. 107.	Patents, Designs, Copyright and Trade Marks (Emergency) Act 1939.	In section 10(1), the definition of "copyright".
1945 c. 16.	Limitation (Enemies and War Prisoners) Act 1945.	In section 2(1) and 4(a), the reference to section 10 of the Copyright Act 1911.
1949 c. 88.	Registered Designs Act 1949.	In section 3(2), the words "or original".
		Section 5(5).
		In section 11(2), the words "or original".
		In section 14(3), the words "or the Isle of Man".
		Section 32.
		Section 33(2).
		Section 37(1).
		Section 38.
		In section 44(1), the definitions of "copyright" and "Journal".
		In section 45, paragraphs (1) and (2).
		In section 46, paragraphs (1) and (2).
		Section 48(1).
		Schedule 1, paragraph 3(1), the words "in such manner as may be prescribed by rules of court".
		Schedule 2.
1956 c. 74	Copyright Act 1956.	The whole Act.
1957 c. 6.	Ghana Independence Act 1957.	In Schedule 2, paragraph 12.
1957 c. 60.	Federation of Malaya Independence Act 1957.	In Schedule 1, paragraphs 14 and 15.
1958 c. 44.	Dramatic and Musical Performers' Protection Act 1958.	The whole Act.
1958 c. 51.	Public Records Act 1958.	Section 11.
		Schedule 3.
1960 c. 52.	Cyprus Independence Act 1960.	In the Schedule, paragraph 13.
1960 c. 55.	Nigeria Independence Act 1960.	In Schedule 2, paragraphs 12 and 13.
1961 c. 1.	Tanganyika Independence Act 1961.	In Schedule 2, paragraphs 13 and 14.

Chapter	Short title	Extent of repeal
1961 c. 16	Sierra Leone Independence Act 1961.	In Schedule 3, paragraphs 13 and 14.
1961 c. 25.	Patents and Designs (Renewals, Extensions and Fees) Act 1961.	The whole Act.
1962 c. 40.	Jamaica Independence Act 1962.	In Schedule 2, paragraph 13.
1962 c. 54.	Trinidad and Tobago Independence Act 1962.	In Schedule 2, paragraph 13.
1963 c. 53.	Performers' Protection Act 1963.	The whole Act.
1964 c. 46.	Malawi Independence Act 1964.	In Schedule 2, paragraph 13.
1964 c. 65.	Zambia Independence Act 1964.	In Schedule 1, paragraph 9.
1964 c. 86.	Malta Independence Act 1964.	In Schedule 1, paragraph 11.
1964 c. 93.	Gambia Independence Act 1964.	In Schedule 2, paragraph 12.
1966 c. 24.	Lesotho Independence Act 1966.	In the Schedule, paragraph 9.
1966 c. 37.	Barbados Independence Act 1966.	In Schedule 2, paragraph 12.
1967 c. 80.	Criminal Justice Act 1967.	In Parts I and IV of Schedule 3, the entries relating to the Registered Designs Act 1949.
1968 c. 56.	Swaziland Independence Act 1968.	In the Schedule, paragraph 9.
1968 c. 67.	Medicines Act 1968.	In section 92(2)(a), the words from "or embodied" to "film". Section 98.
1968 c. 68.	Design Copyright Act 1968.	The whole Act.
1971 c. 4.	Copyright (Amendment) Act 1971.	The whole Act.
1971 c. 23.	Courts Act 1971.	In Schedule 9, the entry relating to the Copyright Act 1956.
1971 c. 62.	Tribunals and Inquiries Act 1971.	In Schedule 1, paragraph 24.
1972 c. 32.	Performers' Protection Act 1972.	The whole Act.
1975 c. 24.	House of Commons Disqualification Act 1975.	In Part II of Schedule 1, the entry relating to the Performing Right Tribunal.
1975 c. 25.	Northern Ireland Assembly Disqualification Act 1975.	In Part II of Schedule 1, the entry relating to the Performing Right Tribunal.
1977 c. 37.	Patents Act 1977.	Section 14(4) and (8). In section 28(3), paragraph (b) and the word "and" preceeding it. Section 28(5) to (9). Section 49(3). Sections 72(3). Sections 84 and 85. Section 88. Section 104. In section 105, the words "within the meaning of section 104 above".

Chapter	Short title	Extent of repeal
1977 c. 37. —*cont.*	Patents Act 1977. —*cont.*	Sections 114 and 115. Section 123(2)(k). In section 130(1), the definition of "patent agent". In section 130(7), the words "88(6) and (7),". In Schedule 5, paragraphs 1 and 2, in paragraph 3 the words "and 44(1)" and "in each case", and paragraphs 7 and 8.
1979 c. 2.	Customs and Excise Management Act 1979.	In Schedule 4, the entry relating to the Copyright Act 1956.
1980 c. 21.	Competition Act 1980.	Section 14.
1981 c. 68.	Broadcasting Act 1981.	Section 20(9)(a).
1982 c. 35.	Copyright Act 1956 (Amendment) Act 1982.	The whole Act.
1983 c. 42.	Copyright (Amendment) Act 1983.	The whole Act.
1984 c. 46.	Cable and Broadcasting Act 1984.	Section 8(8). Section 16(4) and (5). Sections 22 to 24. Section 35(2) and (3). Sections 53 and 54. In section 56(2), the definition of "the 1956 Act". In Schedule 5, paragraphs 6, 7, 13 and 23.
1985 c. 21.	Films Act 1985.	Section 7(2).
1985 c. 41.	Copyright (Computer Software) Amendment Act 1985.	The whole Act.
1985 c. 61.	Administration of Justice Act 1985.	Section 60.
1986 c. 39.	Patents, Designs and Marks Act 1986	In Schedule 2, paragraph 1(2)(a), in paragraph 1(2)(k) the words "subsection (1)(j) of section 396 and" and in paragraph 1(2)(1) the words "subsection (2)(i) of section 93".
1988 c. 1.	Income and Corporation Taxes Act 1988.	In Schedule 29, paragraph 5.

Index

434